About

Chris Sullivan has been a DJ, club runner, band leader, painter, style commentator, stylist, a designer of men's suits and an entrepreneur but for the last 20 years has concentrated on writing mainly prose.

In the 1980s he formed and fronted the Latin funk band, Blue Rondo à la Turk, who were signed to Virgin for a record breaking advance and achieved a number one in Brazil and top tens across Europe, and founded The Wag Club in Wardour Street, where he was host, director and DJ for 18 years. From the mid-eighties onwards he has DJ'd in the best clubs and parties across the world.

As a journalist he has worked at The Face, Boy's Own and Loaded, and for three years until 2000, he was GQ's style editor. Since then he has freelanced for among many others, *The Times, Esquire, Telegraph, Independent, Guardian, Big Issue* and *L'Uomo Vogue*. He has written two previous books, the international bestseller *Punk* (with Stephen Colegrave) and the definitive chronicle of club culture of the '80s, *We Can Be Heroes* (with Graham Smith) and conceived and co-wrote a nine-part TV documentary series, *Gangs of Britain*.

His first film, *Anarchy in the UK* (an Aesop's tale for the 21st Century), is in pre-production with Hacienda films while his TV series, *The Fire People,* adapted partly from the book by Alexander Cordell, is doing the funding rounds. Finally, almost 40 years since he first stepped into St Martins College of Art he is back as Associate Lecturer specializing in subculture, a subject he is rumored to know something about, and has resuscitated his painting career with an exhibition scheduled for Autumn.

Rebel Rebel

Rebel Rebel

Mavericks Who Made Our modern World

Chris Sullivan

Unbound Digital

This edition first published in 2019

Unbound

6th Floor Mutual House, 70 Conduit Street, London W1S 2GF

www.unbound.com

© Chris Sullivan, 2019

ISBN (eBook): 978-1-78965-002-0
ISBN (Paperback): 978-1-78965-003-7

Illustrations by Chris Sullivan
Cover design by Miles English
Cover images by Chris Sullivan

Printed and bound in Great Britain by Clays Ltd, Elcograf S.p.A.

*Dedicated to my mother Brenda without whom this book
would never have existed!*

Contents

What's this then?

Fed up with blandness? Bored rigid with punching the clock? Sick of toeing the line? Are you tired, listless and lacking enthusiasm?

If your answer to any of these questions is 'yes', *Rebel Rebel* might just be the remedy for you. It's a chronological compendium of thirty-four articles on mavericks, intended to remind us all, in this age where to kowtow is a prerequisite, where doing what one is told is essential and where showing the remotest sign of independence or individuality is frowned upon, that most of the people and things of lasting significance didn't play by the rules.

Thinks of it less as an encyclopedia and more as an exceptional party. It's got musicians (Fela Kuti, David Bowie, Siouxsie Sioux, Liam Gallagher), actors (Louise Brooks, Erich von Stroheim, Robert Mitchum, Daniel Day-Lewis), artists (Egon Schiele, Jackson Pollock), directors (Orson Welles, Martin Scorsese), a photographer (Robert Capa), criminals (Brilliant Chang, Jacques Mesrine, Salvatore Giuliano), places (Paris, Vienna, Berlin) and movements, all of them turning up for one reason: they did their own thing in their own way. Not all are heroes – James Brown was a wife-beating misogynist control freak with impossibly bad dress sense after the age of thirty, but by rewriting the rules of music he created a brand new fresh form called *funk*, and went on to influence more musicians than anyone on earth.

Some of the pieces are new, some have been published in magazines, but all appear here in their original form, prior to edits and unconstrained by word count. They are full of the life and energy that was often previously left on the cutting room floor, now fully restored by yours truly with a few updates to boot.

So, dig in. Your paperback manifesto of originality awaits. I'd keep it in the smallest room for regular dipping or in your workbag to while away a tedious train journey. It might be just the encouragement you need to throw caution to the wind and, if you haven't done so already, be the person you know you are… or at least think about it.

Chris Sullivan
Maida Vale
November 2017

The Aesthetic Movement: Whistler, Wilde and Beardsley

According to Isaac Newton's third law, for every action there is always a reaction equal in size and opposite in direction. This rule also exists in art, style, music and culture, which often react against both the prevailing style of the day and its socio-political and economic trends. This was never truer than in the mid-nineteenth century, when a gang of barking mad, decadent, hedonistic artists and writers formed what became known as the Aesthetic movement, which except for Pop art is the only international art movement ever born in the UK.

Their clarion call was 'art for art's sake', as to them taste in all things was paramount. They held that art should have no moral or didactic purpose but simply be beautiful and reward the viewer with a pleasure solely drawn from aesthetics.

As such, they embarked on a mission to inject overwhelming pulchritude into what was a new and very ugly Britain, where every aesthetic consideration had been bludgeoned to death. What followed was an outpouring of paintings, objets d'art, interiors, sculptures and calligraphy full of swirling lines, exotic birds, flowers and oriental sensuality tinged with a *soupçon* of medievalism.

Architects, writers, philosophers, poets and craftsmen jumped on this conceit, which went on to dominate every aspect of UK culture for the next forty years and influence the world.

Arguably, the Aesthetic movement was the first 'youth' cult – albeit an upper-middle-class one – that, like punk rock, was spearheaded by some of the most controversial, self-confessed libertarians of the era. It had its own mottos and contentious manifesto that self-consciously rebelled against staid Victorian morals. It had its own dandified, often rakish, style of dress. The women – typically thin, deathly pale and intense – wore long diaphanous gowns, were corsetless and favoured dizzy spells while their narcissistic, often effeminate men favoured long hair, green breeches, extravagant silk neckwear, canes and complex jacket configurations available only to the moneyed. Sexual ambiguity was suggested by the wearing of a green carnation in one's buttonhole, which served as a green light to those of a similar persuasion.

The movement also had its own writers, acolytes, propagandists, and loose mores that included unbridled sexual congress and a lot of drugs and strong drink. All the rage were opium (the British having introduced its use as a pleasurable narcotic in China) and laudanum – a potent opium tincture sold without prescription as cough medicine, which was very much abused by everyone from ageing septuagenarians to tetchy mums to bored farm workers.

Cocaine, then considered a harmless stimulant, was a fashionable substance, as illustrated by Conan Doyle's coke-sniffing aesthete Sherlock Holmes (who first appeared in print in 1887). The aesthetically inclined dandy Robert Louis Stevenson, meanwhile, wrote *The Strange Case of Dr Jekyll and Mr Hyde* in 1884 during a six-day binge on the marching powder. He based the story on a rather affable associate who turned into a monster after just a few alcoholic beverages.

Thrown in for good measure was the mind-bending, psychosis-inducing absinthe (with the original wormwood extract), the favoured tipple of Toulouse-Lautrec, Wilde, Van Gogh, Verlaine and Baudelaire. By 1900 it had reached sales of 36 million litres a year in France and was said to be responsible for the country's packed mental asylums.

The aesthetes, never afraid to suck influence from whatever quarter, were all over these racy continental French ways like custard on a tart. But primarily, the protagonists of the Aesthetic movement were *reacting* against the industrial rape of their country. In their days there were no campaigners protecting an almost extinct breed of caterpillar whose habitat was about to be obliterated by industry, no naturalists protecting woodland for its Davall's sedge, and no activists championing the cause of the *Cortinarius cumatilis*. Factory owners just stamped their way through the UK in heavy hobnails, smashing all that stood in their way.

Of course, it is impossible for us to grasp what Britain must have been like in the mid-nineteenth century. The industrial revolution had not only changed almost every aspect of daily life but also scarred the landscape beyond our imagination. In less than sixty years Britain had gone from a largely arable community, where most people lived and worked the land, to a country governed by cities full of foul factories where every human concern (especially about the health of the workers) played tenth fiddle to the financial feeding frenzy.

Foul centres of industry were hastily knocked up and, in their wake, even uglier slums to accommodate the influx of poor workers that followed. Manchester boasted some 1,600 mills, where kids as young as thirteen worked day and night producing fabric for almost the whole of the western world. It was hell.

'The noxious sulphuric smoke from the factory chimneys was so dense no object could be seen from one hundred yards away and sunlight never penetrated,' wrote French chronicler Alexis de Tocqueville after a visit to Manchester in 1835. 'The foul smell mixed with that of rotting, uncollected refuse, and dormant animal and human excrement permeated the air... Here humanity attains its most complete development and its most brutish; here civilization works its miracles, and civilised man is turned back almost into a savage.'

London had also grown out of all proportion, its population housed in overcrowded ghettos where sanitation was nil, squalor was endemic and cholera was epidemic. The latter killed some 25,000 people in London, culminating in the Broad Street outbreak in 1854. John Snow, the doctor who discovered it was the result of drinking water contaminated by raw sewage, described it as 'the most terrible outbreak of cholera which ever occurred in this kingdom.' People were throwing their buckets full of faeces upriver, while folk were drinking from it downstream. 'Gong farmers' (people employed to remove excrement from privies and cesspits) made a decent living collecting human and animal defecation from the river's edge and selling it to *proper* farmers as fertiliser.

In the summer of 1858, the sewerage problem reached its peak when the Great Stink brought the whole of London to a standstill. Due to the overflowing of 200,000 cesspits into the streets, the stench was so bad that the House of Commons soaked their heavy draped curtains in chloride of lime, and people walked the streets with handkerchiefs over their noses. Understandably, sales of lavender water and perfume rocketed.

I'd like to think that such olfactory repugnance prompted artists to seek a return, albeit aesthetically, to a time when their world was beautiful, bucolic, beatific – and did not smell of fresh turds. I might be wrong. But if one considers that this mephitic outrage was but one manifestation of the horrors of the industrial revolution, then this starts to seem like a very plausible theory.

Some say Aestheticism began in 1861, when renowned socialist William Morris opened a design studio – Morris, Marshall, Faulkner & Co. – with Edward Burne-Jones, Ford Madox Brown and Pre-Raphaelite Brotherhood founder Dante Gabriel Rossetti. Morris and his gang's entire shtick was a conscious return to an age when individual craftsmanship was paramount. These pioneers stood in obstinate opposition to the era's substandard decorative arts and the asinine covetousness that had swallowed up the country.

William Morris, the Arts and Crafts movement's main protagonist, had been influenced by architect, designer, artist and critic Augustus Pugin – who had himself pioneered the Gothic Revival – and the much-travelled poet, writer, art critic and patron John Ruskin, who later tutored Oscar Wilde. Ruskin championed environmentalism, sustainability, craftsmanship, medievalism and the Pre-Raphaelite Brotherhood, who, formed in 1848, comprised Rossetti, William Holman Hunt and John Everett Millais, who, all barely twenty at the time, were the errant rock stars of their day and trailblazed the aesthetic ideal.

The PRB believed that liberty and accountability were indivisible and, particularly fascinated by medievalism, had used their art – often otherworldly, almost phantasmagorical – as a stand against industrialism. Deliberately borrowing from the Italian Quattrocento school – whose artists, such as Botticelli, were active between 1400 and 1499 – they believed that the past could be harnessed to revitalise the present, and threw whimsy, colour and elegant line into our filthy, smog-infested, wheezing cities.

As much as the PRB raged against the machine, however, it was the machine that made them the first celebrities of the embryonic modern world. Their works were mass-produced as bestselling prints, while the burgeoning popular press sold copies off the back of their madcap antics that titillated the general public. They were the first media stars. Accordingly, drug addiction, insanity, infidelity, obsession, neurosis and sexual anxiety were enjoyed in abundance. So notorious were they that even their life models risked social ostracisation by posing for them. Thus, each night the gang went off on the prowl in search of beautiful women to paint, and found barmaids, prostitutes and seamstresses willing to not only pose nude but gladly fornicate with them.

Rossetti had every intention of marrying the voluptuous Annie Miller, often described as a prostitute, although there is little evidence to support this, until he discovered she had been doing the deed with all of his confederates, while the insane yet sexually chaste Ruskin (then aged thirty-nine), who had allied himself with the PRB, boasted of the love letters he received from a thirteen-year-old Irish girl named Rose, and which he wore next to his skin. He would be arrested today without doubt.

The Aesthetic movement carried on from where the Pre-Raphaelites left off, both hedonistically and ideologically. They also followed the writings of the professor Walter Pater, Oscar Wilde's mentor, who, in the conclusion to his 1873 book of Renaissance essays, advocates living for the moment, and that no experience can be turned down.

'Not the fruit of experience, but experience itself, is the end,' he wrote. 'To burn always with this hard gem-like flame, to maintain this ecstasy, is success in life… Of this wisdom, the poetic passion, the desire of beauty, the love of art for art's sake…'

Pater also name-checks Victor Hugo, a leading figure in the French Decadent movement, often compared to Aestheticism. Other 'decadents' included Baudelaire, who first translated into French the works of Aesthetic idols and fellow opiate addicts Edgar Allan Poe and Thomas De Quincey. Baudelaire declared in 1845 that 'everything that gives pleasure has its reason,' while fellow decadent Théophile Gautier coined the 'art for art's sake' motto, itself adapted from a phrase in Poe's essay *The Poetic Principle* (1850). Aestheticism was one big old tangled mess of groovy influence.

Its genesis can be traced back to the eighteenth and nineteenth centuries, when the British Empire had grown eastwards. Travellers such as Lord Byron had returned to the UK with cases full of arcane foreign treasures, pots of opium and tales of adventure that unveiled a corporeal, distinctly non-British emancipation. New trade routes opened and the traders became rich. Exotic curios were all the rage. Then, in 1858, after 200 years of zero trade with the British, Japanese goods flooded Europe, inspiring a new artistic bent. In Paris, Japonism, as it was called, was a huge fad amongst fashionable Bohemian circles. When American painter James Abbott McNeill Whistler moved to London from Paris in 1859 he encouraged artists and designers to embrace the Nippon ideal. Apart from raw fish, he took to all things Japanese with religious fervour.

Indeed, each and every member of the Aesthetic movement was drawn to all things eastern, including flowers, plants and birds, all of which were delicately realised on vases, glassware and interiors. The immensely successful painter Frederic Leighton, who had painted *everyone* of note, including Queen Victoria, added an Arab Hall to his magnificent Holland Park house in 1877 to complement his Greek statues and Arts and Crafts wallpaper. Leighton had a penchant for North Africa and the Middle East and was as camp a row of tents; he was thus rumoured to be homosexual, which, even though many men had suffered the indignities of the private school system, was something you kept out plain view and certainly did not flaunt in Victorian England.

But the finest of all the eastern-influenced Aesthetic interiors was the Peacock Room, the dining room in the magnificent London home of notoriously rude Liverpudlian shipping magnate Frederick Leyland.

The room was originally created by interior architect Thomas Jekyll but Whistler, whose painting *The Princess from the Land of Porcelain* eventually formed the centrepiece of the room, usurped him and offered to retouch some of the walls, leaving Leyland to go back to his business in Liverpool. In his absence the American let rip and made the interior his own, painting over the whole room. Whistler wrote to Leyland telling him that his dining room was 'brilliant and gorgeous while at the same time delicate and refined to the last degree', finally advising his patron to stay in Liverpool until the room was finished.

Without Leyland's knowledge, Whistler then threw lavish parties in the house in order to show off 'his' creation to both the press and guests. His employer's response was to cut Whistler's fee by half. Whistler's retort was to paint two huge peacocks on Leyland's expensive rare leather walls. The more aggressive-looking bird, baring its plumage, is an obvious caricature of the shipping tycoon, while the slighted peacock in the foreground, its tail down, is himself.

Declared a *persona non grata* by Leyland, Whistler never saw the room again. It was eventually dismantled and bought by a wealthy American industrialist, and now sits in the Smithsonian Institute's Freer Gallery of Art in Washington.

However belligerent, Whistler was held in the highest esteem by his fellow aesthetes. Born in Lowell, Massachusetts, in 1834, he spent part of his youth in St Petersburg and London, enrolled in West Point military academy (but was dismissed for poor grades) and trained as an artist in Paris from 1855.

While in the French capital, he was part of the great Gustave Courbet's group, which included painter Édouard Manet, and the aforementioned Baudelaire and Gautier. Whistler, who frequently passed himself off as a wealthy southern gentleman, moved to London in 1858 and was subsequently attracted by the artistic flavour of the time: Albert Moore's cadenced friezes of toga-clad Greeks, Edward Burne-Jones's medieval mysticism and Thomas Armstrong's virtual surrealism.

Thus rooted in both Paris and London, Whistler crossed the channel frequently, like a bee pollinating each side with the other's bohemian notions. Evidently, everyone listened to this erudite, caustic, combative Yank whose signature was, characteristically, a butterfly with a sting in its tail.

Accordingly, Whistler, with his curling moustache, monocle and the ostentatious attire of a dandy, was the main man behind the Aesthetic movement. His painting of 1861, *Symphony in White No. 1: The White Girl,* an incredibly accomplished and beautiful painting of a young girl dressed in white against a white background, is in many ways a precursor to the movement, but was overshadowed by Manet's controversial *Le Déjeuner sur l'herbe* (1863), featuring a nude woman at lunch with two fully dressed and rather foppish men in a woodland copse.

The French man's work was a deliberate affront to the propriety of the time and thus a major influence on the Aesthetic movement. But, however peeved Whistler was that his thunder was stolen by another, he went back to his easel and in 1864 created *Caprice in Purple and Gold: The Golden Screen,* featuring his mistress in a kimono in a profoundly Japanese interior, and *Purple and Rose: The Lange Leizen of the Six Marks* – with the same woman in Chinese garb surrounded by ceramics from said country. Just as the Sex Pistols defined the punk milieu with 'God Save the Queen', these works, with their Japanese influence and acknowledgement of the importance of everyday objects and everyday poses, epitomised the Aesthetic genre.

After a visit to Chile, Whistler moved back to London and produced a few outstanding paintings, one of which was *Nocturne: Blue and Gold – Old Battersea Bridge* (1874), which showed the old wooden bridge etched against a golden green skyline and river. The picture achieved a certain notoriety after John Ruskin wrote that Whistler was asking 'two hundred guineas for flinging a pot of paint in the public's face.'

Whistler, in bristling form, sued for libel and received one farthing in damages, which he forever wore on his watch chain. Unfortunately, the court costs together with the debts he had accrued building his lavish pad in Chelsea's Tite Street (designed in partnership with E. W. Godwin) bankrupted him in 1879, prompting an auction of his work, collections, house and chattels. Leyland oversaw the sale. Whistler's obituary in the *New York Times* on 18 July 1903 described him as 'The maker of paradoxes, the epigrammatist, the master of the "gentle art of making enemies"'.

While Whistler had pioneered on canvas in the early 1860s, up the road William Morris had been busy reinventing the Victorian interior with his distinctive wallpapers, tapestries and textiles. Harking back to the country's Arthurian folklore, Morris's designs were an attempt to create a beautiful utopian ideal that merged with the flowing lines of eastern art. All the rage in the late nineteenth century, no upmarket bohemian home was complete without Morris's wallpaper or textiles.

Accordingly the time was nigh for the movement's commercialisation and, in 1874, entrepreneur Arthur Lasenby Liberty, previously a trader of eastern bric-a-brac, opened the now famous store off Regent Street and took to producing the hitherto hand-made Arts and Crafts/Aesthetic objects in bulk, employing craftsmen to design and oversee production.

Among these craftsmen was one Archibald Knox, who, raised on the Isle of Man, drew heavily from the intricate Celtic imagery so prevalent on his island and incorporated it in graphics, calligraphy, fonts, and even gravestones – including that of his employer, Lasenby. An expert in enamel, pewter and silverware, Knox was Liberty's main designer; he created objects that, fundamentally Art Nouveau, influenced the world. Looking at many of the great Nouveau masterpieces in comparison with the work of Knox, it's impossible not to notice his huge impact. The entrances to the Paris Metro stations, designed by Hector Guimard, are pure Knox, while Alphonse Mucha, the most well known of the Nouveau poster painters, would have been dead in the water without Knox, the unsung hero of nineteenth century design.

Of course one of the reasons that Liberty influenced that world was because of their recently realised mail-order catalogue, which made the company a huge global brand in the same way that Amazon is today. Now you could order an item, pay with a cheque and it would be sent to you. This hadn't been possible before. Consequently, in Italy, Art Nouveau (the child of Aestheticism) was known simply as *Stile Liberty,* in Spain it was named *Modernismo,* in Czechoslovakia *Secese,* in Denmark (drawing from the Viennese Secession, which was also influenced by the Aesthetic movement) *Skønvirke,* and *Jugendstil* in Sweden and Germany.

It's safe to say that said British movement influenced the world of design from the armchair to the water closet.

It was also thanks to home furnishings that the most famous figure associated with the Aesthetic movement, the latecomer Oscar Wilde, stepped into the fray. Wilde appeared on the London scene in the early 1880s, describing himself as a 'Professor of Aesthetics' and an arbiter of taste. In truth he was a blagger who, entirely bereft of any knowledge of art, had not one published work to his name. He had, however, been editor of *The Woman's World*, where he promulgated the ideas outlined in *The House Beautiful*, a book written by American author Clarence Cook in 1878. He became an art critic and breathed fresh air into the Aesthetic milieu.

His late arrival was greatly derided by Whistler, who embarked on a severe rivalry with the Irishman. Wilde was said to often parrot Whistler's many witticisms. On one occasion Wilde is alleged to have responded to a quip of Whistler's by saying 'I wish I had said that', to which Whistler replied, 'You will, Oscar, you will.'

Although undeniably rivals, Wilde and Whistler perplexed the Victorians and upset their apple carts. They and their Aesthetic movement chums, like punk rock in the 1970s, were the source of both humour and bewilderment. Accordingly, in 1879 the humourist George du Maurier embarked on a series of satirical cartoons in *Punch* entitled 'Nincompoopiana', which mocked the aesthetes' every step. *Patience*, a comic opera by Gilbert and Sullivan, ridiculed the Aesthetics' affectation, while Royal Worcester fashioned the Patience teapot, half of which depicted a caricatured female aesthete and the other her male counterpart. They were big news.

And yet Wilde, with his novel *The Picture of Dorian Grey* (1890), encapsulated the Aesthetic ethos by exploring themes of decadence, duplicity and beauty, while also outlining its corrupt and dire consequences. The tome, influenced by J.-K. Huysmans' *À Rebours*, described a world that infuriated and offended the Victorians, but still took its author to, not only notoriety, but also fame and success. He and his book epitomised this Aesthetic ethic that captivated the young adventurous rebel. Soon Wilde was the grooviest cat in London.

Lured by the opportunity of exploring the Aesthetic consideration before a larger audience, Wilde took to penning plays and soon became the most successful playwright of his day, his work shown with regularity at the Criterion Theatre, after which he and his minions would retire to the magnificent Criterion bar and restaurant. Designed by the architect Thomas Verity and built at a cost in excess of £80,000 (around £8 million today), it opened in 1873 and remains intact today, a true testament to the overwhelming magnificence of Aesthetic interiors.

Another of Wilde's hangouts was the Grill Room at the Café Royal, where he met Lord Alfred Douglas, the profoundly camp young man who would hasten his demise. Sixteen years his junior, Bosie, as he was nicknamed, became Wilde's sexual partner – to much public condemnation. In 1895, the younger man's father, John Sholto Douglas, 9th Marquess of Queensberry, described Wilde as a 'sodomite', after which the playwright sued him for libel and the Marquess was arrested. The trial became the talk of the town and front-page news, but Queensberry's lawyers turned the screw on Wilde, describing him as an older degenerate homosexual who preyed on young, innocent men, and threatened to call a barrage of young male prostitutes to testify against him.

Wilde, without a leg to stand on, dropped the charges and was bankrupted by court costs. The Marquess sent the evidence of Wilde's bawdy ways to Scotland Yard and the writer ended up serving two years' hard labour and abject humiliation in Reading Gaol. He exited a broken man, his health and reputation in tatters, and went into exile, dying ten months after Queensberry, at the Hôtel d'Alsace in Paris on 30 November 1900.

With his extravagantly camp demeanour, Wilde had scandalised Victorian society yet still garnered myriad devotees who took up the Aesthetic flag. One such adherent was the young Aubrey Beardsley, who travelled to Paris in 1892 and witnessed the poster art of Wilde's friend Toulouse-Lautrec and the Gallic fascination with Japanese woodcuts. Beardsley returned to London with enough chutzpah to approach Wilde with an offer to illustrate his 1894 play *Salome*.

An immediate sensation, Beardsley, who was also influenced by Burne-Jones, Morris and Whistler, was catapulted into the upper echelons of the Aesthetic movement, his simple use of pen and ink, 'whiplash' line and block colour immediately marking him as a genius of the age. He died of tuberculosis aged twenty-five in 1898.

By the turn of the century, with the exception of the stubborn Whistler, who died in 1903, all of the major aesthetes – Rossetti, Morris, Burne-Jones, Ford Madox Brown, Wilde and Beardsley – were dead and buried, and thus some might argue that the movement was also dead, but it wasn't so. The idea had spread worldwide, hit the high street and morphed into Art Nouveau.

In 1899 the architect George Skipper designed the Royal Arcade in Norwich in what is arguably Aesthetic-meets-Art Nouveau style, and engaged the services of ceramic sculptor and Arts and Crafts artist W. J. Neatby to tile his creation.

In 1902, Harrods recruited Neatby to design their food hall in a purely Aesthetic style, depicting a medieval Arcadian Albion that, albeit magnificent, never existed. And the trend continued. Neatby went on to design even more Aesthetic-Art Nouveau-style shopping arcades (the forerunner of shopping malls) nationwide.

In Glasgow the notion was taken to its splendid conclusion by the undervalued Aesthetic visionary, Scottish-born Margaret Macdonald, and her husband Charles Rennie Mackintosh. As young art students they had been influenced by Beardsley's hugely controversial drawings. The couple went on to create a style that, purely Aesthetic, leans heavily on the restraint and economy of means of Japanese design. It was most evident in the magnificent Glasgow townhouse they designed to showcase their talents. Now preserved at the Hunterian Museum in Glasgow, it is a temple to faultless design and gentle understatement. Macdonald died in Chelsea in 1933, leaving just £88, but in 2008, her work *The White Rose and the Red Rose* (1902) was auctioned for £1.7 million. Mackintosh, meanwhile, is now revered as one of the greatest ever British architects and designers. The Viennese painter Gustav Klimt admitted that the frieze Macdonald exhibited at the eighth Viennese Secession exhibition in 1900 had a great influence on his work.

Aestheticism was the one British art movement that influenced the whole world for decades. What were the aforementioned Klimt and his Viennese Secessionist acquaintances if not a branch of the Aesthetic movement? Alphonse Mucha, the undisputed king of Art Nouveau, was entirely influenced by the Aesthetics. René Lalique, the great glass designer, took a massive leaf out of their book, and the bisexual dancer Isadora Duncan was 100 per cent aesthete, while composers Claude Debussy and Erik Satie simply applied the Aesthetic consideration to music.

The Aesthetic movement lived by sucking in influence from all over the world but ended up influencing the entire globe. Its reign ended quite appropriately as World War I and its new industrial killing machines smashed every consideration bar survival out of the ballpark, and a new, darker, more cynical and destructive ethic took centre stage. The party was over.

But what is most impressive about the Aesthetic movement was that, unlike we inhabitants of the new age of complacency, the Aesthetics did not let the tide of industry, globalisation, capitalism and greed sweep over them like a gaggle of beached whales. They stood up and made a stand, albeit artistically, and, notwithstanding their detractors, changed the way the world looked and the way we looked at the world.

Their influence is still evident. Only today I saw a burly York-shireman in the park with a bald head and several tattoos, one of which was a Celtic design that was pure Archibald Knox and one a copy of Hokusai's *The Great Wave off Kanagawa*.

The Aesthetic ideal lives on.

Viennese Modernism

Anyone who travelled on the London Underground in 2017 will have noticed the huge advertisements featuring Egon Schiele's controversial nudes replete with a white banner covering their genitalia that proclaimed: 'SORRY, 100 years old but still too daring today. #ToArtItsFreedom: Viennese Modernism 2018. See it all in Vienna.'

Initially, the ads were rejected by marketers in both the UK and Germany due to regulations governing 'morality in the public domain'. Only when the Viennese Tourist Board covered up the nude's offending private parts were the displays allowed.

The adverts were a fittingly risqué promotion for Vienna's massive year-long, city-wide enterprise 'Beauty and the Abyss' – a series of exhibitions to honour the centenary of the deaths of four of the city's most famous sons (artists Gustav Klimt, Egon Schiele and Koloman Moser and the architect Otto Wagner), as well as celebrate the influence of *fin de siècle* Viennese Modernism and the end of the Viennese Secession.

All four men are synonymous with Modernism and especially the Secession, on whose headquarters – an exhibition pavilion on Vienna's Friedrichstrasse – sits that hashtagged aphorism in full, *Der Zeit ihre Kunst. Der Kunst ihre Freiheit* – 'To every age its art. To every art its freedom'.

The furore caused by the posters is, of course, entirely appropriate since Vienna circa 1900 was one of the naughtiest, most liberated cities in the world, where every distraction was available and every controversy courted. It was during this period that the city's best-known art, architecture and design masterpieces were created, music composed and notions conceived. Back then, Vienna was not just the geographical centre of Europe and the capital of the continent's biggest political entity, the Austro-Hungarian Empire, boasting some eleven chief ethno-language groups – it was also a melting pot of cultures, philosophies and arcane mischief.

What is less appropriate is that the Secession's maxim should have been purloined by Austria's current government, a union of the centre-right People's Party and far-right Freedom Party founded in the 1950s by previous Nazi bureaucrats. Their coalition agreement is contained in a 182-page document, which includes a section on their plans for culture, and how freedom for the arts is a given, while also stating 'engagement with our common cultural heritage... contributes significantly to Austria's sense of identity'. But, what has really got the Viennese art cognoscenti's goat is that the Secession's almost sacred motto, 'To every age its art, to every art its freedom', is also used in the manifesto. In answer, the Secession board (who are still very active, with groundbreaking exhibitions) issued a public declaration that included the following: 'Freedom of the arts is necessarily premised on internationality, pluralism, and dialogue. The notion that art's purpose is to buttress a national collective identity presses it into a service that runs counter to its thematic diversity... An open society is the air that art needs to breathe.'

Certainly, when we think of Vienna circa 1900 we don't think of jingoist right-wing politics. We think of Sigmund Freud, the son of a Jewish Moravian who pioneered psychoanalysis; the great composer Gustav Mahler, born in Bohemia; Jewish twelve-tone composer Arthur Schoenberg, of Bratislavan parenthood whose work was considered decadent by the Nazis; and of Joseph Maria Olbrich, the Silesian architect who created the Secession building. One might conclude that this concoction of influence, this open-mindedness that was *fin de siècle* Vienna, is responsible for creating our modern multimedia, multinational, multifaceted world – sitting on a Koloman Moser chair, looking at a Klimt painting while listening to Mahler and thinking about Freud.

This liberal ethic lay at the heart of the Viennese Secession, which included Olbrich, Klimt – who was the society's first president – illustrator Max Kurzweil, designer Josef Hoffmann and all-rounder Moser, who designed everything from stamps to jewellery to stained glass windows and clothing.

Undoubtedly, these Viennese visionaries were hugely influenced by Britain's Aesthetic movement. And while the Brits rebelled against the rapacious industrialisation of their country, so did the Secession revolt against the conformist, reactionary Austro-Hungarian Empire and its lapdog, the Vienna Künstlerhaus (Artist's Society), which foiled any attempt to show either foreign or avant-garde art in their country.

Consequently, the vehemently internationalist Secession fielded exhibitions of arts, photography and crafts from far and wide. Glasgow's Charles Rennie Mackintosh and his wife Margaret Macdonald exhibited at the eighth Secession in 1900, madcap expressionist dancer Isadora Duncan performed in their building, and the gang themselves were proud to count Polish painter, artist and poet Stanislaw Wyspiański, Russian painter Teresa Feoderovna Ries and Hungarian architectural sculptor Othmar Schimkowitz (who created the three Gorgons on the Secession building) amongst their number. Not surprisingly, all this free-thinking modernity and fraternising with foreigners ruffled a few feathers but, as hard as the wheezing old guard huffed and puffed, they could not blow the Secession house down.

To put the Secession in context, the clique were not unlike Brit punk rockers of the 1970s in that they, deliberately contentious and controversial, created a new style of 'art' for the people, by the people. So teachers preached against them, the press ridiculed them and clerics called them the Antichrist, while they just carried on regardless, held their own events, made their own posters and published their house magazine, *Ver Sacrum* (*Sacred Spring*), which featured reproductions, poetry, illustrations, graphic art and object design. The Secession helped Vienna throw off the shackles of nineteenth-century inhibition and march into the new century like a lusty teenage libertine.

A city that proffered all manner of distractions, Vienna in 1900 vied with Paris as the hedonist's paradise. Prostitution of all kinds was rife, sparking numerous appeals by upstanding citizens who decried Vienna's descent into so-called dissolution and depravity. The city became known as the homosexual capital of Europe, its numerous public bathhouses renowned throughout the empire as the premier hang-out for well-heeled urbane gay male. As Magnus Hirschfeld, the Berlin-based pioneer of the German gay movement, wrote in a 1901 article regarding the flourishing secret homosexual life of Vienna: 'We saw men whose appearance gave nothing away, and others in make-up, powdered and decorated with beauty spots and dripping with real or fake diamonds... there whooped a group of eighteen-to twenty-year-olds full of the joy of youth, playfully teasing each other with girls' names.' Alternatively, lesbian women were catered to by sapphic cabaret at the likes of Eisvogel, one of the largest revue bars in the Prater, and its ladies-only orchestra.

To add to this free-for-all, no-holds-barred society, diacetylmorphine – sold over the counter under its well-known trademark (Heroin) as 'the sedative for coughs' – was as common as paracetamol. And, as they were yet to discover its own addictive qualities, heroin addiction was so rife that doctors prescribed the easily available cocaine as a cure. Sigmund Freud was all over the marching powder and as early as 1884 published his papers, 'Über Coca', in which he wrote about the marvellous effects of cocaine: 'It causes exhilaration and lasting euphoria which in no way differs from the normal euphoria of the healthy person,' he wrote. It's hard to imagine the high jinks as folk discovered the fun they might have with these new pharmaceutically pure wonder drugs considered not only harmless but also beneficial. Add the fashionable yet mind-altering absinthe to the mix, shake vigorously, and the consequences were hardly mundane.

And leading the charge was the Secession, created in 1897. Any celebration of Viennese creativity should focus on the group, especially Klimt, Schiele, Wagner and Moser as each played a unique role in not only the city's, but also the world's, aesthetic.

Its most famous member is Klimt (his work *Portrait of Adele Bloch-Bauer* is the thirteenth most expensive painting ever sold, at $158.7 million, adjusted for inflation) and he epitomised the crew's tenet by smashing every convention to smithereens. In 1888, aged twenty-six, he was the establishment golden boy and received the Golden Order of Merit from Emperor Franz Josef for his murals. Four years later, after his father and brother suddenly died, Klimt created a new style that, mainly paintings of the nude female body, was unashamedly erotic (and, by some standards, pornographic) and surfed the city's preoccupation with sex that so coloured the work of Freud. Undoubtedly, Klimt was punk rock. He was front-page news. He was controversial beyond the pale. He took traditional themes, added a primitive sexuality-orientated subtext and blew the bloody doors off.

After Klimt embarked on his 'golden period' (named so because this was when he painted his most celebrated works and he used a lot of gold leaf) he caused a humongous fuss and embraced a hippy, free-loving lifestyle, wore no underwear, sported long man-dresses, open-toed sandals and a scruffy unkempt beard. He fathered some fourteen children with a succession of women – none of whom he married – while his permanent companion, fashion designer Emilie Flöge, with her unconstructed, corsetless, free-flowing garments and liberal sexual mores, was a hero of the Viennese feminist movement.

And yet Klimt still had time to encourage others. In 1907, seventeen-year-old Egon Schiele (who'd previously been ordered not to visit the Secession by his art tutor) met his idol Klimt, who became his mentor. Klimt introduced the absurdly talented teenager to the Wiener Werkstätte (the Secession's community of artists) and consequently invited him to exhibit in the 1909 Vienna Kunstschau, alongside Edvard Munch and Van Gogh. Schiele took the master's lead and concentrated on depicting explicit nude figures, employed bar girls and prostitutes as models and had sex with almost all of them. Thus, between 1909 and 1910 Schiele moved from being merely Klimt's protégé to Austria's premier terror of the bourgeoisie.

In 1911, Schiele met the seventeen-year-old former Klimt model (and supposed mistress) Valerie (Wally) Neuzil and moved with her to his mother's birthplace, Krumau, where he employed the town's teenage girls as models, was arrested and charged with seduction and abduction of a minor, only for the police to raid his home and confiscate over one hundred 'pornographic' drawings and imprison him for three weeks. The more serious charges were dropped, but he was found guilty of exhibiting erotic drawings in a place accessible to children and served another three days in jail.

Indubitably, Schiele's antics were rather off-piste even for the madhouse that was Vienna back then and caused uproar even amongst his colleagues. Apart from drawing nude minors from life he also depicted a woman masturbating, while his painting *Eros* portrayed an emaciated naked male with his legs open holding his huge red, erect penis. Still, it wasn't until after a barnstorming solo show in Paris in 1914 that the international art world suddenly twigged to the man's inestimable genius.

But the Secession was not just about nude paintings, it was also about innovation and, even though the lives of Koloman Moser and Otto Wagner were not quite so controversial as either Klimt or Schiele, both adequately illustrated the Secession's will or *Gesamtkunstwerk* – the idea of the complete artwork, achieved through everyday living surrounded by Art Nouveau. The former was born in Vienna in 1868 and, like Schiele and Klimt, was recognised as something of a genius and, as such, aged just twenty-four was appointed drawing master to the heir to the throne, Archduke Franz Ferdinand.

Still, he threw it all in to form the Secession, design the Secession's stationery, its *Ver Sacrum* magazine and create the famous wreath-bearer frieze on the Secession building. Then, in 1903 Moser established the groundbreaking Wiener Werkstätte (Vienna Workshop) that embraced a host of architects, artists and designers who worked in all manner of design, from ceramics to fashion, silver, furniture and graphics. He is also credited as world's first graphic designer.

Yet the most evident of all the Secesssion's contributors is Otto Wagner, who came up with an entirely innovative language that reflected the vitality of this crazy city, revolutionised architecture and changed the face of Vienna. His series of internationally celebrated buildings such as the Postal Savings Bank and the Karlsplatz Stadtbahn Station feature in any and all tours of the city and have yet to be bettered.

The Secession's elder statesman, he personified the essence of Secessionist Vienna by embracing design, urban planning and entrepreneurialism and believed that practical objects needed no more and no less design than was essential for them to be efficient. Wagner's influence can be seen the world over in Art Deco constructions such as New York's Chrysler Building, the Palais de Tokyo, Paris, London's Broadcasting House and Lisbon's Teatro Eden.

Meanwhile, all had changed, not just for the Secessionists but the entire western hemisphere as the First World War introduced a darker, more malevolent machine age. And all around, the party was over.

As if on cue, the secession's greatest exponents all died in 1918. Klimt pegged it on 6 February 1918, Wagner died of erysipelas on 11 April, while on 18 October Moser passed away after losing a battle with head and neck cancer, followed by Schiele on Halloween. Klimt and Egon were victims of the great Spanish flu epidemic that, in two years, killed between 50 and 100 million people in Europe, including many Viennese artists. 'Twas a bad year for the Secession.

I'd like to think that *fin de siècle* Vienna was rather like Paris in the 1920s, Berlin in the early 1930s or even London in the 1960s – full of mad artists and thinkers drawn from all over Europe running about, off their trolleys, trying to make a difference. Consequently, every artist, musician and intellectual from the Austro-Hungarian Empire flocked there to be the new Mahler, the new Freud or the new Gustav Klimt. One of them was the sixteen-year old Adolf Hitler. But that's another story.

Viennese Modernism 2018 runs until 2019; for more information, visit wienermoderne2018.info

Otto Dix, Kaiser Wilhelm and Berlin in the Twenties

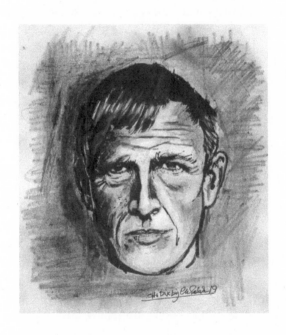

Otto Dix comfortably sits amongst the pantheon of artists who used their craft to criticise and discredit the society in which they lived. His artworks, despised by Hitler and the Third Reich, depicted the chronic aftermath of World War I and the excesses of twenties Berlin – the beggars, the prostitutes, the physically maimed veterans, the sadomasochists and the hedonists. 'All art is exorcism,' he explained. 'I paint dreams and visions too; the dreams and visions of my time. Painting is the effort to produce order; order in yourself. There is much chaos in me, much chaos in our time.'

Indeed, Dix was born at a pivotal time in European history. It was 1891 and Kaiser Wilhelm II – the last German Emperor and King of Prussia – had, only three years before, acceded to the throne. The grandson of Queen Victoria, Wilhelm was a pugnacious monarch who favoured not only warfare, but also all the chivalric pomp that came with it. The esteemed German historian Thomas Nipperdey (1927–1992) described him as 'romantic… unsure and arrogant, with an immeasurably exaggerated self-confidence and desire to show off – a juvenile cadet, who never took the tone of the officers' mess out of his voice, and brashly wanted to play the part of the supreme war-lord'.

Some have suggested that his truculent, belligerent attitude was intended to over-compensate for his weak and noticeably withered, short left arm, which he thought was a misfortune commonly known as Erb's palsy, caused by the use of excessive force during his difficult breech birth. Thus he blamed the British doctor and his English mum for his deformity – which led to a strong anti-British sentiment which ultimately contributed to the 1914–1918 world war. The affliction, now known as Kaiser Wilhelm Syndrome, was actually caused by a fall his mother took when four months pregnant.

A curious fish, he'd loved his grandmother (who was in fact three-quarters German) but hated the English ruling classes, who he thought were 'Freemasons thoroughly infected by Judah' and alienated them with his naval expansion, his policy of aggressive German colonial expansion and his support of the Boers against the British. He also believed in the superiority of the German race and aimed to rule as well as reign.

Still, the new century was certainly beckoning while the old, personified by the Kaiser, was hanging on by its bloody fingernails. It was into this world that Dix was born. One might say that the Kaiser's decisions not only dictated and maybe caused the worst upheavals and horrors of the twentieth century (and history) but the artist's whole life.

Dix was born in Gera, Eastern Germany, the eldest son of a foundry worker and a seamstress. Encouraged by his painter cousin, Fritz Amman, between 1906 and 1910 he served a painting apprenticeship, after which he entered the Dresden Academy of Applied Arts to learn decorative wall painting and studied the methods of the Old Masters. All was going swimmingly until 1914, when the Kaiser turned the whole world on its head.

In short, the Kaiser's childhood buddy, Franz Ferdinand, Archduke of Austria, had been assassinated in Sarajevo on 28 June. Emperor Wilhelm offered to support Austria-Hungary in crushing the 'black hand' – the secret organisation composed of Serbian military who had plotted the killing of his pal – and to further back Austria in its declaration of war against Serbia. The Russians backed the Serbs and Wilhelm, believing that 'England, France and Russia have conspired themselves together to fight an annihilation war against us', attacked France through neutral Belgium after Austria invaded Serbia. The atrocity that was World War I had begun.

Consequently, young Otto volunteered, somewhat eagerly, for service, and was drafted into a field artillery regiment. 'I have to experience all the ghastly, bottomless depths for life for myself; it's for that reason that I went to war, and for that reason I volunteered,' he later said. And he certainly got his wish. By 1915 he was a machine gunner at the front lines in France – his task to mow down oncoming soldiers as they charged to their death over no-man's-land. From this vantage point he saw all the horrors that modern warfare might provide and some that no one had ever imagined.

So there was Dix, knee deep in mud, blood, shit and death at the front. He fought at the Somme Offensive that claimed a million lives across both sides. In 1917, his unit was transferred to the eastern front where he remained until the Russian October Revolution deposed the Czar and hostilities with Russia ended. Dix then returned to the western front, took part in the German Spring Offensive, earned the Iron Cross (second class) for valour and reached the rank of vice sergeant major. Remarkably, even though he'd been wounded five times, he'd served the whole of the Great War on both fronts and was thus honorably discharged one month after the debacle ended. More than 70 million combatants were put into the field, 20 million were wounded and an estimated 17 million killed, including 2.5 million Germans.

'As a young man you don't notice at all that you were, after all, badly affected,' he informed. 'For years afterwards, at least ten years, I kept getting these dreams, in which I had to crawl through ruined houses, along passages I could hardly get through...' No one can doubt that the experience had embittered the artist's enthusiasm for such conflict or that the sketches he made of the horrors fuelled his work for the next twenty years.

In 1919, Dix formed the Dresden Secession with Oskar Kokoschka and Conrad Felixmüller and created quite excellent woodcuts such as *Apotheosis (Apotheose)* that exhibits the better aspects of both Futurism and Cubism. At its centre it features the grossly oversized genitalia of a prostitute dressed in a corset that exposes her sagging breasts. Dix had found his artistic direction.

Meanwhile, the Kaiser had been forced to abdicate. 'The deepest, most disgusting shame ever perpetrated by a people in history,' wrote the disgraced warmonger, pre-empting the forthcoming Nazi anti-Semitic, anti-Versailles ethic, 'the Germans have done onto themselves. Egged on and misled by the tribe of Judah... Let no German ever forget this, nor rest until these parasites have been destroyed and exterminated from German soil!'

What followed was the German Revolution and the founding of the Weimar Republic (the first democratic government in the country's history, whose parliament was based in the city of Weimar) that, however optimistic, was doomed to failure. Germany had signed the Treaty of Versailles, on 28 June 1919. It charged the Kaiser with supreme offence against international morality and gave, among other possessions, Alsace-Lorraine back to France, West Prussia back to Poland, and Northern Schleswig to Denmark, while its many colonies were given to the allied powers. Post-World War I Germany was in fact 13 per cent smaller than during Imperial times and severely weakened. The country was also ordered to pay, according to what became known as the War Guilt Clause (Article 231), financial reparation (269 billion gold marks – the equivalent of around 100,000 tonnes of pure gold or 834 billion dollars) to the allied victors for the cost of the war. To add, Germany was now home to two million orphans, two million invalids, and one million widows. Added to this the Weimar Republic found itself handicapped, with a lack of experienced politicians and a surfeit of political parties all jockeying for power. Thus Germany was thrown into one of the worst economic depressions in history. In the early post-war years, inflation was growing at an alarming rate, but the government simply printed more and more banknotes to pay the bills. Then the monthly rate of inflation rose to a staggering 3.25 billion per cent which, equivalent to prices doubling every two hours, brought the US dollar-to-mark exchange rate to 80 billion. Famously, by 1923 it took a wheelbarrow full of notes (200 billion marks) to buy a loaf of bread.

But if the economy was up the creek, the opposite was happening to the arts. Indeed, the maxim 'many a masterpiece was written on an empty stomach' had never rung so true. Berlin in the 1920s was one of the most creative cities in the history of the world. Rather like the financially strapped New York of the sixties and seventies, poverty and need fuelled artistic endeavour and while, even though the work of Dix, George Grosz and John Heartfield (both of whom Dix met at the Berlin Dada Fair in 1920) was a condemnation of Weimar society, said culture still produced remarkable results. Many of the creatives were joined by one common aim, and that was to eschew old Expressionist habits and to look outside their windows at the factory floors, the hospitals, the shipyards, the brothels, the dens of iniquity and capture the excess, prodigality, despair, revolt and trivial amusements of their brave new world.

Both Dix and Grosz had followed such a path since 1919. Dix had certainly set the tone with the likes of *Crippled War Veterans Playing Cards* (1920), *Butcher Shop* (1920) and *War Wounded* (1922), but it wasn't until 1923 that this 'movement' found a name – Neue Sachlichkeit, or New Objectivity.

Naturally, Dix led the movement by example. In 1924, he'd joined the Berlin Secession and exhibited his series of fifty-one etchings, *Der Krieg (The War),* which were consciously modelled on Goya's (1746–1828) equally famous and equally devastating *Los Desastres de la Guerra (The Disasters of War)* which chronicled Goya's own experience of the horrors of the Napoleonic invasion and the Spanish War of Independence from 1808 to 1814. Art historian George Heard-Hamilton describes Dix's cycle as 'perhaps the most powerful as well as the most unpleasant anti-war statements in modern art'.

Equally unsettling are his paintings of prostitutes, *Salon* (1927) – four prostitutes bored and hideous, one of pensionable age, deathly pale with sagging breasts and pot belly – and *Three Women* (1926), which shows three prostitutes in a brothel – one hideously fat, another painfully thin and the third on her hands and knees like a dog, her pendulous breasts touching the floor. Erotic they certainly are not.

Indisputably, Dix was highlighting the degradation suffered by the German working classes. During this time countless war orphans and widows turned to crime and prostitution just to put food on their tables. The terms prostitute and war widow became interchangeable, and Berlin became one of the world's leading 'sin cities', where any type of sexual distraction could be bought.

Alongside Grosz, George Scholz and the voyeuristic hyperrealist Christian Schad, Dix was part of the New Objectivity's left wing. Called the Verists, they concentrated on what some might call ugly, sordid and certainly satirical material and enveloped Dada's abandonment of any pictorial rules or artistic language. 'I'm not that obsessed with making representations of ugliness. Everything I've seen is beautiful,' enlarged Dix.

Under the banner of Neue Sachlichkeit came the work of Bertolt Brecht (such as *The Threepenny Opera*), the architecture and design of the *Bauhaus* (which was founded with the idea of bringing all the arts together under a functional dictate) and the photography of August Sander, László Moholy-Nagy and Albert Renger-Patzsch.

Berlin especially led the way in cinema, with films as G. W. Pabst's *Pandora's Box* (1929), Joseph von Sternberg's *Blue Angel* (1930) and Fritz Lang's *Metropolis* (1927) and *M* (1931), all of which, even though often described as Expressionist, explore Neue Sachlichkeit themes.

Undeniably, Berlin in the twenties had seized Vienna's mantle as the Paris of the East. It was now a racy metropolis housing some four million people – a third of which were under thirty years of age. Many had drifted there from all over Germany and Europe, attracted by its reputation as a libidinous party central where one's sexuality raised little or no concern. Two hundred thousand Russians had fled the Revolution and settled alongside the artistic avant-garde, the underworld and the licentious, all of whom sensed imminent disaster and fiddled before *their* world burned. Lest we forget, between 1918 and 1920, the Spanish flu claimed more lives than World War I. Worldwide, an estimated 20 to 70 million people fell victim to the pandemic. The pointlessness of the war, the flu, the post-war famine and the hyperinflation strongly shaped attitudes throughout the country, particularly Berlin. The perception being: 'Why bother saving if the money is worthless, and why bother studying if death is around the corner?'

No wonder then that many behaved as if today was their last. Dance clubs, strip clubs, brothels, vaudeville and sexually provocative cabaret flourished while sex between those of the same gender and everyone else was indulged in, along with drugs of every kind. Accordingly Berlin became the cocaine capital of the world, the whole city burning the candle at both ends.

'In some circles, especially in the Berlin art world, cocaine was considered an interesting and fashionable vice,' chided Carl Zuckmayer, who penned the *Blue Angel* screenplay. 'I never got involved myself even though buckets and sacks of the stuff was snorted in my company. I was disgusted by their inflamed nostrils.'

Even though cocaine had recently been made illegal in the UK and the US (except with an easily obtained prescription), no such prohibition seized Berlin and high jinks was virtually compulsory. Also popular was diacetylmorphine, which, from 1898 to 1910, was marketed under the trademark name Heroin as a non-addictive morphine substitute and cough suppressant. It was banned elsewhere but was freely available in Weimar Berlin, where all bets were off.

One of the city's most legendary imbibers was one of Otto Dix's sitters, the scandalously androgynous nude dancer Anita Berber, who wore her hair in a bob dyed blood red, sported a monocle and roamed Berlin with her pet monkey on her shoulder. He captured her in 1925 wearing the tomato-red 'Morphine' costume. Not one to hide her drug use, her preferred substances were cocaine, opium and morphine aided and abetted by chloroform and ether mixed in a bowl which she then stirred with a rose, eating its petals. Her style inspired Marlene Dietrich, who launched her acting career as Berber's understudy and copied her every move. Berber personified Berlin's roaring twenties, dancing to words by her first husband, the expressionist poet and notorious international con artist Sebastian Droste. The pair were banned from most European venues and expelled from Vienna and in their book *The Dances of Vice, Horror, and Ecstasy* envisioned a dance with Berber catching Droste's sperm in her mouth as he hangs from a rope above her. She died of TB aged twenty-nine and was buried in a pauper's grave.

Berber's death metaphorically signalled the forthcoming end of the Weimar Republic and the decadence, liberalism and open-mindedness of Berlin's Golden Twenties. All through the decade discontent had come from both the political far right and left. Adolf Hitler had attempted a coup in his Beer Hall Putsch of November 1923; that failed, but membership to his Nazi Party (a term that stems from *Nationalsozialist*) still went from 27,000 in 1925 to 108,000 in 1928 even though his prediction of further economic disaster was considered unwise. Yet before the Wall Street Crash of 1929, 1.25 million Germans were unemployed. By the end of 1930 the figure had reached nearly four million. Wages dropped and people suffered. Many Germans began to say that if Hitler was clever enough to predict the depression maybe he also knew how to solve it. Many also agreed that the War Guilt Clause had destroyed their country's economy. Virtually all Germans believed they were not responsible for the outbreak of World War I and that the Treaty of Versailles had robbed them of ancestral lands, while Hitler's anti-Semitism was only a minor part of his popular appeal to Germans.

In the General Election of September 1930, the Nazi Party increased its number of representatives in parliament from 14 to 107. Hitler was now the leader of the second largest party in Germany. On 30 January 1933 Adolf Hitler was appointed German Chancellor of the Exchequer, and in August 1934 was formally named *Führer und Reichskanzler* (leader and chancellor), which allowed him absolute power. So he banned all other political parties and a new era of living hell began.

The Nazis condemned much of the work of the Neue Sachlichkeit as degenerate art or Entartete Kunst (a term that they applied to all modern art) and destroyed much of the movement's work and prohibited many of its artists from painting. In 1933, Dix was dismissed from his teaching post at the Dresden Academy and was allowed only to paint landscapes.

In 1937 the Nazis put on their infamous Exhibition of Degenerate Art, which featured any remaining art deemed modern, degenerate, or subversive. Intended to incite further revulsion against the 'perverse Jewish spirit' penetrating German culture, it featured over 650 artworks gathered from thirty-two German museums by 112 mainly German artists (including Dix, Grosz, Beckman and Kandinsky), only six of whom were actually Jewish. It opened in Munich on 19 July, and remained on view until 30 November before touring eleven other cities in Germany and Austria. The artworks were hung in a cramped basement of the Institute of Archaeology. Above the works were scrawled slogans such as 'The Jewish longing for the wilderness reveals itself – in Germany the Negro becomes the racial ideal of a degenerate art.' Some 2,009,899 visitors attended it – an average of 20,000 people per day – while the Nazi-sanctioned Great German Art Exhibition attracted a fraction of that number of visitors. Subsequently, Goebbels destroyed some 4,000 seized works of art. Today they'd be worth a king's ransom.

Meanwhile poor old Dix, who'd said, 'People were already beginning to forget what horrible suffering the war had brought them. I did not want to cause fear and panic, but to let people know how dreadful war is and so to stimulate people's powers of resistance', not only saw his message completely ignored but, after he was arrested in 1939 and charged with involvement in a plot on Hitler's life, was conscripted into the army for World War II. In 1945 he was captured and put into a prisoner of war camp. After the war he returned to his beloved Dresden, which had been thoroughly razed to the ground by allied bombers in 1945. Some of his paintings now followed a more religious path while others, such as *Ecce Homo II* (1948), looked at the misery caused by World War II. He died in Singen, Germany in 1969. The Kaiser died aged eighty-two in Doorn, Netherlands – where he'd been exiled since 1918 – on 3 June 1941, just weeks before the Nazis' fateful invasion of Russia.

To view Julien Bryan's short film of the Exhibition of Degenerate Art: https://bit.ly/2GAObx7

Paris in the Twenties

After a visit to the Man Ray exhibition at the National Portrait Gallery in 2013, I was struck not only by the diversity and idiosyncrasy of the people he had photographed in Paris in the 1920s, but also how they collectively defined arts and culture for the coming century.

Drawn from his immediate circle of friends and associates, his cast of characters includes the following: James Joyce, whose *Ulysses* was the first word in modernist literature; Marcel Duchamp, who created the blueprint for modern art as we know it; two of the greatest composers that ever lived, namely Igor Stravinsky and Erik Satie; the twentieth century's most influential and important painters, Picasso and Matisse; the architect whose ideas shaped the modern world, Le Corbusier; and Coco Chanel and Elsa Schiaparelli, two fashion designers who forever changed the way women looked.

Certainly, when one considers that these individuals not only moulded the world in which we live but were also chewing the fat together in the same cafés and the same parties at the same time in the same city, it is hugely impressive. It's like an artistic *Stella Street*. Imagine the conversation: 'I just bumped into that Picasso in the café. He was sitting with Matisse discussing the nature of art with James Joyce and Samuel Beckett, and then in came Coco Chanel. She waved to Le Corbusier – who was at the bar next to Aleister Crowley – but sat down with those lovely composers, Satie and Ravel, who were talking to Diaghilev – you know, that Russian chap who does the Ballet Russes.'

A few months after said exhibition ended I could think of no better gift for a friend's birthday than the book that accompanied the show: *Man Ray Portraits*. And so I toddled off to the gallery's bookshop and bought one.

'I'm just reading that,' said the girl behind the till, pointing to an open copy on her desk.

'Can you imagine what it must have been like living in Paris in the twenties?' I pondered out loud.

'I can't honestly think of a better time and place to have been in the history of the world,' she replied enthusiastically. On the Tube home

I gave her comment some thought and duly agreed, but still had to ask myself: why? What caused this city to play host to such a huge explosion of creativity, the like of which had not been seen before and hasn't since? Why did it happen then? And why Paris?

Of course the city has a distinct and unique personality every bit as powerful, emotive and all-consuming as those who sipped from its innovative cup. Its inhabitants are fiercely proud of their city and its ideologies, which they have always fought to preserve.

A great big boisterous heaving genius that never slept, Paris in the twenties was the hub of the artistic world, where debate, single-mindedness, sexual experimentation and liberty ruled the roost. Its ambience encouraged the cross-pollination of the avant-garde, whose protagonists were not only indulged but celebrated, and attracted the greatest artists, writers, adventurers and the *beau monde* into its hedonistic bosom.

The French capital had been bubbling away creatively and politically since 1850. Revolutionary painter Gustave Courbet had thrown the baby out with the bathwater and rejected any and all Romanticism in art, instead painting the 'real world', featuring prostitutes, peasants and the poor.

He also asserted that anyone could paint, and championed freedom of speech, artistic expression and political anarchy. As Courbet, the original punk rocker, declared in 1869, 'I am fifty years old and I have always lived in freedom; let me end my life free; when I am dead let this be said of me: "He belonged to no school, to no church, to no institution, to no academy, least of all to any regime except the regime of liberty."'

Political anarchist Courbet was universally considered both a terrible socialist and a savage but boldly encouraged the country's perception of him as an uneducated rube. Courbet was knowingly hand in glove with the realist writers of the day, such as Honoré de Balzac, George Sand, Gustave Flaubert and his pupil, Guy de Maupassant. All described a world that was hitherto regarded as 'untouchable'. And the authorities weren't happy.

Even the influential poet, dandy and opium addict Charles Baudelaire, very much an avowed monarchist, was prosecuted in 1857 by

Napoleon III's authoritarian regime for his volume of poems, *The Flowers of Evil*, and charged with *outrage aux bonnes mœurs* ('an insult to public decency').

Accordingly, freedom of speech, art and literature was a hot topic in nineteenth-century France. Unsurprisingly, the establishment thought that reading about prostitutes, alcoholics and drug addicts – or seeing paintings of them (or in Courbet's case their pudenda) in a gallery – was simply unacceptable.

On the other hand, the likes of Courbet (whose maternal grand-father fought in the French Revolution) believed such censorship unconstitutional and felt that the Napoleonic dynasty had tainted the ethos of the magnificent French Revolution of 1789 to serve their own personal gain. And the likes of Courbet were not wrong. Indeed, after his famed *coup d'état*, Louis-Napoléon Bonaparte, aka Napoleon III, declared himself emperor and adopted a distinctly authoritarian bent, censoring drawings, caricatures, the press, books, art and the theatre to avert the opposition's rise.

He also manipulated elections, denied Parliament any real power and restricted collective male suffrage by imposing a three-year resi-dency requirement that prevented a large proportion of the itinerant lower classes from voting. One could well imagine a Parisian of the time saying, 'Excuse me, but didn't we just get rid of this lot in that Revolution?'

Parisians in particular were not pleased. They wanted not only freedom of expression and a democratic republic, but demanded that Paris should be self-governing, with its own elected council. But the tide was turning against the ruler and his minions. On 11 Janu-ary 1870, journalist Victor Noir was shot dead by the ruler's cousin, Prince Bonaparte, after an argument over a decidedly anti-monar-chist editorial that criticised both Napoleon I and III in his newspa-per, the radical *La Revanche*.

Over 100,000 people attended the funeral parade. Later that year Napoleon III took his country into the Franco-Prussian War and took personal control of the army. He lost the war, 150,000 French soldiers were killed, and on 2 September he was captured.

When news reached Paris, thousands took to the streets, and two days later his empire was overthrown. Consequently, the Germans entered Paris, and left again in January without incident. The city was asked to shoulder an unreasonably large percentage of the financial compensation made to the Prussians. The Parisians rebelled and, led by the politically left-wing National Guard, took over the city in the middle of March.

They formed the Paris Commune, adopted the red flag of communism rather than the tricolour, and entertained a revolutionary socialist stance with definite pro-feminist codicils. Unfortunately, on 21 May the French army attacked the insurgents. During *la semaine sanglante* (or 'the bloody week') that followed, the army crushed the Communards (supporters of the Paris Commune); 30,000 were killed and 43,000 prisoners were taken. Afterwards, a military court pronounced about a hundred death sentences, more than 13,000 prison sentences and more than 7,000 deportations. It had been civil war: Paris – a hotbed of working-class radicalism – against the French government.

The regime that followed, the Third Republic, based itself on parliamentary supremacy and was marked not only by social stability but also the status quo. '*Liberté, égalité, fraternité*' became the official motto of the administration.

Thus, by the 1890s, with insurrection out of the way, the city was in full swing – dining on a sea of *liberté* and the all-consuming decadence of *la belle époque*. Epitomised by the work of the post-Impressionist, prostitute-loving alcoholic Toulouse-Lautrec, and the knickerless can-canning at the Moulin Rouge, Paris flung caution to the wind and floated on a virtual sea of mind-altering absinthe, opium and cocaine.

In 1900 the city held the Exposition Universelle, a world's fair seen by millions, which exhibited such mind-boggling state-of-the-art inventions as magnetic tape recording, talking movies, diesel engines, Ferris wheels and escalators.

With this fair, and the recently constructed boulevards and new Metro system, it was if the city was establishing itself as the most modern, forward-thinking, libertarian city in the whole world. In the decade that followed, Paris expanded both culturally and geographically, its citizens embracing the new century with the zeal of a religious convert, testing the waters with new ideas, throwing out the rulebook and making up the future as they went along.

Cubism, a movement coined after art critic Louis Vauxcelles described the work of Braque and Picasso as *bizarreries cubiques* ('cubic oddities'), sprang to life in this atmosphere and flummoxed a generation. As good an example as any of the progressive attitude of Parisians at the time, Cubism evolved from a marriage between Cézanne's experiments with angles, facets and perspective, and African art.

Picasso, having been shown a mask of the Fang tribe from Cameroon at the ethnographic museum in the Palais du Trocadéro in May 1907, was so taken by it that he repainted the faces of the two figures on the right of his seminal Cubist work, *Les Demoiselles d'Avignon,* in the mask's style, and thus the Cubist die was cast.

Thus African art was absorbed into modern art and the effect was mercurial. No one had seen *anything* like this before and Picasso, as a result, became the cock of the walk, spawning a slew of major painters such as the Section d'Or, the second wave of Cubism, who included, among others, Jean Metzinger, Robert Delaunay and Fernand Léger.

And then came World War I – four years of carnage the like of which the world had never seen or dreamed of. The number of men mobilised totalled 65 million; 8.5 million were killed, 21 million were wounded, 7.7 million were made prisoners of war, and Paris came close to falling, the front line at one point being just fifteen miles away from its confines. The city was saved by the 'miracle on the Marne', when thousands of Parisian taxis were commandeered to transport French soldiers to the front lines, where they pushed the Germans back to Oise – seventy-five miles from the city – where the front lines stayed for the next four years.

Hostilities ceased in 1918 and Paris kicked into action, positively throbbing with unique creativity, decadence and flair. The citizens, having seen both their and their city's existence under threat, lived as if every day was their last, while foreigners (such as the White Russians) flocked there to escape death and persecution.

Others, particularly black American soldiers, simply stayed on after the war. Most of Harlem's 15th New York National Guard Infantry Regiment – the most highly decorated American combat unit in the Great War – remained living the life, along with former members of James Reese Europe's military band. They loved Paris and Paris loved them. Back home, coloured folk were still being lynched down south. No wonder they stayed. The French capital, with its burgeoning egalitarianism and fascination with African arts, was *the* destination for these *exotique* African-Americans. They brought jazz to the party and the Parisians loved it. No hip soirée was complete without such a band.

Appropriately, American jazz musicians flooded Paris. Harlem moved to Montmartre and a community emerged that consisted mainly of young itinerant unmarried male musicians. One of these was Louis Mitchell, who led the white band at the infamous Casino de Paris. So popular was Mitchell that the club's owner, Léon Volterra, demanded black musicians and not French, then sent Mitchell back to New York, requesting he return to Paris with fifty black musicians. He came back with five, headlined the Casino for a few more years, and in 1921 opened his own restaurant-cum-club, a combination of Harlem and Paris that featured a jazz band in the corner and an all-night American breakfast. There were queues around the block.

Other clubs opened to cater to the city's love for *le jazz hot*. One such establishment was le Bal Nègre, which was created by the parliamentary candidate for Martinique, Jean Rézard des Wouves, as a campaign headquarters in 1924. It later morphed into a dance hall where fashionable young Parisians danced the black bottom or the Charleston to the house band, led by fellow Caribbean reedman Ernest Léardée.

Another was Chez Bricktop, opened on 66 rue Pigalle in 1924 by Ada Beatrice Queen Victoria Louise Virginia Smith, aka Bricktop. Initially a singer and dancer from Virginia, she became the 'doyenne of Parisian café society' and entertained the Duke and Duchess of Windsor and F. Scott Fitzgerald.

Another haunt, Le Grand Duc, was owned by Eugene Bullard of

Columbus, Georgia, and served up jazz and soul food in equal proportions. One of only two black combat pilots in World War I, the former drummer was just one of many who created *le tumulte noir* ('the black noise') of Harlem in Montmartre.

By the mid-1920s you could almost hear the vibrant jazz rhythms emanating from Paris all the way across to New York, prompting more jazzers to follow. On 15 September 1925, the first great jazz saxophonist, Sidney Bechet, sailed to Paris along with nineteen-year-old Josephine Baker, and opened at *La Revue Nègre* at the Théâtre des Champs-Élysées on 2 October.

Soon the incorrigible young singer and dancer eclipsed Bechet and became the toast of Paris – often dressed in an outfit consisting only of fake bananas and appearing on stage with her pet cheetah dressed in a diamond collar. As Ernest Hemingway said, she was 'the most sensational woman anyone ever saw.'

But it wasn't just black Americans who settled in Paris after World War I. A lot of rich white folk came in search of a conurbation where anything and everything went.

The outrageously camp Cole Porter, composer of such standards as 'I get a Kick out of You' and 'Night and Day', was ubiquitous in the city. The grandson of lumber and coal speculator J. O. Cole, the richest man in Indiana, legendary songsmith Porter moved to Paris in 1917 to work with the Duryea Relief organisation, before serving, he claimed, in the French Foreign Legion. A hedonist to the core, he lived in a palatial house with platinum wallpaper and chairs upholstered in zebra skin and threw wild, fabulous parties for Europe's rich and famous, alongside arty ne'er-do-wells. His legendary soirées were the talk of the town, with cross-dressers, exotic musicians, oodles of gay and bisexual congress and much imbibing of cocaine, opium, absinthe and absurdly expensive champagne.

Porter was not alone. In 1920 there were an estimated 8,000 American expats living in the city, but by 1925 they numbered 40,000. And then there were the hundreds of thousands of US tourists who descended on the city annually.

Lest we forget, the prohibition of alcohol had come into force in the United States at midnight on 17 January 1920. Understandably, creative American sensualists were not at all happy having their civil liberties clipped, and thus literally jumped ship. Liberal 'gay Paree', as it was known, with its all-night bars, eccentric sex shows, cross-dressing, gay bath houses, brothels and overt cocaine use, was unmitigated heaven for these American émigrés. You could find students parading through the streets almost naked in all night saturnalias, nudists running through the parks at night, and couples engaging in sexual acts both furtive and uninhibited in public places and bars. Said Americans could not believe their luck.

Many of those who fetched up in Paris were wealthy heirs and heiresses eager to sup at the cup of this creative maelstrom. Shipping heiress Nancy Cunard, who arrived in the city in 1920, immediately set about writing poetry and designing jewellery whilst allying herself with the surrealists and modernists, her obsession with all things African immediately satiated. The muse of, among others, Tristan Tzara, Ezra Pound and Louis Aragon, she could count Ernest Hemingway, Constantin Brâncuşi and Man Ray amongst her lovers, and embraced the bohemian affectation of an eccentric heiress, dressing in a mixture of mannish clothes and ethnic jewellery, dubbed the 'barbaric look' by the fashion world. But her love of both alcohol and Class A narcotics soon got the better of her, and she descended into mental illness and poverty. She died in the Hôpital Cochin, Paris in 1965, aged sixty-nine, weighing just sixty pounds.

The undisputed king of excessive American expats in Paris in the 1920s, however, was Harry Crosby. The son of one of the richest banking families in New England and the nephew of J. P. Morgan Jr, he had been an ambulance driver in the war and seen more deaths than any eighteen-year-old should. As a result, he became one of the youngest American recipients of the Croix de Guerre in 1919. That year he went back to America, only to return to Paris in 1922 with his new wife Polly, who he renamed Caresse – a rather well-endowed beauty who actually invented and patented the first bra.

Ensconced in Paris, the pair embarked on an infinitely decadent and entirely bohemian lifestyle financed by Crosby's $12,000 a year trust fund ($170,000 today, and the exchange rate was outrageously kind to the dollar). The couple were farahead of their time, indulging in exotic African holidays, religious flirtations, spectacular bacchanals, open marriage, seven-in-a-bed orgies, ominous tattoos, and airplane joy-rides and gambling sprees. They took so many opiates, cocaine and hashish that they'd make today's most indulgent young reprobates feel distinctly pedestrian.

Harry, handsome in that clean-cut, all-American, Brad Pitt sense had a mop of blond, greased-back hair and sported black suits, blackpainted fingernails and a black flower in his buttonhole. In July 1925, he slept with a thirteen-year-old Berber girl in North Africa and a young Arab boy in Jerusalem. And during bacchanalian orgies of the annual Four Arts Ball (Bal des Quat'z'Arts) he turned up in nothing but a loincloth covered in crimson ochre, with a necklace of dead pigeons around his neck, while Caresse showed up topless wearing a turquoise wig, riding a baby elephant.

'Harry seemed to be more expression and mood, than man,' wrote Caresse. 'Yet he was the most vivid personality I've ever known, electric with rebellion.' With their money they established the Black Sun Press and published each other's rather accomplished books of poems (with illustrations by Max Ernst).

They were also instrumental in getting the likes of James Joyce, Hemingway and T. S. Eliot published, while their sexual permissiveness attracted other notables such as the then twenty-five-year-old painter Henri Cartier-Bresson (the grandfather of reportage photography). With Harry's nod, Cartier-Bresson embarked on a passionate relationship with keen photographer Caresse, who encouraged and helped the neophyte painter become *the* Cartier-Bresson, now considered one of the greatest photographers of all time. Caresse later said in an interview that Cartier-Bresson 'looked like a fledgling, shy and frail, and mild as whey.' Unfortunately, Harry was found dead on 10 December 1929, aged thirty-one, with a .25 calibre bullet in his right temple. Next to him was the body of his mistress, twenty-year-old Josephine Noyes Rotch, who had a matching hole in her left temple. It was a suicide pact.

The previous day, Harry Crosby had written his final entry in his journal: 'One is not in love unless one desires to die with one's beloved. There is only one happiness – it is to love and to be loved.'

The coroner reported that Crosby had a Christian cross tattooed on the sole of one foot and a pagan icon representing the sun on the other, while his toenails were painted red. Crosby certainly epitomised a generation of writers that American-born author Gertrude Stein dubbed 'the Lost Generation'. This referred to a disaffected group of young men who had fought, lived through and often witnessed first hand the atrocities on the front line of World War I and were now adrift and writing in Paris. Others included Ernest Hemingway, F. Scott Fitzgerald, John Dos Passos and Erich Maria Remarque. Indeed, by 1922, the city was drenched in words. By then it had already seen Proust finish *À La Recherche du Temps Perdu*, James Joyce complete and publish *Ulysses* and Ezra Pound polish *The Cantos,* while Parisian writers such as Francis Carco were penning the likes of *Perversity* which, written in underworld slang, the argot of the Apache gangs, told of 1920s Parisian slum life as no one had before.

If you were a writer in the twenties, you went to Paris.

The first wave of writers who settled in Paris (many of whom are still household names) lasted roughly from the end of World War I to the onset of World War II. The era reached its peak in the 1920s, when Paris's literary residents included Ezra Pound, Hemingway, James Joyce, F. Scott Fitzgerald, William Faulkner, Henry Miller and Anaïs Nin – none of whom were particularly sound psychologically. Certainly, Ernest Hemingway's *A Farewell to Arms* is not the product of a contented mind. Neither is *Manhattan Transfer* by Dos Passos or *Tender Is the Night* by Fitzgerald.

But troubled or not, all of the above revolved around Gertrude Stein. An advocate and critic of artists of every kind, Stein held gatherings every Saturday at her sumptuous home at 27 rue de Fleurus. Here she encouraged a confluence of talent and thinking that would help define modernism in literature and art. On any one night you might find Picasso, poet and erotic novelist Guillaume Apollinaire, Henri Matisse, F. Scott Fitzgerald, James Joyce, Georges Braque and Henri Rousseau sitting around discussing culture with the esteemed harridan.

As Ernest Hemingway, a frequent visitor, states in his book *A Moveable Feast*: 'She [Stein] was angry at Ezra Pound because he had sat down too quickly on a small, fragile, and doubtless uncomfortable chair that it is quite possible he had been given on purpose, and had either cracked or broken it ... That he was a great poet and a gentle and generous man and could have accommodated himself in a normal chair was not considered. The reasons for her dislike of Ezra, skilfully and maliciously put, were invented years later.'

However manipulating and critical was the sapphic Stein, she did however nurture, encourage and help her charges, as did many wealthy residents of twenties Paris. Many writers hung out at Sylvia Beach's Shakespeare and Company on the Left Bank – an informal writers' club-cum-bookshop-cum-flophouse, where literary types hung out and crashed if they were broke. More than a shop, it was also the best-stocked library in Paris.

'I was very shy when I first went into the bookshop and I did not have enough money on me to join the rental library,' explains Hemingway in *A Moveable Feast*. 'She [Sylvia] told me told me I could pay the deposit any time I had the money and made me out a card and said I could take as many books as I wished.' James Joyce nicknamed the shop 'Stratford-on-Odéon' and used it as his office, while Beach bravely published his novel, *Ulysses*, in 1922. It caused a scandal and made her reputation.

Certainly, it appears that this sense of community, and the pooling together of resources, was another significant factor that provoked the prodigious artistic output of twenties Paris. It was the norm for a writer or artist to come up with a valid concept, form a group of fellow writers, poets, sculptors and painters around said conceit, present a manifesto underlining their aims, come up with a name and thrive. It gave the papers something to write about, created a buzz and could be enormously beneficial. One group that grew directly out of the emancipation and autonomy of twenties Paris and epitomised not only this ethic, but also the progressive, libertine, internationalist nutbag abandon of the times were the Surrealists.

Surrealism, via the auspices of poet André Breton, was created on the back of Dadaism, as seen through the eyes of the great Marcel Duchamp. The latter had caused a big stink in 1917 when he submitted a porcelain urinal signed 'R. Mutt' for the exhibition of the Society of Independent Artists in New York. He not only broke every rule of art there was, but also exhibited a work that was more about an idea than an aesthetic and, in doing so, created today's art world. Without Duchamp there'd be no Warhol, Hurst or Chapman Brothers. Undeniably, he pioneered the ready made and the contentious before the concepts were even considered.

Thus, Breton saw the importance of Duchamp (whom he admired for his 'disdain of the thesis') and his works, but describing Dada as a 'ship in distress', he used his interest in Freudian psychology – especially the role of the unconscious and dream analysis – to steer the form into Surrealism.

As big a bag of extrovert oddballs as one might ever encounter, the Surrealists hailed from all over the world and descended on the city like a swarm of mad-arsed wasps. Like-minded poets, painters, sculptors, photographers, dramatists and filmmakers rallied to Breton's assertion that the movement would 'break with things as they are. The essence of the Surrealist image consisting in this call for a freedom of the mind in that life and poetry are "elsewhere"... only the word freedom still exalts me.'

Amongst their number were some of the biggest, most interesting and influential names in the lexicon of modern art. You had, among others: Parisian-born Yves Tanguy, who, with his spiky punk-rock haircut, painted otherworldly globular forms; Frenchman André Masson, whose automatic linear works still excite; Catalan Joan Miró, a total one-off by anyone's measure; and the aforementioned Man Ray, a Pennsylvania-born Russian Jew who, allied to Duchamp in New York, moved to Paris in 1921, became a leading light in first Dada and then Surrealism, and captured all on film.

Since its inception, Surrealism has taken a lot of flak from the art cognoscenti, its visual wisecracks considered cheap jokes that have meagre artistic merit. In some instances I would agree, but even by contemporary standards, who can criticise the films of Luis Buñuel or Germaine Dulac, the sensual sculptures of Jean Arp, the outrageously contemporary sexually charged dolls of the German Hans Bellmer, or the evocative poems of Federico Garcia Lorca or Tristan Tzara?

Surrealism's most noticeable impact on the world, however, was in photography, in particular fashion photography. Norman Parkinson was an advocate of the movement, as was Horst P. Horst and later Erwin Blumenfeld and Martin Munkácsi. Following in the footsteps of Man Ray, they together created the blueprint for all fashion photography to come. Challenged to make photographs of skinny pretty girls in trendy clothing look interesting and groovy they went surreal on their ass.

Indeed, the visual punning and juxtaposing of Surrealism has since permeated every aspect of the media, with the advertising world especially still in its thrall and filmmakers still name-checking its influence. Much of today's contemporary art is at best a reworking of the initial concept, and at worst blatant plagiarism.

Surrealism was all about freedom of thought, and as such its influence has been massive – arguably more so than any other art movement of the twentieth century. The same might be said of much of the creative outpouring from Paris in the 1920s. The city was home to more influential art movements than one could count. It was the hub of an ever-growing photographic community and the epicentre of a massive fashion movement that revolutionised not only how men, and especially women, dressed, but also behaved.

Chanel opened her first boutique on 31 rue Cambon in 1921, pushing the 'flapper' style that swept the world. Androgynous in appearance, it suggested that its wearer was on equal standing with her male counterpart and not a passive dependent. It echoed the rise of female emancipation and equal voting rights that came to being in the UK in 1928, but curiously not in France until 1944. The style, devoid of corsets, long gowns and hair that took hours to achieve, was a deliberate slap in the face to the establishment. Said feminists were a walking, talking demonstration of women's independence and free spirit, and thus this became the uniform for the young lady who refused to accept the shit. Marching en masse down the Rive Gauche, these funky young chicks made a huge statement that changed the twentieth century forever and opened the door for women to dress in pants, T-shirts and flat shoes. This was totally revolutionary.

Paris also led the world on the silver screen in the 1920s with the feature-length work of directors Jean Renoir, Carl Theodor Dreyer and Abel Gance, while the shorts of Fernand Léger (namely 1924's *Ballet Mécanique,* a template for modern pop promos) or Jean Vigo (*A propos de Nice*, 1930) bled cinematic innovation.

Of course the common denominator between all of the above is encapsulated in the maxim '*Liberté, égalité, fraternité'*, without which none of this might have occurred. This attitude allowed the grandsons of black American slaves to sit and drink with intellectuals, the world's most influential artists, *le beau monde* and the filthy rich, all of whom appreciated each other for their uniquely individual gifts.

Finally, if the phrase 'every dog has his day' rings true, then it stands to reason that every city has its decade. Vienna had its golden age from the *fin de siècle* until the First World War, Berlin's was the 1930s, until Hitler and his jack-booted pals came and squashed it, and from the end of World War I until the 1930s Paris had it *all*, and a whole lot more.

Brilliant Chang

'Chang dispensed Chinese delicacies and the drugs and vices of the Orient,' reported the *World Pictorial News* in 1922. 'He demanded payment for his drugs in kind.' The rag went on to further advise its women readers, 'who retained sufficient decency and pride of race', that they turn down 'this fellow with lips thin and cruel, tightly drawn across even yellow teeth.'

So who was this demon, this embodiment of the 'Yellow Peril' that so seized London in the 1920s? He was indeed the first society drug dealer. Billy 'Brilliant' Chang – whose surname is used as slang for cocaine to this day – was an acquaintance of stars and socialites throughout the decade. He dressed in spats, astrakhan-collared over-coats and pinstripe trousers. He was suave, fast and amicable. He was exotic, funny and Chinese. And for a time he was the West End's chief purveyor of cocaine.

Of course, this irrational fear of all things Oriental was hardly new. In 1918 the press had been whipped into a frenzy after a popular young and beautiful actress called Billie Carleton was found dead in her bed after starring at the Victory Ball at the Albert Hall. At her bedside in her Savoy Hotel suite a gold box was found containing cocaine given to her by Reggie de Veulle, a well-known costume designer of the day. He had bought the drug from a Scottish woman called Ada and her Chinese husband, Lau Ping You, who both lived on the Limehouse Causeway, London's original Chinatown.

Usually staid publications reported that both de Veulle and Carleton had been at an all-night orgy in a Mayfair flat where the women wore flimsy nighties and the men silk pyjamas while smoking opium. Ada and de Veulle were sentenced to five and eight months' hard labour respectively. The prosecution painted de Veulle in the worst possible light, describing him as somewhat foreign, with an effeminate face and mincing little smile, while Lau Ping You escaped with a £10 fine.

The death of a beautiful white girl from an overdose of drugs, in combination with the participation of a Chinese man, led to the first big drug scandal of the twentieth century. The press whisked them-selves into an uncommon frenzy and the *Pictorial News* ran a series of pieces about the East End of London, Limehouse and what they described as the encroaching 'Yellow Peril.'

In reality the Yellow Peril was actually a small, relatively law-abiding Chinese community, which had been based around the Limehouse docks area from the beginning of the nineteenth century. By the twentieth century two separate communities emerged: the Chinese from Shanghai, who were based around Pennyfields and Ming Street (between the present Westferry and Poplar DLR stations) and the immigrants from southern China and Canton, who lived around Gill Street and the Limehouse Causeway. By 1911 the area was known as Chinatown by the rest of London.

At the time the area had a bad reputation, as it wasn't just the gutter press who had it in for the Chinese. Writers, novelists and even film-makers were accountable for greatly exaggerating the danger and immorality of the area. H. V. Morton, the famous travel essayist and journalist, wrote about Limehouse in his book *The Nights of London* in 1926:

The squalor of Limehouse is that strange squalor of the East which seems to conceal vicious splendour There is an air of something unrevealed in those narrow streets of shuttered houses, each one of which appears to be hugging its own dreadful little secret… you might open a filthy door and find yourself in a palace sweet with joss-sticks, where queer things happen in a mist of smoke… The silence grips you, almost persuading you that behind it is something which you are always on the verge of discovering; some mystery of vice or of beauty, or of terror and cruelty.

Of course the reality was that the Chinese community liked to gamble and smoke opium. This was bad enough, but it was the mortal fear of interracial sexual relations (which the drug-taking seemed to facilitate) that terrified the newspaper editors of the era.

'White Girls Hypnotised by Yellow Men,' screamed the *Evening News*, adding that it was the God-given duty 'of every Englishman and Englishwoman to know the truth about the degradation of young white girls'. Substandard writers leaped on the bandwagon *ad nauseam*. Thomas Burke, writing for a lacklustre readership that lapped up his work, wrote a number of 'sordid and morbid' short stories and newspaper articles about the Limehouse Chinatown. One of his stories, 'The Chink and the Child', from a collection entitled *Limehouse Nights*, was actually made into a successful film called *Broken Blossoms* by the equally racist D. W. Griffith and starred Lillian Gish.

Another opportunist was former journalist Sax Rohmer, who used his questionable knowledge of Limehouse to write the incredibly successful Fu Manchu novels, about a depraved Chinese man whose evil empire was based, improbably, in the slums of Limehouse.

'Imagine a person, tall, lean and feline, high-shouldered, with a brow like Shakespeare and a face like Satan,' wrote Rohmer, 'a close-shaven skull, and long magnetic eyes of the true cat-green. Invest him with all the cruel cunning of an entire Eastern race, accumulated in one giant intellect, with all the resources of science past and present… Imagine that awful being and you have a mental picture of Dr Fu Manchu, the yellow peril incarnate in one man.'

Indeed the man who was rumoured to have inspired Fu Manchu was Billy Brilliant Chang himself. At the fulcrum of all the furore, Chang, a former contractor in Limehouse, initially ran a restaurant in the area called Shanghai, which was synonymous with extreme hedonistic excess. The establishment attracted all manner of groovy upper-class socialites who wanted to sniff on the coca that Chang had appropriated from the many chemists who still had it in their back rooms (it was only made illegal in 1920, so there was still plenty about), smoke some opium and taste the seamier side of life.

Eminently successful, Chang moved his restaurant to Regent Street, where he became even more notorious for peddling drugs and seducing young white upper-crust women – whose parents were understandably livid. The papers couldn't get enough of him and the police were constantly on his back, but he delighted in winding them up, safe in the knowledge that his enterprise was administered with caution.

And after all, there was no law that decreed a Chinese man could not have sex with a white girl, no matter how long his moustache. And so Chang continued plying the chicks – including gorgeous West End showgirls – with pharmaceutical-grade cocaine.

Unfortunately for Chang, things were about to take a turn for the worse. After a young dancer, Freda Kempton, died of a cocaine over-dose in 1922, it was discovered that she had been with Chang on the night of her death. Pulled in for questioning, he said: 'She was a friend of mine. But I know nothing about the cocaine. It is all a mystery to me.'

With no evidence to suggest he was guilty of the crime, he was released, and shortly after opened the Palm Court Club in Gerrard Street, Soho, thus becoming the first Chinese man to open a business in what was to become the centre of the Chinatown we know today.

Gerrard Street, with its maze of underground tunnels that lead to Great Newport Street, became a haven for drug dealers. The 43 Club at number 43 was especially notorious. Run by Irishwoman Kate Meyrick, it dodged the draconian licensing laws, sold alcohol all night and, due to a secret escape route to Newport Place (which still exists), was favoured by dealers such as Chang and heroin kingpin Eddie Manning. Socialites who patronised the place included painter Augustus John, novelist Aldous Huxley, and Stephen Tennant (the inspiration for Cedric Hampton in Nancy Mitford's *Love in a Cold Climate* and Sebastian Flyte in Evelyn Waugh's *Brideshead Revisited*). Regular patron Tallulah Bankhead, who readily admitted to a penchant for cocaine, described the club as 'useful for early breakfasts' – breakfast time for her being 'about 10pm'.

As for Chang (who was estimated to control 40 per cent of London's cocaine trade), he was harried by the police to the point of persecution. He sold the Palm Court and moved back to Limehouse, where he opened the Shanghai Restaurant. His flat was at 13 Limehouse Causeway (coincidentally just four doors away from where Mr and Mrs Lau Ping You lived) and it was here in 1924 that his luck finally ran out.

The police had already raided his Limehouse flat twice, and although they found no drugs, on one occasion they found two chorus girls in his bed. On the third attempt they came armed with the evidence from a drug-addicted actress called Violet Payne. Finding a wrap of cocaine behind a loose wooden board, they arrested Chang.

During the trial the press had a field day. The *World Pictorial News* wrote: 'Sometimes one girl alone went with Chang to learn the mysteries of that intoxicatingly beautiful den of iniquity above the restaurant. At other times half-a-dozen drug-frenzied women together joined him in wild orgies.'

At his trial the judge told him, 'It is you and men like you who are corrupting the womanhood of this country,' and sentenced him to fourteen months in prison, after which he was deported. The *Empire News* wrote, 'Mothers would be well advised to keep their daughters as far away as they can from Chinese laundries and other places where the yellow men congregate.'

These words seem to have come directly from a Sax Rohmer Fu Manchu novel in that they fed off the massive anti-Chinese sentiment that filled the tabloid pages of the day. Blamed for every drug that entered the capital, accused of white slavery, and harried to virtual extinction, the Chinese and their Limehouse were swept away.

As for Chang, the *Daily Telegraph* reported a few years later that he had gone 'blind and ended his days, not in luxury and rich silks, but as a sightless worker in a little kitchen garden.'

The cause or whereabouts of his death remains unknown.

Erich von Stroheim

Few actors have ever commanded the screen with such indefatigable presence as the great Erich von Stroheim. As the World War I German officer and aristocrat Rittmeister von Rauffenstein in Jean Renoir's immense *La Grande Illusion*, the monocle-donning actor – dressed in a body and neck brace (his idea) underneath his tight officers' uniform – drove the bolt well and truly home. And who could forget him in *Foolish Wives* (which he also wrote and directed) with his precariously tilted white cap, Sam Browne belt, white gloves and cigarette holder?

Stroheim's most significant creation, however, was himself. Long after his death his claims of having had a career as a cavalry officer, being an Austrian nobleman and his right to prefix his name with the word 'von' (illegal in Austria until 1919 unless you were nobility) were proven to be complete and utter falsehoods.

Erich Oswald Stroheim was born in Vienna in 1885 to practising Jews Benno Stroheim, a middle-class hat-maker, and Johanna Bondy. Despite having the fortune to witness the rise of the Secession and the golden age of Viennese art and culture, wanderlust grabbed him and in 1909, aged twenty-four, he stepped off the SS *Prinz Friedrich Wilhelm* and onto Ellis Island, New York. There, without a penny to his name, he declared himself Count Erich Oswald Hans Carl Maria von Stroheim und Nordenwall. His timing was perfect.

Stroheim gradually made his way to Hollywood, where filmmakers were already congregating en masse. Curiously, one of the main reasons for this sudden flurry was geographical. California was about as far away from the New York headquarters of inventor Thomas Edison (who actually stole many of the inventions he is credited for) as it was possible to go without actually leaving the US, and land was cheap. Edison held most of the patents on motion picture cameras and litigated anyone who didn't fit in with his draconian plan to control the film market. California was simply uneconomical to police; Edison's agents were sent out undercover to seize offending cameras, but ignored Hollywood as it was 2,500 miles away, and thus filmmaking carried on regardless.

The Biograph Company (whose owner William Kennedy Dickson had worked as an inventor at the Edison laboratory) produced the first film made in Hollywood. Biograph was based in New Jersey, but Dickson avoided his former employer's wrath by using the costly large-format film measuring 68 mm wide rather than Edison's 35 mm.

In 1908 D. W. Griffith joined Biograph as an actor/writer. He was soon directing a film a week and established a lot of the film techniques – such as close-ups, cross-cutting and flashbacks – that we now take for granted. Two years later California was on the lips of every filmmaker and Griffith, along with the Biograph acting company, travelled to Los Angeles to make a film. They decided, however, to venture a little further north to a small village they'd heard was beautiful and friendly. It was called Hollywood.

In 1910, D. W. Griffith made the first motion picture in Hollywood, the seventeen-minute-long *In Old California*, a Latino melodrama about the early days of Mexican-owned California. This landmark movie also coincided with the area's annexation to the City of Los Angeles, which, unlike Hollywood, not only had a decent water and sewage system but also allowed cinemas to operate.

An enterprising young chap, Stroheim seized his chance, his finger firmly on the zeitgeist. Hollywood was the centre of this new art form, cinema, which not only combined photography, theatre, literature, fashion and music, but could also be seen by the masses worldwide. Nothing like this had ever happened before, and this tiny village in southern California – which beckoned chancers and adventurers from all over the globe – was *the* place to be.

By 1914 Stroheim was working full time in Hollywood movies as a stuntman, filling bit parts, and as a consultant on German culture and fashion, strutting around town in jodhpurs, riding boots and trademark cane. In 1915 he claimed to have had a small part in Griffith's entirely racist *The Birth of a Nation*, but others say otherwise. He did, however, get a small role in the director's three-and-a-half-hour epic *Intolerance,* for which he also claimed to be the assistant director but was actually a production assistant.

By now World War I was well under way and Stroheim, who had already been married twice, didn't miss a trick. He rose to the bait and became the film industry's token Kraut – America's 'man you love to hate' – appearing in such films as *The Heart of Humanity*. Playing the evil Erich von Eberhard, he tears the buttons from a Red Cross nurse's uniform with his teeth before having his way, and throws a crying baby out of a window for distracting him. Most Americans saw Germany as a dangerous monarchy dominated by autocratic militarist thinking, including a hidden agenda to undermine democracy and US power. Stroheim was the Hun's on-screen personification. Undeniably, Stroheim epitomised the opportunist.

And so he sailed through World War I unscathed, milking the German stereotype replete with the severest of crew cuts, starched collars, spats and monocle. After the war he decided to write, and subsequently directed his own script, *Blind Husbands* – the first of his adultery trilogy – which was well received both critically and at the box office. An example to us all, Stroheim had no formal training. He made it up as he went along. What he had in abundance, though, was *self-belief*.

By 1919 he had also perfected his persona. It has been said he did such a great job that he even convinced himself. He became the blueprint for the sadistic northern European and unashamedly made the most of it.

In 1922 he wrote, directed and starred in *Foolish Wives* as Count Wladislaw Sergius Karamzin, a captain in the Imperial Russian Army. Costing, according to the studio, a whopping million bucks, it was a film vastly ahead of its time. In it, Stroheim is a Russian émigré ensconced in Monte Carlo who leases a villa and (as Stroheim had once done) poses as a count. His two mistresses pose as his cousins while he, using his rather camp militaristic, aristocratic behaviour, seduces gullible rich women, lusts after a retarded teenager, and attempts to undo an innocent American. In truth, the plot plays second fiddle to Stroheim's rather outré appearance. With his make-up, monocle and plucked eyebrows (in 1922!) Stroheim is utterly unforgettable. His profile is one of the great images of silent cinema.

'Since that first showing of *Foolish Wives*,' said Stroheim at the time, 'I have seemed to walk through vast crowds of people, their white American faces turned towards me in stern reproof.' Indeed,

Stroheim's look was as uncompromising as his persona. Described by esteemed film critic Derek Malcolm as 'one of the most extraordinary filmmakers of all time', when in the driving seat Stroheim took no prisoners, winding up his actors, stomping around shouting the odds, both dictatorial and demanding.

Unfortunately, Stroheim's antics and some might say inflated opinion of himself (I disagree) knew no bounds. After shooting half of *Merry-Go-Round,* the first in another trilogy that looked back to the days of the Habsburgs in pre-World War I Austria, he was fired by studio bigwig Irving Thalberg.

Next up for the monocled one was *Greed*, an adaptation of the 1899 Frank Norris novel *McTeague* starring the amazing Zasu Pitts and Gibson Gowland. Regarded as one of *the* great films of all time, it tells the story of a rather dim, poor dentist, McTeague, who opens a shop in San Francisco and falls in love with one of his patients. She wins the lottery, they marry, and then she becomes utterly obsessed with her money. A jealous best friend, Marcus, then informs city hall that the dentist has no licence. He loses everything and turns to drink, but still his wife will not dip into her winnings. Furious, he beats her to death and escapes to Death Valley, where Marcus finds him. The film ends with McTeague killing Marcus, who has handcuffed himself to his murderer, leaving McTeague now stranded in one of the world's hottest places with a corpse to drag around. Dark.

Greed is incomparable by virtue of Stroheim's uncompromising realism, the great performances and the actual locations, like the sewer where the lovers meet, the slums of San Francisco or Death Valley where Mac meets his nemesis.

Stroheim worked unpaid on the edit for a year. Still, the initial cut he submitted to the flabbergasted Goldwyn Company was an outrageous eight hours long. Lest we forget, it was silent and this was 1924. Under pressure, he relented and cut it to four hours to be shown in two parts. Still unhappy, Goldwyn got his story editor June Mathis (who, Stroheim complained, hadn't read either the book or the original screenplay) to chop it, and the eventual released version came in at two and a half hours.

Years later, Henri Langlois, the head of the Cinémathèque

Française, showed Stroheim the disfigured version. The Austrian sobbed as he watched it. 'This was like an exhumation for me,' he explained afterwards. 'In a tiny coffin I found a lot of dust, a terrible smell, a little backbone and a shoulder bone.'

Langlois assured him that the movie, however mutilated, was still a masterpiece. After watching the film, fellow Austrian director Billy Wilder told him he was ten years ahead of his time. 'No, twenty,' replied Stroheim. I couldn't agree more.

Amazingly, the untiring Austrian kept on going and subsequently notched up his biggest box office hit with the black comedy *The Merry Widow* starring John Gilbert and Mae Murray, in which both Clark Gable and Joan Crawford had uncredited roles. Strongly Stroheimian, the film was rich in cruelty, perversion and sadism.

He followed this up with *The Wedding March,* in which the entirely egotistical Austrian directed and starred as another monocle-wearing aristo who this time marries the daughter of an industrialist for convenience. Things take a turn for the worse on their wedding night when he removes her shoes and stockings with fetishist gallantry and is visibly repulsed by her deformed foot. (Two recurring features hallmark Stroheim's films – there is always a scene with a janitor, and they always feature the physically malformed. Don't you just love him?)

Unsurprisingly, Stroheim's unwillingness or inability to modify his artistic principles for the commercial cinema, his extreme attention to detail, his insistence on near-total artistic freedom and the resulting costs of his films led inevitably to fights with the studios. As time went on he received fewer directing opportunities. His last proper directorial outing was the even more crazy, opulent and perversely erotic *Queen Kelly* (1929), which starred Gloria Swanson and tells of a convent girl who ends up running a brothel in Africa. Unfortunately, Stroheim got a little too lewd (in one scene Swanson is whipped by the mad Queen Regina V of Kronberg while her guards grin with excitement), so the actress sacked him and the film was stalled. By now talkies had stolen silent's thunder and Hollywood was turned on its head – Stroheim with it. The film was never released.

But Stroheim wasn't done yet. He went back to acting and moved to Paris where adoration for him and his films knew no bounds. In 1936 he met Jean Renoir, son of Impressionist painter Pierre-Auguste Renoir, who cast him in *Le Grande Illusion*. It has since been cited countless times as one of the greatest films ever made.

Le Grande Illusion tells of the futility of war and stars the great Jean Gabin, Pierre Fresnay and Marcel Dalio as French PoWs in a World War I prison camp where Stroheim is the honourable camp commandant. It was released in 1937, and so powerful was its message that, when the Germans annexed France, Goebbels made sure that the original print was the first thing the Germans seized.

Stroheim's affiliation with Renoir almost led him to direct another movie, *La Dame Blanche*, based on an original story by Stroheim of the same name, which saw Renoir writing the dialogue. Unfortunately the auteur was scuppered by fellow Austrian Adolf Hitler, who had the audacity to invade France and caused Stroheim to head back to the USA, where he continued to act to type (he played Rommel in *Five Graves to Cairo*). Even though it might have helped him in an era of staunch anti-Germanic feeling, he never dropped his guard and admitted his Jewish heritage.

After the war he made a living out of being 'the Great' Erich Von Stroheim. 'If you live in France and you have written one good book, or painted one good picture, or directed one outstanding film, fifty years ago, and nothing ever since, you are still recognised as an artist and honoured accordingly,' he opined.

He acted in a few films a year, mainly in France, and lived the good life, but it wasn't until 1950 that he would play a prominent part in another masterpiece – *Sunset Boulevard*, directed by Billy Wilder.

It stars William Holden as poor young writer Joe Gillis, who agrees to write a screenplay for barking mad faded silent movie star Norma Desmond (Gloria Swanson), while Stroheim is Max von Mayerling, her faithful chauffeur/butler/right-hand man who previously directed her in some of her greatest triumphs. The film that Desmond makes Joe watch in her screening room is none other than the unreleased *Queen Kelly*, directed by Stroheim.

After *Sunset Boulevard*, Stroheim moved to France, where he continued to be celebrated and played out his life as mad German scientists and criminal masterminds. He died in 1957 of cancer in Yvelines, Île-de-France, aged seventy-one, leaving a trail of unrealised projects behind him and many a film fan surmising what greatness he might have achieved had he been given a fairer crack of the whip.

It was Stroheim who introduced sophisticated plot lines and perverted psychological and sexual undercurrents, which essentially harked back to his Viennese contemporary Freud, to cinema. It was he who opened the can of worms that galvanised Hitchcock, Fritz Lang, Orson Welles and John Huston, and fuelled the whole film noir movement. In fact, much of the great cinema of the last hundred years might not have happened without him.

He was a true visionary, and certainly one of a kind.

Louise Brooks

'Louise Brooks was the most seductive sexual image of Woman ever committed to celluloid. She's the only unrepentant hedonist, the only pure pleasure-seeker I think I've ever known,' remarked eminent critic Kenneth Tynan, who spent two days interviewing her in 1978. 'And when men bored her she left them and when Hollywood bored her she left and went into retirement from which she never emerged.'

Primarily known for just two European masterpieces, *Pandora's Box* and *Diary of a Lost Girl*, directed in Berlin by Georg Wilhelm Pabst, Brooks made only twenty-four films during a movie career that began in 1925 and ended, with inscrutable abruptness, in 1938. At the time she was regarded as a second-tier star, but today is more well known and admired than any of the huge Hollywood stars who overshadowed her, such as Theda Bara, Mary Pickford, Gloria Swanson and Lillian Gish, her failure having lasted much longer than their success.

A single-minded maverick, she was one of the first, most famous and infamous 'flappers' – brash young women who, in the 1920s, wore short skirts, excessive make-up, smoked, drove automobiles, listened to jazz and visibly flaunted their disdain for the acceptable behaviour and sexual mores of the day. Indeed, these attractive, reckless, style-obsessed flapper girls were not only *perceived* as, but actually *were*, a threat to a society where women were expected to be seen, not heard, obedient and servile – rather like a nanny you had sex with when drunk, who produced offspring for you to further your line. Flappers changed all that in a decade and, as such, were infinitely more controversial than rockers, hippies or punk rockers and caused even greater hullabaloo.

'The social butterfly type... the frivolous, scantily-clad, jazzing flapper, irresponsible and undisciplined, to whom a dance, a new hat, or a man with a car, were of more importance than the fate of nations,' wrote Dr R. Murray-Leslie in 1920 in an article entitled 'Too many Women. Is it the cause of Social Unrest?' With her short pioneering bob haircut, flimsy dresses, flat chest, open sexual proclivity, baffling recalcitrance and passion for drinks, drugs and fags, Brooks (who slept with both Garbo and Charlie Chaplin, though not at the same time) was the unrivalled Queen of the Flappers. She epitomised the Roaring Twenties and led the way for international female emancipation and is one of *the* biggest and most influential style icons of all time.

She was born on 14 November 1906 in Cherryvale, Kansas to lawyer Leonard Porter Brooks, a saintly man who, according to Louise in her memoir, was 'so honest his secretary makes more money than he does', and doctor's daughter Myra Rude, a talented pianist who thought that their four children, all under ten, 'should take care of themselves'. Inevitably, this meant a lot of reading so that, by the time Louise was a teenager, she had already immersed herself in Dickens, Thackeray, Twain and Darwin – which, as she readily admitted, did her Hollywood career no favours at all. Indeed, the Brooks clan seems a rather arcane bunch. Initially poor English farmers, they settled in Tennessee in the late eighteenth century, fought against the slave owners in the Civil War and in 1871 journeyed a thousand miles in a covered wagon to settle in Kansas. Maybe it was this blood that gave Brooks her spirit, as by the age of ten she was, as she stated in her memoir, 'what amounted to a professional dancer'.

Of course, her teachers gave up on her because, as she said in her diary, 'I am fed up with teaching my teachers what to teach me', so her mother parcelled her off to New York aged fifteen, with her stout matronly chaperone, Alice Mills. Here she was taught modern dance by Ted Shawn, whose assistant Martha Graham has been said to have had the same impact on dance as Picasso had on art. Already a beauty *sui generis*, in 1922 Brooks, now just sixteen, joined the rather arty Denishawn Dance Company and met Barbara Bennett (sister of soon-to-be Hollywood stars Joan and Constance Bennett), who introduced her to New York café society and Wall Street brokers. Her trademark bob already in place, cropped at what Christopher Isherwood described as 'that unique imperious neck of hers', Brooks – a virtual Pygmalion who was given elocution lessons by a soda jerk, and learned dining etiquette from waiters and dress sense from Miss Rita, a salesgirl from the Bronx who worked in a fashionable store – had millionaires fawning at her feet and showering her with gifts aplenty. But, as she later wrote, 'Sexual submission was not a condition of this arrangement.'

By 1924 she had entirely reinvented herself as a New York Ace Face and then, without warning, slipped off to London, where she performed the Charleston on stage at the Café de Paris and started a nationwide craze. Quite naturally, she was loved and embraced by the so-called 'bright young things', a notoriously bohemian group of drink- and drug-addled aristocrats who included the politically suspect Mitford sisters, stately homosexuals Cecil Beaton, Stephen Tennant and Edward James and the literary-minded Sitwell brood. Typically, Brooks found them rather dull and, after reading Evelyn Waugh's *Vile Bodies,* which was based on them, remarked, 'Only a genius could write a masterpiece out of such glum material.'

And so, disillusioned with the English toffs, she borrowed the boat fare and returned to New York, where she announced: 'At last my beloved New York was able to present a Louise Brooks who was neither Kansas nor Broadway nor Hollywood nor Park Avenue but uniquely herself.' Alighting from the boat she was met by Florenz Ziegfeld, who immediately signed her up to appear on Broadway in the revue *Louis the 14th.* 'The director detested me,' she wrote in *Sight & Sound,* 'because on occasion when I had other commitments I would wire my non appearance to the theater.' Twelve months on, aged just nineteen, she first appeared as a scantily clad chorus dancer in the controversial *Scandals.* She then joined W. C. Fields and cowboy Will Rogers as a cast member of the 1925 edition of the *Ziegfeld Follies* as a speciality dancer.

A 'social butterfly', Brooks stayed out all night at the speakeasies, lived in hotels and was thrown out of both the Algonquin (where she met with Harpo Marx, George Cohan and Dorothy Parker) and the Martha Washington hotel for 'bad behaviour'. Still her admirers were legion. One of them was the peevishly witty *Times* critic Herman Mankiewicz, who went on to write the screenplay for *Citizen Kane*; another was Charlie Chaplin, with whom who she had a two-month affair: 'A true genius, a glistening creature who never said a bad word about anyone and was radiantly carefree and absurdly generous,' reported Louise in her memoir.

W. C. Fields became her close companion and close friend ('a solitary person… He abhorred bars, nightclubs, parties and other people's houses'). Another ardent admirer was thirty-six-year-old Walter Wanger, an executive at Famous Players-Lasky (later to become Paramount Pictures), who was so besotted by her that he offered her a five-year film contract. Over the following year she made twelve movies – most of which are now lost.

Her first audience with the press was with Ruth Waterbury of *Photoplay,* who turned up at the fledgling actress's hotel and, much to her annoyance, found the actress still in bed, from where she conducted the interview. The writer embraced the studio press release line about the 'young chorus girl who should feel so very lucky to be cast opposite great star, Adolphe Menjou, in *A Social Celebrity*'. She soon discovered, however, that Brooks was not at all impressed by the pompous Menjou or the annoying scribe.

'Whereas she looked at me as a stupid "chorus girl" who didn't know how lucky she was,' wrote the diminutive Brooks, just five feet, two inches in stocking feet, 'I looked at her as artistically retarded not to know that ten years of professional dancing was the best possible preparation for "moving pictures"; I asked her if she had seen, or even heard of, Martha Graham's sensational success in the Greenwich Village Follies. She had not. I didn't realise then that that this cultural conflict with this writer was merely the first instance of the kind of contempt that would drive me out of Hollywood.'

Very much impressed, Waterbury wrote, 'Describing Louise presents its difficulties. She is so very Manhattan. Very Young. Exquisitely hard boiled. Her black eyes and sleek black hair are as brilliant as Chinese lacquer. Her skin is white as a camellia. Her legs are lyric. She is just nineteen.'

Brooks was on a roll as the single-minded flapper who captured the imagination of a million young girls. She shone in *Love 'Em and Leave 'Em* as the sly and conniving shop girl Janie Walsh, who uses her feminine wiles to make her way in the world, and appeared with Fields in *It's the Old Army Game* in 1926. Meanwhile she had also, uncharacteristically, married *Army Game* director A. Edward Sutherland – the hard-drinking London-born playboy and author/

screenwriter who novelist Anita Loos described as 'the Beau Brummell of the era'. The couple moved to Hollywood, where she entertained the cream of 'interesting' Hollywood society such as Buster Keaton, Zelda and F. Scott Fitzgerald, Clark Gable, Pola Negri, Tallulah Bankhead and John Barrymore. 'When I went to Hollywood in 1927,' wrote Brookes in her memoir, 'the girls were wearing lumpy sweaters and skirts... I was wearing sleek suits and half naked beaded gowns and piles and piles of furs. But I just didn't fit into the Hollywood scheme at all. I was neither a fluffy heroine, nor a wicked vamp, nor a woman of the world. I just didn't fit into any category.' That is why we love her, why she has stood the test of time, why even today gals sport the Brooks bob. She was unique.

The couple divorced after just two years. 'The men I liked most were the worst in bed, and the men I liked least were the best,' she admitted. 'I liked the bastards... English men are the best. And priest-ridden Irishman are the worst.'

Later in life Brooks attributed her almost masochistic sexual bent to her being sexually molested aged nine by a fifty-year-old man named Mr Feathers. She told her mother, who blamed her. 'My mother told me I must have led him on,' she explained. 'But for me soft easy men were never enough – there had to be an element of domination – I am convinced that's all tied up with Mr Feathers.'

In 1928 Brooks, now aged twenty-one, made *A Girl in Every Port*, directed by Howard Hawks (who also helmed *Scarface* in 1932 and *Red River* in 1948), which sees her succeed as yet another amoral pleasure-seeker who turns bullyboy Victor McLaglen into a simpering bowl of shuddering jelly. She followed up with *Beggars of Life*, directed by World War I war hero William 'Wild Bill' Wellman, in which she plays a girl who kills her stepfather, who tried to rape her, and goes on the run dressed as a boy. Young flappers looked at Brooks with total and utter adoration. On film she was using all at her disposal to conquer men. She was a new kind of woman. She was Louise Brooks.

Being a feisty twenty-one-year-old who held less respect for Hollywood than she did an ice cream, she hardly ingratiated herself with the likes of Paramount bigwig producer B. P. Schulberg, with whom she argued relentlessly and later described as a 'coarse exploiter who propositioned every actress and policed every set'. But by this time she was bedding multi-millionaire playboy laundry magnate George Marshall, who took over her business affairs and told her that her contract was up with Paramount and that the Austrian Expressionist cineaste G. W. Pabst was offering her a thousand dollars a week to appear in a movie in Berlin. Schulberg had given her a choice: stay at her old salary or quit. 'And, just for the hell of it,' Brooks wrote, 'I quit.' A few days later she was on her way to Germany.

'At the Eden hotel, where I lived in Berlin, the café bar was lined with the higher-priced trollops,' she wrote in her memoirs. 'The economy girls walked the streets outside. On the corner stood the girls in boots, advertising flagellation... Actors' agents pimped for the ladies in luxury apartments in the Bavarian Quarter. Racetrack touts at the Hoppegarten arranged orgies for groups of sportsmen. The nightclub Eldorado displayed an enticing line of homosexuals dressed as women. At the Maly there was a choice of feminine or collar-and-tie lesbians.'

Berlin during the Weimar Republic was a sexual Disneyland for foreign visitors where any and every sexual distraction could be procured for a pittance. The corruption had begun after World War I had created thousands of war orphans and widows, who had little option but to sell themselves to eat. Subsequently, prostitution became utterly entrenched in the city's underground economy, which was itself fuelled by a massive drug culture in which heroin and cocaine were commonplace; the latter, selling for less than a penny a capsule, came from leftover military stockpiles that made their way into the black market, onto the streets, and into the boudoirs of the bourgeoisie.

In some circles, especially in the Berlin art world, cocaine was considered an interesting and fashionable vice, and buckets of the stuff were snorted on a daily basis. The whole city was at it. Thus, in the twenties Berlin became known as a 'powder city' that, according to police reports, was ruled by some sixty-two organised criminal gangs in Berlin, called *Ringvereine*. To add to the city's degradation, hyper-inflation had risen to a monthly rate of inflation of 3.25 billion per cent, which is the equivalent of prices doubling every two hours. It was into this world that this spirited, beautiful twenty-two-year-old was thrust while the picture in which she was to star aimed to mirror it.

Die Büchse der Pandora – *Pandora's Box* (1929), based on Frank Wedekind's mercurial stage play, is an apt depiction of depravity and low life that sits rather comfortably in the aforementioned Berlin. Brooks is Lulu – a seductive, thoughtless sybarite whose raw sexuality and uninhibited quest for the illicit pleasures of life, set amongst a backdrop of male and female homosexuality, brings ruin to herself and those who love her. It might easily have been a cautionary tale, but in the hands of both Pabst and Brooks, it is unquestionably not.

'At the time Wedekind produced *Pandora's Box*,' wrote Brooks, '...it was detested, condemned and banned. It was declared "immoral and inartistic."' Yet nobody who was connected with the film dreamed that Pabst was risking commercial failure with the story even though the newspaper the *Berliner Tageblatt* described Lulu as an 'immoral prostitute who wasn't crazy about her work and was surrounded by the "inartistic" ugliness of raw bestiality.'

Pabst had a suitably unsentimental outlook and was thus the perfect director for such a film, but it was his casting of Brooks that really set the film apart. 'Pabst was looking for a girl that was perfect for Lulu. Absolutely born for the role,' informed *Pandora's Box* assistant director Mark Sorkin. 'Lulu was this beautiful destructive character and so was Louise Brooks and as such she conveyed it perfectly. But Louise was very independent and when she worked she always had an opinion of what she had to do that wasn't always right but was most of the time.'

It was perhaps the finest piece of casting in cinema history. Just like Brooks, for all her feminine charms and seductive guile, Lulu (who in the play had also been molested as a young girl) is never the exploiter but the exploited. And even though we are never allowed to feel sorry for her, she is like a voluptuous bird of paradise in a cage full of hungry predatory vultures.

'As Wedekind said, "Lulu is not a real character but the personification of primitive sexuality who inspires evil unaware,"' said Brooks.

'She plays a purely passive role. Besides daring to show the prosti-tute as a victim, Mr Pabst went onto the final damning immorality of making his Lulu sweetly innocent. I played Pabst's Lulu and she is not the destroyer of men like Wederkind's Lulu. She was the same kind of nitwit as I am. I would have made an impossible wife – stay-ing in bed all day reading and drinking gin. Lulu's story is as near as you will get to mine.'

Lulu begins as the mistress of a respected, middle-aged newspaper publisher, Ludwig Schön, who, feeling Lulu unfit to marry, plans to wed the daughter of a cabinet minister. His aims are shot to pieces after his fiancée finds him *in flagrante delicto* with his former mis-tress, who marries him herself. At the infamous wedding scene, the first lesbian scene in movie history, Brooks dances cheek to cheek with the raving bull dyke Countess Geschwitz, which enrages her new husband, who then finds her in their wedding bed verging on what appears to be both romp and orgy with two wedding guests, Schigolch and Rodrigo. Beside himself, he finds his revolver and, after a struggle, is killed. Consequently, Lulu is convicted of manslaughter and is sentenced to five years, but escapes with the help of Geschwitz – the only person in the film who truly loves Lulu – ending up in London on Christmas Eve. She turns to prostitution to eat and suffers an ignominious and untimely end.

Remarkably, even though *Pandora* seems somehow eminently believable in its depiction of twenties Berlin as a silent picture, it was a commercial failure. Rediscovered by cinefiles decades later, how-ever, it became a huge cult classic, regarded as one of the great works of the silent era, and was a great influence on film noir. Somewhat belatedly, another screen icon was born.

Numerous critics have declared that the untrained Brooks rein-vented screen acting by simply not caring what we, the audience, thought of her, not overreacting, not over acting, not *anything*. 'When I acted I hadn't the slightest idea of what I was doing. I was simply playing myself, which is the hardest thing to do – if you know that it's hard,' she told filmmaker Richard Leacock. 'I didn't, so it seemed easy. I had nothing to unlearn. When I worked with Pabst, he was furious with me as he approached people intellectually and you couldn't approach me intellectually because there was nothing to approach... But I was never an actress as I was never in love with myself.'

Next up for Pabst and Brooks came *Diary of a Lost Girl* (1929), based on the million-selling novel of 1905, *Tagebuch einer Verlorenen,* by Margarete Böhme. It is the story of Thymian Henning (Louise Brooks), the naïve and virginal daughter of a pharmacist, Robert Henning. In a moment of distress Thymian is ravaged by her father's assistant; she subsequently becomes pregnant, has the baby taken away, is banished to a draconian reformatory, escapes and, with no place to go, ends up a prostitute in an upmarket brothel.

Today, such a tale that might seem rather commonplace but, in the twenties, by empathising with the plight of the prostitute, it was explosively controversial, hit the zeitgeist head on and, even though many women in the city had suffered the same fate, ruffled more than a few feathers and failed at the box office.

Brooks's final European film, *Prix de Beauté,* produced by Pabst and directed in Paris (where she was a huge fashion icon) by former Italian theatre critic Augusto Genina, stands out purely because of the actress's then-derided naturalist acting style. The perfect vehicle for Brooks, *Prix de Beauté* should have made her a worldwide star, but it came out just as talkies were taking over, and even though a French actress dubbed Brooks, the general public considered it dated.

By this time she had fallen out with Pabst, with whom she'd had a one-night stand. She gave, as she describes, 'the best sexual performance of my life. I jumped into the hay with him and delivered myself body and soul.'

'At one point in Paris Pabst was annoyed with me for spending time with my every hour away from work with my rich American friends,' she wrote in her memoir. 'He thought they prevented me from being a serious actress and would discard me like an old toy when done with me. "Your life is exactly like Lulu's," he said, "and you will end the same way."'

This third flop in a row drove Brooks back to Hollywood, where Paramount had carefully converted her last film with them, *The Canary Murder Case* (with William Powell and Jean Arthur), to a talkie by overdubbing lacklustre American actress Margaret Livingston's jarring voice and using a Brooks lookalike for added scenes. Brooks, whose voice Tynan described as a treasure Hollywood failed to realise, was incensed. Paramount's response was to place her in small insubstantial roles, effectively stifling her career, but of course Brooks, typically, did not give a hoot about Hollywood or this 'silly business', so didn't help herself one iota.

'This intricate man [Bill Wellman] offered me a part in *The Public Enemy*,' she told Richard Leacock. 'But when I turned it down to make a trip New York he passed it onto Jean Harlow.' *The Public Enemy* was one of the year's biggest box office successes and made huge stars of its two leads – James Cagney and Harlow.

After a few even more lacklustre Hollywood films, Brooks – disenchanted with what she described as 'Hollywood fools' – retired in 1931, aged twenty-five, declared bankruptcy in 1932, and began dancing in nightclubs to earn a living. She attempted a comeback in 1936 but was told she would have start again at the bottom as a chorus girl. Columbia chief Harry Cohn summoned her to a series of meetings in his office. He greeted her naked from the waist up and explained that good parts would appear if she played the 'game' with him. She refused and was denied a contract. A veritable pig of a man, Cohn vengefully publicised her aborted 'comeback' by circulating a still throughout the country's newspapers with the caption, 'Louise Brooks former star who deserted Hollywood seven years ago at the height of her career for Germany has come back to resume her work in pictures but seven years is too long for the public to remember and Louise begins again at the bottom.' Her last film was *Overland Stage Raiders* (1938), opposite John Wayne and a ventriloquist's dummy. In her own estimation, she'd made $124,000 (almost $2 million in today's money) during her career and spent the lot.

'The only people who wanted to see me [about work] were men who wanted to sleep with me,' she told Kenneth Tynan. 'Then Walter Wanger warned me that if I hung around I'd become a call girl. So I fled to Wichita, Kansas where my family had moved in 1919. But that turned out to be another kind of hell. The citizens of

Wichita either resented me for being a success or hated me for being a failure. And I wasn't exactly enchanted with them.'

After an unsuccessful attempt at operating a dance studio for 'young people', and an unsuccessful booklet, *The Fundamentals of Good Ballroom Dancing*, she returned east to New York. 'I found that the only well-paying career open to me, as an unsuccessful actress of thirty-six, was that of a call girl and I was too proud for that,' she admits in her autobiography, 'and began to flirt with the fancies related to little bottles filled with yellow sleeping pills.'

Like many, she struggled through the war but still didn't sell out. In 1943 she was paid $1,500 for the rights to publish her ghostwritten story in the *American Weekly* magazine, but it never saw the light of day as Brooks refused to provide salacious details or name any names.

After World War II and brief stints as a radio actor and a gossip columnist, she shocked New York. In 1947 the proud, snooty Louise Brooks started work as a salesgirl at Saks, Fifth Avenue. 'They paid me $40 a week,' she told Tynan. 'I had this silly idea of proving myself an "honest woman" but the only effect it had was to disgust all my famous New York friends who cut me off forever.'

During this period she wrote an autobiographical novel called *Naked on My Goat*, a title taken from *Faust,* but after working on it for several years, she destroyed the only copy of the manuscript by throwing it into an incinerator. She attributes this to a sense of *pudeur*, embarrassed by her candour regarding her sexual proclivity. She later summed herself up as a typical Midwesterner, 'born in the Bible belt of Anglo-Saxon farmers who prayed in the parlour and practiced incest in the barn... I too am unwilling to write the sexual truth that would make my life worth reading. I cannot unbuckle the Bible belt.'

Between 1948 and 1953 she then eked out a living as a courtesan, supported at various times by three millionaires (one of whom was CBS founder William Paley, who provided her with an allowance for the rest of her life) who she declined to marry because, as she said, 'I wasn't in love with them. In fact I have never been in love. And If I had loved a man, could I have ever been faithful to him? Could he have trusted me behind a closed door? I doubt it. It was clever of

Pabst to know that, even before he met me, I possessed the tramp essence of Lulu.'

She swerved marriage by becoming a Catholic who, in the eyes of the Church, was still married to Eddie Sutherland, but her young priest fell in love with her and was banished to the west coast. 'He wanted to give me special instruction in my apartment but I resisted,' she said.

By 1954 she hit an all-time low. 'There was no point in throwing myself in the East River because I could swim, and I couldn't afford the alternative, which was sleeping pills.' Depressed, she had become an overweight alcoholic recluse, forgotten by all and sundry until in 1955 Henri Langlois, the energetic head of the Cinémathèque Française, organised a massive exhibition entitled 'Sixty Years of Cinema', the entrance to which was dominated by two huge blowups – one of French actress Falconetti in Dreyer's *La Passion de Jeanne d' Arc,* and one of Brooks in *Pandora's Box.* When a critic demanded to know why this nonentity Brooks occupied centre stage and not Garbo or Dietrich, Langlois went ballistic and shouted, 'There is no Garbo! There is no Dietrich! There is only Louise Brooks!' Later that year silent film enthusiast and film curator at George Eastman House James Card tracked her down to what she described as her 'grubby hole on 1st Avenue at 59th Street'.

'It was such a shock to see someone who had looked like her in the most deplorable, unimaginable physical condition from having lived on nothing but alcohol for years and years and years,' stated Card. 'She was enormously bloated and her hair was unkempt, hanging around her face like the witch of Endor and she wore a rusty old overcoat and huge space slippers that she called her uniform. She was like a Lon Chaney in reverse, somebody so remote from the person I'd seen on screen that it was unlikely it was the same person.'

Card set about her rehabilitation. He moved her to Rochester, New York, where he was the curator of the George Eastman Museum. Here he screened many of her movies for her, most of which she had never bothered to watch. 'I still haven't seen them… not right through,' she admitted in an on-screen interview with Richard Leacock. 'Jimmy Card screened them for me during my drinking period. So I would watch through glazed eyes for about five minutes and sleep through the rest. I still haven't seen *Pandora*. I've been present at two screenings but was drunk both times.'

Card persevered and eventually persuaded her that film, which she had never taken seriously, was indeed a valid art form. Consequently, she looked back at all the years of misery, the twenty years of obscurity, and started to re-evaluate her worth and began writing a series of tough, fastidious, yet rather elusive articles about her experiences in film. Brooks had been a heavy drinker since the age of fourteen but remained relatively sober while writing her incisive essays on colleagues and contemporaries such as Garbo, Dietrich, Chaplin, Bogart, Fields, Zasu Pitts and Pabst. These essays, published all over the world in rather serious film journals such as *Sight & Sound* and *Positif*, cemented her iconicism and allowed her a second career. Brooks, above all a gorgeous failure, now initiated a new kind of marketing strategy that exonerated the beauty of stubborn recalcitrance and was rewarded with an instant cult following.

Then, in 1957, Langlois presented a festival in Paris, an homage to Louise Brooks, and flew her over. In Paris she was greeted with wild acclaim from, among others, Jean-Luc Godard, who in 1962 made his own Brooks tribute with his movie *Vivre Sa Vie,* whose heroine, a prostitute played by Anna Karina, was a Brooks lookalike who the director described as 'a young and pretty Parisian shop girl who gives her body but retained her soul.'

But by the time Godard's film was out, Brooks had become a recluse who only ventured out to either doctors or dentists. 'I would drink a pint of gin once a week and become what Dickens called "gincoherent", sleep and drowse for four days and read, write and see the odd visitor for the other three, but no priests, I gave up on the Church in 1964.'

After seeing a Brooks season, the eminent critic/playwright/scriptwriter Kenneth Tynan tracked her down in 1979 and wrote about her in the *New Yorker,* where he described her as 'the Ravishing Hermit of Rochester.' 'You're doing a terrible thing to me,' she told him. 'I've been killing myself off for twenty years, and you're going to bring me back to life.'

This ushered in the publication of her book, *Lulu in Hollywood,* which became an international bestseller, and a documentary entitled *Lulu in Berlin,* helmed by Richard Leacock. The film won over audiences all over the world for the enormously pragmatic and down-to-earth Brooks, and secured her 'car crash' status alongside the likes of other destructomaniacs James Dean, Judy Garland and Orson Welles. Arthouse cinemas showed her movies relentlessly at late night screenings all over the world, sparking another Brooks renaissance. Her look, candour, uninhibited sexual proclivities, and the suggestion of her bisexuality (a result of her penchant for men's suits in the twenties, *Pandora's* sapphic scene and her admission of sex with Garbo) was a huge hit with a generation brought up on David Bowie, Warhol and Roxy Music. 'When I am dead, I believe that film writers will fasten on the story that I am a lesbian,' she wrote. 'I have done lots to make it believable. All my women friends have been lesbians... But that is one point upon which I agree positively with Isherwood. There is no such thing as bisexuality... Out of curiosity, I had two affairs with girls – they did nothing for me. I only loved men's bodies.'

Her amazingly prescient and thoroughly refreshing attitude towards sex was always a draw; so too was her unimpeachable sense of style, epitomised by her eponymous hairstyle, the Louise Brooks Bob. Almost seventy years after she first adopted it, it was still deemed incredibly stylish, its sharp androgynous lines giving its wearer an altogether devilish edge. Said hairstyle has been adopted by the likes of Cyd Charisse (in *Singing in the Rain*), Brigitte Bardot (in *Mepris*), Melanie Griffiths (in *Something Wild*), Audrey Tautou (in *Amélie*) and Cate Blanchett (in *Indiana Jones),* while Isabella Rossellini, Madonna, Winona Ryder, Halle Berry and Lady Gaga have all taken to the style off camera. If a lass wants to look a little bit naughty, independent and dangerous, they go for the Brooks Bob.

But of course Brooks was much, much more than a pretty haircut. She was incredibly modern, a beautiful loser who marketed her superior defeatism, dazzling recalcitrance, stubborn masochism and rejection of material wealth and won ceaseless cult love in the process. She was without doubt her own singular creation, her own walking work of art, decades before the idea of being your own walking taking art piece (as in Leigh Bowery) was ever considered. It might be said that her life was her art, both of which converged in Lulu, but never met again.

Louise Brooks, maverick, hedonist, bohemian, bibliophile and dyed-in-the-wool socialist who positively refused to accept the restrictive role that women had in American society, died in 1985, aged seventy-eight, just two years after her bestselling cult memoir was published.

As she said, 'If I ever bore you it will be with a knife.'

The Zoot Suit

Few articles of clothing have caused riots that resulted in hundreds of arrests, scores of injuries and international headlines. But then again, few have the history or social gravitas of the zoot suit. More than just a jacket and trousers, it's an item of clothing that defined its wearer as part of a culture that chose to stand outside of accepted society, unafraid of the consequences.

More than just an outlandish fashion fad, its silhouette defied an era of wartime conformity and racial prejudice and was undoubtedly a declaration of freedom and auto-determination amongst beleaguered minorities.

The suit itself comprises a wide-lapelled, often knee-length 'killer-diller coat with a drape shape, and shoulders padded like a lunatic's cell' (as Malcolm X succinctly put it), while the deeply pleated trousers ballooned to some thirty-two inches at the knee and fourteen inches at the ankle, below the inevitable long, looping watch chain.

Worn with a large felt fedora with feather, a fat tie and a spear-collared shirt, the look, when it first appeared amongst late 1930s hep cats in urban jazz saloons, was radical to say the least – its unmistakable silhouette as confrontational as any outfit from the punk era. As American author Ralph Ellison's narrator in his 1952 novel *The Invisible Man* described:

Walking slowly, their shoulders swaying, their legs swinging from their hips in trousers that ballooned upward from cuffs fitting snug about their ankles; their coats long and hip-tight with shoulders far too broad to be those of natural western men.

Exactly who invented the zoot remains under debate. Claimants have included Beale Street tailor Louis Lettes of Memphis, Charles Klein and Vito Bagnato in Manhattan, Lew Eisenstein on 125th Street, and a Detroit retailer known as Nathan (Toddy) Elkus.

Chicago tailor and bandleader Harold C. Fox, asserts he made the first zoot suit with the reet pleat, the reave sleeve, the ripe stripe, the stuff cuff and the drape shape in 1941, influenced by underprivileged urban black teenagers. 'The zoot was not a costume or uniform from the world of entertainment,' he once said. 'It came right off the street and out of the ghetto.'

Many others have also claimed that its creation belonged to poor black youth of the Great Depression era. Many, too broke to buy new kit, adapted their dads' suits, nipping the jackets in at the waist, leaving the unalterable big shoulders and length, and taking the trousers in at the waist, hips and ankles.

Another great style that came out of necessity, this new look – smart yet loose enough to dive about doing the Big Apple (the thoroughly gymnastic grand pappy of jive) – became an essential part of Afro-American culture.

Indeed, the word 'zoot' was common currency in the jazz circles of the 1930s. Some say it was employed to denote all that was extravagant and slipped into the vernacular to specifically describe said item. Some say that since it was common jazz slang to put a 'z' at the beginning of words, so the suit became a zoot, while others claim it was first coined by Mexican-American 'pachucos' as part of their street cant, 'Caló', and evolved from the Mexican Spanish pronunciation of the word 'suit', with the 's' taking on the sound of a 'z'.

However all are unanimous in their belief that the zoot is undoubtedly the most bizarre raiment ever worn by the heterosexual American male.

And just as the word itself came to define something, the zoot suit became a badge of ethnicity, a subcultural manifestation of its owner's steadfast refusal to kowtow to the racist confines of the USA in the 1930s when, lest we forget, lynching was still common.

What is also certain is that the zoot spread through the working classes like wildfire (much like the modern-day hooded sweatshirt) and was a most coveted item that some today might describe as bling. In his autobiography, Malcolm X (then Malcolm Little) remembers the exhilaration of buying his first zoot suit at the age of fifteen:

I was measured, and the young salesman picked off a rack a zoot suit that was just wild: sky-blue pants thirty inches in the knee and angle narrowed down to twelve inches at the bottom, and a long coat that pinched my waist and flared out below my knees. The salesman said the store would give me a narrow leather belt with my initial 'L' on it. Then he said I ought to also buy a hat, and I did – blue, with a feather in the four-inch brim. Then the store gave me another present: a long, thick-lined, gold-plated chain that swung down lower than my coat hem. I was sold forever on credit... I took three of those twenty-five cent sepia-toned, while-you wait pictures of myself, posed the way 'hipsters' wearing their zoots would 'cool it' – hat angled, knees drawn close together, feet wide apart, both index fingers jabbed toward the floor. The long coat and swinging chain and the Punjab pants were much more dramatic if you stood that way.

And, just as in recent hip-hop times, Mexican-Americans and Hispanics robbed of their customs, values, beliefs and language adopted a style of clothing that was first pioneered by their black brethren and spoke of upward mobility and pride.

Undeniably, due to the amount of material used, you needed a good few bucks to acquire a zoot – a luxury item brought out on special occasions and worn by the sharpest dudes. The flamboyant outfit set them apart from the crowd and, rather like the skinhead, punk or Ted clothing of the UK, was a look that told you all about its wearer's interests and culture.

For African-Americans it was jazz-lovers, and for Mexican-Americans it was 'pachucos' – tough, vehemently heterosexual urban Hispanic dandies – who, more than anyone, dressed to impress, adopted an arrogant posture and were prone to drug-taking, minor crime, juvenile delinquency and followed their own very distinct lifestyle. Said attire marked you as part of that particular subculture.

Accordingly, the zoot suit, like the styles of many a youth cult that followed, acutely polarised the community. It's not hard to imagine the hatred felt by some poor white Americans (116,000 families had travelled from the dust bowls of the Oklahoma to the west in search of work in the 1930s, many of whom became policemen) as they saw these upstart dandies parade their finery. Little did they know, or care, that many of these black and Hispanic 'zooters' had toiled on the lowest rung as bus boys, labourers and factory workers for perhaps months and saved their every last penny to buy their threads. They didn't spend their money in the saloons drinking away their misery. They dressed up instead.

Separate from these racial anxieties, the youth of the day embracing jazz – basically black music that was an ideological manifestation far removed from the hit parade played on mainstream radio – was a bone of contention.

Jazz spoke of sensuality and joy and openly defied segregation – its adherents, white, black and Hispanic, mixed both on stage and on the dance floor. And the zoot suit was the easily recognised uniform of this new jazz ideology that visually challenged the norms of apartheid.

But it wasn't just the rise of the scandalous 'jazz' that precipitated what some observers called 'the worst mob violence in Los Angeles history', aka the Zoot Suit Riots of June 1943. A number of other factors contributed. The first was the war. The whole country, overwhelmed by an almighty surge of nationalism and paranoia regarding fifth columnists, included a citizenship that excluded minorities and those who weren't white. Curiously, while the US was fighting the forces of fascism abroad the nationalist racist pro-Aryan extremes that so marked the Third Reich were thriving and encouraged at home.

Civil rights were denied to most blacks, while anti-Mexican sentiment has long prevailed in the West. In the early 1930s, Los Angeles County deported more than 12,000 people of Mexican descent – including many American citizens – to Mexico. Those left were corralled in run-down corners of East LA and made to work for below minimum wage. It was in this climate that Chicano youth (and gang) culture emerged, while many whites, fuelled by racially contentious articles in Californian newspapers, especially those owned by William Randolph Hearst which traded in the frenzied stirring-up of unabashed hatred, believed that pachucos were Mexicans who refused both to speak English and to contribute to the war effort.

To further exacerbate the furore, in March 1942 the US War Production Board restricted the use of cloth by 26 per cent, resulting in what *Esquire* magazine called 'streamlined suits by Uncle Sam', causing the manufacture of the zoot suit to be banned. Underground tailors all over the US still produced the item, however, and reinforced a most visible divide between the predominantly white serviceman and the black and Hispanic zooters, whose outfit was viewed as a deliberate, scandalous and most obvious flouting of wartime rationing by drug-using unpatriotic hoodlums.

The zoot was a red flag to the already pissed-off redneck bulls. The truth is that many pachucos had enlisted in the forces, while much of the cloth used existed way before war broke out and was old stock.

Another prescient factor was an incident known as the Sleepy Lagoon Murder, which in no way impinged on white California, yet still fuelled animosity between whites and Hispanics. Accused of the 1942 murder of José Diaz, the gang known as the 38th Street Boys (comprising twenty-two defendants) was allegedly led by Henry Leyvas (who had enlisted in the merchant marines). It was the largest mass trial in Californian history. It played out 'like a Hollywood movie', and as such captivated the city.

The Sleepy Lagoon Defence Committee was formed by civil rights pioneer Carey McWilliams and consisted of leftists, communists, unionists, and Hollywood celebrities like Orson Welles and Rita Hayworth, all of whose involvement further aggravated this controversial affair.

Normally the LAPD kept well out of minority murders but on this occasion felt the need to clamp down on what white Angelinos saw as a worryingly dangerous and violent zoot suit subculture. Of course, the trial was a farce. Presiding Judge Charles Fricke allowed jurors to go home at night where they read LA journalists' racist slurs directed against pachucos, while the usually immaculate defendants were refused haircuts, a wash and a clean change of clothes.

The result was that seventeen of the twenty-two defendants were duly convicted, which emphatically reminded LA's Mexican community that they were indeed second-class citizens who would never be accepted in the land that had been theirs until the 1848 Treaty of Guadalupe Hidalgo. The agreement, perhaps one of the most unjust treaties in history, was created to end the war (1846–48) between the United States and defeated Mexico and 'forced' the US to pay the paltry sum of $15 million to Mexico and to settle the claims of American citizens against Mexico up to $3.25 million, for which they took ownership of the whole of California, half of New Mexico, most of Arizona, Utah , Nevada and huge chunks of Colorado and Wyoming

(the southern parts of New Mexico and Arizona were peacefully purchased under the Gadsden Purchase of 1853 for $10 million, which is
equivalent to $280 million today), while Mexicans in those annexed
areas were offered the privilege of becoming American citizens or
moving back across the new border. The ancestors of these pachucos
were some of the 90 per cent who chose to become US citizens.

Meanwhile whites, whipped up by a press that characterised all
Mexican youth as dark-skinned hoodlums, became overwhelmingly
paranoid, indeed terrified, of those who sported the zoot.

The fact that some poor working class whites also wore the fashion
was immaterial – it was regarded as anti-American and those who
wore it deserved a good beating (often from US servicemen or
policemen) and that was that.

As a result, altercations broke out between serviceman and zooters
all over California, two of which had a particular effect on the
forthcoming riots. On 30 May 1943, a group of sailors and soldiers
harassed a group of pachucas (female zooters) on Main Street in
downtown LA and were battered by the ladies' male counterparts as
a result. Four days later, sailors were again routed by a gang of zooted
Chicanos, causing a mob of off-duty LA coppers, who called themselves the Vengeance Squad, to further attack Hispanics on Main
Street. The shit really hit the fan the following day after a barrage of
taxis containing about 200 sailors turned up in East LA, attacked a
group of mainly twelve- and thirteen-year-old boys, clubbed them
to within an inch of their lives, stripped them naked and burned their
clothes in a big pile.

And thus the riots began.

As the journalist Carey McWilliams, a witness to the attacks,
wrote:

*Marching through the streets of downtown Los Angeles, a mob of several
thousand soldiers, sailors, and civilians, proceeded to beat up every zoot
suiter they could find. Pushing its way into the important motion picture
theatres, the mob ordered the management to turn on the house lights and
then ran up and down the aisles dragging Mexicans out of their seats.
Streetcars were halted while Mexicans, and some Filipinos and Negroes as*

*young as twelve, were jerked from their seats, pushed into the streets and
beaten with a sadistic frenzy.*

On one occasion a gang of sailors dragged two Chicano zoot suiters onto the cinema stage and, while the film carried on playing, stripped the boys naked and urinated on their clothing. Meanwhile the press stated that said attacks were perpetrated by 'heroic servicemen' who were 'cleansing their cities of human garbage.'

The most heinous violence occurred on Monday 7 June, after one Los Angeles paper printed a guide on how to 'de-zoot' a zoot suiter. 'Grab a zooter. Take off his pants and frock coat and tear them up or burn them,' it instructed.

That night a crowd of 5,000 civilians gathered downtown alongside soldiers, marines and sailors and headed south to the black neighbourhood of Watts, and east for Mexican-American East Los Angeles, beating up not only zooters but any Mexicans or blacks they could find. As *Time* magazine later reported: 'The police practice was to accompany the caravans of soldiers and sailors in police cars, watch the beatings and jail the victims.' Six hundred Chicanos were arrested and incarcerated.

One policeman was quoted after the riots as saying: 'You can say that the cops had a "hands-off" policy during the riots. Well, we represented public opinion. Many of us were in the First World War, and we're not going to pick on kids in the service.' Accordingly, after Councilman Norris Nelson called the zoot suit 'a badge of hoodlumism', the LA City Council criminalised the suit within the confines of the city.

Of course, to put this into perspective one has to realise that in 1943, at the height of the riots, the hugely successful black jazz musical feature films, *Stormy Weather,* directed by Andrew Stone, and *Cabin in the Sky,* directed by Vincente Minnelli, were released, featuring zoot suits, while in the same year America's favourite comedy duo Laurel and Hardy wore zoots in the film *Jitterbugs.*

Furthermore, the song 'A Zoot Suit (For My Sunday Gal)' was a huge hit in 1942 for several artists. 'Dig a zoot suit with a reet pleat and a drape shape and a stuff cuff to look sharp enough to see your Sunday gal?' said the lyric.

The zoot suit had found a place in mainstream contemporary culture and *still* it caused riots.

The debacle was eventually contained not on any humanitarian basis but for purely economic reasons. California's state senators were only concerned about the adverse effect that events might have on the relationship between the United States and Mexico. The government declared, 'The riots might endanger the program of importing Mexican labour to aid in harvesting California crops.'

Accordingly, the Mexican Embassy formally complained to the State Department, and US Service Chiefs had no choice but to intervene on 7 June, declaring Los Angeles off-limits to all military personnel and confining sailors and Marines to barracks.

By the middle of June the situation had calmed down in LA, but riots erupted elsewhere in California, as well as in Texas, Arizona, Detroit, Harlem and Philadelphia, where two zoot-clad members of Gene Krupa's chart-topping band were given a hiding. Meanwhile Detroit suffered the worst race riot in its history.

A prime manifestation of the old adage 'you reap what you sow', the zoot-suit riots had a profound effect on a whole generation of socially underprivileged teenagers who themselves would exert their influence on the US itself.

It was during the riots that young zoot suiter and soon-to-be Chicano union activist Cesar Chavez became involved with community politics, which transformed California. Elsewhere, a certain young pimp, 'Detroit Red', aka Malcolm Little, due to his role in the Harlem riots, embarked on a political journey that ultimately transformed him into the radical black leader, Malcolm X.

Furthermore, the seeds of Eme, the Mexican Mafia – the most powerful crime syndicate in the US today – were sown during the conflict. Eme founder and leader Rodolfo Cadena's father fell victim to navy thugs in 1943 and the mob boss never forgot. The melee also gave gang culture an almighty boost as, even though many Mexican and black gangs already existed (such as the White Fence and the Businessmen), the riots served to validate their existence, strengthen their resolve and attract recruits, all of which created a massive surge in armed ethnic street gangs in post-war America.

And looking back, who can blame them? If I had gangs of sailors strolling into my neighbourhood and beating up innocent people, I too would form a resistance group. Ultimately, then, the debacle achieved the opposite of what was intended. It did not cleanse the area of mobsters; it actually turned many law-abiding young men on to the gangster life. Just as NF activities in East London in the seventies provoked the rise of Asian gangs like the Brick Lane Massif, so did the zoot suit riots prompt the rise of Californian gang culture.

But as you are now aware the furore wasn't *just* about a suit.

Certainly, the item exerted considerable influence elsewhere. UK spivs took to big suits as proof, as with their Mexican counterparts, that they could afford and source the cloth denied to mere mortals by cloth restrictions during and after World War II. Jamaican settlers sported their versions as they alighted from the S.S. *Windrush* in London's Tilbury Dock in 1948, thus influencing young Brits.

Also, post-World War II, Dior launched his New Look for women in which everything went big. American male fashion responded with a style that was heavily influenced by the zoot – high-waisted, pleated peg trousers, heavily shouldered jackets with big lapels, wide kipper ties and spear-collared shirts – which became almost a uniform for the stars of film noir such as Alan Ladd, Victor Mature and Jack Palance. Shortly after, I played my own part in the zoot suit's inimitable journey.

Unnaturally obsessed with film noir as a lad in 1973, I was overjoyed to see a fashion shoot in a *Club International* nudie mag I'd purloined from a newsagent in my home town, which featured tailored zoots from Malcolm McLaren and Vivienne Westwood's Let It Rock store.

Almost sick with excitement, I realised that I could dress like that now, and two years later found myself in London buying vintage suits from Beaufort Market, big ties from Retro and black-and-white shoes from Acme Attractions. I'd wear this gear dancing to raw US imported funk in Crackers.

I even managed to get myself an ice-cream-pink Mal and Viv zoot from their store, which was now called Sex. Meanwhile I became a teenage zoot spotter – eyes glued to the TV, clocking every stylish nuance of the aforementioned movies of 1943.

Subsequently, in 1980, having no truck whatsoever with some of the rather antiseptic futurist music and absurdly camp fashions that were all the rage at clubs like the Blitz, which I frequented, I turned the clock back and started DJ-ing funk and Latin and wearing 1940s clothes again.

That summer, after a trip to New York, I decided to form my own Latin-funk band – Blue Rondo à la Turk – and, having discovered a book, *The Zoot Suit Murders* (which climaxes with the aforementioned riots), realised the social importance of the silhouette.

I also realised that the suit was ripe for revival, and that was how we, as a combo influenced by seventies funk and sixties jazz, should dress. Forties punk, no less.

In the meantime, Blue Rondo penned its first composition – 'Me and Mr Sanchez', after the author of *The Zoot Suit Murders*, Thomas Sanchez. I then designed my very own zoot and commissioned Bob the Tailor of Aldgate – whose pattern cutter was coincidentally a Chicano who had been involved in the aforementioned riots as a teen – and started a night at Le Kilt (the first of the clubs to devote itself almost entirely to rare groove), which served as a necessary haven for all those of a similar stylistic persuasion.

Of course, the band, the club and the style took off like rocket, and soon I launched my own range of ready-to-wear zoot suits, in partnership with ex-Amen Corner saxophonist and style entrepreneur Alan Jones under the brand Sullivan Suits, which sold all over the country in shops such as Demob in London and Paradise Garage in Bristol.

Amazingly, headlines in *The Face*, *L'Uomo Vogue*, the *New York Times*, *LA Times* and *Paris Match* (which led with the headline 'Zoot Alors') proclaimed the global return of the style while uber designers such as Giorgio Armani and Jean-Paul Gaultier created collection after collection featuring watered-down versions of the style until the oversized, large-shouldered, peg-trousered suit became the signature eighties style. Afterwards, I had fashion shows all over the world and designed zoot suits – albeit with my own odd twists – which were made by tailor Chris Ruocco of Kentish Town. They were worn by chart toppers Spandau Ballet, Ultravox, Adam Ant (who wore it for Live Aid) and Madness, to name a few. It still tickles me that a style created by dirt-poor black teenagers ended up on the backs of global chart-topping British chaps fifty years later. I guess it wasn't the first or the last time.

As a result of my endeavours, the country was soon festooned with fellas in oversized suits, long chains and correspondent shoes. The conceit was further propagated in 1982 when August Darnell of Kid Creole and the Coconuts fame fell on the zoot as his chosen look and, due to his chart success, totally eclipsed our usage (oddly Darnell was born on the same day as me, but ten years before), and fair play to the man. He did it very well.

Today, as clued-up hep cats find the fashions of today rather predictable, the zoot is enjoying another renaissance. I just hope that any would-be Zootie McVouties can find a tailor like Bob of Aldgate and Chris of Kentish Town to produce one of the quality it so rightly deserves.

Salvatore Giuliano

Since his death in 1950, forty-four books have been written about the Sicilian bandit Salvatore Giuliano, including one by his sister and a bestselling novel, *The Sicilian,* penned by Mario Puzo, which entwines the life of Giuliano with that of the fictional character Michael Corleone – the all-powerful Italian-American Mafia boss who first appeared in Puzo's *The Godfather*.

The Sicilian, adapted for the big screen in 1987, was directed by Michael Cimino and starred Christopher Lambert as the man in question. However most agree that the definitive movie about the outlaw, simply titled *Salvatore Giuliano*, was directed by Italian film-maker Francesco Rosi in 1962.

Critic Derek Malcolm described it as 'almost certainly the best film about the social and political forces that have shaped [Sicily,] that benighted island.' *New Yorker* critic Terrence Rafferty was equally impressed: '*Salvatore Giuliano* manages to sustain an almost impossible balance of immediacy and reflection. It's such an exciting piece of filmmaking that you might not realise until the end that its dominant tone is contemplative, even melancholy.' It is also one of Martin Scorsese's all-time favourite films.

Shot in a documentary, non-linear style, the film, which wasn't released in the UK until September 2014, tells Giuliano's story by following the lives of those involved with the 'Gentleman Bandit', who rose to prominence after the invasion of Sicily in World War II. A high-profile, handsome, charismatic and remarkably stylish robber, Giuliano courted and made full use of the press and, owing to his movie-star good looks, flamboyance and audacity, hit the front pages of newspapers worldwide. Even *Time* magazine felt it necessary to quote the bedtime prayer of an eight-year-old boy in Rome in 1949: 'God bless mother and father and save Giuliano from the police.' Eminent historian Eric Hobsbawm described him as 'the last of the people's bandits (à la Robin Hood) and the first to be covered in real time by modern mass media.'

Yet apart from the splurge of interest in the 1980s (including an opera based on his life by Italian composer Lorenzo Ferrero) the man has slipped under the radar and has been consigned to a dusty bottom drawer in the annals of history – which begs the questions: who was Salvatore Giuliano? Why was there such global interest in him? And what was the political and social climate that created such a man?

To understand him, or bandit culture, or indeed the Mafia, one has to acquaint oneself with the uncommonly mercurial Sicily, the island where an alphabetical guidebook published in 1905 sandwiches Murder between Mules and Museums, stating that, 'Murders in Sicily are not rare. But foreigners are never murdered, murder being reserved for vendettas and quarrels.'

The island was first inhabited by the Elymians, the Sicanians and the Siculi. Subsequently, the Greeks, Phoenicians and Carthaginians fought over the land until the Roman Republic's victory at the Battle of Carthage in 149 BC. Things calmed down and the island prospered until the middle of the fifth century, when in stomped the Vandals and Ostrogoths, Teuton races from the plains of Hungary who swept down through Italy and populated Sicily and the North African coast. One hundred years later the Byzantines marched in and declared it their own for the next three centuries, even though they were continually harassed by Arabs and Berbers, who eventually took over in the early ninth century.

Muslim rule existed until the next wave came. This time it was the Normans who routed the North Africans, and for the next century ruled with a surprising religious tolerance that elevated the island to a state of rare prosperity.

All this ended when the second Teuton conquest came in 1194, the first German king flexing his muscles in an avalanche of sadism, rape and murder. As bad as he was, he was outdone in 1266 when the French Angevins subjugated the island in a torrent of bloodletting, brutality and butchery which for the first time prompted the ragtag islanders to rise as one against their oppressors.

The revolt started with the ascent of the Sicilian ballad, sung out of earshot of their subjugators, which told of the tortures and atrocities they had suffered, and urged the locals to kill the hated French. This culminated in 1282 in the carnage known as the Sicilian Vespers, whereupon the islanders rose up and slaughtered thousands of French.

The resulting war lasted thirty years and was uncommonly blood-thirsty.

The Sicilians called on Peter of Aragon to be their king, and, for the first time, the island was independent. It enjoyed relative stability until 1412, when Peter's bloodline ended and the ruling barons, in order to avoid a civil war, proclaimed King Ferdinand of Spain as King of Sicily in 1412.

The Spanish ruled for 300 years, bringing with them the Inquisition, who tortured the significant Jewish population into religious conversion, death or expulsion. Even though this was the longest rule since the Romans, culturally the Spanish made little impact on the Sicilians. The war of secession ended their rule, only for the Duke of Savoy to step in for a year, followed by Austria, which ruled for sixteen years.

Next up was Carlos Bourbon, the prince of Spain, whose leniency allowed the rot to set in. Corruption and apathy reigned, provoking periodic revolutions which, apart from the ten-year occupation by Britain, which regarded the island as nothing more than a strategic point from which to wage war on Napoleon, continued until Sicily was conquered by Giuseppe Garibaldi during the Risorgimento of 1860.

Notably, this invasion was made possible by the Sicilians themselves, who were not only thrilled to be a part of this new unified Italy for the first time but proud to be regarded as *Italian*. Joy soon turned to despondency as their part in the Risorgimento was forgotten, along with their voluntary vote of allegiance. Ignored by Rome, taxes were raised, conscription was introduced and all the money made in Sicily was taken out and not put back in. By the turn of the twentieth century, Sicily was, despite being part of Italy, severely disillusioned .

After World War I, Sicily descended into the chaos that has blighted it ever since. In Palermo a murder a day was not uncommon, while the sound of gunfights permeated the air regularly – twenty-four hours a day, seven days a week. Countless bandits roamed the country doing what they do best. It was out of this maelstrom of upheaval and malcontent that Giuliano eventually emerged.

Indeed, *everything* about Sicily is a direct result of the succession of rulers and their proclivities. It is said that houses are painted in different colours according to the owners' ancestors – blue for Greek descent, white for Norman, red for Saracen, and yellow for the converted Jew. Until fairly recently (and certainly during Giuliano's years) unmarried women could only show their faces in special circumstances, a legacy of the Muslim occupation, while post-pubescent girls were not permitted to walk the streets to church unless accompanied by a chaperone. Priests often asked for proof of a would-be bride's virginity before agreeing to perform a wedding ceremony, which was a direct result of the Spaniards and their Inquisition. Even the Sicilian mother tongue – more a dialect than a language – is infused with Greek, Arabic and French words. Little wonder that Rosi's historically accurate movie employs Italian subtitles, as few mainlanders fully comprehended Sicilian even in 1962.

But then again, few Italians understood Sicily, its bandits or the Mafia – the ultimate Sicilian government, whose activities are not 100 per cent criminal. But to completely comprehend the bandit, and the Mafia as a whole, some knowledge of the history of said island is integral. Successive potentates were regarded as foreign interlopers, ripe for thieving from, while the homegrown Mafia were the only 'rulers' the locals kowtowed to. Thus, the Mafia was the only entity that had the power and the respect to govern, albeit in their own most unusual way.

Nearly all of the Mafia's actions are replicated by other so-called constitutional elected governments – the likes of which were absent from the island for centuries. One such example is 'protection', which the mafia bestows with far more efficiency than most police forces, whose existence is maintained by taxes that if not paid will result in a jail term, the threat of which can only be described as demanding money with menace. Furthermore, few police forces guarantee immunity from theft or burglary, while the mafia *certainly* does.

Undeniably, the Mafia has changed almost as much as the island; the big transformation occurred after World War I when young Mafiosi returned from the front lines, not only disenchanted with their older counterparts, who, by virtue of their rank, had dodged the draft and were now fat with profit, but with a knowledge of firearms far exceeding that of their shirking countrymen. Thus, warfare erupted amongst the Sicilian Mafia, the distracted dons lost their ability to regulate crime, and unlicensed brigands sprang up all over the country.

Into this melee strutted Il Duce, aka Benito Mussolini, who called upon Sicily to openly defy the Mafia and appointed Colonel Cesare Mori as prefect of police to eradicate them. 'Let nobody speak of the nobility or chivalry of the mafia, unless he really wishes to insult the whole of Sicily,' said Mussolini.

In truth, Cesare Mori made little impact throughout Il Duce's reign, and once he was toppled the Mafia carried on exactly as before. No one can doubt that Sicily under Il Duce was a mess in which disorganised crime flourished. Indeed, Giuliano was a case in point. Having taken the oath, he controlled western Sicily with despotic zeal and was as ruthless a killer as any of them. A much-loved figure idolised by Sicilians, he robbed from the rich and gave to the poor. But he existed at the behest of the Mafia, and when he crossed them his candle was extinguished at the age of twenty-eight.

Unusually, Giuliano was conceived in New York but born in Sicily. His parents, unlike many of the estimated 400,000 Italians who emigrated to the US during the early part of the twentieth century – many of whom were Sicilian – turned their noses up at what to many was a lifelong dream, and returned to Sicily after eighteen years. Giuliano was born on 16 November 1922 in the mountains in the hamlet of Montelepre – which Sicilians pronounce *Muncialebre* – some seventeen miles from Palermo.

One of four children (the average Sicilian family then numbered ten) Giuliano was, in the great Italian tradition, worshipped as a boy by *la mamma*. Although described by his teacher as a 'quick learner' who devoured every book he could lay his hands on, Giuliano left school aged fifteen to work with his father after his elder brother was conscripted. Nicknamed 'Turiddu' – the Sicilian shortening of Salvatore – he listened to his papa tell tales of the great, the good and the gold-covered sidewalks of New York and from an early age idolised the US. Thus, when the allies landed in Sicily, he rejoiced along with the rest of his countrymen (most of whom had relatives in the US).

Unfortunately, the invasion did not in any way relieve the utter chaos that existed in Sicily in 1943. Life without the black market was impossible as rations allowed just half a pound of bread and five ounces of pasta a day and criminal racketeering thrived. All roads had been bombed and bridges demolished, while the weapons of four armies were just another commodity to be sold to the highest bidder and law enforcement ceased to exist. To add to the Sicilians' misery the US had bombed Sicily indiscriminately, killing 3,000 locals in just one raid, while British troops raped and looted and lolled around drunk out of their skulls on the local wine that, at 13.5 per cent alcohol, was four times as strong as the beer they were used to.

Giuliano was now twenty-one, full of the same piss and vinegar that fills many of his age, and was therefore more than a little indignant regarding the status quo.

A law had been passed to force the release of hoarded foodstuffs that prohibited the transport of grain, particularly from one province to the next. The Carabinieri enforced said laws by searching travellers at strategic borders and, if not offered a bribe, seized what they found. Therefore, only the poorest and the hungriest were caught – an old man with a bag of pasta only big enough to feed his family, a young girl with a small bottle of olive oil, a child with half a loaf of bread. Not one for either observing or accommodating such actions, Turridu started organising the smuggling of small amounts of grain to his village, increasing the load when he had saved enough for a mule.

All went swimmingly until 2 September 1943, when the young man passed a checkpoint and had his goods confiscated. He refused to offer the officers a bribe and thus his identity card was demanded, while he was threatened with a beating with a rifle unless he informed on his supplier. In true Sicilian tradition he refused to tell tales, but begged for them to let him go, only for another mule laden with grain to amble over and pay the Carabinieri a bribe.

Seeing this, it seems that Giuliano, now held by only one Carabinieri, attacked him and fled, only for the other three to open fire and hit him. Bleeding profusely, he fired on his pursuers using a gun he had concealed, killing one while the other three backed off. Finding his ID card on the floor and refusing to risk their lives chasing a young man with a gun who would possibly die of his wounds, the Carabinieri were confident of rounding him up sooner or later.

They could never have guessed that it would take seven years, around 2,000 troops and millions of lira to apprehend him.

The young man might have turned himself in and spent the rest of his life in a rat-infested prison, but was turned to the life that was to make him famous when the authorities arrested his uncle and father (who shared the same name). Turridu's answer was to ambush the Carabinieri vans on the way to the prison. Despite killing one and wounding another, he was no match for seven men armed with machine guns, and promptly vanished. But he wouldn't let it lie. Disguised as a gardener, he smuggled a file to his cousin in the Monreale Gaol that facilitated a mass breakout of twelve men who had equipped themselves with much of the prison's armoury.

It was this merry band who formed the nucleus of the Giuliano gang, while the escape served to fuel his soon-to-be folkloric reputation. Giuliano's career as an outlaw was gathering pace, yet his dad languished in the decrepit Palermo prison.

His next move was a stroke of genius. He allied himself within the Sicilian separatist movement, whose leaders saw that he was just what they needed: a fiercely ambitious, charismatic young man who hated the Carabinieri but who lacked the usual sordid criminal history of his contemporaries – in other words, a hero. Accordingly they offered him the coveted post of chief of police and minister of justice should they succeed in their aims.

When he asked for £6,000 to put together a force, they suggested he raise the money by kidnap and ransom. 'I am no bandit!' protested Giuliano, after which they gave him £1,500 to found a new army, promised arms and uniforms, and made him colonel of the New Western Army.

He could now kill those he hated with impunity and as a soldier fighting for a just cause that many believed in. He would be a heroic rebel commander instead of a criminal robber. The party leaders promised him immunity for all his actions if they won, and a passage abroad if not. They now had Giuliano in the palm of their hands and were primed to have him do their dirty work.

The first task was to gather together an army. Initially, it was a family affair, all unpaid, but they had uniforms – loose red and yellow tunics with the emblem of Sicily sewn on the breast. And they had anti-Carabinieri songs to sing.

On 28 April 1945 Mussolini was executed. A week later the Nazis capitulated in Italy, causing the Italians themselves to declare war on Japan – an act that put them on the same footing as all the other allied belligerents. Knowing that England and America would no longer side with them, the separatists realised they had to act now before Italy sorted itself out and took control of the island.

The separatist army now numbered some 5,000 soldiers, with Giuliano commanding half of them, but they were still routed by the Italian forces in October 1945, their propaganda made illegal and their leaders, with the exception of Giuliano – still a fugitive, who fought more of a guerilla campaign – exiled.

Yet still he showed his tenacity. On 28 December 1945, accompanied by eighty men, Giuliano attacked the Carabinieri barracks at Bellolampo, blew its doors off, stole their guns and daubed the inside walls with separatist slogans. He followed that up with daily raids and ambushes, and a raid on the Palermo–Trapani train, where he relieved a rich passenger of a large wad of cash, treated passengers – including a few women and a British officer – with uncommon courtesy, and gave an impromptu interview to an Italian journalist who just happened to be travelling on the train. He then ambushed an army officer, shot him, tended to his wounds, and let him go. Giuliano didn't see himself as a common brigand and murderer but as a man who reflected the people and their needs. Simply killing an officer had no intrinsic public relations worth, but saving him did. Giuliano was very aware of his reputation as the Sicilian Robin Hood, as the man of the people, as the just and principled leader, and so did all he could to protect this.

But there was another side to the man. One time he caught a boy, who he had nurtured like his own son, spying on him for the Carabinieri and let him go. The foolish youth, lured by the 2,000 lire (around £30) the cops offered him, did it again and was caught. Showing no mercy this time, Giuliano put him up against a wall, made him say his prayers and shot him.

To the corpse he then pinned a note: 'So Giuliano will deal with all those who spy on him.' A week later another spy was found dead with a note pinned to his breast. A few days later another man, a Carabinieri officer who posed as a separatist, was killed – the note written this time in rhyme. Many others followed.

Under a new amnesty granted to all separatists not charged with criminal acts, many of his cronies fled to respectability, but Giuliano, still the leader of a large band of outlaws, carried on regardless, robbing the rich and giving to the poor. In his absence he was tried for his crimes and sentenced to twenty-four years of imprisonment, while his mother and sisters were arrested and imprisoned.

Hearing this news, Giuliano exploded with rage. Posters appeared signed by the man himself, warning the public not to travel on buses in which the Carabinieri were riding for fear of ambush. And when his family were released twenty-three days later, he issued more posters, this time stating that passengers would now remain unmolested on the buses and apologising for any inconvenience caused.

Without the political backing needed to be seen as champion of the poor and oppressed, he executed those of his men who ignored such rules and robbed the unfortunate, leaving their corpses in prominent places with the note 'Giuliano does not rob the poor' pinned to their chests.

Acting as defender of the impoverished, he shot a shopkeeper who extended credit to his poor customers at extortionate rates of interest and seized their homes when they were unable to pay. He shot a post office clerk for stealing letters containing money intended for the underprivileged relatives of American immigrants. 'I will not tolerate injustice,' he declared. 'I am on the side of justice for its own sake.'

Accordingly, as he seems to have accumulated no money himself from his daring robberies, we can conclude that whatever was left after he paid the Mafia was given to his beloved peasants. Thus it was difficult to argue against Giuliano's reputation as a latter-day

Robin Hood. By the summer of 1946 almost all major crimes on the island were attributed to the handsome young rebel who, much to the embarrassment of the authorities, still evaded capture.

The first months of 1947 brought fresh humiliation when a New York journalist, Michael Stern, looking for a sensational story to bolster his career, received a commission from his editor to interview Giuliano. Stern, a former war correspondent who dressed in his entitled uniform of a captain in the US army, simply drove to Montelepre, where he successfully sought out Giuliano senior, who subsequently led him to junior. He photographed the man and conducted an interview which was eventually published all over the world in a dozen different languages. The article painted Turiddu as a hero and certainly not a brigand, thus securing the Giuliano legend.

'He was a nice guy, a sincere guy,' said Stern. 'He had just one thing wrong with him: he rather liked killing people.'

Events escalated after the allies handed Sicily over to the Italians, who dispatched an army to aid the Carabinieri. In February 1947 they clashed regularly with Giuliano and his men, who continued to hold up and kidnap rich civilians, the man himself present at every occasion, treating any women who accompanied his victims with exaggerated gallantry.

By this time Giuliano was hand in glove with the Mafia, who made the ransom demands on his behalf, receiving 10 per cent for their troubles. He also carried out their strong-arm work and was guaranteed full protection for doing so. Still, a reward of a million lira (£100,000) was posted for capturing him, dead or alive.

Meanwhile, the separatist leaders were set free from exile and denounced their cause, leaving Giuliano and his men stranded. So he formed a new group: the Movement for the Annexation of Sicily to the American Confederation.

News got out that Giuliano had written a letter to President Truman, delivered by Stern, requesting he add Sicily to the United States as the 'forty-ninth Golden Star', stating that he would purge the island of communism and refuse financial aid from Stalin. Whether Truman replied is unknown.

What is known is that the Communist Party, now the dominant

party on the island, were enraged and accused the openly right-wing Giuliano of collusion with the *polizia*. The bandit replied by backing the Monarchist Party (who offered him amnesty if they succeeded) and launching a major offensive against the communists.

On 1 May 1947, Giuliano made the first of a succession of mistakes. The communists of Portelle della Ginestra had decided to hold their May Day celebrations locally. Giuliano got wind of it and by his own admission planned to upset the hoedown by firing over the heads of the revellers and executing the communist Senator Li Causi in front of the crowd.

At ten o'clock that morning the crowd started to arrive – peasant families dressed in their Sunday best on gaily painted donkey carts, ready for a day of fun with the children. Fifteen minutes later, the party secretary took to the stage.

Seconds into his welcome, the machine guns opened fire, killing eleven men, women and children, nine donkeys and horses, and wounding thirty-three others.

Giuliano claimed he was horrified by what he described as an accident. But less than two months later, on 24 June, he bombed the Communist Party's headquarters in six different villages, blew up an industrial plant in Palermo, and scattered thousands of anti-communist leaflets throughout the city.

The reaction amongst the left-wingers was marked to say the least. Protest strikes occurred throughout Italy and debate raged in the Italian senate, while the left-wing newspaper *L'Unità* led with the headline 'American spy Stern supplied Giuliano with arms'.

Consequently, the Carabinieri moved in on Montelepre with renewed vigour, using tear gas and machine guns to intimidate the 6,000 townspeople, many of whom were arrested and taken in for questioning. Giuliano, meanwhile, continued with his routine attacks, robberies and kidnappings. His mother and sister were again arrested and imprisoned, which provoked a swathe of letters from Giuliano that threatened to up the ante. In the meantime, many of his core soldiers left him. It seemed as if the writing was on the wall.

As if to underline the above, on 17 July 1948, Giuliano did the unthinkable. He killed five high-ranking Mafiosi, including a *capo* –

Santo Fleres. Suddenly, his roof came falling down. His mother and sister were arrested and sentenced to five years' imprisonment. His father received an extra five years.

Things were to get even worse for Giuliano. Two thousand Carabinieri were stationed around Montelepre, 2,000 villagers were dragged in for questioning, and 400 were jailed, while a reward of five million lira was put on his head, dead or alive. Giuliano's response was to kidnap politicians, dukes and princes, for which the ransom was reported to be in excess of 100 million lira.

Consequently, the Italian government set up an anti-bandit squad whose main job was to bring down Giuliano. It was commanded by two crack officers, Antonio Perenze and Ugo Luca, who brought in a gang of hard-nosed, un-bribable northern Italians to garrison Montelepre. In the meantime, the Mafia started betraying and setting up Giuliano's core gang members, leaving few of his trusted players for the last act.

On 5 July 1950, Giuliano was killed in the east coast town of Castelvetrano. His body lay in a courtyard, on his side facing downward. He was dressed in a sleeveless singlet, drill trousers and sandals. Near his face lay his pistol, while a Beretta submachine gun sat next to his right hand. A huge bloodstain covered his singlet. But who killed him and how was he caught? Whoever did it and in what circumstances were as elusive as the man himself. The police offered a number of explanations. One was that he was lured to the town by Luca, who had spread the rumour that a film crew were there to interview him. Another said that he was there to visit a prostitute, Maria Caradonna, while it was also suggested he was preparing to escape the country from the nearby coast.

As for who killed him, *The Times* printed a story that claimed he fell foul of police machine guns. Some of the Italian press, in the absence of the truth, concentrated on his clothes, describing the minute details of his beautifully cut jacket that lay nearby and his highly polished brown sandals. There was even doubt as to whether the body was actually Giuliano. Scepticism remained until his mother (now released from prison) identified his body.

Subsequently, his cousin and right-hand man, Gaspare Pisciotta, stated at the trial that he had fired the fatal shot, a claim that was disputed, even though it was substantiated by the Mafia lawyer in whose house the killing took place and who claimed he saw the corpse carried out of his house. Undoubtedly Pisciotta was there in the house, but whether he did kill Giuliano or merely claimed he did under police pressure remains a mystery. Four years later he was murdered in prison, his morning coffee laced with enough strychnine to kill a horse.

A year later, writer Gavin Maxwell, while investigating Giuliano's death, met with an unnamed source from Montelepre. 'Everyone knows that Gaspare was *innocentissimo*,' the source claimed. 'The real killer was the same man who killed Pisciotta – but the orders in each case came from high up. The arm of the Mafia is much longer than that of the law.'

Film Noir

It is inconceivable to imagine life without film noir. Indeed, I both pity and envy those who have yet to feast on this particularly sumptuous cinematic banquet. Pity them since they don't know what they're missing, and envy them as they have a veritable smorgasbord of celluloid delights ahead of them: wise-cracking private dicks, bad-ass criminals, beleaguered leading men ushering in their own demise and the feisty femmes fatales who suck them deep into their subterranean world where all honest bets are off and scruples are decidedly old fashioned. And that is just the beginning.

Noir splits itself into sub-categories. There's amnesia and nightmare noir, gangster noir, heist noir, woman-in-distress noir, grifter noir (based on a confidence trick), runaway noir, psycho noir, gothic noir, docu-noir (which often uses real crime footage), prison noir, fantasy noir and occult noir – many of which overlap.

What they all have in common, however, is that the audience knows things aren't going to work out *at all* well. It's just a matter of when and how. An adult form that deals with emotions, motives and prejudices that are beyond the comprehension of most multiplex patrons, it occupies a massively important place in cinema history.

Despite being perceived as a fundamentally American genre, the term 'noir' was in fact coined by the French publisher Gallimard, who had decided to print all the hard-boiled crime novels by the likes of Raymond Chandler, Dashiell Hammett, Horace McCoy and James M. Cain, which screamed out for a Gallic airing since they were unavailable in France during the war due to Nazi occupation.

Thus in 1945 *Série Noire* was born, which translated as 'the black series' but was also a play on words, since *une série noire* also describes a succession of dire events. Said series of books was a great success and the following year Nino Frank, an Italian-born film critic living in Paris, began referring to all the American crime movies that were made in the early 1940s as 'film noir'. The moniker refers not only to the dark, brooding, pessimistic tone of the films but the way they look; much in film noir occurs at night and is shot in sharply contrasting black and white, where shadows reign supreme.

In America, such films were known simply as *melodramas* up until the 1970s – a term the Oxford English Dictionary defines as 'a sensational dramatic piece with exaggerated characters and exciting events intended to appeal to the emotions.' Add a large measure of cynicism, a *soupçon* of sex and a large measure of darkness and the result is noir.

Of course the *look* of noir is as American as its handle and can be easily traced back to the German Expressionist cinema of the 1920s and 1930s. And while some cite Robert Wiene's silent *The Cabinet of Dr Caligari* (1920) as the grandaddy of noir, I would ascribe some of this honour to the likes of Erich von Stroheim's *Foolish Wives* (1922), G. W. Pabst's immensely decadent *Pandora's Box* (1929) starring Louse Brooks, and F. W. Murnau's dark *Sunrise: A Song of Two Humans* (1927) – a virtual blueprint for the form.

Indeed, silent film directors including Sergei Eisenstein, Tod Browning and Carl Dreyer often employed the 'gothic' noir tones, outdoor night-time locations and the expressionist camera angles that later epitomised the form. It was only when the talkies came along that banality and studio shoots took over, as the necessary equipment became too big to cart around to locations.

That said, as much as we can tip our titfers to the silents, few can doubt that the roots of noir stem from the Berlin of the 1930s, after Germany had been ordered to pay the War Guilt Clause – amounting to a sum of 269 billion gold marks (the equivalent of $834 billion today) – to the victorious Allies for the cost of World War I. Hyperinflation rose to 3.25 billion per cent (see the chapter on Otto Dix). And then there was the rise of the Nazi party. Believing that the end of the world was nigh, the denizens of the city drank, drugged, gambled, perverted and fucked themselves to death.

Two distinctly different films set the ominous, dank tone for decades to come. The first was Josef von Sternberg's *Der blaue Engel* (1930) starring Marlene Dietrich as Lola Lola, a raunchy, stocking-clad, predatory singer-cum-hooker working in the Blue Angel 'speakeasy' who attracts the attentions of an aged bachelor, Professor Rath. Like many subsequent male noir protagonists, Rath is hopelessly attracted to this femme fatale, who he knows will never love him. And as we watch his life go down the plughole, she is positively nonplussed.

Next up came the dark and disturbing *M* (1931), directed by the monocled Fritz Lang. The film stars Peter Lorre as the child murderer Hans Beckert, who repeatedly evades capture, despite giving the police clues about his identity. Beckert loathes himself for what he is yet can't refrain from killing very young children. The police work round the clock but the killer continues unfettered, causing systematic raids on the city's felons until a criminal known as 'the Safecracker' (Gustaf Gründgens, immaculate in bowler hat, leather coat and gloves) organises a meeting with the conurbation's crime lords. They organise their own manhunt and use the city's petty criminals and beggars to watch the children and, ultimately, find their man.

Both films epitomise noir, not only in the way they look – dark and disjointed – but also in their subject matter. The first takes the classic noir construct that sees a man dragged down by an insatiable addiction. Usually it is the femme fatale to whom the protagonist is fatally attracted, but it might also be money, power, drugs, drink or, as is frequently the case, all of them together. *M* on the other hand takes a story in the news (Lang based it on newspaper cuttings of a latter-day child killer) and, however brutal, weaves a psychiatric maze around it that both contradicts and confounds.

Both films echoed the early twentieth century German/Austrian obsession with psychology (personified by Freud and Jung), wrapping said fascination up in a yarn that allowed a glimpse into society's netherworld and the so-called lowlifes that populated it. And lest we forget, Berlin between the two wars was the global epicentre of sleaze, where sex was cheap, drugs were cheaper and sexual experimentation ruled the roost.

Writers had caused huge controversy by examining and describing the so-called lowest rung on society's ladder for decades. In 1880, the French novelist Émile Zola penned *Nana,* the story of a prostitute, while Charles Dickens's *Oliver Twist*, though not plunging the darker depths that Zola inhabits, might be described as realist, and Robert Louis Stevenson's *Dr Jekyll and Mr Hyde* is certainly noir in its ambitions. A landmark publication translated into English by Jean Rhys, Francis Carco's *Perversity* used underworld slang to describe a hooker and her pimp's life in a 1920s Parisian slum and is pure pulp fiction. Carco et al were thus named poetic realists, a moniker subsequently appropriated in the 1930s by Parisian filmmakers such as Jean Grémillon, Jean Vigo and Jean Renoir, who produced quite remarkable movies that, though tagged poetic realism, had all the hallmarks of noir.

No surprise then that France should provide another key to the story. After Hitler's rise seemed unavoidable, most of the truly innovative – and predominantly Jewish – filmmakers based in Berlin quickly upped and left and found a home in Paris. Their numbers included the finest exponents of the form, such as Anatole Litvak, Robert Siodmak, Billy Wilder, Max Ophüls and Curtis Bernhardt, who was arrested by the Gestapo before making a narrow escape.

In fact the only filmmaker who wasn't Jewish and learned his trade in Berlin and left to take the noir stage was Alfred Hitchcock. Consequently, after settling in the French capital, they all realised that this was no place for creatives in general, let alone Jewish filmmakers. As the Nazi tanks moved south, they hot-footed it to Hollywood, along with Duvivier, Renoir and Tourneur. It might be said that Hitler played quite a big part in the creation of film noir. I wonder if he ever knew.

Over in Hollywood, Josef von Sternberg had taken the look he had perfected with *The Blue Angel*, and employed it in a series of Hollywood movies starring Dietrich, the most influential of which was the thoroughly noir-looking *Shanghai Express* (1932). Tod Browning's *Freaks* (1932) had the look and pessimistic tone of the form. But it was Fritz Lang who led the field with his 1937 outing *You Only Live Once*, starring Henry Fonda as a former convict making a fist of trying to go straight.

The jury is out as to what the first American noir picture was. Many claim that it is the sixty-four-minute B-movie *Stranger on the Third Floor,* released on 16 August 1940. The story and script were written by Nathanael West, born Nathan Weinstein, a Lithuanian Jew born in New York. It was directed by Boris Ingster, a Latvian Jew who worked with Sergei Eisenstein and went on to produce *The Man From U.N.C.L.E.* series. The film stars Peter Lorre as a stranger on the third floor who somehow manages to embroil reporter Mike Ward (John McGuire) in his grisly throat-slashing antics.

The film carries all the assurances of noir: the voice-over, an urban setting, a dream sequence and an innocent protagonist falsely accused of a crime. Shot by Italian-born Nicholas Musuraca, it employed heavy shadows, off-kilter low camera angles, lots of darkness and *Dr Caligari*-like sets. Ingster's movie, although less well directed, acted and scripted than much film noir, somehow epitomises the ethic. It is dark, dank, melodramatic and more than a little barking.

But before *Stranger* came Raoul Walsh with his dark 1940 melodrama *They Drive By Night*, starring Ann Sheridan, Ida Lupino as the seething femme fatale, and George Raft and Humphrey Bogart as the truck-driving brothers Joe and Paul Fabrini. A film that carries all the hallmarks of the genre, it is almost a blueprint for the future of the milieu.

The year after *Stranger* made its mark, the émigrés, led by Anatole Litvak (who in that year knocked out both *Blues in the Night* and *Out of the Fog*) stormed forth. Von Sternberg made *The Shanghai Gesture* (starring Victor Mature and noir queen Gene Tierney), which specifically anticipated elements of classic noir, while German-born director William Dieterle twisted the conceit with his sublime 1941 picture *All That Money Can Buy*, which sets a classic noir yarn in 1840s New Hampshire. Meanwhile Fritz Lang had made the excellent *Man Hunt*, which verged on noir.

But even though the Europeans had laid the genre's foundations, it was the Americans who made the biggest noir noises in 1941. With his incomparable (though to many, not pure noir) *Citizen Kane*, Orson Welles influenced the milieu's finest directors, while John Huston's adaptation of Hammett's *Maltese Falcon* was the first major film noir of the classic era which, along with *High Sierra*, placed Bogart at the top of the darkly monochrome ladder.

The following year another actor, Alan Ladd, would don the noir hat and raincoat and achieve fame and fortune with two classics of the genre: *The Glass Key*, written by Hammett, and *This Gun for Hire*, based on a Graham Greene story and scripted by Burnett.

Meanwhile, Ladd's co-star, Veronica Lake, became the femme fatale numero uno.

Undeniably, noir's time had arrived. Hard-boiled crime 'pulp' fiction (so named because the books were made from paper constructed from cheap wood pulp) was massively popular, while its authors lived mainly in Los Angeles, eking out a living writing movie scripts.

Back then, just as today, Hollywood turned bestselling books into movies. But the difference was that in the late 1930s and early 1940s, bestsellers were written by the likes of Dashiell Hammett and Raymond Chandler, whose protagonists, such as the latter's Philip Marlowe and the former's Sam Spade (both played by Humphrey Bogart), were tough private dicks who passed moral judgement on what they considered an immoral society full of inconsequents and deadbeats.

This attitude couldn't have been more timely. Previously, in the depression-hit 1930s, America had seen gangsters such as Al Capone, John Dillinger, Meyer Lansky and Lucky Luciano hit the country's front pages. Hollywood, seeing their money, power, extravagance and anti-establishment glamour as the perfect antidote to the hard times, glorified them on the silver screen in films such as *Little Caesar* (1931), *The Public Enemy* (1931) and Howard Hawks's *Scarface* (1932).

And even though said villains were undoubtedly aggrandised, the films still warned of how power and money corrupts, a message that fell on deaf ears as most Americans didn't know where the next meal was coming from. Most were only too glad to see the bank that had taken away their homes and livelihood robbed, both in real life and on the cinema screen.

This led to the creation of the National Legion of Decency, who warned against the 'massacre of innocence of youth' and urged a campaign for 'the purification of the cinema'. This prompted Wyler (another German Jew) to helm *Dead End* in 1937 and Michael Curtiz (a Hungarian Jew) to direct *Angels with Dirty Faces* in 1938 – both of which featured the once impressed but subsequently disillusioned group of child actors the Dead End Kids, and firmly posited that crime began in the slums and certainly does not pay.

When Hammett and Chandler came on the scene with their morally intact detectives, then, it was good timing. Chandler hit pay dirt in 1939 with his novel *The Big Sleep* and in 1941 Hammett's *The Maltese Falcon* (which had been adapted previously, in 1931) was a cinematic sensation.

But it was the immigrants, particularly the Berliners, who took the noir saga a quantum leap further, albeit on the screen. They had worked on shoestrings in Germany and knew exactly how to turn a dog's balls into a fashionable wallet. They grafted all they had learned in their native land onto a slew of stories that might have been written for them. Furthermore, new lighter cameras were produced for newsreel use in World War II, which allowed cinematographers to experiment again. Many, such as Joseph LaShelle, Hal Mohr, George Barnes and Nicholas Musuraca, had written the rulebook for silent movies, so when noir popped up they were ready, willing and able to show the world just how to layer tone, light and shadow.

The drop in the international film market also gave noir a surprising boost. Hollywood suffered immeasurably and budgets were cut to zilch. Darkness and shadow were put to use to mask the lack of set, while location shoots became cheaper than the studios. Necessity became the mother of invention and Hollywood entered its most creative period ever.

Despite all that had happened so far, it was a mere preamble. The first really big noir year was 1944, when all the elements came together. Wartime cameramen, who had honed the use of small, lighter cameras in the most hazardous locations, were returning home, anxious to film low-budget noir. Meanwhile, writers such as James M. Cain and Cornell Woolrich had notched up a steady stream of mainly short noir stories, while the European directors stepped up to the plate as if they had been sitting on the substitutes' bench. One of the first truly *great* noir movies, *Double Indemnity* (1944), was co-scripted by Raymond Chandler and the film's director, Billy Wilder (a gay German Jew who had fled Berlin), and was based on Cain's 1943 novella and shot in LA.

Hot on its heels, six months later, came another classic: *The Woman in the Window,* directed by Fritz Lang. Then there was Otto Preminger's brilliant *Laura,* and another Chandler adaptation, *Murder, My Sweet*, directed by William Dieterle and starring crooner Dick Powell as Marlowe. The marriage was made and the die was cast.

By the time the war was over, most of the film-watching world were noir crazy, so the studios pumped them out. *The House on 92nd Street*, directed by Henry Hathaway, was the first docu-noir. Made with the full co-operation of the FBI, it used real footage and allowed the public insight into a hitherto clandestine world. The last barrier was down and, from now on, no holds were barred.

Noir was not only the biggest thing since the doughnut, it was infinitely credible, cheap to produce and darned glamorous. Consequently, almost all of the *great* Hollywood movie stars of the 1950s and 1960s made their names in noir. Rita Hayworth became an icon after Charles Vidor's *Gilda* (1946). Both Burt Lancaster and Ava Gardner became stars after Robert Siodmak's *The Killers*, Lana Turner was deemed a headliner after *The Postman Always Rings Twice* (1946) directed by the blacklisted Tay Garnett, while Jacques Tourneur's *Out of the Past* (released in the UK as *Build My Gallows High*) made stars out of Robert Mitchum, Kirk Douglas and Jane Greer. Even Monroe got a foot in the door as Louis Calhern's luscious mistress in *The Asphalt Jungle* (1950), directed by the great noir auteur John Huston, before cracking it with *Niagara* (1953).

And the actors were not alone. Many of the world's finest directors cut their teeth on noir. *The Set-Up* launched the directorial career of former editor Robert Wise. *The Narrow Margin* (1952) put Richard Fleischer in the driving seat. Nick Ray broke through with *They Drive by Night* (the first couple-on-the-run noir), while Robert Aldrich's debut was the brutal *Kiss Me Deadly* (1955), based on Mickey Spillane's novel. Otto Preminger was pure noir. *The Killing* (1956) set Kubrick on the road to success, while the bulk of Hitchcock's output until 1960 was noir. And lest we forget, it has been said that Orson Welles was said to have ushered in the form with *Citizen Kane* and ended the golden age with *Touch of Evil* (1958), a film that is everything the genre can proffer. Even three of Akira Kurosawa's earliest films are noir.

But it wasn't all plain sailing. Hollywood, and noir in particular, was decimated between 1947 and 1957 after the powers that be decreed that any Hollywood talent who had been involved with the American Communist Party or any left-wing organisation must be blacklisted and barred from working in the entertainment business. The idea (in part initiated by Walt Disney and propagated by the columnist Hedda Hopper) was to limit said creatives' ideological influence on the country. Known as the Second Red Scare or, later, McCarthyism (named after one of its fiercest hounds, Senator Joseph McCarthy), thousands of innocent Americans during this period were accused of being either dyed-in-the-wool communists or communist sympathisers. They were subjected to aggressive investigations and interrogations before government panels, committees and agencies – the most notable led by McCarthy himself. And it was the film business, especially those involved in noir, which suffered the most.

According to Mississippi congressman John Rankin, Hollywood was 'the greatest hotbed of subversive activities in the United States'. People were hauled in front of the House Un-American Activities Committee and asked to implicate colleagues. Ten men refused to testify, refused to name names, citing their First Amendment rights to freedom of speech and assembly, and were sentenced to one year in prison. These included Ring Lardner Jr, who worked on *Laura*, Albert Maltz, who scripted *This Gun for Hire* and *The Naked City*, Dalton Trumbo, who wrote *Gun Crazy* (and who won two Academy Awards while blacklisted), and Edward Dmytryk. The latter, on release, implicated some twenty-six colleagues, many of whom never worked again.

Other witnesses who blew the whistle on colleagues were director Elia Kazan, writer Budd Schulberg (whose film *On the Waterfront* is seen as a work created to defend the director and writers' scumbag actions), and actors Lee J. Cobb and Sterling Hayden, who said in his autobiography, 'I don't think you have the foggiest notion of the contempt I have had for myself since the day I did that thing.'

All in all, four hundred people were blacklisted, including Leonard Bernstein, Charlie Chaplin and writer Dorothy Parker. Even Dashiell

Hammett was imprisoned for his political stance. No one with a mind was safe.

The fact was that noir (and its predecessor, poetic realism) was an egalitarian conceit and spoke of the troubles of the man on the street. Its writers were fundamentally left wing. Among those imprisoned were *Algiers* co-writer John Howard Lawson, the first president of the Writers Guild of America and head of the Hollywood division of the Communist Party USA, which, adhering to Marxist-Leninist philosophy, initially fought for racial integration in the workplace and rights for the working man.

Many were Jewish free-thinking liberals who had seen the onslaught of the Nazis and the horrors of World War II and reacted accordingly in both work and politics. Curiously, one might say that film noir was prompted by one right-wing regime, the Nazis, and almost killed by another: the post-war, so-called Democratic administration of President Harry S. Truman.

There was a silver lining. One industry's loss was another's gain. Many creatives moved to New York, where they invigorated the fledgling television industry, creating some of the finest TV shows and plays ever made. It has been said that the only reason that pulp fiction fan, political activist and anti-war campaigner Rod Serling – creator of *The Twilight Zone* – wasn't blacklisted was because (a) he worked in TV and (b) he was a highly decorated war hero.

Indeed many blacklisted actors, such as Sam Jaffe, Burgess Meredith and Zero Mostel, appeared in Serling TV productions. Others moved to Europe. Some became cab drivers. Still, between 1945 and 1960 more than 500 noir titles came out of American studios, some of which are the finest films ever made.

Over the pond, the Brits had cottoned on. Carol Reed's *Odd Man Out*, *The Fallen Idol* and *The Third Man* were as good as anything that came out of Hollywood, while John Boulting's *Brighton Rock* is seminal. Of course, the French were all over the concept. Jules Dassin, the blacklisted American-born director, moved to France and made the staggeringly excellent *Rififi* (1955), an adaptation of Auguste Le Breton's novel, for which he was awarded best director at Cannes.

For his superlative *Casque d'Or* (1952), the great Jacques Becker set the proceedings among Paris's notoriously violent Apache gangs during *la belle époque*, while his 1954 *Touchez Pas Au Grisbi* (*Hands Off the Loot*) stars the great Jean Gabin as an older, world-weary gangster. In 1955 Jean-Pierre Melville made *Bob Le Flambeur*; Louis Malle helmed *Lift to the Scaffold* in 1958; and in 1960, Jean-Luc Godard directed *Breathless*. All of these are pure noir.

Indeed, the list of the world's greatest ever noir reads like a selection of cinema's great triumphs. Boorman's *Point Blank*, Scorsese's *Taxi Driver*, Polanski's *Chinatown*, Scott's *Blade Runner*, Verhoeven's *Basic Instinct*, the Coen Brothers' *Blood Simple*, Tarantino's *Pulp Fiction* and even Winding Refn's *Drive* are essentially neo-noir.

But the question remains: is noir a visual style, a mindset, a psychology, or just a catch-all conceit? Hundreds of books have been written on the subject, yet the jury is still out. What we can say is that the primary moods of classic film noir were, and are, desperation, disaffection, melancholia, isolation, disenchantment, pessimism, ambiguity, paranoia, malevolence, self-reproach, guilt and moral depravity. And perhaps its ability to encompass so many different themes is the reason behind its enduring popularity.

Whatever noir may be, it is certainly the most beguiling, charismatic and thoroughly mesmerising of all cinematic genres.

Here are five noir movies that stretch across the great divide, each one a total gem.

Double Indemnity (1944)

Directed by Billy Wilder, who cleverly cast the sapphic Barbara Stanwyck as the deceitful femme fatale, Fred MacMurray as her hapless victim, and Edward G. Robinson as the clued-up investigator, this is pure unadulterated noir. From the opening credits, etched against the silhouette of a man on crutches walking towards the camera, to its protagonist's final cigarette, this is paradigmatic film noir that set the standard for everything to follow. It was nominated for seven Oscars. A landmark achievement.

Scarlet Street (1945)

Following the 'older guy who falls for the femme fatale who will be his undoing' theme, this masterpiece is based on the French novel *La Chienne* (*The Bitch*) by Georges de La Fouchardière. It was directed by Fritz Lang and stars Edward G. Robinson as Chris Cross, a meek amateur painter and cashier for a clothing retailer who saves prostitute Kitty (Joan Bennett) after she is attacked by a man in the street. What he doesn't know is that the attacker is Kitty's brutish boyfriend, Johnny (Dan Duryea), and that Kitty is a chiselling bitch. But like a moth to a flame, Cross can't get enough. What follows reveals Lang's genius. It was temporarily banned in Milwaukee, Atlanta and New York State for erotic innuendo.

Nightmare Alley (1947)

This was a disturbing, contemporary chunk of darkness based on the book by William Lindsay Gresham. It was directed by Brit Edmund Goulding and shot by Oscar winner Lee Garmes. It stars Tyrone Power as Stanton Carlisle, a thoroughly ambitious carnie sideshow artist who, alongside phony mentalist Zeena (Joan Blondell) and her alcoholic husband Pete, run scams a-go-go. Next to *Freaks*, this might be the finest evocation of the freak show in existence, especially as it hinges on the 'geek', who was a very popular carnie sideshow. He was either an extreme heroin addict or an alcoholic who had been turned that way by the carnie owner, and his speciality was to run around in a cage grunting like an animal, biting the heads off live chickens and eating them. He was paid in drugs or drink, usually held captive and – forever on the edge of withdrawal – suspended in a state of complete and utter delirium.

Flesh and Fantasy (1943)

A portmanteau of three loosely connected stories of an occult nature, this film is one of two collections (the other is the excellent *Tales of Manhattan*) directed by the under-appreciated Julien Duvivier, who in 1937 set the noir tone with the superlative *Pépé le Moko*. This cracking film stars *New Yorker* satirist Robert Benchley alongside Edward G. Robinson, Charles Boyer and a barrage of great character actors.

The Devil and Daniel Webster (1941)

Directed by the supremely talented William Dieterle, who previously excelled with *The Hunchback of Notre Dame* and went on to helm the landmark *Portrait of Jennie*, this film, despite being set in the 1800s, ticks every single noir box in blood-red ink. It is the Faustian tale of one Jabez Stone, a down-on-his luck farmer who finds Mr Scratch, aka the Devil (beautifully rendered by *Maltese Falcon* director John Huston's father, Walter), chilling in his barn. Old Nick offers Jabez prosperity in exchange for his soul. He even throws in a gorgeous French chick (Simone Simon) for good measure. But things don't go as ol' Jab expects, so he calls on lawyer Daniel Webster to get him out of his satanic pact.

Orson Welles

'I don't want *any* description of me to be accurate,' chuckled Orson Welles. 'I want it to be flattering. And there is no point in asking me anything as no matter what, I will tell you a pack of lies.'

Writing anything about Welles will therefore always be a tough task as one attempts to sort the wheat from the chaff, the blind alleys from the high streets and the truth from the porky pies. What is certain, however, is that time has served the auteur exceedingly well.

For the last forty years there has not been one filmmaker, actor, producer or writer who has not regarded the man in the highest esteem. This is a remarkable achievement by anybody's measure, especially as between 1941 and 1958 he made just six Hollywood movies, some of which have yet to be rivalled.

Indeed, Martin Scorsese described him as 'the most influential director ever'. In 1977 the eminent *Chicago Sun-Times* film critic Roger Ebert said, 'Orson Welles can make better movies than most directors with one hand tied behind his back', while Welles's biographer and *Vanity Fair* writer Barbara Leaming described him as 'a titanic figure in twentieth-century popular culture... his list of achievements is unmatchable. He revolutionised modern drama on stage and made cinematic history.'

Orson Welles is also famous for burning whatever bridges he had built shortly after their construction. As the old rascal told Leaming, 'I started at the top and worked down. All the good fortune I ever had all happened before I was twenty-five. After that... nothing.'

And you have to hand it to the man: his first movie, *Citizen Kane*, made when he was twenty-five, is a masterpiece that has been voted the best film ever made on numerous occasions by critics and the public alike. Yet on its release it was sabotaged and sank like a golden nugget.

An outrageously audacious picture, it tells of the life of 'fictional' multi-millionaire newspaper magnate Charles Foster Kane and his scurrilous ascendance. But it is in fact the gossamer-veiled story of William Randolph Hearst, who had been the most powerful newspaper mogul in the US but fell from grace after he attended the Nuremberg Rally, flirted with Hitler and Mussolini, and considered himself America's great white saviour.

Still, at the time of the film's release, Hearst, despite having been removed as his company's top dog, nevertheless controlled many leading local newspapers, while his lackey, the right-wing Hollywood gossip columnist Louella Parsons, was one of the most widely syndicated, read and influential movie journalists in the USA and could easily make or break any movie, actor or director.

The film itself paints a picture of a man who claims to set out to make newspapers that tell the truth, then resorts to supporting the Spanish–American war in Cuba just to sell more papers. Welles stars as Kane, at first fresh-faced, handsome and upbeat, but ending up bitter, broken and decrepit.

The script speaks volumes about the corruptive influence of power and money. If his depiction of Kane as a power-mad lunatic wasn't enough, there was also the infamous 'rosebud' body blow. The whole picture begins when Kane dies, his last word being 'rosebud', which triggers a media frenzy as newspapers attempt to discover what the word actually means. This triggers the telling of his story, as various associates are interviewed and recount Kane anecdotes. And, even though Welles had fun with this by suggesting to the viewer that Rosebud was the young Kane's favourite toboggan, the barb in this particular McGuffin was that Rosebud, according to insiders, was Hearst's nickname for the vulva of his mistress, showgirl Marion Davies.

Allegedly, Hearst wasn't so much incensed at Welles as he was at the film's scriptwriter, Herman J. Mankiewicz, a friend who had betrayed his trust and knew only too well of this peculiar nomenclature. Nevertheless, as director, star, producer and co-writer Welles had the last call on this most controversial detail. Can you imagine a filmmaker today making a movie with a major studio whose story is based on Rupert Murdoch and his affectionate nickname for his wife's pudenda?

Hearst's initial reaction was to try to buy the negative for the $80,000 it cost, but he was refused. He then blackmailed studio bosses by threatening to reveal the rather sordid details of their sex lives if they screened the movie in their theatres.

Consequently, Loews, Paramount and Warner Brothers refused to screen the film, leaving only RKO (who made the film) to show it in their cinemas in Los Angeles and New York. Hearst, on the rampage, banned all of his newspapers from mentioning any RKO product. As a result the film, though loved by the critics, failed to break even. Though nominated for nine Oscars, it won just one, for best screenplay, which was in itself a kick in the teeth for Welles.

Yet no one can deny that *Citizen Kane* is an amazing accomplishment that influenced thousands of films, including a whole milieu, film noir. Its beautifully dark palette, bravura silhouettes, ingenious camera angles and hugely inventive set pieces remain a joy to behold. And then there is the story, a mature narrative that stands as one of the most accurate and provocative cinematic commentaries on the meaning of life and death to date.

On one hand it's as entertaining as any picture, but underneath the surface lie themes that are just as relevant today as they were when the film was released. It is mind-boggling to think that this is the work of a twenty-four-year-old. But perhaps this young man, thrown in at the deep end, didn't know that certain rules and limitations existed, so in true a punk rock style, he made it up as he went along and, using pure instinct, thus created a masterpiece.

No one but Welles could have made *Kane*. He could act, direct, write, paint, play the piano and pass himself off as a first-rate magician, but what he couldn't do is resist mischief – even if that entailed driving one of the era's most powerful media moguls to apoplexy. In short, toeing the party line was impossible for the man to countenance, and given his background it's hardly surprising.

Orson Welles was born on 6 May 1915, in Kenosha, Wisconsin, of Scottish, Irish and German heritage and with what he later described as 'an unfortunate personality'. His father Dick was something of a wag, who by day invented lights for motorcars and worked in a bicycle factory and by night was a womanising dandy who dressed in spats and three-piece suits. He also drank and gambled heavily.

Welles seems to have seen little of his father, instead calling a local doctor, Maurice Bernstein, 'Dadda'.

Bernstein spent a rather unhealthy amount of time with Welles's mother and showered the child with educational gifts. Welles's mother, meanwhile, was a talented pianist, champion rifle shot and suffragette who served time for her political views. Both parents and 'Dadda' considered Orson a veritable mastermind who, by all accounts (mostly his), could read aged three and memorise pages of classical script.

'The word "genius" was whispered in my ear, it was the first thing I ever heard, while I was still mewling in my crib,' Welles told Barbara Leaming. 'So it never occurred to me that I wasn't until middle age.' Little Orson made his first stage appearance aged three as a walk-on at the Chicago Opera House (shamelessly urged on by Bernstein), and two years later showed signs of musical talent on the piano.

The family moved to Chicago and Bernstein, now platonically infatuated with both mother and child, followed like a stray dog. 'He [Bernstein] was no stranger to the bedroom; but he preferred to stay on the balcony,' remarked Welles in conversation with Peter Bogdanovich in 1969. When Welles was six his parents parted for good. As reported by the *New York Times* in 1985: '"When they separated I felt no partisanship," says Orson, who blamed neither parent for the rift. In a curious way, young Orson thought of himself as having actually benefited from the separation, because seeing his parents individually afforded him "twice the love".' Subsequently his dad (who had inherited a fair chunk of change) aimlessly travelled the world drinking, gambling and womanising, while his mum (along with Orson) was swiftly accepted into the Chicago arts set.

Yet life with Beatrice could be a challenge. 'Children could be treated as adults as long as they were amusing,' chuckled Welles. 'The moment you became boring it was off to the nursery for an early night.' Accordingly, Welles's older brother – the less talented Richard – spent much of his time alone, then bounced from one mental institution to another, eventually finding solace as a monk in a secluded monastery.

Disaster struck in 1924 when his mother died of acute yellow atrophy of the liver. Welles, aged nine, abandoned the piano, while Bernstein stepped in to look after the sickly child, who had already suffered a plethora of illnesses, including malaria, scarlet fever, diphtheria and rheumatism. He also had flat feet, weak ankles and asthma. His father set about broadening the boy's mind by taking him along on his travels to Europe, Africa and Asia.

The young boy's precocity blossomed even further. Aged ten he adapted, directed and starred in his school production of *Dr Jekyll and Mr Hyde*, then caused uproar by delivering a lecture at his local school that lambasted his teachers' 'lack of creativity'. For his troubles he ended up as the subject of an article in the local newspaper, the *Madison Journal*. Under the headline 'Cartoonist, Actor, Poet and only Ten', it went on to describe Orson's activities, which included illustrating and editing the *Indianola Trail* – an outdoor adventure camp newspaper.

That's not to say he was a model pupil. After running away from home with a young girl, Welles, now aged eleven, was found performing blackface on an Illinois street corner and marched to the Todd School for Boys. Intended to straighten him out, this institution was, as one alumnus recalled, 'an island of lost boys', from where his elder brother had already been expelled.

Typically, Welles, instead of falling foul, thrived at the school, mainly under the auspices of teacher and mentor Roger 'Skipper' Hill. In his first year he appeared in four plays, wrote a musical revue and then went on to design, direct, act in and paint the scenery for, among others, Molière's *The Doctor in Spite of Himself*, Marlowe's *Doctor Faustus*, Shakespeare's *Julius Caesar*, and Shaw's *Androcles and the Lion*.

During his summer holidays he accompanied his now perpetually inebriated father first to Europe and then, in 1930, Japan and China. At one point his father was so drunk he lost his trousers in public and Welles had to find them and dress him.

Consequently, Welles told his addled papa that he would stop seeing him unless he refrained from drinking. A few months on, tragedy struck yet again. Three days after Christmas, on 28 December, Dick

Welles, who had bought a rundown hotel and narrowly escaped death as it burned down around him when drunk, died in a Chicago flophouse of heart and kidney failure caused by alcoholism.

Welles, who in an effort to stop his father's life-threatening imbibing had been persuaded to sever ties with his dad, was utterly devastated. 'I have always thought I killed him,' he told Barbara Leaming some fifty years later, still in despair. 'I think he deliberately drank himself to death. I was not prepared for his death in spite of the fact that he thought he was dying just the summer before.'

Welles was now officially an orphan. His father's will had left the boy the right to choose his own guardian, so after Roger Hill declined in stepped Bernstein on 31 January 1931. After graduating from Todd in May 1931 Welles, as everyone expected, was offered scholarships to Harvard and Cornell, but instead plumped for the Art Institute of Chicago where his tutor, Boris Anisfeld, strongly suggested a career as a painter.

Typically Welles resisted, having been spurred on by an editorial in Hearst's *Chicago American* daily newspaper by eminent theatre critic Ashton Stevens, who penned, 'Orson Welles is likely as not going to become my favourite actor. True, it will be four or five years before he has attained his majority and a degree... I am going to put this clipping in my betting book. If Orson is not at least a leading man by the time it has yellowed I will never make another prophecy.'

Welles, who had inherited a tidy sum from his father, responded by placing an ad in *Billboard* that read, 'Orson Welles is willing to invest a moderate amount of cash and own services as Heavy, Character and Juvenile in good summer stock or repertory position.' Dadda Bernstein hit the roof, but cleverly managed the situation and proposed that Welles should go on a sketching tour of Ireland. A few weeks later, Welles was hiking through Galway and, having done very little sketching, discovered a soft spot for 'shindy' (Irish dances), stout and whisky.

Inevitably his travels led him to the Gate Theatre, Dublin, where the now six-foot, two-inch youth with the bass-baritone speaking voice persuaded director Hilton Edwards that he was an eighteen-year-old professional actor from New York. He read for a part and was accepted. 'Step back John Barrymore, Gordon Craig and John Clayton. Your day has passed, a new glory glows in the East. I am a professional!!!" he wrote in a letter to Skipper Hill.

'I had a very high opinion of myself as an actor, which I have never lost, one which is seldom shared by anybody else,' he told Leaming. 'So it didn't seem to me that I was at hazard in any way. I'd seen the other actors and it was clear to me that I could walk away with the play – and I *did* you see.'

Over the next nine months the young Welles appeared in some seven major productions, acted in several other local plays, directed another handful and, under the pseudonym Knowles Noel Shane, penned a weekly column about theatre (which included much praise for his own work) entitled 'Chitchat and Criticism' in a Dublin tabloid.

The next year he was back in New York but, filled with wanderlust, travelled to Morocco and Spain where he did 'a little bull-fighting on the side', wrote a few pulp detective stories and generally explored.

Back in the US, still full of piss and vinegar, he continued to write play after play at breakneck speed and then secured a part in the thirty-six-week theatre tour of *The Barretts of Wimpole Street*, followed by 200 performances of *Romeo and Juliet*, starring Basil Rathbone. He then published a series of textbooks entitled *Everybody's Shakespeare*.

It was now 1934, and after directing a whole summer of theatre on the grounds of the Todd School, Welles, aged nineteen, surprised everyone by marrying socialite Virginia Nicholson. 'We only got married so we could live together,' recalled Welles. 'It wasn't taken very seriously by either of us.' They moved into what Welles described as 'the loveliest English basement apartment', situated in the West Village next to a Chinese laundry and a flophouse.

Welles thrived in New York. As well as a spouse he also found himself a radio platform, which helped open some major doors. He became friends with composer Bernard Herrmann, who wrote the scores for *Psycho*, *The Twilight Zone* and *Taxi Driver*, among others, and attracted the attentions of another admirer and mentor – actor, writer and theatrical entrepreneur John Houseman, who gave him a starring role in Archibald MacLeish's play *Panic*. The play was staged at Broadway's Imperial Theatre in midtown, which seated 1,400 people and had previously hosted musicals by Irving Berlin and Cole Porter, to name two. You might say that Welles had arrived.

His next stroke of luck came from an unlikely source. In 1935 the Franklin D. Roosevelt administration, faced with 15 million unemployed, established the Works Progress Administration (WPA), which undertook the re-employment of hundreds of thousands of able workers. One of the plan's initiatives was the Federal Theatre Project, led by Hallie Flanagan, which aimed to bring quality theatre to Americans at affordable prices, while employing actors, musicians, writers and crew whose careers had been decimated by the Great Depression. The enterprising Houseman got his feet well and truly under the WPA table when he was chosen by African-American theatre actress Rose McClendon – head of the Negro Theatre Unit in Harlem – to help direct their productions. He subsequently brought in 'wonder boy' Welles, entirely cognisant of the furore his appointment had caused amongst seasoned theatre directors, many of whom were still unemployed. Houseman knew he needed to produce something very special to tick all the WPA boxes and justify Welles's appointment. And so, at his wife's suggestion, he proposed an all-black version of *Macbeth*, set in voodoo-infested Haiti, to be staged at Harlem's Lafayette Theatre.

Welles auditioned hundreds, many of whom were not only unfamiliar with Shakespeare but couldn't read. But he was still impressed by the abundant talent, even if he went through hell to get it to the stage. One man, fearing that the production would be an insult to black folk, attempted to slash Welles with a cut-throat razor. The black Communist Party picketed the rehearsal, and the cast initially refused to listen to this 'young white boy' director. The production's acclaimed lighting director, Abe Feder, thought him too young and ignorant.

Welles, though, carried on regardless. He brought a dance troupe from West Africa to perform the on-stage voodoo ceremony. They were led by a dwarf and an actual witch doctor, Abdul, who'd requested twelve black goats to kill and skin to make the 'devil drums' he required for the scene. Welles acquiesced and the goats were purchased at the expense of the federal government (something he was very proud of) while suggestions concerning occult activity backstage flooded the superstitious streets of Harlem.

The production opened on 14 April 1936.

'Suddenly, for no apparent reason, on opening night it seemed that all Harlem decided that this was the greatest night of their lives,' Welles told Leaming. 'Traffic stopped for five blocks. You couldn't get near the theatre in Harlem. Everybody who was anybody in the black or white world was there. And when the play ended there were so many curtain calls that finally they left the curtain open, and the audience came up on the stage to congratulate the actors. And that was magical. It was described as the greatest opening in Harlem's history if not the world's.'

Most of the critics agreed. In the *New York Daily News*, Burns Mantle wrote, 'A spectacular theatre experience. This West Indian Macbeth is the most colourful, certainly the most startling of any performance of this gory tragedy that has ever been given on this continent.' One critic, however, Percy Hammond of the *Herald Tribune*, lambasted the unseasoned cast with excessive severity. 'What surprised me last night was the inability of so melodious a race to sing the music of Shakespeare,' he wrote. 'The actors sounded the notes with a muffled timidity that was often unintelligible. They seemed to be afraid of the bard, though they were playing him on their own home grounds.'

Consequently, one of the African drummers who Welles had brought over created a voodoo doll of Hammond, stuck pins in it and hung it backstage for all to see. He brought Welles in on the ruse with the proviso that the director would accept responsibility for the critic's death. Welles, finding this most amusing, gave his assent. Of course no one, least of all Welles, gave the notion another thought until Hammond died of pneumonia shortly afterwards.

The show was a complete sell out. The Negro Theatre Unit, realising that locals couldn't afford tickets, announced that on Mondays two thirds of the seats were to be free, prompting 3,000 souls to turn up to take advantage of the offer. A riot ensued and the cops were called en masse.

'I'd conquered Harlem!' Welles told Peter Bogdanovich. 'I'd go up two or three nights a week to Harlem where I was The King. I really was The King... I lived in nightclubs... I liked screwing the chorus girls... and I liked staying up until five in the morning.'

Flushed by such success, Welles took the production on an exhaustive 4,000-mile tour and, after his lead went missing and his understudy went ill, he took on the lead role. 'This was the only time anyone has blacked up to play Macbeth,' laughed Welles. 'This was a negro *Macbeth,* so why was anybody going to think I was *passing.* The cast thought it very funny.'

It was now the summer of 1936 and Welles was twenty-one.

Hallie Flanagan, fully aware that if she did not act fast and give this ingénue a job he would be snapped up by someone else, gave him his own theatre in New York – the old Maxine Elliott Theatre at 109 West 39th Street – where he could stage anything he wanted.

Typically Welles, who called it his 'magic box', dived straight in and directed a series of government-funded plays, including *Horse Eats Hat, Doctor Faustus, The Second Hurricane*, and *The Cradle Will Rock*.

The latter was a stinging musical allegory that tells of corruption and corporate greed in fictional Steeltown, USA, and was shut down by the WPA, who claimed budget cuts. Others asserted that the musical had been censored and subsequently closed because its pro-union, pro-socialist, anti-establishment stance was far 'too radical' for the US.

Welles and producer Houseman took it in their stride and created the Mercury Theatre, a repertory company that went on to famously produce a string of hugely acclaimed theatre productions that broke the mould and set new levels of excellence. Not that Welles had to do it. By now he had a formidable CV as a radio actor. He had also completed a twelve-month run as the immensely popular crime-fighting psychic vigilante the Shadow, and was a regular on *The March of Time* – a news documentary and dramatisation series. Naturally his next move was to bring theatre to the airwaves and so he created *The*

Mercury Theatre on the Air for CBS, whereby he produced at least one radio play per week.

His career was in its ascendancy and he was doing so well that when Hollywood asked him to star in a film he cheekily asked for $2,500 a week ($42,000 in today's money), purely because he had need of nothing.

He was as happy as a sand boy. He'd moved from the West Village to a country house on the Hudson and to get to work he took a speedboat followed by a chauffeur-driven Rolls Royce. You could say he was living life to the full. But as far as he was concerned he was simply following in his father's footsteps.

'I had a playboy father who never shaved himself in his life,' he said, 'and he ate in the best restaurants, wore tailored clothes, drank in the finest clubs and, unbeknownst to his wife, dated a string of beautiful ballerinas.'

Welles was everywhere. Welles was New York's premier playboy. Welles was just twenty-three years of age and about to rock the world.

It was on 30 October 1938 that Welles wrote, produced and voiced a radio adaptation of H. G. Wells's *War of the Worlds*. Initially intended as a corny update of the book, the basic premise was that the listener had inadvertently tuned into dance music that would be interrupted with live news flashes about Martians: 'It's large, large as a bear... the eyes are black and gleam like a serpent.'

Of the nine million estimated listeners, some 1.75 million took action by packing up and leaving in a state of complete and utter panic, causing several miscarriages and broken bones. The next day Orson was on the front page of the *New York Times* as the cruel perpetrator of a hoax that had terrified the nation. Lawsuits to the tune of £200,000 flooded into CBS.

Welles promptly became a household name – albeit a rather scandalous one.

What followed was an offer from George J. Schaefer, RKO's new president, to come to Hollywood. But Welles was not interested. He preferred debuting his new twenty-minute vaudeville act, *The Green Goddess*, where he impersonated John Barrymore and Charles

Laughton six times a day at the Palace in Chicago. 'Nobody had ever done worse than me in vaudeville,' admitted Welles. 'But it was great to be a vaudeville headliner, even if there was nobody out front.'

Begrudgingly, Welles headed for Hollywood, where he first moved into a suite at the Chateau Marmont. Shortly after, he transferred to a house next to Shirley Temple and Greta Garbo in Brentwood, replete with maids, a butler and a pool.

Soon he was spending $800 a week (around $13,000 today) on living expenses. It was outrageous by most people's standards, but not for Orson, who knew the gravy train was on its way and didn't comprehend the concept of financial caution.

Indeed, the RKO deal was for two movies, which paid Welles's Mercury Productions $100,000 for the first picture, and £125,000 for the second and a recoup of 20 per cent. Plus there would be 25 per cent of profits after RKO recouped its $500,000 production costs.

Hollywood was aghast. Directors choked on their soup. No one could believe that anyone would pay so much to a novice who had never even made a picture, never mind let him write, direct, produce and star in a half-million dollar production. This was in addition to giving him carte blanche to do what he wanted (after the initial green light from RKO), thus denying themselves the right to tamper with the end product in any way without the man's approval. No wonder Orson was hated.

'I think people resented him for the power of his ambition,' said Martin Scorsese. 'It was like, "How dare he take credit for everything?"'

So why was Orson allowed one of the best movie deals in Hollywood to date? According to George Schaefer, it was because Orson had the knack of attracting publicity and, just by signing, it put RKO and any film he made in the public eye. It was in essence a publicity stunt, which was all well and good, but now Welles, entirely under scrutiny, had to make a *great* film.

At first Orson prepared to do an adaptation of Joseph Conrad's *Heart of Darkness* – on which *Apocalypse Now* was later based – and ran around desperately trying to learn all he could about making a movie from technicians and directors. But the project was postponed due to its budget.

Meanwhile, he divorced his wife at great cost, wound up in debt and, pressured to justify his existence in Hollywood, came up with the idea for *Citizen Kane*. He pulled in co-writer Herman Mankiewicz to write a draft based on his concept, and a game of ping-pong ensued, with each rewriting the other's drafts, back and forth, until Welles was happy.

Next he brought his Mercury Theatre actors, such as Joseph Cotten, Everett Sloane and Agnes Moorehead, from New York, comfortable in the knowledge that they were all theatre actors and would not question either his authority or novice filmmaking techniques.

Another vital cog in the film was the cinematographer Gregg Toland, who had revolutionised the form with movies such as *Wuthering Heights* and *The Grapes of Wrath*. Toland was a big name, but anxious to experiment and contravene the unwritten rules that governed his trade. Maverick Orson – a man who defied convention – was the perfect collaborator. Thus, in June 1940, under the guise of shooting tests, they surreptitiously started filming.

After the film bombed, Welles, though critically accepted, was still something of a pariah in Hollywood. To many people's annoyance he had proven that you didn't need years of training to direct a film, yet no matter how amazing *Kane* was (and still is), Hollywood is all about bums on seats. Therefore it was now absolutely essential he make a successful film to continue directing, and he had to make it quickly.

His search for a new project was exhaustive. He toyed with stories by Ernest Hemingway, Fyodor Dostoevsky, Somerset Maugham and Mark Twain. He considered an adaptation of Charles Dickens's debut novel *The Pickwick Papers,* with himself or W. C. Fields in the lead. He also contemplated bringing Edmond Rostand's 1897 play *Cyrano de Bergerac* to the big screen, and wrote a script based on the story of the twentieth-century French serial killer Henri Désiré Landru, which he eventually sold to Charlie Chaplin (who turned it into his excellent movie *Monsieur Verdoux*).

Finally he settled on *The Magnificent Ambersons,* based on Booth

Tarkington's Pulitzer Prize-winning novel – the sombre story of a wealthy Midwestern family at the turn of the century.

By all accounts the original cut, at 135 minutes long and shot by the great Stanley Cortez, was an inspired piece of filmmaking, but it emptied the cinemas at previews.

'People just didn't understand it,' said co-editor Mark Robson. 'It was so ahead of its time.'

While the previews were screened, Welles was in Brazil filming the Rio carnival for a semi-documentary project entitled *It's All True* for RKO, and had intended to finish the edit with co-editor Robert Wise in Rio de Janeiro. Unfortunately Wise, due to a wartime embargo on civilian flying, was unable to take a plane, so he cheekily cut it while trying to contact Orson for instruction. Wise eventually shot extra scenes and forty-five minutes were edited, taking it down to eighty-nine minutes. And although the film is still watchable, it isn't a patch on some of Welles's other work.

'Using the argument of editing out what was not central to the plot, what they edited out was the plot,' chided Welles thirty years later. 'I would not have gone to Brazil without the guarantee that I could finish the picture there. And they absolutely betrayed me by not letting me do it. As far as I was concerned what was screened was a rough cut intended solely for a preview.'

The carnival lasted just three days but Welles was there for months, relentlessly sampling all that Brazilian women might offer. 'He had not just one-night stands,' recalled actress Shifra Haran, 'He had afternoon and after-dinner stands. Quickies by the thousand.'

'Welles's appetite for everything was enormous – work, art, food and women,' explained his biographer Simon Callow. 'He was modest about his prowess as a lover, but essentially he was a classical Don Juan: find 'em, fondle 'em and forget 'em. His three marriages were scuppered from the beginning by his sexual restlessness: a man who can cheat on Rita Hayworth a week after marrying her must certainly be in the grip of a peculiarly perverse compulsion.'

Unsurprisingly the failure of *The Magnificent Ambersons* ushered in the end of his RKO contract, so Hollywood ganged up on Welles, who they considered an incorrigible, cheeky young upstart. In hindsight he should have gone back to New York and the theatre, but one person kept him in California. Her name was Rita Hayworth.

He had met her at a party held by the actor Joseph Cotten and, instantly enamoured, persuaded her to join the magic act he was staging at a tent in Hollywood. Characteristically Welles wooed her by sawing her in half on stage. They married on 7 September 1943.

The press dubbed the union 'the Beauty and the Brain', and predicted the worst. But she openly admitted that she was not the sharpest tool in the box. 'I've been on stage since I was twelve with no time for books or learning,' she said. Orson, on the other hand, faced with this image of loveliness, 'sought to impress her mind' by flooding it with literature penned by the likes of Turgenev and Molière, with classical music by Bach and Mahler and a list of prescribed museums. All was going swimmingly, after a fashion, and in December 1944 their daughter, Rebecca, was born.

He delighted in his wife's astonishing beauty and loved the attention of being married to one of the world's biggest film stars, but when he returned to acting in films, rather than directing (he played Rochester in *Jane Eyre* and a war veteran in *Tomorrow is Forever*) he found himself overshadowed by his wife, then at her peak. Never one to bathe in reflected glory, Welles looked for other avenues to explore that would not put him in 'competition' with his wife.

Welles changed tack and began to write weekly political columns for publications such as the *Free World* magazine. He gave lectures in huge stadiums on ethical appreciation and the evils of racism. He took on a weekly radio show and championed black causes, at one point using the airwaves in an attempt to track down the South Carolina police officer responsible for the blinding of Isaac Woodard, an African-American World War II veteran.

Strongly left wing and pro-union, he spoke out against right-wing Republicans and the evils of the day using his unrivalled eloquence as the voice of reason.

'Welles was one of the great political speakers of his time,' wrote his biographer David Thomson. Not surprisingly Welles had, from 1937, been under the vigorous surveillance of the FBI, but much to their frustration they could never uncover any evidence that proved he was a communist.

Of course none of this helped his career in post-war Red Scare Hollywood. It was now 1946 and the only offers Welles received were small character parts in movies he had little time for. He, along with many others, thought his directing days well and truly over. That is until tough guy producer Sam Spiegel offered him *The Stranger*. Signed up to play the bad guy, he eventually landed the job of directing the film. 'I never regretted it,' declared Spiegel years later. 'Orson did a remarkable job.' Indeed, the film was brought in under budget, on time and even made money.

The story of a Nazi war criminal hiding out in the Midwest, only to be pursued by a detective (Edward G. Robinson), the film is pure Welles – a characteristically potent hunk of film noir. Shot by Russell Metty, it is darkly lit and exquisitely framed, like a series of stills replete with bravura set pieces.

And yet, on its release, Welles was not happy, claiming that his best work was cut. Robinson, the film's weak point, unconvincingly swimming in the shallows like a drugged goldfish, was even more downbeat. 'Welles seemed to have run out of genius while making this,' he said. 'It was bloodless and so was I.'

Meanwhile, his marriage had hit the rocks. He was a notorious womaniser, while Hayworth (born Margarita Carmen Cansino) was seething with explosive Latin jealousy. To exacerbate things, he had dallied with the likes of Judy Garland and Eartha Kitt. A jaded Hayworth finally left him, saying, 'I can't take his genius anymore.'

But the indomitable Welles carried on regardless. At the time, he had started a monster project – a lavish Broadway musical of *Around the World in Eighty Days*, with Mike Todd producing and Cole Porter writing the music – but had run out of cash. As a result he went to Harry Cohn, head of Hayworth's studio, Columbia.

'I called Cohn in Hollywood,' Welles told Bogdanovich. 'And I said, "I have a great story for you. If you send me £50,000 by telegram in one hour I will make it." "What story?" Cohn said. I was calling from a pay phone and next to it was a display of paperbacks... the title of one of them [was] *Lady from Shanghai.* I said, "Buy the novel and we'll make the film." An hour later I got the money.'

Of course the other stipulation was that Hayworth would star with Welles, as Cohn thought that their recent break-up was a good publicity angle. Initially reticent about Welles as director, he was reassured by Spiegel, who was confident that Welles would behave.

The budget was set at under a million dollars, but due to the star's recurrent ill health, which left her exhausted and inept, location shooting in Acapulco was delayed. Welles rewrote the script daily and the cost doubled.

To add to Cohn's frustration, Welles had cut Hayworth's trademark luscious auburn locks and dyed them blonde. Louella Parsons, never a Welles fan, wrote that Welles had de-feminised his ex-wife as an act of revenge because he was all washed up. And if that wasn't bad enough the film was a disaster – loathed by critics and the public alike.

Described by some as boring and incomprehensible and others as bizarre and experimental, it is indeed a puzzling slice of film noir, viewed by many as memorable only for its brilliantly realised climactic shoot-out scene in a hall of mirrors. As Cohn said after a screening, 'What the fucking hell was all that about?' Welles later described it as 'an experiment in what not to do.'

This almost put the kibosh on Welles's Hollywood career. He did one middling version of *Macbeth* for bottom-of-the-heap studio Republic, who specialised in cheap B-movie westerns. He was thirty-three and he had had his fill with the City of Angels, while Hollywood had had enough of him.

It was a gloomy period for Welles. He lost his well-paid weekly political column mainly because the 'serious' readers didn't take him seriously, while those who did only wanted to read about Hollywood and filmmaking. With only a few radio shows to look forward to, Welles left for Europe in 1949 to play Harry Lime in director Carol Reed's majestic *The Third Man.* Here he not only excelled but, in one of the greatest cameos of all time, provided an ad lib that is now regarded as one of the greatest paragraphs in cinema history.

Like the fellow said – in Italy for thirty years under the Borgias they had warfare, terror, murder and bloodshed, but they produced Michelangelo, Leonardo da Vinci and the Renaissance. In Switzerland they had brotherly love, they had five hundred years of democracy and peace – and what did that produce? The cuckoo clock. So long Holly.

Welles, again in need of cash to finish a film – this time *Othello*, which he was shooting in Morocco – took the $100,000 fee as payment instead of the 20 per cent of the picture's gross.

'There was never such a [box office] hit in twenty-five years in Europe,' he lamented. 'I could have retired on that!' Once again, having too many irons in too many fires banjaxed the auteur.

Over the next decade Welles aimlessly travelled throughout Europe trying to raise money for various projects and appearing in the occasional movie. In 1955 he directed and starred in the adventure-mystery *Mr Arkadin* (later retitled *Confidential Report*). Hopelessly over-ambitious in terms of locations, it took him to seven European countries. Again way over budget, Welles was sued by the film's producer Louis Dolivet, who claimed Welles had drunk excessively in nightclubs whilst filming, resulting in lost time. The lawsuit, however, was withdrawn.

The director, on the other hand, claimed that the editors and producers destroyed the movie more than any picture he had ever done. '[They] completely changed the entire form, changed the whole point of it. So it's not my movie.'

Even so, the *New York Times* was gushing, describing it as 'from start to finish, the work of a man with an unmistakable genius for the film medium.'

Meanwhile Welles impregnated his co-star, Italian aristocrat Paola Mori (née Countess Paola di Girifalco), whose family, in abject fear for their family's reputation, insisted on a wedding – and so they married.

Now Welles had *too* many reasons to stay in Europe and used his newfound status to his advantage. He directed and starred in a marvellous documentary series, *Around the World with Orson Welles*, which saw the man travelling Europe meeting Basques and bohemians alike. There was also *Orson Welles's Sketch Book,* a series in which he simply talks to camera about the many sketches he produced and the adventures he had whilst travelling.

In the same period, his many bit parts in the likes of John Huston's *Moby Dick* and the TV series *I Love Lucy* still impress, but nothing can compare with what many (including yours truly) consider his finest work – *Touch of Evil*. A monumentally dark, brooding noir masterpiece, it is as effective today as it was on release in 1958.

Welles came to direct, act and script the picture after he was asked to play the bent, sadistic cop Hank Quinlan in an adaptation of the book *Badge of Honour*. Charlton Heston, then at his peak, had read the initial script and, informed of Welles's involvement, suggested he direct.

Amazingly Universal propositioned Welles, who agreed only if he could rewrite the script. The result starred Heston as a Mexican narcotics cop, Miguel Vargas, controversially just married to the blonde and thoroughly American Janet Leigh. While looking for a honeymoon bed in a border town they witness a car bombing and get sucked into a murky world of hoodlums, Mexican drug cartels, corruption and claustrophobia. Vargas is attacked with acid and his wife is kidnapped and taken to a seedy motel where, in one of the most harrowing scenes in cinema, she is injected with heroin by a leatherjacketed bull dyke (Mercedes McCambridge) and left for dead.

Meanwhile Welles, taking ugliness to a new level as the grotesquely obese cop Quinlan – he resembles a fat, wrinkled, sweaty, oven-ready chicken – is on the rampage, framing anyone darker than an albino, while consulting his former paramour, clairvoyant Marlene Dietrich, as to his obviously blighted future.

Welles, apparently not learning from past experience, delivered his version and then went to Mexico to shoot *Don Quixote* (a project that began in 1955 and was never completed), leaving the studio to maul his masterpiece. On his return he argued with the new editor and film company and got fired then banned from further participation. As with *The Magnificent Ambersons,* new scenes were shot and Welles disowned the picture.

'You cannot leave a studio holding on to an unfinished film surely, not without talking to them,' said Charlton Heston, who sided with

Welles all the way. 'Orson was infinitely charming with cast and crew but went out of his way to deliberately insult studio heads. Very dumb. They have the money and if they don't give you any, you can't make films.'

What Marlene Dietrich told Quinlan in the film might as well have been said to Welles himself: 'Your future's all used up.'

The resulting studio film was ignored in the US; critics found it terrific but hollow. Not surprisingly it was an instant cult hit in Europe, where François Truffaut wrote, 'Welles adapted for the screen a woefully poor little detective novel and simplified the crim- inal intrigue where he could match it to his favourite canvas – the portrait of a paradoxical monster which he plays himself, under cover of which he designed the simplest of moralities: that of the purity of the absolute and absolutists.'

An utterly brilliant film whose attention to the tiniest detail is astonishing, it is a testament to Welles's utter genius, but was offen- sive to the palate of the US public, who were happy to see Welles flying off to Europe once again. The film subsequently won awards aplenty and Orson quickly changed his tune, telling Oxford students, while dressed in a blue silk tuxedo and Chinese silk waistcoat, that, though ripped from his grasp, the picture came closest to his inten- tions.

Luckily two versions exist. The director's cut was restored to Welles's vision – i.e., complete and uncut with reinstated footage that had previously gone AWOL (before his death he left instructions on how he wanted the film to be edited). Meanwhile the original stu- dio version ended up being entirely dwarfed by Welles's posthumous creation.

Once again ensconced in Europe, Welles was a gun for hire, play- ing just about anyone if the price was right. 'Being in show business we are like cherry pickers,' he told the UK press at the time. 'We go where the crops are. Whatever's going we take, except I'm more choosy about what I direct than what I act in.'

Welles hammed it up marvellously as King Saul in *David and Goliath*. In 1961 he upped the porcine ante when he played a warlord opposite Victor Mature in *The Tartars*, directed by Richard Thorpe.

Though a box office success, it was as bad as its tagline, 'Seize your swords, hide your women, here come The Tartars. The awesome saga of their fury and their lust!'

'It was a perfectly legible drive-in movie,' uttered Welles rather patronisingly.

He then narrated director Nicholas Ray's thoroughly ridiculous telling of the first testament, *King of Kings*, which not only had All-American blue-eyed boy Jeffrey Hunter playing Jesus, but saw John Wayne as a centurion famously uttering in his broadest cowboy drawl, 'Truly, this man was the son of Gahd.'

Next Welles adapted and directed Kafka's *The Trial*, starring Anthony Perkins. As usual the production, shot in Yugoslavia, ran out of money, only for Welles to save the day and get it finished. Once completed, he dusted himself down and petitioned to adapt Joseph Heller's *Catch-22* for the screen, but was unable to secure the rights (although he did deliver a splendid performance as Brigadier General Dreedle in Mike Nichols's 1971 rendering).

In 1963 he appeared in director Anthony Asquith's rather dull *The V.I.Ps* alongside Elizabeth Taylor and Richard Burton, then in 1965 played Long John Silver in *Treasure Island* and Marco Polo's tutor in *Marco the Magnificent*, none of which stretched him in the slightest.

That year also saw him push through yet another labour of love, *Chimes at Midnight*, which he directed, adapted and starred in as Sir John Falstaff. Shot all over Spain and backed by Spanish money, it was a gloriously authentic monotone masterpiece. 'Spain was the only country in the world that didn't know black and white wasn't commercial,' chuckled Welles.

Based on selections from Shakespeare's *Henry IV*, the film is a brilliant tribute to Falstaff – perhaps Welles felt a comradeship with his subject this time – and tells of Prince Hal's renunciation of his hugely corpulent, sloppy, wenching, lovable old drinking buddy, Falstaff (Welles) to appease his father, the king.

Welles is superb and so is the film. Roger Ebert described it as 'a film to treasure'. It is certainly my favourite adaptation of Old Will's work, but it again failed to dent the box office.

Unbelievably, though Welles was now only fifty years old, his directorial career was in tatters, while his acting career was hardly in better shape. Over the next few years he narrated endlessly, did a few silly costume epics that have sunk without trace, and acted in any film that provided him sufficient remuneration. Yet one terrific performance from this period stands out. In *The Southern Star* (1969) he played a rather nasty heavy. 'I did it as a comic gay cockney,' he told Bogdanovich. 'But nobody noticed it. The picture bombed.'

By the 1970s Welles had embarked on his very own version of crowdfunding, appearing in commercial after commercial and earning the contemporary equivalent of $75,000 a day while advertising contracts paid him as much as half a million dollars a year, plus residuals.

Welles, no matter what his critics said, saw nothing wrong in this. 'I do not suppose I shall be remembered for anything,' he once said. 'But I don't think about my work in those terms. It is just as vulgar to work for the sake of posterity as to work for the sake of money.'

Welles was getting paid very well, made a comfortable living and was proud of the fact that for the first time in his life he owned credit cards, but still, things did not sit well with the great genius. He often made light of his situation but inside it was killing him, to the point where social engagements with even his closest friends were too painful to endure. Towards the end of Welles's life, the writer Gore Vidal would often invite him to dine at his Los Angeles home. Though Welles was always game, he backed out an hour before, invariably phoning with the excuse, 'I have an early call tomorrow. For a commercial. Dog food, I think it is this time. No, I do not eat from the can on camera, but I celebrate the contents. Yes, I have fallen so low.' He accepted his lot, but it was destroying him.

As a result of being ubiquitous during TV commercial breaks, he was now known primarily (especially by the younger generation) for providing voice-overs for adverts. These included Carlsberg ('Probably the best lager in the world') and Paul Masson wine. But he also did Japanese whisky, Vivitar cameras, frozen peas and photocopiers.

Clearly he was doing almost anything to bankroll his lavish lifestyle, which insiders have said never waned, even when he was broke. Welles continued to travel the world in five-star hotels and eat at the finest restaurants. But as he once said, 'Living in the lap of luxury isn't bad, except you never know when luxury is going to stand up.'

Yet there was a method to his madness: he was still doing such work to fund his now almost entirely self-financed film projects. He funded *The Other Side of the Wind* to the tune of $750,000 and pulled in John Huston and Susan Strasberg to act in what was a quintessential 'mockumentary'. Shot between 1970 and 1976 and decades ahead of its time, it is a satire that tells of a director who needs backers to finance his 'hip and with-it' comeback film in the style of Antonioni.

The last film he physically finished directing and editing was *F for Fake* (1973), a documentary about fakes and frauds, including the professional art forger Elmyr de Hory. It certainly has its moments and demonstrates how the director could make a film out of very little, but it didn't challenge him in the slightest. In my opinion it is a rather dull affair that illustrates the undeniable reality that Welles was just plain tired.

He saw out the 1970s as Lew Lord in *The Muppet Movie*, and went through the 1980s narrating various productions, including a couple of animated features and the popular TV series *Shōgun*, starring Richard Chamberlain. He shone as a star on TV talk shows and continued to push his own projects.

Since 1965 he had lived with his mistress, the Croatian actress Oja Kodar, who was twenty-four years his junior. Towards the end of his life the actor weighed in at over 350 pounds and could barely walk.

'My doctor told me to stop having intimate dinners for four. Unless there are three other people,' he once quipped. He had heart problems, diabetes, and gout, was a heavy drinker and addicted to big fat Cuban cigars.

He died in his bed on 10 October 1985, aged seventy. A typewriter sat on a nearby table and in it a blank sheet of paper waiting for Welles to type stage directions for a project he and Gary Graver were planning to shoot at UCLA the following day. It's reassuring to realise that the great man died with an artistic venture still on his mind and hope in his heart.

His no-frills private funeral was attended by his ex-wife, Paola

Mori, Welles's three daughters, who had never met before, and a handful of close friends. His memorial a few weeks later attracted Hollywood's finest.

At various times in his chequered but remarkable life Welles had been a painter, writer, actor, director, radio comedian, professional magician, newspaper columnist, political activist and documentary-maker. But he is chiefly remembered as a maverick, a flawed genius, and an outsider who had to do things his own, often ill-advised way. As Roger Ebert said in 1978, 'Orson Welles can make better movies than most directors with one hand tied behind his back. His problem, of course, is that for thirty-five years the hand has remained tied. His career is a study in lost possibilities.'

Of making movies Welles said, 'This is the biggest electric train set a boy ever had!' But I'd say he treated his train set as would a naughty boy – chuckling mischievously as he created crashes and bombing his own track.

Welles to me was a man without fear – someone who was not only prepared to fail but also had the courage of his convictions and, unlike many others, actually stood by them.

Maybe the final words in this essay should go to Marlene Dietrich who, despite referring to his character Quinlan from *Touch of Evil,* could have easily been talking about Welles.

'He was some kind of a man... What does it matter what you say about people?'

Robert Capa

In 1938 the UK's *Picture Post* magazine described twenty-five-year-old Robert Capa as 'the greatest war photographer in the world.' During his career he covered five armed conflicts in ten countries, left 70,000 negatives and bequeathed an extraordinary record that told not only of the darkness of war but of the human condition.

'I worked with Capa a lot,' wrote esteemed author and former war correspondent John Steinbeck. 'His work is the picture of a great and overwhelming passion. No one can take his place. He could photograph motion and gaiety. He captured a world and it was Capa's world.'

Indeed, the more I've read about the man the more convinced I am of his genius. Not only that, he seems like a chap with whom you'd want to hang out, chew that fat and then go on a humongous bender – a man who was charismatic, brave, egalitarian and funny. It seems that many others would agree. As journalist Simon Kuper once said, 'Capa was the perfect hero, equally brilliant on either side of the lens: impish smile, cleft chin and jet-black hair; poker player, champagne drinker and lover of beautiful women; a cosmopolitan so footloose he didn't even have a favourite hotel.'

Capa was born Endre Ernő Friedmann on 22 October 1913, on the Pest side of Budapest, Hungary. According to many his birth was somewhat remarkable for three reasons: his head was wrapped in the caul (a membrane that covers the neck and face in the womb), which apparently is extremely rare, occurring in fewer than 1 in 80,000 births; the midwife discovered a head of thick black hair more in common with a one-year-old; and lastly, he had an extra finger on his left hand. Many have opined that such seemingly unsavoury aspects suggested that this baby would grow up to be someone *very* special. Call me old fashioned, but if I was the father I would have said, 'Oh shit!'

Capa came from a well-to-do middle-class Jewish family. His mother Júlia was the proprietress of a thriving fashion business, while his father, Dezső, was the company's head tailor. She was the matriarch – demanding, shrewd and hard working – while he was an extremely well-dressed reprobate who loved drinking, gambling and women. She believed that hard work would get you everywhere. He believed that charm, connections and chutzpah would get one by. Capa was a mixture of both, albeit immensely more curious.

Just a year after his birth, World War I began, inadvertently altering the course of his life, to the benefit of the world and especially lovers of great photography. In 1918 Hungary's prime minister, Mihály Károlyi, dissolved its union with Austria and Hungary became an independent republic. In March 1919, communists led by Béla Kun ousted the Károlyi government and declared the Hungarian Soviet Republic.

There was no respite from the political tumult that swallowed Hungary. In November 1919, rightist forces led by former Austro-Hungarian admiral Miklós Horthy entered Budapest and assumed leadership. In January 1920, parliamentary elections were held and Horthy was proclaimed regent of the re-established Kingdom of Hungary. Gangs of right-wing thugs seized the moment and roamed the streets, beating up Jews indiscriminately. Understandably, this left an indelible mark on the young man's psyche, prompting him to devote his adult life to fighting fascism in his own inimitable fashion.

As with many, Capa's life journey was influenced by an older man, Lajos Kassák, who was forty-two when he met the sixteen-year-old ingénu. A poet, a painter, a novelist, a graphic artist and a socialist who embraced Futurism, he was the man around which Hungary's avant garde revolved. In 1929 Kassák founded a magazine that, against the grain of the zeitgeist, featured photographs of Hungary's poor by Tibor Bass and Kata Kálmán. Capa couldn't help being influenced.

The right-wing Horthy wasn't that accommodating to either Jews or the working classes. As an eighteen-year-old, Capa, with fire in his veins, took to demonstrating against the regime, often ending up in fights with right-wing supporters. By all accounts he wasn't a chap to tangle with and, as such, was courted by the Communist Party, but after meeting with an insubstantial representative was unimpressed.

'He found that I was a fuzzy-headed intellectual with five half-digested books and a bourgeois father,' Capa wrote in his excellent book, *Slightly Out of Focus,* first published in 1947. 'I found that his views were far less radical than I had hoped for and that his looking over his shoulder was a rather pretentious act. I decided not to join the Communist Party.'

After he returned home and went to sleep he was woken by 'two rather big gentlemen in bowler hats'. They took him to the police station and repeatedly beat him until he passed out unconscious.

'When I awoke,' he wrote, 'I was lying on the floor in a cell... a lot of names were pencilled on the wall. The last two were Sallain and Furst, two young Hungarian Communists who after returning from Moscow had been caught and executed.'

Luckily, the police chief's wife was a customer of his parents, so Desző persuaded the officer to release his son on condition that he left Hungary. Having suffered enormously since the Wall Street Crash of 1929, their wealthy customers were not so wealthy anymore and neither were they so they could spare very little, but still he managed to get to Berlin by August 1931.

Here, he studied journalism until his parents' financial aid stopped entirely. Forced to leave college, he regularly slept on park benches and almost starved, while all around him the Nazis and their brown-shirted fools created havoc.

As a foreign leftist Jew, Capa was certainly in the wrong place at the wrong time, but he persevered. He borrowed a camera, found a job on a newspaper – first as an errand boy, then as a darkroom assistant-cum-trainee smudger – and was soon photographing local events for the rag while wandering the streets capturing whatever caught his eye.

And then he got his big break.

'The newspapers carried a story that Trotsky would speak in Copenhagen,' he wrote. 'But realised that all their photographers were covering events in Germany, so they sent me.'

Capa's shots were instantly heralded. He was elevated into the publication's hierarchy as its top photographer. He was nineteen. Unfortunately, the photographer's buoyancy was not to last. On 30 January 1933, Hitler became chancellor and life for anyone of Capa's disposition became decidedly dangerous. He was jeered at, threatened and abused as he walked the streets. 'Berlin,' he wrote, 'seemed suddenly very unfriendly.'

Understandably, he left for Austria and then Budapest, and eventually arrived in Paris poorer than a junkyard dog.

Capa, who was yet to be called Capa at this point, was known as Bandi, but on entering Paris decided to be called André. Still broke, he hung out in the cafés of Montmartre to keep warm and met fellow photographers André Kertész, David 'Chim' Seymour and Henri Cartier-Bresson.

He also met Gerda Pohorylle, a German-Jewish refugee. Love blossomed. They moved in together. She typed his captions and he taught her how to take photographs. Times were tight so the pair came up with the notion of inventing a character, a successful yet elusive American photographer named Robert Capa, who was so sought after, so glamorous and so brilliant that any publication worth their onions would be honoured to use his shots, which were of course taken by André Ernő Friedmann.

The surname was derived from that of Sicilian-born Hollywood director Frank Capra, whose movie *It Happened One Night* had recently won five Academy Awards, while the Robert was borrowed from Robert Taylor, star of the 1936 film *Camille*. Gerda, on the other hand, found her second name, Taro, from the young Japanese artist Tarō Okamoto. It wasn't long before Capa became famous and the ruse was discovered, so André held his hands up and became Robert Capa full time.

'Dear Mother,' he wrote. 'I am working under a new name – Robert Capa – it's like being born again but this time it doesn't hurt anyone.'

Capa had to live up to the persona he had created. It was August 1936 and his answer was to thoroughly and passionately cover the Spanish Civil War – a conflict that touched a particularly raw nerve with the egalitarian young man. This war was between the Republicans – who supported the established democratically elected anti-monarchist Spanish Republic – and the right-wing Nationalists, a rebel group led by General Francisco Franco, who'd attempted a coup d'état and received support, munitions and soldiers from Nazi Germany and Fascist Italy.

For Capa, a fervent anti-fascist, there was no other place to be on the planet. His subsequent photograph of a Spanish loyalist falling after having been fatally shot was published internationally to massive acclaim. Capa had arrived.

'I think the picture was a fluke,' reflects John Morris, Capa's editor at *Time* magazine. 'I doubt he knew he'd captured the moment until he saw it published. I think it was a painful subject for him. Who wants to profit from the death of another man – a comrade, if you will?'

And as Capa himself testified, 'It's not easy to stand aside and be unable to do anything except to record the sufferings around one.'

Soon Capa was to suffer himself. In July 1937, after he had left for Paris to attend to business, his now fiancée, Gerda, was accidentally crushed to death by a loyalist tank while she was shooting a battle in Brunete near Madrid. The news reached him in the pages of a newspaper. It was said he never fully recovered.

Disinclined to go back to the war that had killed the love of his life, he instead ventured to China with filmmaker Joris Ivens to record the locals' fight against the invading Japanese who, now allied to Hitler, were pushing through the eastern front of the international war on fascism. This, the Second Sino-Japanese War, saw Japanese forces torture and murder up to 300,000 Chinese (mostly civilians and surrendered soldiers), rape tens of thousands of women during the Rape of Nanking and commit atrocities largely forgotten by the West as they surged to appease the Japanese after World War II. Capa saw the conflict's magnitude. 'I am so crazy all I can do is keep myself together and work hard,' he said, but still his feelings slipped through as he now could perhaps empathise with the aggrieved more than ever.

'Slowly I am beginning to feel more like a hyena,' he wrote. 'Even if you know the value of your work you think everyone thinks you are a spy or are trying to make money out of their misery.'

Six months later he was back in Spain covering the departure of the International Brigades and subsequently captured the battles of the Rio Segre and Mora de Ebro. The *Picture Post* devoted eight pages to his shots.

'Fascist planes backed by German and Italy bombed Madrid,'

reported Capa. 'People are bombed as they buy bread and sleep. It's always the same. The bombs stop and the people go off to see if a son or husband or wife is dead.'

And as Milton Wolff of the Abraham Lincoln Battalion – a US faction who fought the fascists in Spain – emphasised in an interview with PBS, 'You can't talk about the Spanish Civil War until you see the photographs of Bob Capa.'

The photographer had camped with the soldiers and risked his life on countless occasions to get his images. 'He'd be there with his camera and the bombs would be falling all around him,' added Wolff. 'His photos were then published all around the world and it was the first time the people saw what the fascists were doing, and so people like me came from all over to fight against them. The camera was Bob Capa's weapon.'

Capa's fight against fascism was personal, extremely real and enormously relevant. Both he and Gerda had suffered directly at the hand of the fascist machine that was attempting to take over the world, and from 1936 the Spanish Civil War was the undoubted frontline of that conflict.

What exemplifies Capa is his ability to translate the sheer misery of war onto the page and transmit its immutable horror. Many of his Spanish Civil War shots tell of the consequences of war and not the war itself. We see women fleeing bombs, children looking forlornly for their parents, a mother and daughter looking up at the bombers overhead. All force the realities of armed conflict home, devoid of any Boys' Own glamour.

'Capa knew what to look for and where to find it,' wrote John Steinbeck, who as a war reporter travelled with the photographer on several assignments. 'He knew, for example, that you cannot photograph war, because it is an emotion. But he did photograph that emotion by shooting beside it. He could show the horror of a whole people in the face of a child. His camera caught and held emotion.'

Capa's famous dictum was, 'If your pictures aren't good enough, you're not close enough,' which for him was also a moral sanction, in that if you were going to photograph people dying, you had to share their danger.

After Spain, the photographer went back to Paris. It was 1939 and two of Capa's left-wing outlets, *L'Humanité* and *Ce Soir,* had been closed down. When Germany invaded Poland on 1 September and war was declared, the French began rounding up communists and German émigrés and putting them in internment camps. Capa, a communist sympathiser and former Berlin resident, was once again skating on thin ice, so decided to join his mother and brother in New York, where they had moved after his father's death that summer.

On the ship over, he pulled actress Geraldine Fitzgerald, best friend of Orson Welles's wife Virginia. 'Cap conveyed a sense of inner euphoria,' she recalled. 'You got the feeling that he wanted to share this euphoria. You could not offend him. Some people didn't like his wild appearance or his self-confidence and tried to put him down, but after a few minutes they would give up... he always seemed to be having fun and people wanted to join in and share the fun.'

In New York Capa befriended the staff of *Life* – the world's foremost photojournalism magazine – but by March 1940 he faced problems with immigration, so when tough native New Yorker and former fashion model Toni Sorel offered to marry him, he accepted. They never lived together or consummated the marriage.

Time Inc. sent Capa to Mexico for the six-month visa waiting period, where he was to report the turmoil caused by the presidential elections and Nazi agent provocateurs wishing to destabilise America's neighbour and distract the US from the war in Europe. There he met up with Holland McCombs, chief of Time Inc. Mexico and a documentary-maker called Jack Glenn, instantly forming a mischievous brotherhood with the two men, and embarked on a 'reckless, rollicking spree of fun, frolics and brutally bruising work.'

'We chased politics and various stories all over Mexico,' recalled McCombs in conversation with Capa biographer Richard Whelan. 'When we were in town we chased the nightspots, the café society, hangouts where the girls were. We dated a lot. One night we'd had too many hot-buttered rums and we decided to have a fight and we did, mostly rolling about the floor. Of course, the tourists were outraged and called for the manager who came and said, "You cannot do *anything* about this. This is Mr Capa, Mr McCombs and Mr Glenn. I advise you not to try *anything* with them at all.'"

On 20 August 1940, Leon Trotsky, the thinking man's revolutionary, was assassinated with an ice pick through the back of his head by Spanish-born communist Ramón Mercader. Stalin had expelled Trotsky after he had become more and more open in his disagreement with the increasingly totalitarian policies of the Communist Party. Capa arrived in time for the exiled Bolshevik's leader's funeral in Mexico.

He was still there when the Germans entered Paris triumphantly on 14 June 1940. 'Dear little Brother, European news is miserable and it depresses me very much,' he wrote to his younger brother, Cornell. 'The world was never as sad as it is now.'

Three months later, the Germans were bombing Britain. London took the brunt of the attacks. Beginning on 7 September 1940, London was bombed for fifty-seven consecutive nights, destroying one million houses and killing 20,000 people. Around 18,000 tons of high explosives were dropped.

Commissioned by *Time* to shoot the London Blitz, he focused on the Gibbs family – a solidly working-class Lambeth household. The work was entitled *The Battle of Waterloo Road* and Capa more or less moved in, spending all his time with them as they tried to carry on while German bombers decimated their city, reducing houses and factories to rubble every single night.

'You didn't see him taking the pictures,' explained Lilly Gibbs on camera in a PBS Capa documentary. 'You knew he was there but he wasn't up your nose.'

The Gibbs family's nonchalance was testament to the fact that, no matter how many bombs Hitler threw at the UK, the British people would not kowtow. All it did was strengthen their spirit and galvanise their resolve. People were often blasé about it, talking about the latest raid in similar terms as the weather, a bombed-out day, for example, being 'very blitzy'. The Gibbs family epitomised this bulldog spirit.

'When Capa came to do the book, the bombing wasn't anywhere near over,' continued Lilly Gibbs. 'We had an easy night and were all relaxed and Dad said we didn't have to go shelter and it was the worst night we ever had. We used to go to the shelter underneath the church and the Church Army would make us tea, but most of the ladies and gentlemen were all killed one night. We were near where the bomb came in. It hit the altar and blew. When we came out, the church was devastated, so we all set to, cleaned up the church and sorted ourselves out. What his pictures tell you is what we were like – the faces. Not everyone can take a photo like that and show how we felt. No one. It was in him. It was there.'

Back in the USA Capa, now a US citizen, spent a while shooting all over the country for *Life* – cowboys, black jazz clubs, elk hunts, football players – romancing everyone with his special language, which he called Capanese.

'He managed to connect with everyone, even though he had this language which was this horrible crazy English and impossible to imitate,' explained Holland McCombs. 'Capanese was spoken by one man in the world and that was Cap.'

He was desperate to get back to the war, but as a Hungarian when the US entered the war, he was suddenly declared an enemy alien and ordered to surrender his passport and cameras and not leave New York.

In April 1941 he finally got his visa and headed first to London, where he got a Bond Street tailor to make him a special uniform. Then he left for North Africa and joined the US troops in Tunisia as they fought against the Germans. Next he went to Sicily for the allied invasion, followed by seven gruelling months with the army as they fought in Italy.

'I dragged myself from mountain to mountain, from foxhole to foxhole, shooting mud, misery and death,' he wrote. 'Every five yards a foxhole and in each at least one dead soldier.'

As the army advanced, so did Capa, followed by the tanks of General Patton. They reached Naples and entered without opposition.

'Taking pictures of victory is like taking pictures of a wedding ten minutes after the departure of the newlyweds,' he wrote in his book. 'I walked along the deserted streets, unhappy yet glad I had such a good excuse for not taking pictures. The narrow street leading to my hotels was blocked with a queue of silent people in front of a school-house. The people held only their hats. I fell in behind the queue. I entered the school and was met by the sweet sickly smell of flowers and the dead. In the room were twenty primitive coffins, not well enough covered with flowers and too small to hide the dirty little feet of children – children old enough to fight the Germans and be killed but just a little too old to be in children's coffins.'

He added: 'These children of Naples had stolen rifles and bullets and had fought the Germans for fourteen days while we'd been pinned to the Chiunzi Pass. These children's feet were my real welcome to Europe, I who had been born here. More real by far than the welcome of the cheering crowds I had met along the road, many of who had yelled *Duce!* in an earlier year.

'I took off my hat and got out my camera. I pointed the lens at the faces of the prostrated women, taking little pictures of their dead babies until finally the coffins were carried away. Those were my truest picture of victory, the ones I took at that simple school house funeral.'

He had spent a year with the army and was relieved to get back to London. He and every other journalist in the world knew that the invasion of France was imminent and London was awash with scribes. Cap plotted up in the Dorchester with Pinky, a spoken-for lady friend, and proceeded to spend his year's wages in style.

Ernest Hemingway, who Capa had known and enjoyed a father-son relationship with since 1937 in Spain, arrived too, so Capa threw a big party for the man. 'On the day of the event I bought a big fish bowl, a case of champagne, brandy, half a dozen fresh peaches, soaked them in the brandy, poured the champagne over them and everything was ready,' he said. 'The attraction of free booze and Mr Hemingway proved irresistible. Everyone was in London for the invasion and they all showed up for the party.'

Undeniably, Capa was a party fiend, a great bon viveur, raconteur and comic. But he was also a massive gambler who risked everything to win. On one night at Sun Valley, Idaho in 1940 he lost $2,000 (about $35,000 today) – his entire life savings. 'What difference does it make?' he commented. 'It's good for me. Now I have to work harder.'

Indeed, gambling was his life. 'The war correspondent has his stake – his life – in his own hands,' he wrote in *Slightly Out of Focus*. 'And he can put it on this horse or on that horse, or he can put it back in his pocket at the very last minute. I am a gambler. I decided to go in with Company E in the first wave.'

This was the most dangerous mission he had ever taken. He was the only photographer in this wave of troops: E Company, the 2nd Battalion of the Parachute Regiment of the 101st US Airborne. Eventually made famous by the TV series *Band of Brothers*, they were the heroes of the now legendary Operation Overlord who attacked the Germans on Omaha Beach, Normandy, in the early hours of 6 June 1944, and faced their machine gun and mortar fire head on.

As Capa wrote in *Slightly Out of Focus*:

At 4am we assembled on the deck. 2,000 men stood in perfect silence. Everyone was thinking some kind of prayer. The sea was rough and we were wet before the barge left the mother ship. In no time, men started to puke. But this was a polite as well as a carefully prepared invasion, and little bags had been provided for the purpose. Soon the puking hit an all-time low. I had an idea that this would develop into the mother and father of all D-Days.

The boatswain, who was in an understandable hurry to get the hell out of there, mistook my picture-taking attitude for explicable hesitation, and helped me make up my mind with a well-aimed kick in the rear. The water was cold, and the beach still more than a hundred yards away. The men from my barge waded in the water. Waist-deep, with rifles ready to shoot, with the invasion obstacles and the smoking beach in the background I was ready to take my first real picture of the invasion.

I saw men falling back as the bullets hit their bodies and had to push past their bodies. I made for the nearest metal obstacle, my picture frame full of smoke and burnt out tanks and barges. Every piece of shrapnel found a man's body and I frantically shot frame after frame.

Unfortunately, the world never got to see most of Capa's pictures from that day. A nervous darkroom assistant ruined ninety-five of his

106 negatives. *Life* magazine published the eleven remaining images, but the greatest record of one of the most remarkable battles in history was lost forever.

Back in Normandy the unstoppable Capa jumped on a barge along with the wounded. When offered a plane back to London he refused, and instead returned to the beachhead on the first boat available. Around 10,000 US troops died that day. The photographer was thought to be one such casualty.

'Back on the beach that night I found my colleagues... the day was D-plus-2, the drink was a Norman applejack called Calvados and the party was a French wake in my honour,' he wrote. 'I'd been reported dead by a sergeant who'd seen my body floating on the water with my cameras round my neck. I'd been missing for forty-eight hours, my death was official, and the censor had released my obituaries. My friends introduced me to Calvados.'

Still, the mad Hungarian followed the soldiers all the way through France as they pushed the Germans east, putting his life on the line day after day.

'The closer to death you were, the more alive you felt,' testified fellow war photographer Myron Davis. 'When you're taking risks your adrenaline is pumping so fast it's like living in a different sphere.'

'Shells were dropping all around us and I jumped into a ditch and this man jumped in next to me,' explained World War II veteran Walter Bernstein in a PBS documentary on Capa. 'He was very calm and started talking about Tolstoy. You'd hear bombs exploding and screams but he paid no attention. When the shelling stopped he said goodbye and left. I never saw him again. I asked a soldier who he was and he said it was a photographer called Robert Capa.'

Capa continued following the soldiers and saw many die as they pressed on and liberated Paris.

'It was the most unforgettable day in the world,' recalled Capa. 'The road to Paris was open and every Parisian was out in the street to touch the first tank, to kiss the first man, to sing and to cry. Never were there so many so happy so early in the morning.'

Cap had found a ride on a tank manned by Spanish Republicans. It was named after a battle that he'd taken part in.

'I felt that this entry into Paris was made especially for me,' he said. 'On a tank made by Americans who had accepted me riding with Spanish Republicans with whom I had fought against fascism long years ago, I was returning to Paris – the beautiful city where I'd first learned to eat, drink and love.'

As General Patton continued his move east, Capa accompanied his troops with his trusty Rolleiflex and two Contax cameras. It was two days before Christmas during one of the coldest winters in decades, the temperature dropping to way below zero, but Capa and the American relief army pushed on through blizzards. They had marched day and night to bring much-needed manpower to the beleaguered boys of the 101st, who were holding Bastogne near Luxembourg.

Of course, this was just before the infamous Battle of the Bulge, Hitler's last-ditch offensive against the Allies. Capa was there, surrounded by German Panzers, paratroopers and infantry. The German commander had demanded their surrender, only for Brigadier General Anthony McAuliffe to deliver a reply that made Bastogne and its defenders famous and confused the hell out of the Germans. It simply read 'NUTS!'

'Christmas Day came,' remembered Lieutenant Ken Koyen. 'But reinforcements had still not arrived. We, and all of the Third Army, were attacking the left or south flank of the German Breakthrough that had smashed through thinly held American lines in Luxembourg and Belgium. Three German armies, two of them Panzer, had been thrown into the surprise counter attack.

'The Third Army pressed us to attack night and day,' continued the Lieutenant. 'By noon of the next day Capa and I stood on a hillside three miles from Bastogne. The main thrust of our attack had shifted from the main road to the left, or west, to a secondary road where the Germans held the two small towns of Clochiment and Assenois.

'By 16:50 hours on 26 December, after a rapid advance by our column of nine Sherman tanks pushing through the German lines and an air-drop of supplies to the beleaguered American forces, the German grip on Bastogne was effectively broken and we were able to evacuate 652 of our wounded troops.'

Capa's next operation was even more reckless and harrowing. He volunteered to join the 17th Airborne and parachute into enemy territory. In short, they would be jumping into enemy fire.

'It was fearless, even reckless,' says James Conboy, a World War II 17th Airborne paratrooper. 'He would go to any lengths to get the shot. They were shooting at us as we came down. Many didn't make it to the ground alive. I couldn't have done what he [Capa] did. We could shoot back. He had only a camera. You can't shoot [a bullet] with a camera.'

From the Rhine to the Oder, Capa took no photographs. He wasn't interested in the defeated, demoralised Germans. 'All I wanted to do was meet the first Russian and then pack up my war,' he declared.

The army moved on to Leipzig, where the last of Hitler's stormtroopers were holed up. Capa decided to take one last picture of a very young corporal firing a machine gun from the balcony at the German snipers.

'I clicked my shutter – my first picture in two weeks – and the last one of the boy… He slumped back into the room. His face not changed apart from a tiny hole between his eyes and his pulse had long stopped beating… I had the picture of the last man to die.'

Capa was thirty-two and World War II was over. What to do now? He was at the Ritz with writer Irwin Shaw when he saw Ingrid Bergman walk past. He sent a note to the actress's room explaining that he would have liked to have sent her flowers and take her to dinner but could not afford both. She, of course, could not help but be charmed and a relationship ensued.

Isabella Rossellini has said that her mother fell in love with Capa. On her return to Hollywood she appeared in *Notorious* for Hitchcock and Capa was the on-set stills man. 'This was not easy at all,' wrote the Oscar-winning actress in her autobiography. 'I was married [unhappily to Petter Lindstrom] and was so moral and prudish but I wanted so much to be with Capa.'

In Hollywood he embraced the party lifestyle. During the war he had become friends with directors John Huston, George Stevens, Billy Wilder and Anatole Litvak. As the latter exclaimed, 'After only two weeks here, Capa is getting invited to parties it took me ten years to get invited to.'

In 1946, William Goetz, head of International Pictures, hired Capa as apprentice producer/director. 'He was socially acceptable, famous, good-looking and single, but he was not happy,' explained his friend, screenwriter Peter Viertel. 'He hated to go to people's houses. He said, "I like to go to cafés, have a drink and leave when I'm bored!"'

In LA he got a part as Hamza, an Egyptian servant, in a movie entitled *Temptation*, directed by Irving Pichel, but it was not for him. 'Hollywood was the biggest mess I ever stepped into,' he said in an interview.

Unhappy in Hollywood, he enjoyed a moment of respite during his affair with Ingrid Bergman. She wanted to marry him but, as he said, he was not the marrying kind. 'I am a newspaper man,' he stated. 'And it is good to be lonely and stay in lonely hotels.' According to Bergman, Hitchcock wrote his superlative movie *Rear Window* based on her relationship with Capa, James Stewart being Capa the war photographer and Grace Kelly the beautiful model. 'Could you see me driving down to a fashion salon in a jeep wearing combat boots and a three-day beard?' says Stewart in the picture. 'Let's not talk any more nonsense.'

Finally fed up with the Hollywood lifestyle, Capa left for Paris, and in the spring of 1947 opened his photo agency, Magnum. 'He called it that because whenever we met he would open a bottle of champagne,' explained fellow Magnum founder Henri Cartier-Bresson. Magnum was a co-operative of independent photographers that began with his old friends Chim (aka David Seymour), Cartier-Bresson and then Englishman George Rodger.

Capa's first big scoop for Magnum was shooting Russia and its people. John Steinbeck obtained Capa's visa and off they went. The story sold for $20,000 and Magnum held the copyright. Indeed, it was Capa who invented the idea of photographers owning their images and licensing them to publications – he revolutionised the industry.

Other assignments followed. While shooting and getting involved in the 1948 Arab-Israeli War he was almost killed when a bullet pierced his thigh in Tel Aviv, and he vowed never to cover war again. Still, his shots were no less iconic. His photos of Picasso (with wife Françoise Gilet in the South of France) for *Illustrated Magazine* are arguably the best ever of the artist. The same can be said of his shots of Henri Matisse, taken a few months later.

'He'd come and stay for two weeks and spend all day with you and let you get on with what you were doing,' recalls Gilet. 'He didn't seem like a photographer. Nothing was posed. He would entertain you and it was fun to be with him.'

While in the South of France, tales of his drinking, gambling and womanising were legion. 'You'd forgive him for his indiscretions, but he was so charming you'd lend him two hundred dollars [$1300 in today's money] to replace the two hundred dollars he'd borrowed from you the night before and lost in the casino in Cannes,' explained old friend Irwin Shaw, who he stayed with.

Back in Paris his gambling reached new heights. He spent all of his time at the races. He borrowed Magnum money for his bets and when he won he funded the office, which was now at 125 rue de Faubourg, Saint-Honoré. But he was rarely there. He popped in to make calls and pinch the bottoms of the attractive young ladies who kept the office running. Capa conducted the agency's big business in the café downstairs. He would discuss the big stories and where Magnum should place them, usually as he played pinball with a Chesterfield dangling from his mouth and a drink on the side.

'You'd be standing behind him and he'd be tilting the pinball,' recounted Magnum photographer Erich Lessing. 'And he'd shout, "I think you should go to Germany and do a story!" He did this many times with me.'

But Capa was nothing less than unorthodox. When Pierre Gassmann, whose lab processed Magnum's photos, needed the $400 owed to pay his staff, Capa discovered Gassmann had seventy bucks in his possession and suggested putting it all on a horse that he had a hot tip for. Gassmann refused but Capa went ahead and won enough to pay the lab staff, and more.

As time went on, Magnum became the world's most respected photojournalism agency. Capa loved nothing better than to sign up young photographers and help them out. One was the incredible Ernst Haas. Eve Arnold was another, as well as Elliott Erwitt and Erich Lessing. Robert Frank was extremely successful, keen to sign up, and undoubtedly would have massively benefited the agency financially. Capa, however, thought him too difficult and lacking humour. 'He wouldn't work well with us here!' he commented.

Magnum, for many of the staff and photographers, was like a family, with Capa as the big daddy. He would encourage his charges, find them work, feed them when hungry, take them to grand parties in New York, London and Paris and gave them tips on horses.

By now Capa was not only the world's most famous photographer but also a world-famous man-about-town. He dined with lords, ladies, film directors, artists and intellectuals. He shot stories amongst the rich and famous in St Moritz, Biarritz and Deauville – and then it all went wrong.

In 1953 McCarthyism reigned supreme, so the US embassy contacted Capa once more. He was considered a communist, and as such his passport was to be revoked. He couldn't work as a journalist without a passport and so appealed and, after much to-do and a $10,000 lawyers' fee, he won his passport back. But the affair weighed heavily on him. Having grown weary of his superficial playboy lifestyle photographing movie stars and holiday resorts, he saw that his life consisted of 'none of the good things, just the material ones.'

He wrote to John Morris, 'I have now definitely decided to go back to work. What and where I do not know but the Biarritz and Deauville and motley movie money period is over.'

His friend Irwin Shaw wrote of Capa at this unhappy time, 'Only in the morning does Capa show that the tragedy and sorrow through which he has passed have left their marks on him. Then he drinks down a strong bubbling draft, puts on his afternoon smile and sets out carefully light-hearted to these places where this homeless man can be at home.'

In 1954 he received an invitation to show his work in Japan. Here he was treated like a demi-god, as he deserved to be, and consequently got his mojo working once again.

'He took many photographs of children when he was in Japan,' recalls Magnum photographer Hiroji Kubota. 'And these images really stuck a chord with me as they were all taken from the eye level of the children so he'd had to kneel down to take the shots. This explains enough about Capa as a human being.'

After two weeks in Japan, *Life* magazine contacted him and asked him to cover the First Indochina War in Vietnam.

'I called him and told him he didn't have to go,' said John Morris, Magnum executive director. 'This isn't our war.'

His family was distraught at the thought of him covering another war, but Capa needed to do some proper work. He also needed the money and was worried that David Douglas Duncan – who'd covered the war there for the last few months – was eclipsing him as the world's greatest war photographer. He thus took the job and arrived in Hanoi on 9 May, just after Dien Bien Phu had fallen to the Viet Minh.

On 25 May 1954, at 2.55pm, he accompanied a retreating French regiment through the Red River Delta. Although advised not to, he decided to leave his Jeep and go up the road to photograph the advance. 'For a long indecisive minute he crouched behind the protective bulk of our jeep,' wrote Scripps Howard correspondent Jim Lucas. 'He was ready to leap back or spring ahead as if testing the temper of the Viet Minh fire. He decided he would risk it.'

An hour later he stepped on a landmine and died. He was forty years of age.

Capa's family were offered a military funeral for him at Arlington but his mother refused, saying, 'He was not a soldier but a man of peace.' He was buried in a Quaker cemetery just outside New York City.

At the memorial service for Capa, one of the world's greatest-ever photographers, Edward Steichen stood up and said a few words. 'He understood life, he loved life intensely. He gave richly of what he had to give to life... [He] lived valiantly, vigorously, with a rare integrity.'

Robert Mitchum

Ah, little lad, you're staring at my fingers. Would you like me to tell you the little story of right hand, left hand? The story of good and evil? H-A-T-E! It was with this left hand that old brother Cain struck the blow that laid his brother low. L-O-V-E. You see these fingers, dear hearts? These fingers have veins that run straight to the soul of man. The right hand, friends! The hand of love! Now watch and I'll show you the story of life...

So says Robert Mitchum, pitching his tattooed fingers against each other in *The Night of the Hunter* (1955), one of the finest, most menacing, most haunting and most accomplished movies in cinema history. Even more relevant today than it was on release, the picture dares to lambast and question the morality of those who use religion to justify each and every foul and evil deed they commit. As François Truffaut, then critic for the magazine *Cahiers du Cinéma*, wrote on the film's release in 1955, 'This film makes us fall in love again with an experimental cinema that truly experiments, and a cinema of discovery that in fact discovers.'

The Night of the Hunter, directed by that great English thespian Charles Laughton – who Laurence Olivier described as the acting profession's only genius – remained loyal to the novel from which it's adapted. Penned by the southern rich kid Davis Grubb, the book is based on the true story of a particularly loathsome serial killer, Harry Powers, nicknamed 'the lonely hearts killer' and 'the bluebeard of Quiet Dell'. Powers romanced and killed two widows he met through lonely hearts ads, slaughtered three children and was subsequently hanged for his crimes in 1932, aged thirty-nine.

Classic American Gothic, Grubb's book takes inspiration from Poe, Faulkner and Lovecraft, while the movie is similarly part fairy tale, part nightmare, drawing heavily on the German Expressionist cinema of the 1920s to create a bizarre and ethereal twilight zone that defies categorisation.

In this most daring and controversial film of the 1950s, Mitchum plays the misanthropic former convict Harry Powell – an altogether twisted psychopathic evangelist – who wanders the southern backwaters killing strippers, whores and widows in his self-styled 'heaven-sent' mission to rid the world of wanton and immoral sexual undesirables.

As Grubb wrote, 'Sometimes he wondered if God really understood. Not that the Lord minded about their killings. Why, His Book was full of killings. But there were things that God did hate – perfume-smelling things, lacy things, things with curly hair, whore things. Preacher would think of these and his hands at night would go crawling down under the blankets till the fingers named Love closed around the bone hasp of the knife and his soul rose up in flaming glorious fury.'

Having shared a cell with condemned bank robber Ben Harper, Powell overhears the man talking in his sleep, telling of the money he stole and where it's hidden.

'Lord you sure knowed what You was doing when You put me in a cell at this very time,' says Powell in the movie, looking on as his cellmate reaches the gallows. 'A man with ten thousand dollars hid somewhere and there's a widow in the making.'

Thus he trawls West Virginia in search of his former cellmate's widow, Willa Harper (Shelley Winters), who unknowingly sits on the $10,000 ($150,000 today) that her executed husband has robbed. All Powell knows is that the couple's children know something of the money's whereabouts and that he *must* find it.

Like many religious zealots, Powell believes he is the wrath of God, and easily rationalises each and every atrocity he commits by simply believing that God instructed him:

'Well, now. What's it to be, Lord, another widow? How many's it been, six? Twelve? I disremember. Lord I am tired. Sometimes I wonder if You really understand. Not that *You* mind the killings.'

Laughton was introduced to the book by his producer partner, Paul Gregory. Together they bought the rights and agreed that Mitchum was perfect for the lead. 'He was a man of great charm, yet there was this sense of evil lurking beneath the surface,' said Gregory.

'Bob told me he was going to do that one to show people not to follow some character because he's got some Bible in his hands or his collar on backwards,' explained the actor's wife, Dorothy. 'And he was always very sympathetic to the exploitation of children and thought that this would get that out there.'

Mitchum was up for any film that questioned the ethics of church-goers like the Ku Klux Klan, who praised the Lord on Sunday and went lynching negroes on Monday. As Mitchum later said in an interview with Hedda Hopper, 'If you want my interest, interest me.'

But even though the film featured one of the world's great movie actors, the production wasn't all plain sailing. Novelist Grubb, who lived in Philadelphia, wouldn't travel on any form of transport other than bicycle or train, and when asked to co-write the script, instead sent in over a hundred pen and ink sketches of his characters' faces, their expressions changing to match the requisite scene.

Understandably miffed, Laughton and Gregory plumped for *The African Queen* writer James Agee to write the script, but he was at the time trapped in a downward spiral of alcoholism. Eventually Laughton was forced to step in and edit and rewrite much of the script himself.

The fledgling director wanted the movie to look and feel like the antiquated, otherworldly silent films that had captivated him as a teenager (he was born in 1899), and so screened movies by the dichotomous D. W. Griffith, such as *The Birth of a Nation* and *Intolerance*, at New York's Museum of Modern Art. All starred Lillian Gish, who was promptly awarded the role of the fearsome widow Miz Cooper in *The Night of the Hunter*. Laughton told Gish at the time: 'When Griffith was making films, audiences sat bolt upright on the edge of their seats. Now they sit slumped over, feeding themselves popcorn. I want them to sit upright again.'

Now Laughton had to find someone to play Powell's young prey. After Betty Grable – uncertain of the controversial subject matter – turned him down a few weeks before filming, Laughton plumped for a student from his acting class: Brooklyn-born Shelley Winters.

'She looks and sounds as much like a wasted West Virginia girl as I do,' scoffed Mitchum. 'The only bit she'll do convincingly is to float in the water with her throat cut.'

Eventually, Laughton saw Mitchum's point.

'Sometimes Shelley would have little screaming jeebies over something, and Robert used not to be tolerant of it at all,' clarified Mitchum's secretary Reva Frederick. 'Once she was making an awful scene over a piece of wardrobe that didn't fit and Charles walked over and slapped her hard across the face and screamed "Stop it!"'

But Laughton and his lead did not agree on everything either. Mitchum wanted to shoot on location, but his director had other ideas. To achieve the sufficient level of surrealism he decided to shoot on sound stages and at a ranch near LA, and sent off his second unit to shoot on the Ohio River.

To photograph the movie he pulled in Stanley Cortez, who had outdone himself on Orson Welles's *The Magnificent Ambersons* but was now stuck filming throwaway B-movies. The pair met every week for six weeks – Cortez showing Laughton exactly how a camera worked, while Laughton showed the cinematographer films by D. W. Griffith. He then followed suit with untested composer Walter Schumann, who created a score that is as unforgettable as the picture itself.

At this point Laughton was fifty-six years old and, even though he had worked as an actor for well over thirty years, approached this, his directorial debut, like it was the first movie he had ever been involved with.

He employed non-naturalistic stylisation, employing effects such as wipes and iris outs that hadn't been working since the silent movies, and every day after shooting he met with set designer Hilyard M. Brown, assistant director Milt Carter and Cortez to design the following day's shoot.

Nothing was too much trouble. The unforgettably harrowing scene (beware of the spoiler) of Shelley Winters in her car with her throat slashed beneath the lake's waters was achieved in the water tank at Republic Pictures – the camera operator and right-hand man shooting in scuba gear while wind machines carefully blew her hair and the surrounding weeds without making waves. Needless to say it was a dummy and not the actress, though you'd never guess.

Meanwhile, Mitchum, who later credited Laughton as the best director he'd ever worked with, was having a ball, the director allowing him free rein to contribute ideas (it was Mitchum who suggested hanging upside down from his bunk whilst delivering his lines in the prison cell). As Powell, he eschewed his usual laconic tone in favour of a new, more theatrical bravura performance befitting the nutbag preacher.

Whether malevolently singing 'Leaning on the Everlasting Arms' silhouetted against the moonlight whilst astride a barebacked pony, or flicking out his switchblade in anger during a burlesque show saying 'there are jes' too many of them Lord... I can't kill them all', the result was a potent cocktail, sweetened with molasses and laced with strychnine.

Unfortunately, by the end of the shoot Mitchum started losing focus. 'Mitch said all this shit how he loved Charles, but he was on drugs and drink and what have you and there were times when Charles could not get him in front of the camera,' recalled producer Gregory. 'We went through hell and were $200,000 over budget. Things came to a head one day when Mitchum arrived on set late staggering about, but insisted on working. He was puffy-eyed and could hardly see. So I said, "Mitch sweetheart, you're in no condition to go on camera."'

Mitchum considered the suggestion.

'Then he opened his fly, whipped out his dick, then staggered to behind my Cadillac's door which was open,' continues Gregory. 'I thought he was hiding behind it for modesty's sake, but I looked back and see him pissing on the front seat of the car where I'd been sitting.

'And it went on and on, filling up the seat with piss. I could *not* believe it. And then he put his cock back in his pants with a look on his face that was as if this was the *dearest* thing he had ever done in his whole life? And then he staggered off.

'But he was a charmer and an evil son of a bitch,' continued the producer. 'He scared me, to tell you the truth. I was always on guard. He was often in a state and you never knew what he would do next. He'd be drunk and fighting with this flunky he kept around, kicking him all over the place. I'd always worked in the theatre and I'd never met *anyone* like him.'

'The three toughest guys in the movie business were Jack Palance, Robert Ryan and Bob Mitchum,' claims director Budd Boetticher.

'And Mitchum was the toughest. And very soft and tender, like a lot of real tough guys. He didn't have to prove himself in anything. He had done it *all*.'

I doubt if *anyone* had ever met anyone like Robert Charles Durham Mitchum. In the course of my research I've availed myself of his many YouTube clips (do watch them) and found a plethora of Mitchum's past TV interviews. And for the most part, the man seems amazed that anyone should want to know anything about him and baffled as to why these saps should be paid good money to ask him ridiculous questions.

His modus operandi was to take the piss, josh, lie and tie interrogators up in knots. In one interview for the BBC in 1972 Michael Parkinson actually asked the then fifty-three-year-old, 'When was the last time someone took a swing at you?' Mitchum lowered his eyes but Parkinson pushed it.

'The last was a very good one,' replied Mitchum. 'I was in Colorado and a fella came over and threw a piece of used toilet paper on my plate and said, "Sign that." So I picked up my fork and ran it up through his chin and into his upper palette and said, "Take him to the hospital."'

'It's great story,' replied Parkinson 'but I didn't believe word of it.' (Mitchum sighs). 'But did you always want to be a movie star?' continued Parkinson. 'No,' said Mitchum, looking at Parkinson with measured derision, 'I wanted to be the queen, but I couldn't make the weight.'

Indeed, the actor was known not to suffer fools gladly. And looking at the many interviews he did on TV, one can see that he had little respect for journalists or interviewers and not a lot for most actors.

Mitchum, maybe because of his penchant for marijuana, spent a lot of time in Jamaica in the 1950s and even released an album of mento (calypso) that is avidly collected by vinyl enthusiasts. And he disliked actors. Of Steve McQueen he said, 'he sure don't bring much brains to the party, that kid'. He didn't think much of method actors such as Pacino, De Niro and Jack Nicholson ('they're all small'), while John Wayne simply irritated him ('he had four-inch lifts put in his shoes… they probably buried him in his goddamn lifts… And sure, I was glad when he won the Oscar… I'm always glad to see the fat lady win the Cadillac on TV, too!').

But, as he said later, 'The only difference between me and my fellow actors is that I've spent more time in jail.'

Mitchum was born in Bridgeport, Connecticut, on 6 August 1917, to Ann Harriet Mitchum (née Gunderson), the immigrant daughter of a Norwegian sea captain, and James Thomas Mitchum, of Scottish, Irish and Blackfoot descent. His tough-guy father died whilst working on the railroad when the actor was just two, leaving behind his pregnant wife, young Robert and older sister Annette. Things were never easy.

A boisterous child both physically and intellectually, young Bob wrote poems, some of which were published in the Bridgeport local paper when he was seven years old. They moved to a farm in the country shortly after he and his younger brother, John, found themselves fending off the local hick bullies, putting a few in hospital, thus earning the nickname 'them ornery Mitchum boys' – a phrase that brother John would later use as the title of his autobiography.

In 1927, Ann married former English soldier Hugh Cunningham Morris and they had their own child. Two years later Bob was expelled from school, Wall Street crashed, the farm went under and the family moved to a tiny tenement apartment in the tough New York City west-side slum, Hell's Kitchen.

Now it was the brothers who were the hicks and had to fight the local gangs to survive. But young Bob – the consummate chameleon – sounding now like a West Side New York Paddy, fought all comers, earned the broken nose he later attributed to a boxing career (and then denied) and became known as a young man best left alone.

Two high school expulsions followed and, aged fourteen, he left home to work as a deckhand on a salvage vessel. A year later, in 1933, in the midst of the Great Depression, he left home for good and headed for California. When Michael Parkinson asked him in 1971 why he had left home at such a tender age he replied, 'Suddenly I came home and there was no place at the table so it was time to split.

'I got the message and took off, and so I became a hobo, knocking on doors asking the kind for a crust of bread, never offering to mow the lawn, just dealing with the kind lady. I just kept moving. No purpose.'

Annette, his sister, begged to differ. 'He didn't run away. Mother packed his bags for him. He was so, so eager to see all these places he'd read about and so he went.'

In truth, Mitchum had been entirely engrossed by the literature of Jack London and particularly Jim Tully, whose memoir *Beggars of Life* young Bob read until it fell apart. Tully, the son of an Irish immigrant ditch-digger, had been forced onto the road at the age of twelve, had been a boxer and a tree surgeon, and turned to poetry out of angst. A heavy drinker and a notorious brawler, he moved to LA and in 1915 was one of the first reporters to cover Hollywood, albeit scathingly.

Writing such trivia allowed him to pen a series of books about his life on the road and the American poor in his spare time, as well as novels on prostitution, boxing, Hollywood and travel. He is considered the daddy of hard-boiled, no-nonsense American literature. The young Bob Mitchum was entirely enamoured of the writer, but unlike Tully was not forced onto the road. His own trip was fuelled by romantic idealism, wanderlust and books.

But Mitchum never denied his abuse of the truth. 'I learnt early in life that by telling a story far more colourfully than the truth, one's truth would be left alone,' he declared. 'I like to be left alone.' And when a journalist asked if all the stories he had read were true, the actor replied, 'Yep they're all true – booze, brawls, broads, all true. Make up some more if you want to.'

As one pieces the Mitchum jigsaw together, everything about him starts to make sense – sort of. As a fifteen-year-old itinerant, his intention had been to get to California to join his sister, who'd married a navy medic and settled in Long Beach. Unfortunately he was arrested for vagrancy and ended up on a prison farm on another charge.

'The judge accused me of robbing a shoe store on a Wednesday,' he told talk show host Dick Cavett. 'But as I told the judge, I'd been in jail since the Sunday before and was in the bucket, so he threw me in the can anyway – Chatham County Camp Number One, Georgia. I was busted for mopery with intent to gawp. I was only fifteen. They categorised me as a dangerous and suspicious character with no means of support.'

How long he was in for no one knows. Some claim he was in for a week, his brother claimed ninety days. How his incarceration ended is also shrouded in the mists of fabrication, as are the majority of his teenage years.

He often claimed he escaped. 'I just didn't turn up one day and they didn't miss me and I ran, so they fired a few warning shots over my head,' he told Cavett. What is certain is that he returned home with a badly lacerated ankle infected by the leg irons, and his mother refused to allow the doctor to amputate.

As soon as he recovered he was off again and made it to LA, sleeping in the Midnight Mission in downtown LA. Soon back on the hobo express, he was imprisoned for a short while in Texas and ended up working in a coalmine in Delaware for a week. Along the way he had fallen for a young woman called Dorothy Clement Spence and elicited a promise from her that she would marry him just as soon as he found a proper job, after which he left again for California.

Meanwhile, his sister had started working with a theatre group in Long Beach and, in an attempt to keep him out of trouble, she persuaded her errant brother to tread the boards. It was 1937. He was now twenty years of age. The following year he starred as Duke Mantee in a stage version of *The Petrified Forest* and was writing material for comedians and singers (he'd learned to play the saxophone whilst in New York), including an oratorio for the twenty-two-year-old Orson Welles. Another writing job followed for the celebrity astrologer Carroll Righter.

Consequently, he accompanied Righter on a tour that included Philadelphia, where his former paramour Dorothy was now living. They married on 16 March 1940, and stayed together until his death almost sixty years later.

Back in LA, he found work at the Lockheed aircraft factory, assisting a skilled worker named James Dougherty – whose young wife Norma Jean was soon to become known as Marilyn Monroe – and found his first paid job as an actor in an episode of the ham western *Hopalong Cassidy* series, in which he played the bad guy.

'They paid me a hundred bucks a week and I could take all the horse manure home I wanted and a free lunch,' he was oft to say. 'But I never went after a job. They just seemed to come after me. The bread kept getting better and it sure as hell beat punching a time clock.'

Initially, Mitchum had a tough time as a cowboy. He told his employers he had been a ranch hand in Texas, but he couldn't ride for shit. They gave him a troublesome horse that threw him twice, so, with his job on the line, he punched the horse on the nose and it didn't throw him again.

In 1940 Mitchum played a heavy in the Laurel and Hardy vehicle *The Dancing Masters*, while Dorothy had another son, Christopher. The following year America joined the war and his brother and brother-in-law were drafted while Bob was deferred, firstly because his job at Lockheed was classified and secondly because he was the only breadwinner for his ever-growing clan, who now all lived in the same street and included his mother, sister, sister-in-law and all their respective offspring. He was eventually drafted and his service for his country included checking recruits' genitals for venereal disease – 'a pecker checker'. He was honourably discharged as a private first class and received the World War II Victory Medal.

Over time, his reputation as a reliable actor increased, as did his proclivity for drinking, womanising and brawling. On the set of the war film *Thirty Seconds Over Tokyo* he had battered a real-life army sergeant who had the temerity to proclaim in Mitchum's presence that all film actors not in the services were draft-dodging queers. Although managing to avoid the gossip columns, he gained a rep for tupping many a young secretary and starlet.

Thus, Mitchum became a pin-up for the bobby-soxer crowd who loved his bad-boy image. Calamity struck, though, on 31 August 1948, when at a rented house in Laurel Canyon he was caught smoking weed in the company of his best friend Robin Ford, Lila Leeds (one of the most beautiful of all Hollywood starlets) and her friend Vicki Evans.

Mitchum was sentenced to two years of probation, sixty days of which would be spent behind bars. Mitchum had picked up his life-long marijuana habit as a young hobo. In those days the weed grew wild and he and his fellow homeless peripatetics used it during those long train rides to kill boredom, help stave off cold or simply to get to sleep. So when Mitchum made his way west to Hollywood his infatuation with the weed went with him. In 1948 this was a major deal and a huge Hollywood scandal. In my opinion the man was simply ahead of his time.

But perhaps the furore was a good thing. The year before he had made two fine films, both low-budget noirs. The first, *Crossfire*, directed by the great Edward Dmytryk, dealt with the death of a soldier whose only crime was that he was Jewish, while the second, an undoubted classic of the genre *Out of the Past* (aka *Build My Gallows High*), directed by Jacques Tourneur and co-starring Jane Greer and Kirk Douglas, is still hugely regarded.

Now contracted to RKO (Radio-Keith-Orpheum) Pictures, whose boss Howard Hughes cared little about a marijuana beef and saw the actor's moneymaking potential, Mitchum was given a slew of low-budget noirs such as *The Big Steal*, which made a fortune at the box office, *His Kind of Woman*, and *Macao*, directed by one of the men who created noir itself – Josef von Sternberg.

'RKO made the same film with me for ten years,' said Mitchum. 'They were so alike I wore the same suit in six of them and the same Burberry trench coat. Only two pictures in that time made any sense whatever. I complained and they told me frankly that they had a certain amount of baloney to sell and I was the boy to do it. In 1946, I worked with Greer Garson in *Desire Me* and gave up being serious about making pictures. She took 125 takes to say no.'

But, all misgivings aside, Mitchum was still on the up. As he said in a 1973 interview, 'I came back from the war and ugly heroes were in, so I took my chances.'

This was a new and altogether attractive entity for the general public. This was an actor who wasn't that enamoured of the task at hand, was a drinker, brawler and anti-hero. Men, boys, girls, women all loved his attitude.

'Listen. I got three expressions,' he explained in the 1970s. 'Looking left, looking right and looking straight ahead. I've still got the same attitude I had when I started. I haven't changed anything but my underwear.'

For a while Mitchum's nonchalance and disinterest was all too evident. Little he did between 1952 and 1955, including the Monroe vehicle *River of No Return*, is worth mentioning. And then came *The Night of the Hunter*.

Mitchum's performance, even though the film received bad reviews and an even cooler reception from the public, was highly lauded. Most critics regard it as the best performance of his career. As *New York Times* film critic Bosley Crowther put it, Mitchum 'plays the murderous minister with an icy unctuousness that gives you the chills. There is more than malevolence in his character. There's a strong trace of Freudian aberration, fanaticism and iniquity.'

Looking at the film today, it's clear that both director and star were having a creative field day, but they were an odd couple to say the least. In many ways they were diametrically opposed. The actor was physically handsome, nonchalant and enjoyed the fruits of his fame. Laughton, on the other hand, was a full-on English thespian known for immersing himself in a series of truly unforgettable roles such as Quasimodo in *The Hunchback of Notre Dame*, Captain Bligh in *Mutiny on the Bounty* and Henry in *The Private Life of Henry VIII*. By all accounts he was unable to come to terms with both his physical ugliness and rampant homosexuality (a tricky combination), so was much troubled and consequently intense.

Yet undeniably, it is this dichotomy that allowed him to make such a film as *The Night of the Hunter*, which works on so many levels.

Obviously, as a homosexual in the 1950s Laughton was more than cognisant of all the hypocrisies of the so-called puritan Christian right (who morphed into the Christian Coalition of America) and all the hooting-and-a-hollering, Bible-bashing preachers who roamed the South threatening everlasting hell and damnation for all fornicators who succumbed to the ways of the flesh.

As such he was decades ahead of his time. Consider that in 1955, the hypocritical horrors that Irish Catholic nuns perpetrated on young pregnant teenagers (such as selling off their children and enslaving them for years), Catholic priests' abuse of young boys, or indeed the excesses of Muslim fundamentalists, had yet to surface. So the film was highly prescient.

Since its release, the film's reputation as a thoroughly exceptional piece of cinema has grown immeasurably. It is now regarded as one of the great artistic anomalies in cinema history that succeeds against all the odds. Unfortunately, Laughton was never allowed to direct another movie and spiralled headlong into depression. He died seven years after its release.

Mitchum, on the other hand, continued working until he died of emphysema in 1997, but even though he made some fine films and was beyond reproach as Max Cady in *Cape Fear* (1962), and as Eddie in *The Friends of Eddie Coyle* (1973), few of his subsequent performances ever matched his rendering of the psychotic parson in *The Night of the Hunter*.

In later years, when asked about what his career meant to him, he said, 'Years ago, I saved up a million dollars from acting, a lot of money in those days, and I spent it all on a horse farm in Tucson. Now when I go down there, I look at that place and I realise my whole acting career adds up to a million dollars' worth of horse shit.

'But people make too much of acting. You are not helping anyone, like being a doctor or even a musician. In the final analysis, you have exalted no one but yourself... These days young actors only want to talk about acting method and motivation; in my day all we talked about was screwing and overtime.'

Robert Mitchum... what a class act!

Jackson Pollock

It is debatable as to who was the greatest American painter of the twentieth century. Many pundits would agree that it is a close call between Jackson Pollock and Mark Rothko. Both were part of the New York School of Abstract Expressionism, both died relatively young and both extended the role of the painter far beyond its accepted parameters, sucking the viewer into a rarely ventured metaphysical world that is above all confusing and intriguing.

Pollock, the more beguiling of the two characters, was a tortured soul to say the least who, in the words of *Life* magazine, was 'a reckless, restless rebel to the end'. Accordingly, his life sparked controversy, his painting provoked loathing, and his reputation as a rabble-rouser still exists today. But being Jackson Pollock was no stroll in the park. He was like a big jigsaw with lots of missing pieces and others that didn't fit, whose sensitivity would eventually destroy him and who was as equally susceptible to the bad as he was to the good.

Pollock expressed all of his emotions through his painting, believing that he actually became part of his work as it progressed. He was under psychiatric care all his life and, for much of his adulthood, was a raging alcoholic. Yet he was one of the greatest artists who ever lived. His work will suck you in and change your perception of the form; it is both powerful and emotive, overwhelming and spiritual. Indeed, both Rothko and Pollock redefined the role of art, but it was Pollock who put American art on the map and it was Pollock who truly captured the imagination of the nation.

Jackson Pollock was born in 1912 in Cody, Wyoming, the youngest of five brothers. His father, an itinerant farmer and surveyor, was essentially a weak man who was cowed by his overprotective and, ultimately, bossy wife. She in turn mollycoddled and bullied her boys, leaving at least one, Jackson, with lifelong mental problems. School was problematic for Pollock, who never really found his forte until he followed his brother into the arts. At first he studied in Los Angeles, before later joining his sibling at the recently formed Art Students League of New York.

Arriving in New York, Pollock immediately missed the American West and quickly adopted that certain cowboy demeanour – slouching as he walked, always sporting Levi's, 'anecdotes blazing', and driving his battered Model T Ford.

Brooding and non-verbal, he became the inspiration for Tennessee Williams's character Stanley Kowalski in the play *A Streetcar Named Desire*. Pollock was typical of that special kind of 'troubled outsider' that America finds so easy to produce. Not unlike the hero of a fifties western, he was melancholic and antisocial, a loner who was frequently drunk, but ultimately honourable. He was a publicist's dream but he was also the real thing, right down to the pointed cowboy boots.

Undeniably, conformity was very much an issue in post-World War II America, where a multitude of disillusioned servicemen had returned from killing Germans abroad to find themselves ostracised in a world that was thoroughly alien to them. They simply could *not* conform. Many joined biker gangs, one example of the ways in which ex-soldiers railed against conformity and where they might enjoy the same camaraderie and morals they had experienced in wartime. A bestselling book of the day was Robert Lindner's *Must You Conform?* which extolled the virtues of rebellion put to creative use, while Arthur Miller penned the play *Death of a Salesman* – the tale of Willy Loman, a man more or less killed by conventionality. And the two biggest actors of Pollock's heyday of the fifties, James Dean and Marlon Brando, openly exploited alienation, while Lenny Bruce is quoted as saying that to survive one had to 'sell out'. Pollock, very much of his age, was the quintessential renegade, a maverick free thinker who flaunted every orthodoxy, including that of the unconventional artist.

Much of the time, Pollock's concept of painting converged directly with the then extremely hip Actors Studio. Lee Strasberg of the Studio taught that an actor should become the part he plays in the same way that Pollock believed a painter should become the painting. Pollock and the Actors Studio rose to prominence at exactly the same time, both evidence of a more considered view of the arts.

Pollock, along with Brando, was one of the first Americans to wear jeans and a T-shirt socially. It is hard to imagine today, now that the jean is an accepted component of any outfit, but in the 1940s jeans were work clothes and anyone who wore them anywhere else was either pitifully poor, a biker, a gang member or a fruitcake. Pollock worked in his jeans, but his work was painting. Outside of work he was a drinker and a brawler, fascinated and absorbed by violence. One of his hobbies was to drink at the Cedar Tavern in New York, fight strangers then smash the bar to bits. He sounds like a right pain in the arse. As his friend, the sculptor Tony Smith, commented, 'At the funeral, someone said, "He was just like the rest of us." Well, it wasn't true. He had more of the hero about him, and everyone knew it.' The owners of the bar vehemently disagreed.

Nearly all of the Abstract Expressionists conformed to the Pollock blueprint – drinking to excess, racing around in fast cars and living on the edge. Most committed suicide and those who didn't died either violently or in car crashes. In 1956 *Life* magazine described the group as 'baffling', and Pollock's painting as 'haphazard, lawless and chaotic'. The Abstract Expressionists were lambasted by the conservative press of the time who likened them to 'a motorcycle gang such as the Black Rebels in *The Wild One*'. They were accused of lowering the moral tone of the nation, of 'violently slashing traditional values'. But to the hipster on the street, Abstract Expressionism was the artistic expression of the Beat movement, defined by the poet John Clellon Holmes as 'a rawness, a state of being directly pushed up against one's own consciousness'.

The writer Kenneth Rexroth wrote: 'a verse by Dylan Thomas, a solo by Charlie Parker, a painting by Jackson Pollock.' These three were the icons of the Beat movement. As he worked, Pollock listened to recordings of both Dylan Thomas and Charlie Parker and certain critics have pointed out that his technique as a painter could be compared to some of the extemporaneous aspects of jazz. As far as Pollock was concerned, jazz was 'the only other creative thing happening in the country'. He would paint just like a jazz musician, going off on a tangent as the mood took him. He was essentially a *jazz painter*.

Possibly the most recognisable artist in history, Pollock's style consisted of layering thousands of paint swirls or drips, creating a pattern without beginning or end. Simple as they may appear, his paintings were the result of years of painstaking study and research and, as one would expect, his influences are as complicated as the man himself.

His first serious influences were the Mexican muralists David Alfaro Siqueiros and José Orozco, whose work he had seen while studying art in Los Angeles. Always fascinated with American Indians and the ritual of the shaman, he was totally empowered by the monumental work that the Mexicans produced. Siqueiros's aim was to help revitalise North American art by using a graphic language that the working class could understand, and so implement political change. Later, in 1936, Pollock helped Siqueiros at the artist's workshop at 5 West 14th Street. The Mexican encouraged his students to experiment with different paint techniques, found materials and spray guns, trying to find new ways of applying the paint other than with a brush.

Pollock burned with curiosity and, like a sponge, soaked up and applied what, at the time, were extremely radical concepts to become Jackson Pollock the *painter*. From the beginning, he chanced upon many radical thinkers and opened his mind up to each and every philosophy, taking the ideas of the *Der Blaue Reiter* and *Die Brücke* schools of German Expressionism to a new unparalleled height.

At the Manual Arts High School in LA his teacher, Frederick John de St Vrain Schwankovsky, or 'Schwanny' as he was thankfully known, taught his students to meet themselves head on, to expand their consciousness and develop their egos. Soon Pollock was hooked, taking on the pseudonym 'Hugo' and participating in student demonstrations.

Schwanny introduced Pollock to the Theosophical Society and the philosopher Jiddu Krishnamurti who believed, as did the Native American Indians, that we are all one with nature, and should recognise this power, that one's comprehension of the world should be all-inclusive and that we are all unique. These were lessons Pollock readily embraced and held onto till his death.

Philosophically armed, he moved to New York in the fall of 1930 with the express idea of following his brother Charles to the Art Students League and studying under its tutor, Regionalist painter Thomas Hart Benton. Benton, who painted rather twee renditions of America's West, was a heavy drinker who, coming from Missouri, considered all easterners to be faggots. He was also an ardent Marxist who encouraged aggressive behaviour and fighting amongst his students, and by all accounts was also a darn good teacher.

Benton taught Pollock how to look at the old masters and recognise their compositional wealth, encouraging him to pay particular attention to El Greco, Tintoretto and Michelangelo. He would get his students to model their compositions in clay, just as Tintoretto had done, so that they could get an idea of how their works existed in a three-dimensional space.

Benton also made his students dissect classical art. Brueghel, Rubens and Assyrian bas-reliefs all came under scrutiny. He taught his class how to construct a painting using cubes and rectangular slabs; he taught them that knowledge is power. It is this comprehensive understanding of the great masters that gives Pollock's work its monumental power and structure. The artist emulated Benton in other ways too, disappearing for months on end, bumming around America, travelling in freight cars, going to jail, shooting craps and pulling poontang.

There is very little left of Pollock's work from this time and what remains is really quite grim – badly drawn, muddy oils of cowboys at night. One painting, entitled *Going West,* is absolutely dire.

In 1936 Pollock managed to get a job with the Federal Art Project, part of the Professional and Service division of the Works Progress Administration (WPA), which had been set up by Roosevelt to provide realistic economic opportunities for groups especially hard hit by the Depression. Pollock began in the mural division but quickly moved to the easel section, which required one painting per month for display in a governmental building.

But all was not well. Jackson's mental health was beginning to slide. In 1938 he was admitted to a psychiatric unit for four months as his self-destructive alcoholism plunged him to new depths. His time in hospital was well spent, however, as he emerged having thrown off the yoke of Benton's Regionalism and was now producing work such as *Birth* (1938–41) and *The Flame* (1934–38), which were reminiscent of German Expressionists such as Franz Marc, Mexican muralist Orozco and Picasso.

He had also been introduced to a new therapist – Joseph Henderson, a disciple of Carl Jung, the psychologist who espoused the virtues of, and coined the word, 'synchronicity'. Henderson described the fledgling painter as 'a very troubled man whose only salvation would be to find himself as an artist'.

After eighteen months of intensive treatment, Pollock emerged with a renewed interest in the Mexican muralists and a newfound fascination with Picasso. In his work he married these influences with a liberal smattering of American Indian symbolism and the resulting work was, well… better.

Spiritually, Pollock at this time felt a great affinity with the Indian shaman who, it was said, underwent mental transformation while painting. Whether Pollock experienced such a metamorphosis is unlikely, but what is certain is that, like Van Gogh, he had to paint for his sanity. It was a 'physical manifestation of the primitive need to utter'. Without painting he would have been completely and utterly lost.

To look at Pollock's work and just see paint splashes is naïve. The research and information that fuelled his work was immense. Pollock thoroughly investigated the writings of John Graham, who in 1937 wrote a piece in the *Magazine of Art* entitled 'Primitive Art and Picasso', which stressed the influence of African art on that artist. This article had a profound effect on Pollock, who cut it out and wrote to the author, beginning a long and ultimately rewarding intellectual relationship.

Graham, a Russian-born aesthete born Ivan Dombrowski, claimed to be an ex-cavalry officer of the Grand Duke Michael's 'Wild Brigade'. Graham travelled extensively in Surrealist circles, selling primitive sculpture to the likes of André Breton and Paul Éluard and was the best friend of Arshile Gorky. It was Graham who introduced Pollock to Surrealism.

The concept of Surrealism suited Pollock in that it constituted a state of mind that was beyond the canvas. Pollock, though not a Surrealist, harboured certain Surrealist tenets in his painting, in that the production of art relied, in part, on the artist's unconscious. Pollock and Graham also shared an interest in all things primitive. They were fascinated with the art of the American Indians, particularly the Navajo sand painters, who poured different coloured sand onto the floor to create their art.

They avidly studied the cabal, alchemy and spiritualism, as well as the Eskimo shamen who in their primeval circular dance 'give birth' to a new personality. Before he painted, Pollock would often meditate, preparing himself for what was, in essence, a spiritual experience. John Graham taught him to keep every artistic situation spontaneous, to be ever willing to go out on a limb and to court, not deny, accident.

This idea that nothing is accidental and everything is serendipitous was drawn directly from Jungian philosophy. Pollock and Graham both believed that one could spontaneously tap into a 'creative wisdom' stored in the subconscious. Graham believed that using this ability would allow the painter to make 'an imaginary journey into the primordial past'.

It was through Graham that Pollock met another great influence, his future wife, painter Lee Krasner, when they both showed at an exhibition of French and American painting organised by the Russian aesthete. Krasner had every contact in the upper echelons of the New York art world and introduced Pollock to Willem de Kooning, Fritz Bultman and Arshile Gorky – other Abstract Expressionists. She was more conversant with all manner of foreign art than Pollock and actively encouraged his belief in mysticism and magic, which exerted a huge influence on Pollock's later work.

She also believed herself to have second sight, inherited from her father. She, Pollock and Graham experimented with the occult, Graham strenuously believing that he was a Zoroastrian priest and a sorcerer of another age. Pollock and Krasner, even though of entirely different ethnic backgrounds – him Scottish-Irish, her a Russian Jew – enjoyed a relationship that was ultimately rewarding. Pollock was self-conscious and embarrassed in social situations and she often spoke for him; she was more articulate and 'remarkably sure of herself', while Pollock was 'riddled with doubt', silent and withdrawn.

She was more political and aggressive, and he was insular and distant. Her main ability, as far as Pollock was concerned, was that she consciously created an environment in which Pollock could produce meaningful work. She encouraged and coerced the troubled artist into producing his best work. As the critic Clement Greenberg stated, 'I don't feel that Pollock would have gotten where he did without her eye and support.'

Another great influence was the artist Roberto Matta. Matta had been the assistant of architect Le Corbusier and held regular discussion sessions at his home where he encouraged artists to create a travelogue with their unconscious. Matta, who had earlier found success as an artist in Europe, impressed Pollock. His opinion was grist to Pollock's mill. Pollock shared Matta's interest in the occult, primitivist theories, superstitions and the belief that painting was more than just applying paint to a surface.

More importantly, Matta was so impressed with the young cowboy that he lauded him to another highly influential person, Peggy Guggenheim, and it was she who would eventually launch Pollock's career.

Peggy was, as *Time* magazine described her, 'the black-haired, husky-voiced niece of philanthropist copper tycoon Solomon Guggenheim', and 'Surrealism's benevolent angel'. As with Gertrude Stein before her, she was furiously committed to the arts, and she gave Pollock his first show on 8 November 1943.

Guggenheim had lived in Europe right up until the Blitz when, scared that she might lose her precious paintings, she moved back to America. In New York she started her own gallery, the Art of This Century, with three rather eccentric rooms – two devoted to Surrealism and the other to Cubism. She was married to Max Ernst and included Marcel Duchamp, André Breton and Roberto Matta amongst her friends. Initially rather confused by Pollock, at his first exhibition, in 1943, she noticed the leader of the Dutch De Stijl movement, Piet Mondrian, standing in front of Pollock's work. She made a somewhat disparaging comment, to which the Dutchman replied that it was one of the most interesting works he had seen in the US and that 'something important was happening here'.

But the man who was behind Pollock from the start was Guggen-heim's advisor and secretary, Howard Putzel. It was Putzel who per-suaded Guggenheim to offer Pollock a year's contract with a monthly retainer of $150. Spurred on, Pollock quit his job as a janitor and launched into a whole new body of work. He dropped his Jungian shrink, choosing instead to consult a homeopathic doctor. This new work was to be influenced by Pollock's interest in cave painting and palaeontology.

The writer Thomas Hess commented that Pollock's work at this time had a 'whiff of the shaman and Jung'. The sponge was starting to empty, and even though certain works, such as *Blue (Moby Dick)* – which is almost a pastiche of Joan Miró – openly exhibited their influences, others, such as *Composition with Pouring*, showed exactly where he was headed as an artist.

Luckily for Pollock, Peggy Guggenheim split with Max Ernst after his first show. Her reaction was to drop Surrealism entirely and con-centrate instead on a group of young American artists she called her 'war babies', of which Pollock was certainly one.

And America celebrated this new breed of artist with gusto. Indeed, it has been suggested on more than one occasion that the propagation of Abstract Expressionism was a deliberate move by government and industrialists of the age to undermine the strangle-hold that European artists, who they considered to be communists to the last, had on the art world. If one considers the Cold War, the aftermath of World War II and the Hollywood witch-hunts, this the-ory is not beyond the stretch of even the feeblest imagination. Odd to think that such a motley crew as the New York Abstract Expression-ists might be regarded by the American powers that be as eminently more savoury than their European counterparts, but stranger things have happened

Meanwhile, Mr Pollock was growing and changing constantly as an artist. In 1944 he began working with British printmaker Stan-ley William Hayter, who encouraged his students to rotate the plate they worked on to break the traditional 'top to bottom, left to right' approach. By 1945 Pollock went into overdrive, ridding himself of the influence of his two favourite painters, Joan Miró and Picasso. His

Portrait of H. M., painted in 1945, looks restless and downright ugly, but to quote Gertrude Stein, 'All profoundly original art looks ugly at first.' Unfortunately this one still does.

Probably the first work that would carry all the hallmarks of a classic Pollock is the mural he painted in 1943 for Guggenheim's apartment. Apparently he furiously studied the blank wall for some six months, only to execute the painting in one tumultuous session. Here he uses the decorative potential of linear rhythm by rotating curves as taught by Benton, employs the splash and drip technique so favoured by Siqueiros, and eliminates as much as possible the direct contact between brush and canvas as sanctioned by Robert Matta. Other artists, namely Francis Picabia and Hans Hofmann, had used this drip technique before Pollock, but the difference was that, as Lee Krasner said, 'Pollock had the ability to work in the air and know exactly where the paint would land.'

Many of Pollock's works, such as *There Were Seven in Eight* (1945), actually started off as figurative works. He began this painting, Lee Krasner said, with 'more or less recognisable imagery – heads, parts of the body, fantastic creatures'. When asked why he lost this figurative aspect he replied, 'I choose to veil the imagery', which is fair enough, I suppose.

There is, however, an underlying figurative element in all of Pollock's work. As he said, 'I'm very representational some of the time and a little all of the time'. Many in the art world did not see this. Maude Riley of *Art Digest* stated that Pollock's work was 'a chaotic tangle of broad lines, wiry threads and speckles of colour'. This annoyed Pollock so much that he wired *Time* magazine with the following: 'NO CHAOS DAMN IT. DAMNED BUSY PAINTING.'

It was at this time that Pollock earned his reputation as a hard drinker, often getting loaded at Peggy Guggenheim's parties where, on one occasion, he walked into her house stark naked and urinated in her fireplace. Public peeing became Pollock's party trick; once while emptying his bladder, he was overheard saying, 'I can pee on the world.' And after just a few drinks Pollock's pugilistic tendencies would come roaring into the fray, and he would at times attack complete strangers. But, as he claimed, he would 'never hit another artist'.

Perhaps as a means to cure these curious tendencies, Pollock and Krasner moved to a farmhouse in the Springs, a small town near East Hampton, in 1946. The area had long been the habitué of writers and artists and Pollock settled in well, baking, gardening and tinkering with machinery. He and Krasner married and Pollock embarked on what would later be seen as his most fruitful period, a time when he produced much of his best work. Relieved of the demand of the city, he embraced the country, realising the power of nature.

'My concern is with the rhythms of nature. I work inside out like nature,' he said in 1946. When the writer B. H. Friedman chastised the artist for painting from his imagination and not nature, Pollock replied, 'I am nature.' Pollock's work at this time, known as the Accabonac Creek series, reflects this new-found sense of space. Work such as *Magic Light* and *The Tea Cup* made one writer claim that Pollock was in a 'somewhat gayer mood', although I believe that is pushing it just a bit.

Many of the paintings were, as Pollock claimed, 'landscapes'. *Shimmering Substance* could be called Abstract Impressionism, being directly influenced by the later work of Claude Monet, while others expanded the premise of analytical Cubism. *Untitled, 1946* is a direct rip-off of Wassily Kandinsky, and *The Tea Cup* was still heavily reliant on Picasso. But it was in the next year that Pollock would become *the* Jackson Pollock, his influences merging together like a well-honed recipe.

When Peggy Guggenheim moved to Venice in 1947, Betty Parsons, whose gallery was located opposite the Art of This Century, took Pollock under her wing. It was at this new gallery that Pollock really made his mark, with work such as *Reflection of the Big Dipper* (1947) and *Alchemy* (1947), the like of which America had never seen before.

He had completely abandoned traditional painting techniques in favour of throwing and dripping the paint onto the canvas beneath him. Peter Busa questioned Pollock about the accidental quality of his work, to which the artist replied, 'What makes you think it's accidental when I know what I'm going to drip before I work?' His goal in painting, as described by his wife, was to 'formulate unframed space' (whatever that means!).

As he painted, Pollock listened to recordings of the author James Joyce, whose prose was described by Clement Greenberg as 'the reduction of experience to expression, for the sake of expression, the expression mattering more than what is being expressed'. This could certainly have been said about Pollock who, in order to express himself, began incorporating foreign elements into his work such as nails and found objects.

In the painting *Full Fathom Five* (a quote from both Shakespeare and Joyce) of 1947 we find pebbles, buttons, tacks, pennies, nails, combs matches, cigarettes, paint tops and two keys. Maybe he should have called it *Hardware Store*. Another painting created at this period was the superb *Summertime: Number 9A* (1948), a magisterial work that has all the appearance of a moving, swaying, undulating mass of Masai warriors, but then again it doesn't. Pollock had reached his zenith.

By now Pollock's reputation was growing rapidly. One of his paintings, *Cathedral*, was the subject of a round-table discussion for *Life* magazine, with Aldous Huxley, James Johnson Sweeney and Meyer Schapiro all included on the panel. The question raised was, 'Is modern art, as a whole, considered a good or bad development?' That is to say, is it something that responsible people can support or do they neglect it as a minor phase of culture?

One A. Hyatt Mayor, referring to Pollock's painting, said, 'I suspect any picture I think I could have made myself.' Huxley said, 'It seems to me like a panel for wallpaper which is repeated indefinitely on the wall.' Professor Green of Yale thought it 'a pleasant design for a necktie', whilst Leigh Ashton of the V&A stated that it would make 'an enchanting piece of silk'.

Today it is hard to imagine the furore Pollock caused; he was considered Public Enemy Number One and a threat to the moral wellbeing of the USA. When *Life* posed the question, 'Is Jackson Pollock the greatest living painter in the US?' the magazine received 532 letters of complaint criticising the publishing of such nonsense. Snide in their appraisal of the artist, *Life* said that Pollock 'drools enamel paint' while 'cigarette ashes and an occasional dead bee sometimes get in the picture inadvertently'. This piece provoked both criticism and praise for Pollock, but the man himself found the former extremely hard to live with.

Even so, Pollock had been on the wagon for a while and, happy both at home and in his marriage, he sought only the counsel of a local doctor. When the doctor Edwin H. Heller died in an automobile accident Pollock went completely off the rails, drinking all he could lay his hands on with a ferocity only matched by the likes of Oliver Reed. And yet he was the darling of the Beat Generation – those crazy peace-loving daddyos who adored reefer, goatees, open-toed sandals and all things poetic. In fact he was *Beat* before *Beat* existed.

The only film ever shot of Pollock testifies to the claim that the artist transmogrified whilst painting. At the beginning he has all the elegance of an upturned bull, but as he gets deeper into his work he takes on the grace of a ballet dancer. 'It was great drama,' says Hans Namuth, who shot the film, 'the flame of explosion when the paint hit the canvas, the dance-like movements, the eyes tormented before knowing where to strike next, the tension, then the explosion again. My hands were trembling.' As soon as filming was finished Pollock marched into his house, downed a good too many stiff drinks and flew into a rage, upturning the dinner table and screaming like a lunatic, much to the bewilderment of his guests.

By the time the artist had painted *One: Number 31* – a classic Pollock – he had enlarged the size of the canvas and somehow managed to evoke an abstract image of swaying, dancing figures that actually appear to move. These paintings are much influenced by Joan Miró, André Masson, Mark Tobey and Janet Sobel – the untrained, Russian-born Brooklyn housewife who Pollock very much admired. Yet the work on show was still classic Pollock, evidence of his ability to suck in all that he saw and then regurgitate those influences, whilst always remaining his own man.

During 1950 Pollock was like a bubble about to burst. He had reached his peak with works such as *Number 1, 1950 (Lavender Mist)* and *Autumn Rhythm (Number 30)*, but in some work the symbiosis of colour that Pollock had in the past mastered was beginning to disintegrate.

But by 1951 Pollock was back on the booze big time and was beginning to slide. Every move he made was now worth hard cash and this realisation paralysed him. His wife, Krasner, had pushed him to become a huge success, but no one had considered whether Pollock, whose mental state was, at best, precarious, could handle the fame.

In March 1951, Cecil Beaton shot a fashion story for American *Vogue* in which the models wore the 'New Soft Look' against a backdrop of Pollock's latest work in a show at Parsons. His art was now being presented to the American public as an icon of glamour, but to the artist, it was the first of many nails in his coffin.

The show in question featured some of Pollock's finest work, but only one painting was sold. Even though he had produced such amazing work Pollock, in his own words, was 'at an all-time low'. He hit the bottle seriously and it showed. His appearance had altered; he now looked tense, angry and bewildered.

He took to driving aimlessly around East Hampton at all hours of the night and his relationship with his wife began to deteriorate. He tried all manner of concoctions in an effort to raise himself out of this acute depression – protein emulsions prepared by trendy Manhattan pharmacists, herbal remedies by New England quacks, and bourbon.

His work suffered and by 1955 many considered him passé, although only now was he beginning to make real money. He tried to revive his golden years by creating work such as *Scent* and *Search* but he failed to find his old aplomb. The situation was not as it had been and, more importantly, neither was he.

Only one painting from this period, *The Deep* (1953), stands out. It seems to echo Pollock's claustrophobia, a cloud of white encroaching on and covering what may have been an old Pollock. He embarked on a series of more figurative black-and-white paintings such as *Frogman* (1951) and *Portrait and a Dream* (1953), but as the colour drained from his palette so did his sanity. Pollock's paintings when at their best reflect a cohesive man at one with his work, his worst the very opposite. Now, psychologically, Jackson Pollock was in an extreme state of ill health.

It wasn't until his last year, however, that Pollock truly earned his reputation as the wild man of art. As close friend Patsy Southgate says, 'His social life was a continual drunken large party. When I think of it, I don't know how they carried on in this fashion. He was continually drunk, all the time driving around in fast cars.

'It was because artists had a limp-wristed reputation and so they [he and the Abstract Expressionists] over-compensated by being super macho. They were short, ugly men; they were not cutie boys at all.'

In 1956 he embarked on a relationship with Ruth Kligman, but it was to be short-lived. On 11 August they decided to go to a party so he, Ruth and a lady named Edith set off in Pollock's car. Unable to contain his emotions Pollock began crying as they drove and Edith, not understanding his problems, reacted in all the wrong ways. Pollock accelerated ridiculously, laughing as he went even faster. The car swerved and left the road, killing both Pollock and Edith. An obituary of Pollock that week led with the title 'Still Life', and featured a photograph of a hubcap, two cans of Rheingold beer and Pollock's right loafer resting in the grass verge, exactly where they had fallen after the crash.

In the eyes of Kligman, 'he was like the James Dean of the art world'. His death actually helped his image as the romantic artist, and as with many struggling artists his work increased in value enormously after his death. The estate, controlled by Lee Krasner, sold his works piece by piece, limiting the supply and thus driving up the price, until in 1973 one painting was sold to the Australian government for US$2.3 million. Pollock was the first artist to command such figures and is largely responsible for the art market as we know it today. In 2006 his *No. 5, 1948* was sold for the equivalent of $156 million.

Jackson Pollock was many things – the anti-hero of the Beat movement, a loner in the classic western mould and, more importantly, a genius. Two thousand five hundred years ago Plato described the typology of such men of genius as those who suffer from 'divine mania'. Such characteristics have remained unchanged since. Generally, the brilliantly artistic are melancholic, alienated, anxious, extravagant, rebellious and unreliable. Often their character is inherently flawed, with an in-built predilection for drugs or alcohol, requiring madness as a prerequisite to their creativity. Often these individuals succumb to self-destruction. Prime examples include Modigliani, Van Gogh, Watteau and last, but certainly not least, Jackson Pollock.

Pollock had his exact counterparts in other fields of the arts, too. Charlie Parker and Dylan Thomas are perhaps the two closest examples. All three came and went in a blaze of glory, never to be forgotten but ultimately tragic. Thomas, according to the poet John Clellon Holmes, along with Jackson Pollock 'went out without making accommodations to a hostile society' and both died of their excesses. Pollock was a martyr in that he advanced the world of art by his willingness to balance precariously on the edge of disaster. He needed to paint just as the rest of us need food, but what he didn't need and could not handle was the fame, and more importantly the criticism and public scrutiny that comes with it.

Pollock was extremely sensitive and mentally fragile, but was one of the most important painters of the twentieth century. One cannot fail to be moved by a classic Pollock, and that, for an artist, is one hell of an epitaph.

Jack Kerouac

'The only people for me are the mad ones, the ones who are mad to live, mad to talk, mad to be saved, desirous of everything,' wrote Jack Kerouac in his landmark novel, *On the Road*. Famously, he bashed the book out in only three weeks in 1951 on a continuous sheet of teletype paper so as not to hinder his stream of consciousness (or unconsciousness, as some would have it), fuelled by coffee, speed and marijuana. Yet it took him six years to get the book published.

Greeted by mixed reviews when first released, it nevertheless changed many readers' lives and inspired and enthused writers and performers as diverse as John Updike, Jack Nicholson, Ken Kesey, Bob Dylan, Hunter S. Thompson, Norman Mailer, Nick Nolte, and even that crazy mofo Jim Morrison. Since its release it has sold well over three million copies and is regarded as one of *the* great counterculture novels.

I first came across a battered 1967 third UK edition when I was a sixteen-year-old devotee of 1950s Americana. Its front cover tagline hailed it as 'an explosive epic of the Beat Generation', and was accompanied by an illustration of a Beat guy and a hep cat chick. I loved the look. I wanted in. On the back, the *Manchester Evening News* described it as a, 'crazy, mixed-up novel about frustrated youth getting nowhere fast'. It sounded right up my adolescent *strasse*.

A year later, still under the book's influence, I ended up in North Beach, San Francisco, hanging out in the same bookshop – City Lights – and, using a fake ID to get served alcohol, the same bar – Vesuvio – where the author and his Beat pals hung out.

Admittedly the San Francisco I found in 1978 was certainly not the city Kerouac encountered in 1948. Still, the trip, the city and the book changed me forever, as it had him. I later discovered that Kerouac didn't like the book at all and repeatedly described it as a 'crock of shit'. I like him for that.

He was born Jean-Louis Lebris de Kerouac in Lowell, Massachusetts, on 12 March 1922, to Gabrielle and Léo-Alcide. His father was a French-Canadian printer who, after the Great Depression in the 1930s, was left virtually destitute. And so the Kerouacs moved to a rough tenement block.

Consequently, he became a tough kid, excelled as a football player, and in 1939 entered the Horace Mann School in the Bronx with the promise of a football scholarship to Columbia University. The next year he enrolled and spent most of his time on the pitch or in the library reading Céline, Dostoevsky, and especially Thomas Wolfe.

Dropped from the team after constant arguments with his coach, he ended up quitting college entirely. Just over a year later, in early 1942, a few months after the Japanese attack on Pearl Harbor, he joined the merchant marine. He soon left, only to be drafted into the US Navy the following year. He lasted all of ten days, getting an honourable discharge after doctors described him as 'a schizoid personality'.

Back in Manhattan, he wallowed in bohemia and moved into the Upper West Side with his girlfriend, Edie Parker. Very much part of the hep set, he hung out with a gang of Columbia students and fledgling writers who would not only shape his future but that of American literature.

The youngest member of the crew was Allen Ginsberg, a camp, sexually obsessed, strident homosexual whose mother was an active Communist Party member and was as mad as a March hare.

Ginsberg's shtick was vehement opposition to materialism, capitalism and sexual repression. Another cat was the wealthy and privileged morphine addict William Burroughs, whose grandfather owned the Burroughs Corporation – the world's biggest producer of adding machines.

Six years older than Kerouac, Burroughs was twenty-nine when they met and was living on a handsome allowance. He had already resigned himself to a life of unmitigated gay sleaze and the idealisation of unexpurgated means of expression. After a while, they formed themselves into a literary cabal, led by the rakish genius Lucien Carr, who had known Burroughs in St Louis.

Carr penned their manifesto, which called for a 'New Vision' (a phrase borrowed from Rimbaud) and concluded that:

(1) *Naked self-expression is the seed of creativity;*

(2) *The artist's consciousness is expanded by derangement of the senses;*

(3) *Art eludes conventional morality.*

Fair play.

On 13 August 1944, after a night out drinking with Kerouac, Carr stabbed predatory homosexual David Kammerer to death with a scout's knife. '[They] went to Riverside Park where Dave finally pushed too hard; he made a play for Lucien, who stabbed him with his Boy Scout knife, killing him. Lucien weighed down the body and rolled it into the Hudson River,' wrote Brenda Knight in *Women of the Beat Generation.*

The next day Carr turned himself in and was charged with second-degree murder. Burroughs and Kerouac were arrested as material witnesses. Carr claimed that Kammerer had tried to rape him and the furore hit the papers, who went to town on a scandal that involved a popular, gifted student from an uptown socialite family (Carr), New York's leading university, the seedy odour of homosexuality and a gang of intellectual bohemians. And even though the snivelling Ginsberg – forever out for himself – refused to back up Carr's testimony, with the press on his side Carr pleaded guilty to manslaughter and was sentenced to a term of one-to-twenty years in prison, serving only two.

In the meantime their new 'movement' surged ahead like Hitler through Poland. Greenwich Village couldn't get enough of it and coffee bars, fuelled by poetry readings, copious reefer and sandals, sprung up like magic mushrooms on sheep shit. As Norman Mailer said, 'In such places as Greenwich Village, a ménage-a-trois was completed – the bohemian and the juvenile delinquent came face-to-face with the Negro, and the hipster was a fact in American life.'

The gang were soon joined by petty junky criminals such as Herbert Huncke (on whom the protagonist in Burroughs's finest work, *Junkie,* is based). Such reprobates allowed these middle-class kids an insight into the seedy underbelly of New York.

More influential was Neal Cassady. An ex-con brought up on skid row, he was a freewheeling professional imbiber of *everything*. A naughty, macho bisexual who had married the fifteen-year-old Lu Anne Henderson but often moonlighted as a rent boy, he was the real deal – an amoral New York hard-ass who could scrap and take it all.

'Suffice to say,' he once said, 'I just eat every twelve hours, sleep every twenty hours, masturbate every eight hours and otherwise just sit on the train and stare ahead without a thought…'

A rum bunch of miscreants, they had the lifestyle, the words, the attitude and the distinctive style of dress. In post-war New York, men wore suits, ties and hats. They laundered their shirts and polished their shoes.

If you didn't, you were considered, quite literally, a bum. The Beats, as they came to be known, wore army surplus chinos, sweatshirts and work clothes: blue jeans and boots. They had all the aspects of a 'youth cult' – the clothes, the drugs, the attitude, the anti-establishment ethic. The only difference was that none were youths and they didn't yet have a name.

The moniker came in 1948 when sometime Beat member John Clellon Holmes pressed Kerouac to define his cohorts. In response, Kerouac called them 'the Beat Generation'. Consequently, in 1952, after the publication of his novel *Go*, another autobiographical work that tells of fun and games with Ginsberg, Cassady and Kerouac, Clellon Holmes wrote an article for the *New York Times Magazine* entitled, 'This Is the Beat Generation.'

The press loved the name and it stuck. Some say it referred to a generation of disenfranchised ex-servicemen who had nowhere to go after the war and felt 'beat', while others have claimed that it referred to jazz and its groove. Whatever its etymology, the name was perfect. As Kerouac said:

The Beat Generation. That was a vision that we had, John Clellon Holmes and I – and Allen Ginsberg in an even wilder way, in the late forties, of a generation of crazy, illuminated hipsters suddenly rising and roaming America, serious, bumming and hitchhiking everywhere, ragged, beatific, beautiful in an ugly graceful new way – a vision gleaned from the way we had heard the word 'beat' spoken on street corners on Times Square and in the Village, in other cities in the downtown city night of post-war America – beat, meaning down-and-out but full of intense conviction.

In 1947 Kerouac started on his first novel, *The Town and the City,* and in an attempt to cure writer's block embarked on one of the many trips on which the almost entirely autobiographical *On the Road* was based.

For *On the Road*, he takes the name Sal Paradise and criss-crosses the US and briefly Mexico over a three-year period, mainly with Dean Moriarty (Cassady), sometimes hooking up with the likes of Carlo Marx (Ginsberg), Old Bull Lee (Burroughs) and Elmer Hassel (Herbert Hunke). Their escapades revolve around drinking, doing drugs, taking in jazz, women and introspection, while looking for the meaning of life. As Kerouac wrote, 'rising from the underground, the sordid hipsters of America, a new beat generation that I was slowly joining.'

In effect, the book is one long travel story, an in-depth, no-holds-barred diary that reveals the habits – right down to the last Benzedrine inhaler – of a gang of renegade intellectual reprobates. What they did as a group (as the book more than adequately illustrates) is reject the society that made them, reject the mores and trappings of a country that considered itself perfect, and reject any and all of its codes, whether sexual or otherwise. The living embodiment of the Shakespearean maxim to thine own self be true, by being themselves they became the seeds of what was the most beguiling youth movement of all time – a movement that, with its own language, music, literature and film, changed the way the world thought about *everything*.

In 1947 most educated white folk did not smoke reefer, sleep rough, dance to black music, swap partners (both male and female), grow their hair long, dress in jeans, discuss Karl Marx or espouse the virtues of eastern religions. Ten years later, when *On the Road* was published, it was more relevant, appealing to East Village-dwelling, Miles Davis-loving Beatniks who dallied with much of the aforementioned. Ten years later, in 1967, it was the bible for hippies who, following the tome's lead, flocked to San Francisco's Haight-Ashbury for the Summer of Love and let it all go.

Clellon Holmes published his book *Go* in 1952, while Kerouac was still trying to get *On the Road* into print, and a few years later, Ginsberg published his expansive poem, *Howl*, which became the subject of an obscenity trial due to the line 'who let themselves be fucked in the ass by saintly motorcyclists, and screamed with joy'. It was the most popular Beat poem of the day. So one might say that by the time *On the Road* actually hit the shelves, in 1957, the general public had caught up with the Beat ideology. Indeed, it was in 1957 that Audrey Hepburn starred as a Beatnik alongside Fred Astaire in the huge box office hit *Funny Face,* prancing around the Left Bank. Others championed the Beat movement because it struck a chord with a generation of disaffected youth who, appalled by the way their country was going, needed to express their dissatisfaction.

Lest we forget, the USA had suffered an appalling depression in the 1930s and was subsequently saved economically by World War II, after which came what academics and popular economists refer to as 'the Golden Age of Capitalism'. This prompted the biggest surge of materialism in history, which some have compared to that of the USSR after

Glasnost. Advertising companies grew, consumerism boomed and, while some were overjoyed, others saw that the so-called American Dream was little more than a marketing man's catchphrase, used to sell stuff you didn't need.

Furthermore, many were still sickened by the dropping of the atomic bomb on Hiroshima and Nagasaki, and even further appalled by Senator Joseph McCarthy's anti-communist purge, which saw many a left-wing intellectual imprisoned for their thoughts. Much of the population also backed the Civil Rights movement that began in 1955. Adherence to the jazz-and-peace-loving, anti-materialistic Beat or Beatnik ideology showed a certain attunement with all of the above. *On the Road* hit this particular zeitgeist head on. As Warhol photographer Nat Finkelstein told me, 'In 1958 if you wanted to get fucked by some blonde rich chick who wanted to rebel you became a beatnik!'

A few weeks after the book's publication a review appeared in the *New York Times* proclaiming Kerouac a major American writer. 'The most beautifully executed, the clearest and the most important utterance yet made by the generation Kerouac himself named years ago as "beat," and whose principal avatar he is,' it said.

His prose, however forced, was seen as the new vernacular, his characters' attitudes the new human condition. Fame jumped on his bones, gave him a shaking and, along with his fellow Beats Ginsberg, Corso and Burroughs, he was catapulted into literary hyperspace.

The problem was that by 1960 he had become a huge media star, reaped the rewards and found himself regarded as the voice of a generation that he no longer represented. How could he? He was now a thirty-eight-year-old successful author who had never lived up to the promise of *On the Road*. Fame was an albatross around his neck. He was derided, followed around and even beaten up outside a bar in New York. He represented things that many Americans hated – freedom, nonconformity and individuality – and he suffered as a result. As the poet Gary Snyder remarked, 'Around Jack there circulated a palpable aura of fame and death.'

Ultimately Kerouac became a caricature of himself. The TV series *Route 66* (broadcast from 1960 to 1964) aped and sanitised Kerouac and Cassady's travels, while Kerouac fought hard to kill his reputation by appearing on a string of TV shows drunk and out of his mind. In one famous interview on Italian TV with Fernanda Pivano he was so blasted that he couldn't hold his head up and spoke to her first in French and then Spanish – even though she was speaking English (albeit heavily accented). On William Buckley's show in 1968 he berated his host and fellow guests before shouting 'Heil Hitler!' completely out of the blue.

Kerouac drifted into extreme alcoholism, and died as a result. On 20 October 1969, at 11am, he was sitting drinking malt whiskey when he suddenly began to throw up blood. He underwent surgery to tie off all his blood vessels but died due to an internal haemorrhage caused by cirrhosis. He was forty-seven. Further complications came from an untreated hernia and a bar fight he had had a few weeks before.

By all accounts, Kerouac died an unhappy and unfulfilled man, but he needn't have been. The Beat Generation was one of the most important underground cultural movements of the twentieth century. It made individuality fashionable, along with questioning the powers that be, sexual liberation, open-mindedness, egalitarianism, intellectualism self-expression, literature, discussion, black music, art and, perhaps more trivially, beards.

In short, the Beats were proto-hippies, yet also proto-punks (Burroughs was called 'the Godfather of Punk'), but most of all they were blatant nonconformist mavericks who rejected the capitalist, consumerist celebrity-obsessed society that they'd been handed.

Where are they now, when we need them most?

Sonny Liston

On 24 February 1964, world heavyweight boxing champion Sonny Liston lost his title after a puzzling performance against a loud, brash twenty-two-year-old from Louisville, Kentucky. Eyebrows were raised but the matter was never fully investigated, and many were more than prepared to accept that the youngster had beaten Liston fair and square.

Whether he really did or not, we will never know. But as someone once said, anyone can be bought and anything can be fixed if you have enough money, power and balls. And in the 1960s, the American mafia had all three in abundance.

Said twenty-two-year-old was, of course, none other than Cassius Clay, a man who many hold to be one of the greatest heavyweight boxers of all time. Others consider him to have lowered the status of boxing to that of all-in wrestling, where showmanship and braggadocio is more important than dignity.

Before the bout, Clay, as he later did with Joe Frazier (who despised him till his death), taunted Liston with racial insults, saying, 'After I beat him I'm going to donate him to the zoo.' No sportsman had used such language in so public a setting before.

I will admit that Clay – who later changed his name to Muhammad Ali – did rise to the title and become a fine fighter, but back then he was no match for Liston.

An Olympic champion, the middle-class Clay had clawed his way up through the ranks, carefully avoiding class acts such as Cleveland Williams, Zora Folley and Eddie Machen. Instead, he took the easier route, fighting the forty-six-year-old ex-champion Archie Moore, who took him to four rounds, and then in 1963 the twenty-nine-year-old British fighter Henry Cooper.

The South Londoner weighed in at twenty-seven pounds lighter than Clay but still felled his opponent, leaving him hanging on the ropes. Clay's trainer, Angelo Dundee, dived in and unlawfully guided Clay to the corner where he administered smelling salts (a serious violation of UK boxing rules). Dundee also claimed years later that he had opened a cut in one of Clay's gloves, telling the referee that his man needed a new pair. The subsequent delay allowed the Kentuckian to find his legs and deny Cooper the chance to try to knock him out while he was still dazed. The fight was stopped in the fifth round due to a nasty cut over the Brit's eye. Three years later Cooper took Ali, as he was by then known, to six rounds again, only for the same cut to open and thus end the fight.

Liston, on the other hand, had totally demolished everyone in his path, including world champion Floyd Patterson, who he knocked out in less than three minutes on two occasions. He had knocked out 90 per cent of the opposition, smashing every single quality boxer in the heavyweight division.

'Sonny Liston is in the top five greatest heavyweights of all time,' insists boxing historian Hank Kaplan. 'He had the hardest left jab in boxing history.'

No one can doubt that Sonny Liston was the real thing. He was a true fighter in the Tyson mould – a simmering lump of malevolence, who, as someone once said, 'had died the day he was born'.

Characteristically, there is no record of Liston's birth. His name is absent from the 1930 US census but does appear in the 1940 census as being born in 1929 or 1930. For official purposes he later settled on a birth date of 8 May 1932, but it seems as though even he didn't know the exact date. The record of his first arrest says he was born in 1928.

His birthplace was also in dispute. Sometimes Liston said it was Pine Bluff, Arkansas, other times Memphis, Tennessee. According to his mother it was the little town of Forrest City, Arkansas – a desolate township of some 350 inhabitants in 1963, and probably less at the time of Liston's birth.

The truth is even less impressive. Liston was actually born in a lean-to cypress board shack in a barren little backwater called Sand Slough. His mother Helen described it as having 'no ceiling so I had to put cardboard on the walls to keep the wind out'. He was delivered and named Charles L. Liston by an old lady who never mentioned what the 'L' stood for. He was born to be a pugilist – the first thing his mother noticed about her newborn son was his massive hands.

But it wasn't just his physique that hinted at a future champ, it was also his woeful upbringing. Liston grew up in the kind of poverty that only the deprivation of subsistence dirt farming in the Great Depression could provide.

His father had already sired some twelve children, but after becoming a widower in his fifties he moved from Mississippi to Arkansas in 1916 with his sixteen-year-old bride, Helen Baskin, who bore him thirteen children. Sonny, the youngest male offspring, was toiling in the fields with his father by the age of eight. Tobe Liston, a mean, insensitive man, beat his children senseless, especially Sonny, who was later quoted as saying, 'The only thing my old man ever gave me was a whipping.' Liston senior also considered the ability to read and write not only unnecessary but a waste of time. Liston junior therefore went through life totally illiterate, a severe disadvantage in the contractual world of boxing.

Tobe farmed the fifty-acre crop share, Morledge Plantation, near Johnson Township, St Francis County, sharing his profits with the owner. In other words, he rented the land, worked his ass off and then gave 25 per cent of his hard-earned cash to an absentee landowner. No wonder he was pissed off. All through his life Liston junior found this principle hard to shake – he *always* had to pay the man.

Unsurprisingly, in 1948 Liston's mother moved to St Louis, Missouri, and soon the boy followed. Wandering the big city after days of sleeping on the streets, he found his mother with the help of the police. Unfortunately, this initial co-operation with the boys in blue was not to last. He soon turned to crime and led a gang of tough street kids who specialised in mugging and robbery.

Due to his penchant for bright shirts, he became known to St Louis PD as the 'yellow shirt bandit'. In January 1950, he was caught after a gratuitously violent robbery, and having pleaded guilty to three charges of first degree robbery and two of larceny he entered the Missouri State Penitentiary. Liston, along with two accomplices, had robbed three people at gunpoint in a spree that lasted just one night, and was rewarded with five years on each charge, all to run concurrently. The big house was never going to be a stroll in the park, but Liston soon learned how to survive the rigours of the state penitentiary.

Three dominant gangs controlled the Missouri State Pen, all of whom were white. It's been said that Liston, having fallen foul of each gang, challenged the leaders to meet him at six o' clock 'in the hole', a storage room beneath the cellblock. Four men walked in, but only Liston walked out, the rest battered and unconscious on the hole's concrete floor. As Liston remarked later in his career, 'I didn't mind prison.' His pugilistic prowess soon came to the attention of the authorities, who decided the best place for him was the prison boxing ring. The first problem they encountered was the regulation gloves. They didn't fit. Most heavyweight boxers' hands measure some twelve inches in circumference; Liston's measured an astonishing fifteen.

Later in life, Liston's gloves had to be tailor-made to accommodate this mammoth fist, rated the largest of all previous heavyweight champions – larger than those belonging to the six-foot, six-inch Italian champ Primo Carnera, or the six-foot, four-inch Abe Simon. Liston's glovemaker found it almost impossible to keep the weight of a pair of XXXL gloves down to the required eight ounces. Indeed, Liston was a bull of man who, standing at just over six feet, possessed thighs that measured twenty-five inches in circumference, a forty-four-inch chest, a nineteen-inch neck and a reach that stretched to a good eighty-four inches.

For his first fight in prison, however, the gloves were eventually squeezed on and the laces left untied. In the ring Liston, now nicknamed 'Sonny' by the prison chaplain and boxing coach Father Schlattmann, found his feet as easily as his opponents lost theirs.

He strolled through the opposition, knocking the pen's heavyweight champion out cold and almost killing another. Before long, his reputation had spread beyond the prison walls, reaching the ears of Father Alois Stevens.

The priest had heard that 'there was this great enormous convict over there that they couldn't get anybody else to fight. They had to put two men in the ring with him at the same time and he still won.' So Father Stevens, together with a sportswriter for the *St Louis Star-Times* named McGuire, drove down to St Louis in search of opposition for the mighty Liston. With the help of a former boxer and trainer Monroe 'Muncey' Harrison, they came up with the best heavyweight in the city – the thirty-two-year-old Thurman Wilson. After just two rounds with Liston, the formidable pro was said to have quit, ending the bout with the words, 'I don't want no more of him.' Some ten years later, this Sonny Liston would be easily beaten by Cassius Clay – a twenty-two-year-old 'kid' supposedly without a punch.

Monroe 'Muncey' Harrison had been Joe Louis's favourite sparring partner and had trained Archie Moore. In his own words, he had at last found a 'live one'. Harrison and the then publisher of the *St Louis Argus*, Frank Mitchell, campaigned for Liston's release. By 30 October 1952, Sonny was back out on the streets, ready to start his job as a labourer at a local steel plant.

In February 1953, they entered him in the open and novice heavyweight division of the amateur Golden Gloves tournament, sponsored by the *St Louis Globe-Democrat*. Liston trounced the competition, going on to win the Midwest Golden Gloves title, beating an Olympic heavyweight champion, and then the national title, becoming, in March, the Golden Gloves heavyweight champion.

In June that year he defeated Herman Schreibauer of West Germany to become the Golden Gloves world heavyweight champion. In five months, Sonny Liston had gone from unknown ex-con to amateur champion. Evidently, it was time to turn pro.

His first professional fight against Don Smith, an impressive newcomer who had knocked out all of his previous opponents, was marked by the fact that he KO'd the hapless Smith with his first punch of the first round. It lasted a mere thirty seconds.

It wasn't all plain sailing, however. In 1954 Liston fought Marty Marshall and was told to 'carry the boy for three or four rounds'. He knocked Marshall to the floor in the first, only for Marshall to jump back up and catch Liston off guard as he was laughing. The punch broke his jaw. Still, Sonny fought on for the remaining eight rounds, only to lose on a close points decision.

In the rematch, Liston battered Marshall in six rounds. Marshall said after the fight, 'He hit me like no man should be hit. Nobody should be hit like that. He hurts when he breathes on you. I think about it now and I hurt.'

That particular TKO was followed by five consecutive knockouts on the run. Such talent soon attracted the attentions of a number of parties. One was John J. Vitale, boss of the St Louis mafia, a satellite of the Chicago mob. Another was Truman K. Gibson, founder of the now defunct IBC (International Boxing Club). And last, but by no means least, was the man who controlled American boxing in the 1950s – Frankie Carbo.

Born on the Lower East Side of New York in 1904, his real name was Paul John Carbo, although he was known by a number of rather entertaining aliases, including Mr Gray, Frank Martin, Frankie Tucker, That Man, the Ambassador, and Our Friend. Earlier in his career he was also referred to in more derogatory terms as Dago Frank or Frankie the Wop.

A 'killer amongst killers', Carbo was first convicted of murder in 1924. While on parole in 1931 he was arrested for the killing of wealthy bootlegger Mickey Duffy. After his release he was indicted again in 1936 for the double murder of Max Greenberg and Max Hassel, former associates of gangster/bootlegger Waxey Gordon. The pair had unfortunately embarked on a costly bootleg war with Dutch Schultz. And in 1940, along with Bugsy Siegel and Louis 'Lepke' Buchalter, head of Murder Inc., Carbo was indicted with the murder of a Mr Harry 'Big Greenie' Greenberg, a Lepke apostate who had fled to Hollywood. Carbo was identified as the shooter.

But in addition to his day job as a ruthless assassin, Frankie Carbo also managed boxers.

Importantly, the IBC, under Truman Gibson, promoted and tele-vised every major fight in the US. But powerful as they were, they soon came to the inevitable realisation that they could not survive without Carbo and the mob. As a result they installed Carbo's girl-friend, Viola Masters, in a position within the company whereby she received a sum of $40,000 over three years.

Carbo's main man was a certain Blinky Palermo. Initially a book-maker, Palermo lost his licence as a fight manager in every state he had worked in but continued operating under cover. Specialising in fight fixing, the pair embarked on a number of spectacular scams, the first big 'fix' being the Billy Fox–Jake LaMotta fight of 1947, where Carbo convinced LaMotta, the overwhelming favourite, to throw the fight in exchange for a shot at the middleweight title.

In 1942 he 'persuaded' Sugar Ray Robinson to carry Al Nettlow for ten rounds so that Carbo could collect. Robinson, however, angered by a nasty Nettlow right, retaliated and KO'd Nettlow in the third. Robinson had to meet Palermo after the bout outside Blinky's favourite newsstand to explain, apologise and avoid being shot. Carbo and Palermo were very serious men.

The first world title fight that Carbo and Palermo fixed was the 1955 capitulation by Archie Moore against the undefeated Rocky Marciano. And this was certainly not their last venture on behalf of the mob. It was Carbo and Blinky who would eventually come to control the future of Charles 'Sonny' Liston.

Liston's connection to organised crime did not begin with boxing. After his release from the state pen in 1952, all of Liston's non-boxing work was controlled by Local 110, including three months with Vitale's cement contractors in St Louis. The union was controlled by Vitale and Syrian mobster Ray Sarkis. In the words of colleague Terry Lynch, Liston worked as a 'kind of chauffeur, quasi bodyguard' for Ray Sarkis to 'break people's legs and stuff'.

Sonny's partner in the fracture enterprise was Barney Baker, an enforcer for New York mob kingpin Meyer Lansky, himself a partner of Bugsy Siegel and Lucky Luciano. Baker was also the last man Jack Ruby spoke to before the Kennedy assassination, and had been Jimmy Hoffa's right-hand man since the early days of the Teamsters. The plot thickens.

As the mob connections became overpoweringly obvious, both California and Pennsylvania suspended Liston's boxing licence. Consequently, Liston had to appear before a Senate sub-committee investigating organised crime's influence in professional boxing.

Liston admitted knowing Vitale and Baker, stating that he had met Baker in Chicago (the mob capital of the US). In answer to whether these men should remain in the sport of boxing he answered, 'Well I couldn't pass judgement. I haven't been perfect myself.'

This was something of an understatement; Liston had been arrested some six times between 1956 and 1957 for a number of alleged crimes ranging from larceny, careless driving, speeding, suspicion of theft and, most notably, battering an arresting officer in a St Louis alleyway.

The much-publicised account of Liston resisting arrest, even after wooden nightsticks were allegedly broken over his head, abetted his reputation as a ghoulish fiend who felt no pain. For that transgression he was sentenced to nine months in prison. Paroled after six months, he was still banned from boxing for the whole of 1957 and deemed a constant thorn in the side of the St Louis police. Finally, Captain John Doherty took Liston to the outskirts of the city where he put a gun to the side of his head and told him to get out of town. As Liston said later, if he failed to leave, Doherty's men 'would put me in the alley'. And so he fetched up in Philadelphia and in 1958 returned to boxing, winning eight fights that year, mostly by early knockouts.

Around this time, the police were getting busy. They arrested Blinky Palermo, who was found to have a number of important names in his address book. Liston was one, George Raft another. Frankie Carbo had to go to earth after an investigation revealed that he had offered champ Rocky Graziano $100,000 to throw his championship fight against Tony Zale.

Other investigations revealed that Carbo was also an associate of feared New York boss Albert Anastasia, while one of Carbo's lieutenants was Gabe Genovese, cousin to Vito Genovese, aka Don Vito – the former enforcer who, as the head of one of New York's most powerful crime families, the Genovese Family (founded by Lucky Luciano), was the man responsible for starting the city's heroin trade. Frankie was not one to mess with.

Carbo's flight from justice, however, was short lived, and in 1959 he was tried and convicted of conspiracy, undercover matchmaking, undercover management and corruption. Due to his ill health he received a mandatory two-year sentence. But while the trial had gone on, he and Blinky had carefully contrived to own Sonny Liston.

Subsequently, Liston battered all comers. His fights became the place to be for the well-to-do mobster. As one contemporary copper said, 'Every time Liston fights, every hoodlum in the goddamn country shows up.' Sonny's reputation grew daily, and not only in the boxing arena. He became known as 'the mightiest of men and the sharpest of dressers'. Furthermore, his sparring partner, Foneda Cox, said Liston was endowed 'with a prick that could scare a horse'. This monstrous member, Cox continued, would 'put an unbelievable amount of prostitutes in the hospital.' Ouch!

Working towards a title fight with the heavyweight champion of the world, Floyd Patterson, Liston demolished Cleveland Williams (the hardest hitting heavyweight in the world), Niño Valdés and Howard 'Honeyboy' King in three rounds. He defeated the so-called 'perfect fighting machine,' Eddie Machen, in twelve rounds. The latter claimed that Sonny was the strongest man he had ever fought.

His reputation preceding him, Liston scared Patterson shitless. The champ's manager Cus D'Amato (later Mike Tyson's trainer) defended Patterson by saying that the boxer would not fight Liston because 'he was a criminal who represented all that was unsavoury and evil'. Civic leaders feared that Liston was a bad example to the country's youth and that he would hamper the civil rights movement.

According to legendary fight commentator Larry Merchant, Liston 'distrusted everyone, disliked the press, the media, perhaps even the public. He was a man of few words who came across as truly dangerous, replying often with a silent stare from these dead cold snake eyes.'

'He was described as a latter day caveman, a jungle beast, a gorilla, the heavyweight who everyone hated,' recalls Merchant, who was sports editor for the *Philadelphia Daily News* at the time.

'It was really over the top. And of course his name appeared on the front pages as often as the sports pages as he was always in trouble with the police which was rare then for a world-class athlete.'

Former champ Jack Dempsey stated that because of his mob links, Liston should not be allowed to fight for the title. Liston's reply questioned whether Dempsey's failure to serve in World War I gave him the right to judge. Frustrated, Liston changed his management and claimed that Patterson – who had faced only white challengers since becoming champion – was pulling the race card against his own colour. But still the answer was a resounding no.

Liston, undeterred, offered to fight Patterson and the main contender, Ingemar Johansson, both on the same night. Still no joy. Liston became increasingly frustrated and eventually bowled into D'Amato's office asking the frightened and diminutive manager, 'Is you or is you ain't gonna give me a shot at the title?'

In the end Liston had made the controversy so public that Patterson was on the ropes. Then, on 4 December 1961, Liston fought in the opening bout in a double-fixture featuring Floyd Patterson as the main draw. Two minutes in, Liston knocked out West German Albert Westphal (ranked number four in the world), who remained unconscious longer than the fight had lasted. Undeniably, Liston was the only challenger left for Patterson. Thus, in March 1962, Floyd Patterson was left with no alternative. Finally he signed a contract to fight Sonny Liston.

They eventually fought in Comiskey Park, Chicago, on 25 September 1962, in what was described as the most lucrative fixture in boxing history. Patterson was knocked out cold in two minutes and six seconds. It was the third-fastest knockout in a world heavyweight title fight and the first time the champion had been knocked out in the first round. In 1962, Liston went officially from being the poverty-stricken, illiterate child of an abusive tenant farmer in Arkansas to being the heavyweight champion of the whole world. Liston reigned supreme, and yet no one celebrated. The usual homecoming victory parade was absent, no hoo-ha, just a man coming home after work to a disinterested audience.

'When we landed in Philadelphia from Chicago there was nobody there except a handful of reporters and I saw him almost deflate,' remembers former boxer Jack McKinney. 'There was no welcome whatsoever for the world champion. And I saw his huge shoulders sag in front of me.'

In the rematch, Patterson was knocked down three times in two minutes and twenty-three seconds.

Next up was Clay, a rank outsider who, if truth be told, did not deserve a shot at the title – he was a 7–1 underdog. But there were other powers at play. Regardless, Clay still derided the champ during the pre-fight shenanigans, calling him 'the big ugly bear'.

In the face of an unusually placid, almost resigned Liston, Clay declared that he would 'float like a butterfly and sting like a bee', and that 'Liston even smells like a bear'. He turned the pre-bout weigh-in into a farce, screaming, 'Someone is going to die at ringside tonight.' Such antics were unprecedented in the world of boxing.

But the whites in the audience loved it. They didn't want a big, dangerous black man as the champ. They wanted an Uncle Tom, a clown. They wanted a pretty boy, someone they could laugh at and definitely not fear. The press also loved Clay, whose 'tiresome and trying wit, whose harmless and drably colourful shows of playfulness, and whose affected audacity were perfectly suited for the media of the day.'

Many pundits, however, felt that Clay was no match for Liston. Joe Louis said, 'Nobody's gonna beat Liston 'cept old age.' Nat Fleischer, a formidable and knowledgeable sportswriter of the day, wrote, 'Clay must be regarded as no more favourable an antagonist for Liston than was Patterson. Nothing that Clay did against Henry Cooper in London or Doug Jones in New York justifies throwing him to the Wolf.'

Clay was very much the underdog, which was exactly how mobster Frankie Carbo wanted it.

Machinations for the Liston-Clay match had begun, aided and abetted by the latter's trainer, Angelo Dundee, whose brother Chris was now the partner of Carbo's lieutenant Gabe Genovese, aforementioned cousin of Vito.

For several reasons, the fight ended up in Miami Beach under the aegis of Frankie's old pal Chris Dundee. Carbo had recently been convicted of fight fixing and conspiracy, and had started a twenty-five-year prison sentence, but Blinky was still at large. They still controlled Liston and they could smell a lucrative fix coming on.

In the run up to the Clay match, no one wanted Liston to be the champ. He had an extensive police record, had myriad connections to organised crime and there were unsubstantiated rumours that he had raped a chambermaid. He was the baddest black guy in America.

This does not, however, alter the fact that he was more than capable of pulverising Clay. Billy Conn, former lightweight champion, put it this way: 'Clay hasn't the experience. The only experience he'll get is how to get killed in a hurry.'

On the night of the fight, Clay was only too aware of the task before him. His pulse raced to 120 at the weigh-in. He was petrified. At the sound of the bell, Clay rushed at Liston like a madman and claimed the first round. Liston took control in the second, but at the start of the third the younger man impressively landed a barrage of great shots, cutting the champ's eye, only for Liston to again take control until, by the end, Clay looked in big trouble. Between rounds, the TV cameras honed in on the champ. He didn't look angry, tired or frustrated; he looked perplexed and preoccupied.

The fourth was even, but for the fifth, Clay, dealing with some kind of eye problem, was battered by Liston and it looked as if there was no way the challenger could win. In the sixth, however, Liston hardly threw a punch and just plodded around doing very little, while Clay seemed not to believe his luck.

At the start of the seventh, the unimaginable happened. Liston sat in his corner, looked around rather sheepishly and refused to rise, complaining of numbness in his left arm. This was the man who had previously fought seven rounds with a badly broken jaw. This was the man who had almost killed opponents. This was daft. Liston had previously shown no sign of an injured arm.

Clay was ecstatic. Unfortunately, the endearing image one has of the fight is of the loudmouth Clay rushing to the microphone to scream praise for himself.

In boxing, the victor is never aware of the fix and we'll probably never know for sure what really happened that night. Significantly, however, if one places a bet for a fighter to win and he does, you take home a lot of dosh – but if you can specify a round, as Carbo had tried to do with the Sugar Ray Robinson versus Al Nettlow fixture, you win a damn sight more. They had obviously picked round seven.

The hoo-ha that surrounded the event was huge. Some doctors verified Sonny's claim of an injured arm. Others could find no such evidence. The Miami Beach Boxing Commission seized Liston's

$720,000 purse, but afterwards Dr Alexander Robbins – the commission's official physician – said that he had no doubt that Liston, who claimed he hurt his arm when he missed a left hook in the first round, was injured.

Dan Parker of the *New York Journal-American* wrote, 'If he dislocated his shoulder in the first round, he didn't seem to be handicapped in throwing left hooks in the ensuing five rounds.'

There was an inquiry into Liston's holdings. Liston's brother was said to have stated that when he asked his sibling what happened, he replied, 'I did what they told me to do.' Liston's bodyguard, Lowell Powell, who had lost a substantial amount of cash by betting on Sonny, asked him why he didn't tell him that he knew he was going to lose. 'With your big mouth, we'd both be wearing concrete boots,' replied Liston.

All around the country, large sums of cash went out from bookmakers to mobsters in the know. The odds had been kind, and the returns kinder.

In the meantime, the clownish Clay had turned to Islam, adopting a racially separatist philosophy, saying with reference to mixed marriages that, 'In the jungle, lions are with lions and tigers are with tigers, and redbirds stay with redbirds and bluebirds with bluebirds. That's human nature too, to be with your own kind.'

The rematch was planned, but few were prepared to stage such a circus. The country knew the last fight had been fixed and no one wanted a repeat.

Except the powers that be.

The rematch was rescheduled for 25 May 1965, but Massachusetts, which previously endorsed the bout, now refused to comply because everyone knew that the promoters were tied to organised crime. Said promoters couldn't find a new location. Cleveland wanted nothing to do with it and neither did Chicago or Philadelphia. Finally, the fight took place in Lewiston, Maine, at St Dominic's Hall before a crowd of 2,412 – the smallest audience ever for a world heavyweight championship bout.

The reservations were well founded. This fight was more than a farce, it was a one-round pantomime. Liston had all the action but his punches were mere pokes, lacking any power or conviction. Meanwhile Ali just bounced around, hitting Liston with a short ineffectual blow towards the end of the round – a punch not intended to damage, but to parry. Nevertheless, Liston went down.

After a few seconds he attempted to rise and, in a terrible display of play-acting that would have rivalled Johnny Depp, rolled over like a kitten waiting for its belly to be rubbed. He then got up and allowed Clay to hit him a few times, offering no defence, before the fight was stopped.

This was a man who had previously been knocked down only once – and yet here he was, going down like a two-dollar hooker. It was without doubt the most unconvincing KO in boxing history.

The crowd booed and shouted, 'fake, fake, fake', over and over again. No one noticed the winning punch, apart from Ali, who called it his 'anchor' punch. To the rest of the world it became known as the 'phantom punch,' in that it hardly existed. It was a wave, and an ineffectual one at that. I have watched the bout some twenty times or more and how anyone could not see that the fix was on is beyond me. *Sports Illustrated* writer Mark Kram said that years later Liston told him, 'That guy [Ali] was crazy. I didn't want anything to do with him. And the Muslims were coming up. Who needed that? So I went down. I wasn't hit.'

In the years that have followed, even though the FBI strongly suspected that Irving 'Ash' Resnick – Las Vegas gambler and confidante of both Joe Louis and Liston, also a mob associate and alleged friend of Meyer Lansky, Genovese crime family member Vincent Alo ('Jimmy Blue Eyes') and Charles 'the Blade' Tourine – was behind the fix, almost everyone has forgotten this monumental charade, particularly Ali.

Liston's life more or less ended that night. He continued to box for a few years, his power still undiminished. Between March 1968 and September 1969 he fought twelve bouts, losing only one. His last fight, at the Jersey City Armoury, took place on 29 June 1970. His opponent, Chuck Wepner, thirty-one, said, 'After the fifth round I was target practice... my one eye closed, my equilibrium was off. Broken nose, broken left cheekbone, seventy-two stitches.'

The fight was stopped in the ninth round by which time Wepner was a bloody mess.

This was some five years after the Clay match. Wepner, on whom Sylvester Stallone's creation Rocky Balboa was based, went on to fight Ali for the world title a few years later and knocked him down in the ninth, only to lose in the fifteenth after the ref declared a technical knockout after Ali broke Wepner's nose.

Liston eventually moved to Las Vegas. He appeared in a number of films and adverts, most notably a Braniff Airways commercial with the artist Andy Warhol. He hung out with his hero Joe Louis and slipped into drug dealing, heavy gambling and heavier drinking.

On 5 January 1971, Liston's wife Geraldine found him dead in his apartment. The circumstances were more than suspicious, the anomalies many. His body was found sat on a bench at the bottom of his bed. A quarter ounce of heroin was found in the kitchen, as was a bag of reefer. There was a glass of vodka on a table, a .38 calibre revolver (holstered), a stuffed snake, some small change and a wooden cross. A newspaper was found next to the body, yet Liston could not read. There were signs of possible needle marks on his arm. But as Liston's wife emphatically stated, he had refused medical care for illness and cancelled a trip to Europe that involved shots because he was pathologically scared of needles.

Even so, the Vegas police decided on a heroin overdose as the cause of death. An autopsy later revealed traces of morphine in his blood that would normally be the result of a breakdown of heroin in the body, but, as his body had sat there decomposing for six days, tests were questionable. Liston was known as a heavy drinker but not a drug user, which prompted many to believe that he had been killed.

One reason might have been that Sonny had reputedly been ordered by Wepner's mob 'handlers' to throw the fight so that they might pick up a big chunk of readies at the bookmakers. Maybe Liston had simply had enough of throwing fights.

His demise was eventually attributed to 'probable myocardial anoxia due to coronary insufficiency', i.e. lung congestion and heart failure. But Liston, having fought his last bout less than seven months before, was a fit forty-three-year-old man – perhaps younger.

Liston's demise was so inconclusive, the anomalies surrounding his death so uncertain, and the results so open to doubt, that a professional hit was suspected by all. And yet detractors have dismissed the assassination theory with the question, 'Why did the mob wait six months after the Wepner fight to kill Liston?'

They appear to be forgetting one of the most oft repeated and most apt Sicilian sayings of all: 'Revenge is a dish best served cold.'

And Liston always had to pay the man.

In 2014, a year or so after I filed this article, and fifty years on from the controversial second bout versus Ali, four-decade-old documents released to the Washington Times *under the Freedom of Information Act revealed that the FBI's long-time suspicion that the fight was a mafia fix was entirely founded. The reports also revealed that according to Vegas insiders and Houston gambler Barnett Magid, Resnick and Liston made over $1 million betting against Liston. The documents show no indication that Ali was in on the conspiracy.*

Rod Steiger

For any self-respecting cinephile, Rod Steiger needs little introduction. He is regarded by many to be, as Hollywood columnist Louella Parsons said, 'The screen's Number One Bad Man,' and by others, such as Pauline Kael, legendary film critic for the *New Yorker*, 'A genius.'

Steiger was not only one of the few remaining original students of the infamous Actors Studio of New York, he was also one of the world's most underrated and powerful actors. This is the man who gave us the most memorable screen version of Al Capone (the basis for De Niro's characterisation in *The Untouchables*).

This is also the man to whom Brando mumbled those immortal words, 'I coulda been a contender' in *On the Waterfront*. This is the star of *Waterloo, No Way to Treat a Lady, The Illustrated Man, Run of the Arrow, The Pawnbroker* and *In the Heat of the Night,* to name a few. He worked with every great actor and director since the 1950s.

The chance to talk at length with a 'legend' (a term I do not use lightly) is extremely rare, and an opportunity I seized with both hands after looking out the window of my Soho studio one day. Not realising who I was looking at, I remarked to a colleague, 'that bloke in the street looks great. Look at him – bald head, *Easy Rider* sunglasses, polo neck and that great big medallion!'

I continued to watch the elderly gentleman as he talked to a bearded friend. They appeared to be shooting the breeze, enjoying a rare warm afternoon in London. Then it clicked. 'My God!' I said. 'That's Stanley Kubrick... and the bald bloke is Rod Steiger!'

I hurtled down the stairs and into the street and rudely interrupted what had previously been a rather gentle conversation.

'Mr Steiger, could I interview you?' I stuttered nervously. Steiger looked at his companion and smiled before turning to me. 'An interview? What, for a magazine?' I nodded, and he continued, 'Oh sure, you got a card?' I gave him my card and retreated to the comfort of my studio. It was then that I caught my reflection in the studio mirror. My T-shirt, a present from a rather acerbic Welshman, displayed the words, 'No Change, Fuck Off' (his answer to the countless street beggars who, in his opinion, make his life hell).

Add to this my gravity-defying hair and the intriguing mix of acrylic paint splashed around my mouth and I resembled some kind of paint-eating mental patient.

'*C'est la vie,*' I muttered quietly to myself, and got on with the job of creating a masterpiece. Later that day, my assistant at the magazine I worked on (*GQ*) phoned me to say she had received a call from a Mr Steiger, and could I call him back.

*

Born in Long Island on 14 April 1925, Steiger was the only child of Fred and Lorraine, itinerant song and dance artistes who divorced shortly after Rod's birth, leaving the actor with just a vague memory of his father. His mother was, by his own admission, an alcoholic who hit the bottle hard during the Depression of the 1930s, leaving Steiger, for the most part, to fend for himself.

After a more than difficult childhood, and filled with indignation after the Japanese attack on Pearl Harbour, he decided to enlist in the navy. After weeks searching the flophouses of New York's Bowery, Steiger found his mother fully ensconced in one of the area's insalubrious hostelries. Too young to enlist, he had to frog-march his mother to the recruitment office and literally twist her arm to get her to sign the all-important form that stated he was old enough to go to war. He was just sixteen.

'I loved the navy,' Steiger later remarked. 'I was stupid enough to think I was being heroic.' In spite of his age, Steiger garnered enough experience during the war to leave the navy with the desire to do something that *he* really wanted to do.

Chris Sullivan: Do you think the war helped your acting?

Rod Steiger: Well, yes, I have young actors who come to me for advice and I say, 'Do you want or need to be an actor?' and I can tell by the pause whether they should or not. They answer, 'Yeah, I want to be.' But who the hell wouldn't want to be Picasso. To need it means you *have* to fulfil something in your soul that feels empty. Some people paint, others have financial success in business, and you *have* to act because it makes you feel complete, otherwise you should stay the hell out because it's a rotten business. Then I ask them how old they are. They say nineteen, or twenty, maybe, and my answer is that to help them as an actor they should spend a year in the Merchant Marine.

I didn't want to be an actor initially. By the time I was nineteen I had been around the world three times experiencing different cultures, people and languages. My ship had 283 different men. My southern accent that I used for the part of Gillespie, the redneck lawman in *In the Heat of the Night* [for which Steiger received the Academy award for best actor], comes from a guy called King. And by osmosis I realised I'd had one of the best educations for an actor, because I'd seen so many different people doing different things, talking with different accents, with different mannerisms.

CS: Did the war help your characterisation of murderers, such as in *No Way to Treat a Lady?*

RS: When I was at Guadalcanal, we took some marines off – those men were glassy eyed. I realised that they had killed their first human beings. Everything in their life, religion, society, parents, had conditioned them not to kill. They were shocked that they had killed. To see this at first hand was shocking, but it was eventually useful for me as an actor even though it was a very difficult experience. That look in the eye was unforgettable.

After the war Steiger found himself living in a $5 room on West 81st Street, New York, where the GI Bill of Rights entitled him to four years of schooling plus an income of $100 a month. The news that a certain drama group, as organised by the Office of Dependants and Beneficiaries, entertained and educated pretty young women attracted the young Steiger to the class and he was soon starring in the productions. He continued to study his craft at the New School for Social Research, run by German émigré Erwin Piscator, for some two years. Walter Matthau, another student at the time, dubbed the institution the Neurotic School for Sexual Research. As for Steiger, amazed and amused by his reception as an actor, he merely went from strength to strength.

It was around this time that Daniel Mann, one of Rod's teachers, was asked to help a nascent theatrical institution founded by Elia Kazan, Cheryl Crawford and Robert Lewis – the Actors Studio. It spawned the talents of Montgomery Clift, Paul Newman, James Dean, and more recently Al Pacino, Robert De Niro and Dustin Hoffman. Here each actor was taught, in the words of America's first adherent to the form, director Harold Clurman, to 'put the whole gamut of his physical and emotional being into the service of the dramatist's meaning'.

Set up in October 1947, the Studio caused a sensation in December of that year with its first Broadway production, *A Streetcar Named Desire*, starring Marlon Brando and directed by Kazan.

Soon the Actors Studio, aided and abetted by its new rising star, became *the* place to study. Robert Lewis left and was eventually replaced by Austrian-born Lee Strasberg (Hymen Roth in *The Godfather Part II*), and 'the method' entered the dictionary both as a means of preparation for, and style of, acting.

Many of the actors and teachers at the Studio preferred the term 'affective memory', which, as Strasberg explained, '...makes it possible for us to join in the great tradition of acting. When Kean in *Hamlet* picked up the skull of Yorick, he cried, because he said he always thought of his uncle.'

Whatever the rhetoric Strasberg used, many of the Studio's most able protagonists actually deride his style of tuition. Its most famous son, Marlon Brando, cites another tutor, Stella Adler, as changing the style of American acting in the 1950s and 1960s. Strasberg, the man whose name is synonymous with the form, is seen by many as being something of a bully, whose students, in the words of Elia Kazan, see 'little joy in Lee's work'.

Just as recent commentators have sadly overlooked Adler's input, so has the artistry of many of the Actors Studio's more notable talents. Steiger, Karl Malden and Eli Wallach were all destined to be character actors by virtue of their physical appearance, but to the true movie-lover they are the core of every film they appear in. It is they, and not the stars, that make the picture worth watching.

In terms of stardom, rather than artistic accomplishment, Steiger never reached the heights of his contemporaries Montgomery Clift, Brando and James Dean. Many consider him a far more accomplished actor than the aforementioned 'stars', but his size, shape and looks were not the stuff of pin-up. More importantly, Steiger was always his own man – a massive handicap in the Hollywood studio system of the 1950s.

*

CS: 'The method' school of acting technique, *per se*, is a much-maligned form. You have said you don't use it anymore. What is your opinion of it?

RS: I don't like the term method, but for the sake of argument method acting is a means to an end. It is something that helps you get involved in the part personally so that you can communicate with the audience. No matter what, the American actor of the 1950s changed acting the world over. Montgomery Clift was perhaps the actor who started it, Brando caused the sensation and Dean made it a cult.

CS: Did you meet James Dean?

RS: Jimmy was never a great friend of mine, but I knew him pretty well. I liked him and he respected me. I remember when he was making *Giant* with the director George Stevens. He called and asked if we could meet at the commissary at Warner Brothers. He ordered a steak and started to tell me how he thought Stevens didn't know what he was doing.

'Whatever you do, don't argue with the man in front of people. They depend on him for their livelihood,' I told him. 'You don't do that to big egos – don't do that to anyone.' Then I suggested that he should say to Stevens, 'You gave me this idea,' and then ask him, 'How was that? What do you think?' Nine times out of ten it will work and he will be happy to accept the credit. He'll be happy and you get to do it your way. But don't forget, too much discussion can be the death of art.

Meanwhile, Jimmy had eaten about three-quarters of his steak, but he suddenly tells the poor waitress that he doesn't like it. She pointed out that he had almost eaten it all, and he shouts, 'Look, this is Hollywood baby! Take it back!' Here was a nice kid absorbed by his own ego, so much so that it was destroying him. I think he killed himself in that car crash. Shortly before his death he gave me his most prized possession, Ernest Hemingway's book *Death in the Afternoon*, and every mention of death was underlined. The man had a death wish!

Jimmy was surrounded by all these people whom I refer to as not gay, but grey people. An actor is always open to all kinds of feelings and these people indulged in all kinds of weird sexual practices, and he was sucked into that world. He died far too young, but became a legend, and maybe that is what he wanted. At least he avoided the awful flagellatory death of Montgomery Clift. That was terrible.

CS: Did you ever meet Marilyn Monroe?

RS: I remember her as this shy, quiet, vulnerable girl who was already famous when she sat in at the back of the Actors Studio. Very beautiful and very sad. She wanted to know everything, but sometimes knowledge is a very dangerous thing.

CS: The Actors Studio and Kazan led you to the film *On the Waterfront*, for which you received an Oscar nomination. The film received eight Oscars: Brando – best actor; Eva Marie Saint – best actress; best film and best director for Kazan. Were you not disappointed that you did not receive an award?

RS: I wasn't that upset because many more people in the film were nominated. This was my first big part. I'd worked with Brando, been nominated for an Oscar and it was a great picture. What more did I want? That was only my second film and it saved a hell of a lot of time walking around looking for a job.

I did get an Oscar for *In the Heat of the Night*, though. I was incapacitated for about eight years with clinical depression and I walk in to see this new vice president at one of the studios. He says, 'Hello, so nice to see you – can you do a southern accent?' And I say, 'I won an Academy Award with a southern accent!'

It doesn't bother me that he hadn't seen the picture, but he should have been aware of that, at least. Ironically, my career was saved by my old films being shown on TV. Otherwise Hollywood would have ignored me.

CS: You are remembered by many, as is Brando, for the scene in the back of the taxicab in *On the Waterfront*.

RS: Well, yeah, that was my big scene. We shot it in a studio, which was about the width of a rich lady's closet. We got there and they had half a taxicab and a guy sat driving it. You never saw the front .You saw the driver, the wheel, Brando and myself. I was a nervous wreck because I was playing Brando's brother and he was one of the gods of the American theatre and the acting world.

Then Sam Spiegel, the producer, walks in and Elia Kazan starts shouting at him, 'You son of a gun. You promised me a backdrop so that when we shoot we see the two actors in the cab through the window and in the back we see the streets of New York. I can't shoot this damned thing unless there's a backdrop.'

So Spiegel says, 'Gadge [Kazan's nickname], you shouldn't get so excited. I can't shoot the scene.' Then one of the crew said, 'You know Mr Kazan, when I came to work this morning there was a venetian blind in the back of the window of the cab.'

So they got the blind, but the studio was so small you could reach out from the inside of the cab and touch the wall so they couldn't shoot from outside the cab over our shoulders. As a result, Kazan was forced to go in on the actors' faces in close-up. This made it even more difficult for us, but it added a special tension that Kazan was very keen to see. As he said, 'Two young bulls locking horns.' Mr Brando and myself.

When it came to Brando's close-ups, I stood off screen so that he would have somebody to react against. Acting is all about action and reaction, so to have the actor your working with off stage really does help. Only when it came to my close-ups, Marlon went home. I couldn't believe that a great director like Kazan would let him go home, and I couldn't believe that Brando would *want* to go home. It was my big scene and I had to deliver my lines to Kazan, who stepped in to make me feel a little better. Later, Kazan said Brando had to go see his psychiatrist, but at the time he said he was tired.

I didn't speak to Marlon for forty years, until I was accepting an award in Montreal in 1997 and he was in town. He was invited, but didn't go. After the ceremony we went to a Chinese restaurant and there was Marlon, this great three hundred-pound man. He waved and tried to get up, but with his weight... man. So I walked over, we shook hands, embraced and rubbed our bald heads together. It was very emotional. Marlon has had so many problems with his son and his daughter... a terrible time. As we parted, I said, 'This is terrible.' And he said, 'What is?' I said, 'That we'll never be able to say nasty things about each other after a reconciliation like this!' The man has had a tough time.

In the late 1940s and early 1950s, Senator McCarthy and the House Un-American Activities Committee all but paralysed Hollywood. To make matters worse, the Senate ruled in 1948 that studios could no longer own cinemas. This brought an end to the dominance of the system that the studios had always enjoyed. Actors, producers, and directors found themselves out of work for either or both of the aforementioned reasons. Many were blacklisted and never worked again.

The way out for many was television. Each week the new medium aired at least ten new plays showcasing the directing talents of Arthur Penn, Sidney Lumet and John Frankenheimer, to name just three. Actors included Paul Newman, George C. Scott, Jack Palance, Jack Lemmon, John Cassavetes, Lee Marvin, Rip Torn and Sidney Poitier. Steiger, in the period between 1948 and 1953, acted in more than 250 live TV plays, honing his art to virtual perfection. All was not wine and roses, however, as Steiger saw a lot of friends unjustly consumed by the communist witch-hunts, a devastating period in Hollywood where an actor only had to receive a letter from a relative in Russia to literally never work again.

CS: How many of your friends suffered as a result of McCarthyism?

RS: Well, I did. I was blacklisted, but not for long. I was saved because I could do characters, but friends of mine really suffered. That's why I always tangle with Charlton Heston. He wrote to the papers saying he was upset that Elia Kazan didn't get an award from the American Institute – this was before he received one last year. He said that he was appalled. Well, I wrote a letter to the *LA Times* to say that I too was appalled that friends of mine, great talents who were innocent, died of heart attacks because of stress. I'm appalled because of Senator McCarthy. I'm appalled that these friends of mine only wanted to put food on the table. I'm appalled because Senator Joseph McCarthy went for the presidency on the wings of terror, and I'm appalled that Elia Kazan, who used to put Hollywood down, sold his friends out in Washington just to do movies – and at the same time was a millionaire from the theatre. I don't think Charlton Heston likes me. Did you know that Heston said that the second amendment, the right to bear arms, was more important than the first – the freedom of speech? He said that in public. I call him America's favourite fascist.

CS: What about Lee J. Cobb?

RS: A great actor and a great talent, but he went to the wall and ratted on many of his colleagues.

Between 1950 and 1990, Steiger made an abundance of pictures – some fifty-two in total, including *Al Capone*, *The Harder They Fall* (Humphrey Bogart's last film), *The Longest Day*, *The Pawnbroker*, for which he received yet another Academy Award nomination, *Doctor Zhivago*, *Waterloo*, *No Way to Treat a Lady* and *The Illustrated Man*. He has become a household name purely because of his abilities as an actor – a position that many aspire to, but few achieve.

CS: You've worked with some of the world's greatest directors – Zanuck, Preminger, Lumet, David Lean – and, of course, many of the world's greatest actors. Is there anybody you wished you had worked with?

RS: I like to work with people who will allow you to make mistakes. I seem to have a gift for improvisation. I believe that an actor should be able to change everything in a line, except the thought and the cue for the other actors. I don't like to do more than three takes.

CS: What about Darryl Zanuck [producer of *All About Eve* and *Gone with the Wind*]?

RS: That was a surprise. I did *The Longest Day*, a small cameo. Like everybody, I went because it was my first visit to Paris. I would have been the Bride of Frankenstein just to go. Zanuck had a reputation for being tough, but if they respect you they're quite the opposite. Zanuck was so professional and quick with us, people couldn't believe he was done. I scratched my forehead, so he says 'What was that? Do it again for a close up!' I said, 'You want a close up of that? I had an itchy forehead!' These people! Though if someone did not perform or was difficult – God help them.

CS: Tell me how did you get the flies to stay on your face for so long in *The Illustrated Man*?

RS: Jeez, that's another story. That was the greatest acting I have ever done. They mixed sugar and beer and sprayed my face with it, and literally let thousands of flies loose and they just came and came. I had one crawling over my eyelid and I didn't move. I should've known they'd be alcoholics. They just came and came. There's a drunken fly, sir. That movie and *No Way to Treat a Lady* are now really big cult movies on American TV. A lot of young actors ask me, how do I become a TV star? I say, 'Grow another two legs and a tail and call yourself Lassie.' [The telephone rings]. It's my fans. I only have two.

CS: What did you think of Orson Welles?

RS: The man was misunderstood by the commercial world because of his imagination and independence. Hollywood does not understand the words independence or imagination. They use the word difficult as a substitute. In my first Hollywood picture I had come out of this horrendous storm and this bloke came up to me and sprayed my face with this little atomiser. I asked him what it was and he answers, 'You're coming out of a storm, you're getting wet.'

So I go to a bucket full of water and pour it over my head and walk on. 'You see,' he says to his boss to protect himself, 'he's difficult.'

Anybody in Hollywood who they say is difficult has been fighting their ass off to preserve logic. My whole attitude is that when you come out of the rain, you're wet. It's not my opinion, yours, his – you're wet. It's a fact .We could talk for hours about interpretation, so let's stop the bullshit here. Anywhere in the film world there's bullshit. Wet is wet, but in Hollywood, wet is difficult.

CS: Many of your films were independently produced. Are you glad independently produced films are coming back in force?

RS: Well they never went away. *The Pawnbroker*, directed by Sidney Lumet, was an independent, so was *The Sergeant*. They're just coming back stronger because the greed finally ran into a wall, and what proved it was all these small independent films getting nominations and winning awards where all these multi-million dollar films did nothing, and that really shook them up. I would always say the bigger the budget, the less imagination. In the old days, they had designers who, if they had to create a battleship, would get a bit of net and a bit of board and make one. Now there is no imagination. If they want a destroyer now, they ring up the government and get a real one. There aren't any challenges anymore; they're home decorators.

CS: Necessity is the mother of invention.

RS: It is also the basis of progress.

The photographer arrives.

CS: You played W. C. Fields and seem to have a certain affinity with him. Is this the character you most identify with?

RS: No, but my wife said it's the one closest to me – a bitter son of a bitch. Thanks a lot!

Tony McGee [the photographer]: Mr Steiger, we're ready when you are.

We all move to the other side of the room. As Tony begins, the conversation continues.

CS: That's a great medallion. I saw it from four floors up. [The medallion is a big solid circular chunk of gold featuring a figurine of a little boy]

RS: I know, you've told me four times already. My wife gave me this. It features my three greatest achievements: my daughter, my son and my Oscar – and at the bottom is the *Petit Prince*, one of the few people I trust. It's a character from a book by Antoine de Saint-Exupéry.

CS: Your biography recently came out…

RS: I did the book with an old friend called Tom Hutchinson. He was going to call it *Steiger – Superstar Survivor*. That's what I am – three bypasses, two artificial hips. He calls it *Memoirs of a Friendship* because I've known him for forty years.

Tony McGee: Mr Steiger, could we get something serious?

RS: You want me to unzip my flies?

CS: You seem very busy at the moment?

RS: Yeah, I've got five films coming out. I want to die in front of the camera. I have very little fear of death, but the word 'linger' scares the shit out of me. I don't want to be one of those people with pipes up their nose and all that… Jesus!

We continue to talk about courtroom TV, life and the pursuit of happiness, trade a few jokes, take the piss and laugh.

RS: We finished?

CS: Yes.

RS: Well get outta here!

CS: One last thing, Mr Steiger...

RS: Hey, come on...

CS: Could I have your autograph?

He signed the bit of paper with the words: 'To Chris, Up the Welsh, Up the Rebs, Rod Steiger' – an amazingly intuitive couplet to give a Catholic Welshman with an Irish name, but then again Rod Steiger was very special man. He was unique. So many of the people one looks up to in life are actually a disappointment in the flesh. Mr Steiger was anything but. I still feel immensely privileged to have had the luxury to talk to him for a few hours.

Anita Pallenberg

'I seem to have managed to have been quite hip for many years,' says Anita Pallenberg, sitting in her beautiful wood-panelled apartment overlooking the Chelsea embankment. This is something of an understatement. Pallenberg seems to have been at the fulcrum of all that was happening since birth.

Born in Rome during the midst of the Second World War, just as the Americans were attempting to liberate Italy, she bore witness to the widespread devastation it had caused on post-war trips to the Austrian mountains with her mother.

She vacillated between Germany and Italy, attended art college in Munich, and was eventually drawn back to Rome in the early 1960s, aged nineteen.

'I was lucky to be in Rome just as *La Dolce Vita* and all that was happening. I met [Federico] Fellini, Alberto Moravia, [Luchino] Visconti, [Pier Paolo] Pasolini and all those guys,' she says, still obviously impressed by her good fortune.

'I had a boyfriend, Mario Schifano, an Italian artist and filmmaker. We left Rome for New York in 1963 just to check out all the Pop artists. I met [Andy] Warhol, Jasper Johns, and Robert Rauschenberg and hung out with Allen Ginsberg, Gregory Corso, [William] Burroughs and Terry Southern, the *Easy Rider* screenwriter who also wrote *Barbarella* and *Candy*, which I was in. We'd go to jazz clubs in the Village and hang out. This was way before I met the Stones.'

It wasn't long before Anita's looks attracted the attention of the fashion glitterati and soon she was modelling for both *Harpers & Queen* and *Vogue*.

'I was a model in New York, and then went to Paris modelling, which I didn't like very much. In fact, I hated it. I then tested for *A Degree of Murder* for Volker Schlöndorff, the director of *The Tin Drum*, and he needed a German-speaking girl in Paris and I got the part.

'When I stayed at his flat I had a big crash course in cinema. Through him I met Luis Buñuel, who we visited on set, Louis Malle, [François] Truffaut, all those guys. It was a bit like Bertolucci's *The*

Dreamers – watching movies in the Cinémathèque, going out dancing.

'I learned all the new dances in New York, so I just used to get in free to all the clubs. Even though I was in the middle of the French New Wave, as it were, I was getting into rock 'n' roll. I used to go see the Who, Vince Taylor, all those guys, then drive off to Saint-Tropez when it was almost a village. It was great to have done all those things before they became popular.'

It was in Paris that Pallenberg embarked on a *ménage à trois* with Donald Cammell and girlfriend Deborah. It was Cammell who would later direct *Performance* in partnership with eminent cinematographer Nicolas Roeg.

'I met Donald and his girlfriend Deborah in Paris. He had all these movie scenarios, always about rock stars, and I must say he was completely star-struck. He then worked on a rock star movie called *Privilege* with Jean Shrimpton and Paul Jones of Manfred Mann. I then met him on the beach in Saint-Tropez when he was writing *Performance* and all the papers blew into the water. I had to retrieve them and iron them; that was my greatest contribution to the script.'

By this time Pallenberg had begun her long and notorious relationship with the Rolling Stones and Cammell was awestruck. When Anita finally moved into Brian Jones's apartment in South Kensington, Cammell was a frequent visitor. 'He was part of the scene, but was much too hyper for us with all his ideas and constant film scenarios – we were much more chilled out, getting stoned and hanging out.'

Cammell's father had been heir to a massive shipping empire and had written books on Byron, Dante, Gabriel Rossetti and Aleister Crowley.

'It was said that he sat on Crowley's knee,' says Pallenberg. 'He was really well read and was into all his father had been into and more. He was good-looking, into fashion, dressed in hats and scarves with tight pants and all that. He was very talkative, very speedy. He chatted up every girl he saw and was into every sexual thing you could imagine.'

London in the aptly monikered Swinging Sixties was a melting pot for all manner of sexual shenanigans. 'There was a thing at the time where rock stars were mixing with these English intellectuals, and some befriended them and others didn't. Keith [Richards] was sneering from the start – while Donald blabbered in his face for hours, Keith would just sneer. They'd get cracked heads sometimes.'

It is this cross-pollination that provides the basis for *Performance*, a truly seminal picture that is without doubt one of the greatest cult movies of all time. It stars James Fox as Chas, a gangland hitman who, having killed the wrong man, has to hide out in the Powis Square townhouse of faded rock star Turner (Mick Jagger), who lives with paramours Michèle Breton and, of course, Pallenberg.

The movie not only proffers an unabridged version of bohemian London, but also accurately depicts the 1960s London underworld. 'James Fox did a lot of work for the role, hanging out with real gangsters,' says Pallenberg. 'He was introduced to all them, went to their tailors and all the places they hung out. David Litvinoff, who was friends with Ronnie Kray, was a consultant on the movie and took [Fox] around. It was strange to see James Fox, a real posh guy, playing a working-class gangster, and Jagger playing a posh guy when he was sort of common.'

The shoot is rumoured to have left the cast in mental disarray. Fox left acting and spent the next seven years applying himself to Christian vocational work, Michèle Breton never acted again, while Roeg dissociated himself from the movie.

'I am sure people were traumatised as Donald was so good at pushing people to the edge, winding people up and stuff,' says Pallenberg. 'We didn't have trailers like they have today. We were all huddled in a small basement together waiting for our scenes. Nic Roeg would spend like seven hours lighting one shot – and we'd sit and wait all day listening to Dr John and get stoned.

'When we eventually did the scenes, sometimes we would do it like twenty-eight times. It was all very messy. Sometimes I'd have to ask whether I'd done my lines as I was so stoned I couldn't remember. Meanwhile Donald would run around screaming and shouting, trying to put all of these mad, deviant, sexy scenarios into the movie.'

Pallenberg denies, also, that the movie drove Fox into vocational work. 'I saw him after and he said that he was already having these Christian vocational ideas when he did [the 1968 film] *Isadora*. He had already had a breakdown on that and was looking for a way out.

'As for Michèle Breton never acting again, she was never an actress anyway. She thought Mick and I were plotting against her. I don't know what happened afterwards – she just disappeared. The myth is so much better than the truth. But it was not a harmonious shoot at all, it was horrendous and that was what Donald wanted – chaos and paranoia. Donald used my character to wind people up to make them feel ill at ease and that was what I was doing. It was a nightmare.'

But Pallenberg was under an altogether different pressure.

'At night I would go back to Robert Fraser's, the big art dealer's, apartment that I had rented, but he hadn't moved out and he and Keith, who didn't like Donald, would be slagging off the movie, saying things like, "What are you doing with Donald, that fairy?" On and on. And the next morning I got up at six and started again. Keith, even when I was doing *Barbarella*, hated it. He'd ask how much was I getting paid and when I answered twenty-thousand pounds he said he would give me that so I wouldn't do it.'

Keith Richards might well have had reason to be dismissive as Pallenberg, his significant other, had been in a much-publicised relationship with Brian Jones and was now doing raging sex scenes with Mick Jagger.

'But Mick was not the guy for me. I'd seen how he treated his women. I spent a week in bed with him and Michèle and there was a camera under the sheets. It was almost like shooting a porn film. There was all kinds of sex going on, but I put it down to method acting.'

On its release the movie stoked the fires of tabloid hell, with Richards and Pallenberg the object of their scorn, but Pallenberg was gloriously oblivious.

'It was bad for my family but I never really saw it. I never read the papers and still don't. That's my advice to anybody. The whole police thing was happening before the film was released. After the *Performance* shoot ended, Keith, Marianne Faithfull, Mick and I went off to South America for three months and missed it all.

'Keith and I patched up what we had to patch up and then we came back and had Marlon, which was planned. I was getting near to thirty and wanted a baby. I made a conscious decision and did not want to let Keith down as we had such a good relationship and I loved him dearly. And it was so much more exciting than life with Mick. Everybody was always on about how I was a Stones climber because I went through Brian Jones, was with Keith Richards and wanted to end up with Mick Jagger, but that was not my intention at all. Mick was not my type.'

Oblivious or not, Pallenberg was still part of a movie that defined an era like no other in British cinematic history. 'I didn't see it at first,' she says. 'But now I do.'

After *Performance*, Pallenberg did a few movies: *Dillinger Is Dead* in 1969 with Marco Ferreri, director of *La Grande Bouffe*, *Umano Non Umano* in 1972 and in 1976 she starred with the Velvet Underground's Nico in *Le Berceau de Cristal*, directed by Philippe Garrel. A long cinematic hiatus followed.

'I got too busty and too stoned,' she explains. 'If I had been like Sophia Loren I would have had some respect, but I never slept with any of the directors, actors or producers, was really mistreated, and it was really hard. So I said "enough".

'So we then moved to the South of France when Marlon was about two,' says Pallenberg. 'Keith rented this big villa called Nellcôte near Nice. It was the old Gestapo headquarters and had swastikas on the radiators and a leaky roof. Keith took a mobile studio and they recorded *Exile on Main Street,* and we had all kinds of people popping by and staying for a few days or weeks. It was pretty crazy at times.

'I'll leave you to work out how – some things are best left unsaid – but visitors would often come with all kind of drugs. Sometimes we'd have lunch for twenty people, which carried on through the night. Keith was always a great host. Gram Parsons turned up and he and Keith became firm friends. Stash Klossowski [son of painter Balthus], Terry Southern, Bobby Keys, and the sax player… I lost count of the people that came and went.'

But soon things began to turn sour. Several guitars were stolen in a burglary, producer Jimmy Miller joined in with the musicians' heavy heroin abuse and, to top it all off, there was yet another drugs bust. As a direct consequence, the Stones made a rapid departure to America in October.

'We moved to South Salem, New York, for a while, and then had our daughter, Angela. And all was very nice for a while, but we had our tough times. The hardest time for us was after Keith's big Canadian bust in 1977. He got arrested with twenty-two grams of heroin and five grams of cocaine. As a result, I was a guinea pig for all kinds of drug rehabilitation programmes. Three years' probation. Drug urine tests every ten days. It was hell. I lost ten years of my life. It was enough to test any couple. Eventually it was the lawyers who forced us to split. They said I was a bad influence.'

Having retreated to a big rambling house in Westchester, New York, her main mission was now to ensure that Marlon attended school. 'I lived in Long Island and Westchester for about nine years. I was there alone with Marlon and Keith's father, who lived with us in America as well. I had some boyfriends, but nothing serious. I didn't send Marlon to school until he was eight years old. I taught him how to read and write and he was my constant companion and best friend.'

When he did go to school, Pallenberg hit the bottle hard, putting on more and more weight until she hit thirteen stone. Then disaster struck in 1979, when a seventeen-year-old boy shot himself with her gun in her bedroom. She was charged but cleared of manslaughter. In 1987 she went to rehab and, with the exception of a magic mushroom relapse, hasn't touched a drink or drugs since.

'I was a very bad alcoholic and it took me twenty years to come out of it. I was disgusting, aggressive, a very hard drinker. I was morose, not a happy drunk. But I wanted to live. I took care of myself. I went to AA meetings and all that.'

Since then she has studied fashion at St Martins, appeared in films directed by Harmony Korine and Abel Ferrara, and now spends most of her time either at Keith Richards's Jamaican house in the winter, attending to her Chiswick allotment in the summer, or staying with her son Marlon and his family in West Sussex.

'I guess I am what you'd call an old lady now,' she says her eyes still sparkling with mischief. 'And I'm happy with that. Today Keith and I are grandparents, but I don't see him as often as I'd like to as he's always abroad. Amazingly, against all the odds, we are both still here. Now I'm over seventy, and to be honest I didn't think I would live past forty.'

Anita passed away on 13 June 2017, aged seventy-five, due to complications from hepatitis C. I was privileged to have her as a friend, mainly through my friendship with her son Marlon, as she didn't accept any bullshit, was not at all impressed by fame or celebrity, and neither am I. I recall sitting with her at some A-list party looking at some latter-day pop star swanning about giving it the biggest one. 'What an asshole,' she whispered. 'All he's done is release a few appalling records that a load of idiots have bought. I'd have respect for him if he was a doctor or a great writer, but pop star! Come on!'

Anita was one rather marvellous person.

James Brown

There is only one artist whose tunes have kept millions of folk grooving on dance floors from Margate to Manila, Ruislip to Rio, for fifty years and counting, and he is James Brown, a man whose many epithets included Soul Brother Number One, Minister of the New New Super Heavy Funk, Mr Dynamite, the Hardest Working Man in Show Business, and, most famously, the Godfather of Soul.

'I was marked by different names,' explained Brown in his autobiography, *James Brown: The Godfather of Soul*. 'And each one has a different story behind it.'

Brown delivered multiple hits from the late fifties right up until the late eighties, thus it's safe to say that almost everyone has danced to the man's inimitable grooves at some point in their lives – even if they don't know it. Of late, hep cat re-editors such as A.Skillz and the Reflex have beefed up classic Brown tracks such as 'I Got You (I Feel Good)', recorded in 1965, while in 2011 Pharrell Williams laced Kanye West and Jay-Z's 'Gotta Have It' with Brown's 'My Thang' from 1974.

Indeed, Brown's polyrhythmic funk vamps totally restructured dance music while his impact on hip-hop was enormous. To date he has been sampled over 4,500 times by the likes of Biz Markie, Eric B. & Rakim and Public Enemy, while the man's 'Funky Drummer' of 1970 is the most sampled record of all time, its unimpeachable groove having been sampled some 929 times by, among others, Dr Dre and Nas. Add to this to the 50 million records he sold in his career and I'd contest that he is *the* most influential single recording artist of all time.

Millions aped his every nuance, and I was one of them. I first listened to Brown in 1971, when I was about eleven. My Mod uncle used to play the man's *Live at the Apollo, Volume II* over and over, and 'Cold Sweat' and 'Out of Sight' knocked me sideways. It was what made me beg my mother to buy me a record player.

Then in 1972 I heard 'Get Up (I Feel Like Being a) Sex Machine' at a school disco and was utterly smitten. It was a new sound to me, so different from the soul, reggae and glam rock prevalent at the time. I saved up and bought the single.

A few years later I was getting into northern soul, but always had a greater hankering for Brown and his funk, so in 1975, when I first hit the southern soul clubs, which routinely played 'Funky President' and 'Talkin' Loud', I ditched northern soul with its baggy trousers and vest uniform, and opted instead for funk and its pleated peg pants and Hawaiian shirts.

James Brown subsequently changed my life. Indeed, all through the 1970s he kept the hits coming – 'Get Up Offa That Thing' was a particular favourite. By 1979 I was DJ-ing and running my own clubs in London, such as Hell and Le Kilt, and played the Godfather of Soul more than anyone else. I started a band influenced by Brown and founded the Wag Club in Soho, where the self-described Soul Brother Number One was the most played artist bar none.

Then we started on the hip-hop that sampled Brown's work relentlessly – 'It Takes Two' by Rob Base and DJ EZ Rock, 'The Godfather' by Spoonie Gee, and 'I Know You Got Soul' by Eric B. & Rakim being just three massively important tunes that took their heart and soul from a James Brown production. And then there was the rare groove movement that regurgitated his work all over again – particularly 'Same Beat', 'Cross the Track' and 'Funky Drummer'. In fact, I don't think James Brown has ever been off my playlist – be it the originals, or the re-workings and re-edits by the likes of the Fort Knox Five or Featurecast. No one can fill the dance floor like Brown and no one can doubt the influence he has had on British underground youth culture. It is inestimable, while the people he directly influenced are legion.

Michael Jackson, who first saw Brown perform when he appeared on the same TV show as him in 1969 and instantly emulated his moves, said, 'James Brown is magic. I've never dared speak to him, but I consider James Brown my greatest teacher.' Kanye West just recently named James Brown as his favourite artist of all time. Jimmy Page remarked that Brown 'was almost a musical genre in his own right and he changed and moved forward the whole time so people were able to learn from him. He influenced everyone.' Mick Jagger, equally awestruck, said, 'I was obviously learning from it. [Brown's stage dramatics] trying to steal everything I could do.'

So enamoured of Brown was (and is) the Rolling Stone's front man that he recently produced two movies about Soul Brother Number One: the brilliant HBO documentary *Mr Dynamite: The Rise of James Brown*, directed by Oscar winner Alex Gibney, and the biopic *Get on Up*, directed by Tate Taylor. Both movies succeed on different levels, but what's most remarkable is that it has taken this long for someone to make films about this totally off-the-wall, entirely unique human being whose life reads like a preposterous work of fiction.

He was born plain James Joseph Brown in the pinewoods outside Barnwell, South Carolina, on 3 May 1933 (some records give his birth date as 1928) in a one-room lean-to shack without water, windows, electricity or a toilet.

Nearly stillborn, then revived by his aunt Minnie after everyone else had given him up for dead, he should have been named Joseph James Brown, after his father – a physically abusive, alcoholic, gambling sharecropper – but the names were accidentally reversed. His parents were both African-American, but in his autobiography Brown claimed that he was also part Chinese and Native American.

As a young child with no siblings he spent most of his time on his own in the remote pinewoods miles from any neighbours. 'We were so far out I had to be a loner,' he wrote. 'I don't think you can spend that much time on your own as a child and not have it effect you in a big way. Being alone in the woods and in the cabin with no one else there, not having anyone to talk to, worked a change in me that stayed with me from then on. It gave me my own mind. No matter what came my way after that – prison, government harassment, personal problems – I could always fall back on myself.'

Brown suffered badly at the hands of his abusive and drunken father, who made his own liquor and drank most of it himself. 'He'd be away from home and when he come back somebody would tell him I needed a whipping, and he'd whip me good no questions asked.'

Brown's mother left when he was four after his dad tried to kill her. The boy was parcelled off to his Aunt Honey (real name Handsome Washington) in Augusta, Georgia, where she raised him in her brothel, overseen by her brother Jack Scott, who didn't take kindly to the young boy. 'One day he stripped me buck naked, hung me from a ceiling in a burlap sack and beat me with a belt until I almost passed out,' penned Brown.

While living at the knocking shop, the young kid learned the tricks of his forthcoming trade. Aged eight he entertained the GI Johns from nearby by Camp Gordon with his buck dancing. They dropped him the odd coin and soon he was steering them to the house of ill repute. '"Come on," I'd say, "there's some right pretty ones in that house yonder." I'd hook my arm in theirs and start tugging them toward the house, and then I'd lead them into the girls... I guess I saw and heard just about everything in the world in that house, when the soldiers were there with the women.'

Apart from procuring, he shined shoes, delivered groceries, picked peanuts, cleaned churches, picked cotton, and cut sugar cane, while in order to further entertain the troops he learned to play the piano, guitar and harmonica.

His love of music took him to church. Not just one church, but all the churches in the town. 'There was a lot of singing and tambourines and usually an organ,' he said. 'And then the preacher would really get DOWN. I went to a revival service and the preacher really had a lot of fire. He was just screaming and yelling and stomping his foot and then he dropped to his knees. The people got into it answering him and shouting and clapping time. So I went home and imitated them. I wanted to preach. I thought that was the answer... I'm sure a lot of my stage show came from the church.'

'There is no doubt that James Brown was tremendously influenced by the preachers,' states his arranger and trombonist Fred Wesley. 'When they find that one note that becomes a scream, that is James Brown.'

But no matter how enamoured he was of preachers and gospel music, Brown admits that he was a young thug who only really wanted to box. 'My idol was Beau Jack – lightweight champion of the world – who started [to] make his living like me in Augusta's, George St.'

As a teenager he picked up cash as a boxer and ducked and dived to earn a crust. He took part in 'battle royals', boxing matches which, as he says in his autobiography, were to 'entertain the white folks' and entailed a gang of black kids in a ring boxing blindfold with one hand tied behind their backs, swinging at anything that moved until only one was left standing. His prowess allowed him to legitimately earn money, but he still often broke the law with his street gang playmates.

'I was a street kid – a little thug,' he recalled. 'I was sent home from school for insufficient clothes and so I stole them. I was like Robin Hood and stole from the rich to give to the poor, which was me.'

Aged fifteen, he was arrested for robbery, tried as an adult, and received an eight-to-sixteen-year sentence. He subsequently spent three years languishing in a tough boys' detention centre in Toccoa, near Augusta, where, known to the inmates as 'Music Box' because of his ability to play virtually anything, he started a gospel group and organised and led the prison gospel choir.

He met Bobby Byrd (who regularly performed for the inmates with his family's gospel group) at a prisoners-versus-locals baseball match. Byrd's family hastened Brown's release on 14 June 1952 by giving him a home and promising the warden that Brown would not return to Augusta, while Brown did a bit of pro boxing on the side, transported illegal hooch across the state lines, worked at the Lawson Motor Company and as a janitor at a local school, and joined Byrd's band the Gospel Starlighters, who morphed into the Avons and then the Flames.

After a relationship with Byrd's sister, Brown married Velma Warren, and a year later she gave birth to their son, Teddy, followed by his siblings Terry and Larry over the next four years.

'I could see where he wanted something,' said Velma. 'He was very ambitious... He knew that with me he wasn't going back to poverty. He had that determination and was always going to be something.'

'I was a really good boxer,' said Brown. 'But, when I heard the girls scream when I sang... everything else was over.'

In 1954, the band met a wild young piano player named Little Richard, who, taking a break from his own performance, allowed them to play their own short set at Bill's Rendezvous in Toccoa.

Seeing something in James and his band, he suggested they speak to his agent/manager Clint Brantley, who was not only the foremost promoter of black music in Macon, Georgia, but also a tough barbershop proprietor. They auditioned, he took them on and they settled in Macon, where Brown worked at the Greyhound Bus station. Although very much a man's man, he copied Little Richard's every camp nuance. 'The queens of these travelling tent shows had something,' he later admitted.

In 1956 they wrote and released the song 'Please, Please, Please', which reached number six in the R 'n' B charts and eventually sold a million copies. As a result the band soon became *the* Famous Flames, with Brown sometimes on drums or piano, but mainly on vocals, taking a massive leaf from Little Richard's book both in terms of personal style and on-stage antics. 'I've never seen a man work so hard in my whole life,' Bobby Byrd recalled. 'He'd go from what we rehearsed and leap off into something else. It was hard to keep up. He was all the time driving, driving, and driving. This is when he really started hollering and screaming, and dancing fit to burst. He just had to outdo Richard.'

Over the next two years Brown released nine singles that bombed. Then, in 1957, due to group managers Ben Bart and Clint Brantley giving James Brown top billing, renaming the group James Brown and his Famous Flames, the band split up. 'That caused a lot of dissension in the group,' recalled Bobby Byrd.

Nevertheless, it was now that the unstoppable James Brown morphed into another being. As guided by Bart, Brown honed to perfection the James Brown Revue. A dazzling evening's entertainment replete with support acts and a master of ceremonies, the show was painstakingly choreographed, with Brown dancing like no one ever had before. His repertoire comprised shuffling on one foot, fast footwork and multiple splits, eventually pretending to collapse with exhaustion. Then his MC would arrive, help him to his feet and drape his trademark cape over his shoulders (an idea he took from Gorgeous George, the wrestler), guiding him from the stage, only for the man to stop, throw off the cape, and go for it even more – not once but over and over again.

It was pure unadulterated ham, but Brown was a sensation who had queues around the block outside each and every venue he played in. And as a rule Brown, a tough talking, no-holds-barred business-man, would secure his own cash deal and walk away with a suitcase full of readies.

It was then that he earned the title Mr Dynamite.

'The dancing y'all seen later on ain't nothing to what he used to do back then,' said Bobby Byrd. 'James could stand flat-footed and flip over into a split. He'd tumble, too, over and over like in gymnastics.'

Over the next few years he moved into the big time with the likes of *Think!* (1960) and, the following year, 'Night Train' (legend has it Brown played the drums on the hit version when regular drummer Nat Kendrick took a bathroom break). Both were huge amongst Mods and groovers all over Europe. His *Live at the Apollo* LP, financed entirely by Brown, was released in 1962, hit number two, and stayed in the US charts for fourteen months – then unprece-dented for a black music album – while the groundbreaking 'Out of Sight' reached number five on the R 'n' B singles chart.

'You can hear the band and me move in a whole other direction rhythmically,' explained Brown in his memoir. 'The horns, the gui-tar, the vocals – everything was starting to be used to establish all kinds of rhythm at once. On that record you can hear my voice alter-nate with the horns to create rhythmic accents. "Out of Sight" went out of sight across the charts. It just took off across the board. It was the biggest hit I'd ever had.'

In 1965 Brown ditched conventional verse and chorus structure and even eliminated chord progressions. It was now purely about the groove. 'Papa's Got a Brand New Bag' (recorded in less than an hour, in February 1965) subsequently peaked at number eight in the US billboard chart.

'It's hard to describe what I was going for; the song has a gospel feel but it's put together out of jazz licks, And it has a different sound – a snappy, fast-hitting thing from the bass and the guitar,' said Brown. 'We stopped to listen to the first take and see what we needed to do on the next. Everybody – the band, the studio people, *me,* was danc-ing… And that was it. That was the way it went out.'

'What I'd started on "Out of Sight" I took all the way on "Papa's

Bag",' continued Brown. 'They said it was the beginning of funk. I just thought it was where my music was going. The title told it all. I have a new bag.'

He followed 'Papa' with 'I Got You (I Feel Good)', which rose to number three. Brown had arrived, quite literally, kicking and screaming.

'I remember seeing the Mods where I lived in Woking listening to James Brown's "Papa's Got a Brand New Bag" and "I Feel Good" when I was about eight,' recalls Paul Weller. 'It was a huge Mod tune that influenced everyone and kind of stuck with me because of the lyrics.'

In August 1966, Brown bought himself a Learjet, recorded 'Don't Be a Drop-Out' (intended to persuade African-American youth to stay in school) and flew to the White House to give Vice President Hubert H. Humphrey the first copy and tell him about the fledgling programme that paralleled his release.

'That was something I knew about first hand because I didn't have any formal education at all and knew how it could hold you back... He [Humphrey] was glad to see someone do something about it besides talk about it.

'I visited schools, I talked to kids. I told them to stay in school, listen to their teachers, and stay close to their books... During our tour, as part of the campaign, we gave away $500 scholarships to whatever black college was in the area we were playing.'

Brown was fast becoming a figure of national importance. He smashed prime time on *The Ed Sullivan Show,* hosted an enormous civil rights rally in Mississippi and found himself on speaking terms with Frank Sinatra and the Rat Pack.

Now nicknamed the Godfather of Soul, in 1967 he left soul behind and showed the world the future with 'Cold Sweat'.

'"Cold Sweat" deeply affected the musicians I knew,' said Jerry Wexler, who was then producing Aretha Franklin and other soul stars for Atlantic Records. 'It just freaked them out. For a time, no one could get a handle on what to do next.'

Considered by many as the first ever dyed-in-the-wool funk tune, it rocked the whole world. It was just rhythm – Brown basically turned every instrument into a drum, based every lick on a drum pattern, used barely any chord changes, employed jazz horn breaks inspired by Miles Davis's 'So What', and changed the emphasis of the beat from the second and fourth bars to the first, known as 'the one'.

'He'd just hum these lines to us and then we'd try and interpret them,' recalls saxophonist Pee Wee Ellis, a band member from 1965 till 1969. Ellis arranged and co-wrote hits such as 'Cold Sweat' for Brown. 'I wrote the music but had no idea what lyrics he was going to write and heard it for the first time in the studio; then we released it and it turned everything upside down.'

But Brown didn't only influence music, he also changed things politically.

On 5 April 1968, the day after the assassination of Martin Luther King Jr, Brown went on television to plead for calm and, after rioting had broken out in several cities, quelled a race riot in Boston by televising his concert live and demanding peace. He was congratulated for doing so by the president. This outraged the Black Panthers, who thought Brown was siding with the establishment.

'You know, in Augusta, Georgia, I used to shine shoes on the steps of a radio station,' stated Brown. 'I think we started at three cents. But today, I own that radio station. You know what that is? *That's* Black Power.'

Almost every black artist in America jumped on the funk bandwagon, while the man himself, now a cultural hero, was a symbol of self-determination and victory over inherent racism.

In 1968 he released one of the greatest cultural anthems of all time. 'Say It Loud – I'm Black and I'm Proud' hit number ten in the national charts. But, more importantly, it united many African-Americans who, in an era of segregation and widespread racism, had been made to feel ashamed of being black.

'When we first played "Say It Loud" live in front of 20,000 people in a stadium in Houston Texas, James Brown said, "Say it loud!" and the whole audience said, "I'm black and I'm proud!" It sent chills up my spine,' reflects Pee Wee Ellis. 'It was amazing. It was like an anthem.'

Indeed, Brown hit the Black Power zeitgeist head on and said what many African-Americans felt. He sponsored programmes for ghetto youth, spoke at high schools, invested in black businesses, and performed for troops in Vietnam, flying into the front line.

'I was scared to death,' says singer and former girlfriend Marva Whitney, who Brown brought with him to Vietnam. 'Especially in the planes when we kinda peeped out the window and looked down, and all you see is fire, fire, and then they tell you, you have to lay down in the belly of the plane. So we lay down. We were very obedient cause we didn't want to get shot.'

'One night we were in a chopper back from a show,' wrote Brown. 'And tracers [fire from the ground] came at us. It was kind of pretty if you didn't think about the fact that they were trying to kill you.'

Back home James was raking it in.

'I was still playing one-nighters,' he recalled. 'But now they were always in stadiums and coliseums. I rented those places myself, promoted the show, took all the risks. Like Braves Stadium – I rented it and put twenty seven thousand people in there.'

He now enjoyed another moniker: Soul Brother Number One.

'I think Soul Brother Number One meant I was the leader of the Afro-American movement for world dignity and integrity through music,' he informed.

Even so, he then puzzled all by playing Nixon's inaugural ball in January 1969. Nixon not only supported the Vietnam War, but also seemed diametrically opposed to all that Brown had said he stood for. The result was that many African-American organisations boycotted his records and demonstrated outside his shows. Brown declared that he was neither Republican nor Democrat but in future years endorsed Nixon and Reagan as presidents.

Musically, Brown was still a potent force. He kicked off 1969 with 'Give It Up or Turn It Loose', which hit number one in the US R 'n' B charts. But Sly Stone, the Isley Brothers and Norman Whitfield, all of whom were making big funky waves, seriously endangered his crown.

Furthermore, all was not happy in the band as Brown, who insisted that all members call him Mr Brown, fined them for bum notes, missed cues, drinking on the job, and shoes that weren't polished enough. Compared to Brown they were earning peanuts, but whenever money was mentioned Brown displayed the side of him that supported Nixon.

'I was doing a gig in Columbus, Georgia, when the band threatened not to go on,' he growled. 'They wanted more money. I wouldn't give in to a threat like that – never. You cannot lose control of your group. Once you give in to that kind of thing, there's no stopping it.'

Consequently, in March 1970, most of his 1960s band – including Maceo and Melvin Parker, Jimmy Nolen and Alfonzo 'Country' Kellum – who together had created the immense 'Funky Drummer', walked out on him.

Now aged thirty-seven, Brown, always full of surprises, simply brought in eight Cincinnati teenagers – the Pacesetters – who included the Collins brothers: William, aka 'Bootsy', on bass, and Phelps, aka 'Catfish', on rhythm guitar.

'James Brown and his band were our heroes,' said Bootsy. 'We couldn't imagine actually playing with them. To tell the truth, I don't think I ever got used to the fact that I was there. And yes, he was a taskmaster but I really needed it myself. Coming out of a home with no father, my mother was raising us, and so the Godfather really was like a father to me and really helped me and taught me all about funkadelic, and we've been funking on ever since.'

Brown called his band the 'New Breed', before he settled on the JBs – and rolled with the punches, shifting emphasis from the horns to guitar and taking African-American music on another new journey.

The songs they recorded in just eleven months together rank as some of the finest dance tunes ever created: 'Get Up (I Feel Like Being a) Sex Machine', 'It's a New Day', 'Super Bad', 'Give It Up or Turn it Loose', 'Talkin' Loud and Sayin' Nothing', 'Get Up, Get into It, Get Involved', and 'Soul Power'. This was new, this was fresh and this was rocking. Brown thus earned himself yet another moniker: the Minister of New New Super Heavy Funk.

'My older mate from Harrow who was a bit more hip than me

played me "It's a New Day" in 1970,' remembers Dexys main man
Kevin Rowland. 'And it was like jazz, and I didn't get it at first, but
it really grew on me and then changed everything. I went from listening to soul to listening to this new funk. And then a few weeks
later out came "Sex Machine". It went massive and changed music
forever.'

Brown, who in 1970 married Deidre 'Dee Dee' Jenkins, influenced
the world with this new band. 'Sex Machine' was played in almost
every club in the world and has been voted the greatest dance tune
of all time in numerous polls. Fela Kuti saw James Brown live, went
back to Nigeria and started Afrobeat. 'James Brown subsequently has
some fantastic bass lines,' muttered Fela. 'It's like he is African.'

And thus the funk spread. British bands like Cymande flew the
flag, while in France, where Brown almost started a riot with his sensational 1971 performance, they went funk mad. Over in the US, this
became the music of the ghetto. The hard, sparse instrumentation
and rhythmic accent on the one spoke of its African influence, but
funk became a celebration of American blackness: it had its own look,
it brought the community together, it was their *thang*, and Brown
was its emperor.

Even though Brown certainly controlled the show, we have to
credit Bootsy's bass. 'I was just a snotty kid,' Collins says. 'I would listen to Jimmy, smoke weed and take LSD at the back of the bus. But
the deep thing is, every crazy thing I pulled I got away with because
I could hold my own with my axe.' But Brown, the original funk
pioneer, kept his cool as another desertion would have left him high
and dry – so he lightened his discipline, respected their budding talent and gave the JBs room to grow.

"Soul Power" was my most favourite song we did,' explains
Bootsy. 'There was something about the groove that was genius and
it just kind of happened. "Sex Machine" was kinda like that too. The
first one that got released was a big hit. I didn't really feel like I knew
what I was doing but when it was time to cut "Soul Power" I felt like
I wasn't scared anymore, I felt like, yeah let's do this, it was a different
feeling.'

Collins's imbibing rankled the Godfather, however.

'He was accusing me of being high on his set,' he recalls. 'I was like, no, I'm gonna get high after the show but not before the show, we had too much work to do, you had to pay a high price to be high on James Brown's set, and he was accusing me of doing that. But I was a headstrong kid so I thought to myself, if he keeps doing that then I'm going to, so one day I did! I took it. So when he called me back there this last time I was tripping and, after he chastised me, I fell on the floor laughing and he thought I was a total fool. "Get this fool outta here!" he shouted. So he never called me back to give me another lecture, you know, "There's no hope for this fool, he's just a crazy young kid." And I was.'

'I was trying to keep him straight out there because he was a kid who was suddenly pushed into all this show business craziness – thousands of people screaming for you every night, money, women, drugs,' said Brown. 'I couldn't spank him so I lectured him. He wasn't bad or anything. He was just determined to be wrong. I saw a lot of spunk in Bootsy, a lot of life.'

Collins then hitched a ride on George Clinton's P-Funk Mothership. Subsequently, Soul Brother Number One brought in a new band.

'A lot of times a band will start trying to dictate to me, and I don't like that,' said Brown. 'Or they think the music is all them. That's why I've had stormy times with my bands over the years. And my strict rules.'

But no matter how absurd were Brown's regulations, he could still pull in a top band. This next band comprised some new and some old JBs who, directed by the easy-going, Alabama-born, jazz-bred Wesley, continued to knock out the R 'n' B chart number ones, such as 'Make It Funky', 'Talkin' Loud and Sayin' Nothing' and 'Get on the Good Foot' – none of which charted in the UK but were massive on the dance floors.

Meanwhile the performer's endorsement of Nixon was hurting.

'I did a show in Baltimore,' recalled Brown. 'There were pickets outside the arena discouraging people from coming in. Usually I sold out all 13,000 seats there, but that night only about 2,500 showed up. I was disappointed. People just didn't understand.'

The point is that they did.

In 1971, Brown signed his People label to Polydor and the hits – he also wrote and produced for the likes of Lynn Collins, Marva Whitney, Bobby Byrd and Maceo Parker – continued to flow. For UK soul boys and soul girls in the 1970s James Brown was God. Approaching forty, he transformed from an ageing Soul Brother Number One into a venerated Godfather of Soul who could still fill a floor on a wet Tuesday afternoon.

'All that we know, all that we do, James is the father who taught us all how to be funky,' attests Tomi Jenkins of legendary funk combo Cameo. 'He's not called the Godfather for nothing.'

James was riding high until disaster struck on 14 June 1973, when he was told that his oldest son Teddy had been killed in a car crash in upstate New York.

'When I heard the news, it was like the end of the world for me,' wrote Brown. 'We flew to New York but when I got there the officials, seeing how disturbed I was, wouldn't let me go in to identify my son.'

Soon after, Bobby Byrd left the band to pursue a solo career and the Internal Revenue Service, who'd claimed in 1968 that Brown owed nearly $2 million, added another $4.5 million to the tab and stepped up its attempts to collect back taxes. Brown, in the ludicrous belief that President Nixon would protect him from the taxman, jumped political ships and supported the Republican Party. But by now Nixon was going down and the IRS were on to the Godfather like a pack of pit bulls tearing his life and business interests to shreds.

'The government went round to all the coliseums and auditoriums I had played and figured how much I made on each show and they built up a net worth of what I'd made,' groaned Brown. 'They didn't figure payroll, expenses and all of that!'

Simultaneously, Brown became embroiled in a radio payola scandal involving top DJ Frankie 'Hollywood' Crocker. One of Brown's main men, Charles Bobbit, admitted giving the DJ some $6,500 over eight years to play the Godfather's releases. Crocker denied the allegation and was jailed for twelve months for perjury.

'If you give some underpaid Jock $50 to buy groceries, that's payola,' moaned Brown. 'If you're a record company and hand out $750 TV sets as Christmas gifts, that's no payola.'

Brown had had huge problems with his own three stations. He was taken to court after he failed to air thousands of commercials that had been already paid for, violated broadcast regulations over one hundred times, and the American Society of Composers sued his company for not paying royalties. It was then discovered that Brown's station WEBB was not licensed to broadcast any copyrighted music, and he hadn't paid the previous owners a single cent for the station's building in six years.

Still, in 1976, he managed to knock out a massive international dance floor hit with 'Get Up Offa That Thing', but due to his troubles with the IRS, credited authorship of the song to his wife Deidre and their daughters, Deanna and Yamma Brown.

As the seventies progressed, his winning streak faltered. Too hard for disco and not freaky enough for the George Clinton era, he lost sales. Still, he was the most successful African-American musician of the twentieth century, with his own plane, a chain of restaurants, and a TV and radio station. Acts that took their inspiration from Brown received greater advances and more promotion from his label, Polydor, and so his relationship with them soured.

'They weren't flexible about creativity,' growled Brown in a TV interview. 'They expected you to go into the studio on a certain day and a certain hour and finish up at a certain time. Like a factory. At King [his previous label] we worked on a song until we got it right. Polydor might have been fed some bad information about me being difficult to work with. I am difficult if you want to change me from being James Brown.'

James Brown or not, the IRS eventually took away his jet, radio stations and cars, and tried to get his house. And while this was happening disco music was taking over, with live venues turning into discotheques. This meant Brown had fewer places to perform.

Then his wife Deidre ('Dee Dee' Jenkins) left him and took their two kids. Life hadn't been so tough for Brown since the fifties. Accordingly, he went back to playing small New York clubs like the

Lone Star, Irving Plaza and Studio 54, reaching an audience of white bohemian hep cats who'd grown up on Brown's super funk.

It was at New York's Studio 54 that he met *Saturday Night Live* stars John Belushi and Dan Aykroyd, who in 1980 pulled him in to play Reverend Cleophus James in *The Blues Brothers*. The film was a smash. 'That movie exposed me to people who'd never seen me before,' smiled Brown. 'Suddenly I was performing all the time again.'

In 1981 his wife Dee Dee got her final divorce decree after accusing Brown of continued physical abuse. 'Years later, I asked my mom about the beatings,' wrote his daughter Yamma Brown in her book *Cold Sweat: My Father James Brown and Me.* 'I reminded her about the only one I ever actually saw. She said it was that very day she made up her mind to leave my father. That day, something inside her said that if she didn't leave, someone was going to end up dead, and she was pretty sure it would be her.'

Although Brown was losing it in the early eighties, he found himself enjoying a popularity surge in groovy clubs all over the world – especially in London and Paris, where DJs endorsed him like never before. The interest, however, was purely in his back catalogue, the trend back then being to buy old releases second hand. This was of no use to a man with a formidable tax bill on his head. Thankfully revenue did flow in from the aforementioned use of his samples from the early eighties onwards ('There'd be no hip-hop without James Brown,' says rapper Chuck D), while performances in movies such as *Doctor Detroit* (1983) and *Rocky IV* (1985) – which showcased Brown performing 'Living In America' – kept the wolf from the door.

Meanwhile he had met Adrienne Lois Rodriguez, a black Jewish Italian Latina from South Central LA who had grown up in foster homes. They married in 1984 and heavy-duty drugs stepped in, namely PCP (also known as angel dust) – a mind-bending hallucinogenic that causes acute anxiety, paranoia and violent hostility.

In 1984 Rodriguez called 911, claiming she was a victim of domestic violence. She called three times in 1985, once in 1987, and at least seven times in 1988. During the first six months of 1988, Brown was arrested three times and charged with assault and intent to kill, possession of PCP, resisting arrest, and illegal possession of a pistol. On one occasion he was accused of savagely beating his spouse (who had also been arrested for the third time in a little over a month and charged with possession of the drug PCP) with a mop handle and firing a rifle into the car she was driving. Adrienne Brown later dropped those charges. She had filed such charges at least four times before over their ten-year marriage. She also stabbed a woman she thought James was having an affair with in the ass with scissors. A month later she was arrested for setting Brown's clothes on fire in a hotel room and possessing seven ounces of PCP. 'Love's a funny thing,' mused Brown.

The shit hit the proverbial on 24 September 1988, after Brown, then fifty-five, walked into his business office in Augusta, Georgia (where an insurance seminar was taking place) carrying a shotgun and a pistol and told everyone to leave.

He was supposedly riled because someone had used his office bathroom, located in the same office complex, without his permission. Police were called and Brown fled in his pickup truck.

The police subsequently pursued him across two states until they shot out three of his tires and riddled his car with twenty-three bullets as a line of police officers finally stopped him. A Georgia highway patrol officer later said that when he got out of the car he sang the song 'Georgia' and 'did the Good Foot Dance'.

Typically, he refused to plead guilty to driving under the influence of drugs or resisting arrest, but before he was sentenced, he told the judge about the problems he had growing up.

'The only thing that held me together was when I looked at the flag, and that represented a chance,' he said, holding a small Bible. 'I respect police. Without them we have nothing.' He was consequently sentenced to six years in prison but was paroled in 1991 after serving only two and a half. 'It wasn't so terrible,' he later stated. 'I needed the rest *bad*.'

He now acquired yet another moniker: *His Bad Self*.

After his release, he managed to stay out of trouble for a while, released a few records and even went on tour, which – considering his wild stage antics – was quite an accomplishment for a man well into his sixties. He was also back with Adrienne and on the PCP (he called it *go*–rilla), the pair fighting more than ever.

In 1996 Adrienne underwent liposuction treatment at a Hollywood clinic and attempted to recover by imbibing a mix of Demerol, Vicodin, Valium and morphine. She died of a heart attack, which was blamed on the PCP she had in her system. No one mourned her demise apart from Brown who, two years later, after an all-night PCP session, walked onto his lawn naked and shot a .22 calibre handgun and a .30 calibre rifle in the air. He was then put in a facility and observed.

In 1998, Brown was again charged with drug possession – this time for marijuana – and was required to enter a ninety-day drug treatment programme. But you can't keep a good man down. In 1998 he met Tomi Rae Hynie – a gold-digging redhead – in Las Vegas and a year later, whilst still addicted to PCP, survived an operation on his prostate. He was also sued by his daughters for stealing their royalties on songs like 'Get Up Offa That Thing'.

The following year, in 2000, police were summoned to Brown's abode after he was accused of chasing a young electric company repairman with a steak knife after the man called to look into a complaint regarding Brown's overhead lighting.

He married Tomi in 2001, by which time their son James II was six months old. Brown was sixty-eight and Tomi thirty-five.

Meanwhile Brown was mixing Viagra and PCP and still entertaining the ladies. 'What did he do at home?' said Gloria Daniel, a long-time mistress of Brown's. 'Nothing. Fuck, fuck, fuck, fuck, fuck. He operated the remote, watched only cowboy movies and you ate what he ate.'

He also identified with Moses and told many a visitor that God had spoken to him and told him he was chosen to lead the people out of the world.

Undeniably Brown was getting crazier by the minute. At a concert in Tbilisi, Georgia, in 2006, Brown found himself performing above an Olympic swimming pool. Just before finishing a rendition of 'Sex Machine', the last song in the set, he dived into the deep end, fully clothed and wearing cowboy boots. A submerged Brown had to be rescued by his saxophonist and several of his band and backing singers. He then came back on stage and finished the song, giving all who jumped in to save him a £200 bonus.

By now Brown, obviously sick, was trying to retire but couldn't because he thought people needed him to work. On 22 December 2006, when the state of his health sent alarm bells ringing while he was visiting his dentist ('Hair and teeth, hair and teeth – if you have those you have it all,' he once said), he was admitted to hospital and diagnosed with congestive heart failure and pneumonia. Three days later, on Christmas Day, he died of heart failure at a hospital in Atlanta. He was seventy-three.

According to his personal manager and long-time friend Charles Bobbit, Brown stuttered, 'I'm going away tonight', before taking three long, quiet breaths, falling asleep and dying.

Amongst the thousands who attended his funeral were Michael Jackson, Joe Frazier, Ice Cube, Little Richard, Prince, Jesse Jackson, Ice-T, Jerry Lee Lewis, 50 Cent and Stevie Wonder, while the Reverend Al Sharpton officiated.

Since his death he has received numerous accolades and awards, including a star on the Hollywood Walk of Fame, while 22 December is now officially James Brown Day in the city of Cincinnati.

He is also making more money than ever due to the use of his music in ads and sampling fees. The US Supreme Court said it had no idea what Brown's estate is now worth, giving estimates from $5 million to more than $100 million; and even though he left a clear will, a bitter feud over his wealth lingers a decade after his death.

Of course the fly in the ointment is that Brown left behind not only a massive moneymaking machine worth perhaps hundreds of millions of dollars, but the eight women who gave birth to his children. Also vying for a piece of the action are sixteen grandchildren, a truckload of mistresses, a former manager, thirty lawyers, and a long-serving valet.

Perhaps seeing this coming, Brown penned a will in 2000 with the assistance of his lawyer H. Dewain Herring (who himself received a thirty-year sentence in 2006 for killing a stripper) that divided his will into two parts, with his 'personal and household effects' – clothing, bedding, furniture, plates and shot-up pickup truck etc. – bequeathed to the six adult children he fathered from two ex-wives and two fly-by-nights, and a trust fund.

He was very clear about this. 'I have intentionally failed to provide for any other relatives or other persons,' he wrote in the will. 'Such failure is intentional and not occasioned by accident or mistake.' Of course, and here's the rub, the big money, which included his sixty-acre estate in Beech Island, South Carolina, and his catalogue of 800 or so songs and their royalties (which are making more than ever) was put into two trust funds, one of which benefited his grandchildren and another, a much bigger one, estimated at $20 million, to pay tuition for 'financially needy' students of Georgia and South Carolina.

Brown had appointed the trustees himself, so the execution of the will should be straightforward, but all of his children and wives contest whether he was in his right mind (which, as you may gather, is debatable) when he created the trusts. As a result, millions and millions of dollars have been paid to lawyers and the trustees (one of whom, David Cannon, was sentenced to six months' jail time for failing to pay back $300,000 he owed the estate after building a huge house in the Caribbean) and new ones appointed.

To exacerbate things, Brown's first wife Velma has come out of the woodwork claiming that she was never divorced from Brown. Two other daughters, who Brown never acknowledged, also want a share, as well as eighteen years of back child support, while four more potential offspring have made similar claims. And out of six children named in the will, five have demanded the will be invalidated so that the trusts disappear, leaving them equal shares of the total estate. Only one son, Terry, honours his father's wishes, requesting the will and its subsequent trusts to remain.

Then there is Brown's widow, Tomi Rae Hynie, mother of James Brown II. Though James Brown filed his own annulment papers against her, he never followed through with the complaint and vice versa. Recently, a judge declared the former back-up singer to be his legally surviving wife, and she could potentially claim at least a third of the late singer's estate under South Carolina law, after previously being excluded from his final wishes.

This has riled Brown's children – there are at least six and as many as nine, depending on who you believe – who claim Brown had a vasectomy in the 1980s and therefore challenge James junior's legitimacy.

Of course Tomi Rae sees the matter differently. Hynie told the *Daily Mail*, 'James cared passionately about money. He knew what he wanted his legacy to be. He wanted to take care of Little Man and me and the rest would go to a charity helping underprivileged children. He wanted to help poor kids, white and black. He knew what it was like to be hungry and have no shoes on his feet. He often said he wasn't going to leave money to his older kids because he didn't want them living off his legacy.'

She added: 'James was someone who believed everyone was out to get his or her hands on his money. In death he's been proven right.'

Nevertheless in 2014 a South Carolina judge ordered a DNA test, which confirmed that James junior was indeed Brown's son. 'They couldn't do the normal DNA test because of all the embalming fluid in his body so they had to cut off his legs to get to his bone marrow. I wept uncontrollably when I found out. My husband, the greatest dancer in the world, had his legs hacked off in death.'

But that wasn't the end of this macabre farce. The Godfather's corpse was moved fourteen times in the six months after his death and ended up in an impermanent grave in his eldest daughter Deanna's garden in Georgia.

'That is the final insult to James,' said Tomi Rae.

The fight over Brown's estate has been described as 'one of the strangest in recent legal history'. In 2013 the South Carolina Supreme Court overturned a settlement reached by former Attorney General Henry McMaster that divided the estate between a charitable trust, Tomi Rae Hynie and the rest of his adult children, and declared that it didn't follow the singer's wishes. The justices said the arrangement ignored Brown's requests for most of his money to go to a charity for underprivileged children in Georgia and South Carolina. The settlement remains unresolved.

But regardless of what went on in his personal life, his musical legacy is secure.

'I was marked from the get up,' he said. 'You might say that I have a mark on my back that I never knew was there. That's because they fixed it so I couldn't see it myself. But now that I can look back on my life, I realise that what I've done was no accident.'

There is no doubt that James Brown was mad, bad and dangerous to know, a complete and utter genius whose life story is scarcely believable. He was far from perfect, but then so was his upbringing. And we have to look at what he achieved. Love him or hate him, it is totally impossible to consider a world without Mr James Brown.

David Bowie

When it comes to music and style, contemporary or otherwise, only one person has dominated both categories during their own lifetime and that is David Bowie.

Frank Sinatra was a contender, but then he didn't write his own songs. Others, such as Miles Davis or James Brown, certainly had the music, but they lacked Bowie's diversity – and lost the style plot for decades.

Bowie was style personified and wrote not just the lyrics and the music but sang, played various instruments, and arranged and produced much of his own work. Apart from about seventeen albums (nine albums reached number one in the UK) that don't include a single bad track, just listen to the brilliance of singles such as 'Kooks', 'Aladdin Sane', 'Life on Mars', and 'Heroes'. Consider, also, some of the albums he produced for other artists: the Stooges' *Raw Power*, Mott the Hoople's *All the Young Dudes*, Lou Reed's *Transformer*, Iggy Pop's *Lust for Life* – each one a truly seminal album that sounds as good today as it did back then.

The word 'genius' is bandied around willy-nilly, but I firmly believe Bowie fits into that esteemed category with ease. Still, for some, even that accolade might not adequately explain why so many millions of people are obsessed with the man or why his fans deified him. I suppose you had to be there at the height of his career and realise what the man stood for. This was not just music or entertainment; it was liberty – the freedom to take chances, experiment, dress as you pleased and, most importantly, to have the strength to be true to yourself in an extremely intolerant time.

I first met Bowie properly in May 1980 when he popped into Hell, a Covent Garden nightclub that I DJ'd at and ran with Steve Strange and Rusty Egan, both of whom had recently appeared in his 'Ashes to Ashes' video. Accompanied by the model Vivienne Lynn, he came in and humbly introduced himself as 'David'. It was only when I looked into his different-coloured eyes that I realised who he was. We had only just opened the doors and, of the fifteen people there, only my LSD-enhanced pal Christos Tolera approached him, thinking he was an old soul boy he knew from Ilford. Christos launched into conversation while the obviously puzzled Bowie merely smiled and nodded.

Still, looking back, we could have been forgiven for not recognising our idol. He'd turned up in a long tweed raglan-sleeved 1950s-style trench coat and blue peg trousers, his natural brown hair parted to the side, while his demeanour was down to earth. He must have popped in to see Steve, as the release of 'Ashes to Ashes' was imminent. But neither Steve nor Rusty were there and I'd put Beethoven's Ninth choral version on, which lasted the whole side of an LP, allowing me to play host for a while.

He seemed really interested in our little gang of extroverts and even complimented me on my suit. But for the first time in my life I was literally dumbstruck, perhaps because David Bowie in person was not this extraordinary, larger-than-life creature from another planet. He was like your older, funny mate from round the corner, the only difference being those mismatched eyes, which in person were strangely disconcerting.

The next morning I phoned my mum and said, 'David Bowie likes my suit!' I was a twenty-year-old whose whole adolescence was influenced by the great man and whose first suit – bought when I was fourteen years old – was a copy of the one he wore on the cover of the *David Live* album that I had begged, borrowed and saved for. The suit was my pride and joy and I wore it into the ground.

Indisputably David Bowie had a massive effect on my generation and me. He was this omnipresent force – always there at the back of one's mind, being reassuringly reinventive and cleverly chameleon – whose discography charts our journeys from children to adults and beyond.

I acquired my first Bowie recording for Christmas when I was eleven years old. At the same time my mother bought our first record player – a high-fidelity Music Maker – from the Kays catalogue. To accompany the item she let me pick a bunch of LPs from the catalogue, one of which was *Hunky Dory*.

I think I picked it because I loved the movie *The Iron Mistress*, a 1952 drama about nineteenth-century pioneer Jim Bowie. Whatever the reason, I played the record and was duly unimpressed with its rather folksy acoustic tone, which I associated with the smelly hippies who sat cross-legged in the park, smoked funny-smelling roll-ups and giggled constantly. As a result, I didn't really play the album again for a while, preferring the likes of Slade, Dave and Ansell Collins and Desmond Dekker.

It wasn't until June 1972, when I saw Bowie perform 'Starman' on the kids' TV show *Lift Off,* that I gave him any more thought. He was as thin as a broom, wore a horrible multi-coloured jumpsuit and high-heeled boots, and sported a brightly dyed ginger spiky haircut that looked a little like a grown-out girl's skinhead.

My older cousin Susan loved it, though. She played it relentlessly around my granny's house and it grew on me more and more. It was kind of funky and not at all like the ska or Slade-style that rocked my gang. But I wasn't going to jump ship and declare my admiration for this carrot-topped weirdo in a jumpsuit and make-up. In truth, my liking for him as an artist not only confused me at first but also worried me a little.

'A lot of rough working-class kids really adored Bowie,' said Paul Weller. 'But even though he was androgynous and camp, he was held in such high esteem. Round my way there were a few blokes who were brave enough to wear a bit of make-up of a Saturday night, which is chancing your fucking arm in Woking. But Bowie had something. Usually a lot of those tough kids would never have listened to someone like him.'

Perhaps, this is because David Bowie was not unlike the countless millions who adored him – arty yet common people who looked at creativity as a way out of the humdrum.

He was born plain old David Robert Jones in a simple working-class street in Brixton in South London on 8 January 1947, just eighteen months after the end of World War II. His waitress mum Peggy Burns was born in Kent of Irish parents and his dad Haywood Stenton 'John' Jones was from Yorkshire and worked for the charity Barnardo's.

The family moved to leafy Bromley in Kent when he was six, where by all accounts the young boy, though described as 'vividly artistic', wouldn't shy away from a scrap. As a youth he became infatuated with rock 'n' roll – Little Richard, Elvis and Fats Domino – and began learning the ukulele and piano.

Having failed his 11-plus he entered Bromley Tech aged eleven in 1958 and focused on art, music and design under the tutelage of Owen Frampton, father of Peter, the soon-to-be famous recording artist. He wasn't interested in academia. His passion was music, an endeavour he financed by working part-time as a butcher's delivery boy and in a record shop on Saturdays.

After an introduction to jazz from his older half-brother Terry, he saved up and (with a little help from his mum) bought a Selmer Bake-lite acrylic alto saxophone (the type Charlie Parker played). He took sax lessons from esteemed jazzman Ronnie Ross, who toured with the Modern Jazz Quartet and later played on Lou Reed's seminal 'Walk on the Wild Side' (which Bowie produced). He began listening to John Coltrane and Charlie Mingus.

Whilst still at school he formed his first band, the Konrads, with his pal George Underwood, who that year brawled with David for the affections of a girl called Carol Goldsmith. During the scrap Under-wood punched him in the eye, which resulted in two operations for the victim, months off school and a permanently dilated pupil that gave him the unnerving appearance of having two different colour eyes. The following year he left school with an O-level in art and announced to his mother that he would become a pop star. Her response was to get him a job as an electrician's mate.

Undeterred, the sixteen-year-old South Londoner cut his first single, 'Liza Jane/Louie Louie Go Home', as David Jones and the King Bees and contacted washing machine magnate John Bloom, asking him to become the next Brian Epstein and finance 'the new Beatles'. Bloom passed the letter on to Leslie Conn, who booked the band to play a Soho wedding anniversary party. They were so bad that he pulled the plug after ten minutes. David Jones was understandably distraught.

Conn then arranged for David to join his other act, the Manish Boys, and appear on a BBC talk show, *Tonight* with Cliff Michel-more, to discuss long hair as the president of the Society for the Pre-vention of Cruelty to Long-Haired Men. This slot was followed by appearances on TV shows such as *Juke Box Jury, Gadzooks!* and *The Beat Room,* which was pretty impressive for a seventeen-year-old.

Undeniably 1965 was a big year for the man. He turned eighteen on 8 January and released a single with his new band Davy Jones and the Lower Third on 20 August. Realising that there was already a Davy Jones in the pop business, he changed his name to David Bowie after the great Kentuckian hero Jim Bowie, who gave his name to the lethal 'Bowie' knife and died at the Alamo.

By the following year London was swinging like a pendulum, resulting in *Time* magazine declaring it the 'global hub of youthful creativity, hedonism and excitement'. David Bowie found a new manager, Ken Pitt, a flamboyant homosexual and old-school music biz type who had worked with Frank Sinatra, Duke Ellington and Manfred Mann.

'I wasn't sure what he wanted to do,' recalled Pitt. 'He certainly didn't imply he wanted to be a rock 'n' roll star. I was looking for someone who could be an all-round entertainer… and I thought in David we found someone who could be.'

Back then not even the man himself knew exactly what he had created. He released the utterly dire Anthony Newley piss-take 'The Laughing Gnome', which failed to entertain anyone who wasn't either under ten or off their face on LSD, then released his debut solo LP, *David Bowie,* a dire affair that sank without trace.

You'd think that Pitt would have had a strong word to get his star back on track, but he was evidently obsessed. In his book about Bowie, *The Pitt Report,* he talks of David's 'big dick swaying from side to side' and how David's body was almost completely hairless 'apart from a smudging of pubic hair'. Thus it's probably safe to say that Pitt, then aged forty, had a thing for the androgynous would-be pop star. He allowed him to stay rent-free for a year in his flat full of books and gave him an acetate of the first Velvet Underground album, which Lou Reed had given him when he was in New York.

Bowie, a twenty-year-old ingénu from the suburbs, was thrown into Pitt's *omi-polone* arena that comprised secret bars in Soho where *fantabulosa* fruits plucked their eyebrows, flashed their baskets and spoke Polari (an underground cant similar to rhyming slang which was spoken by various subcultures and gays). For this boy from Beck-enham such a cavalcade of camp was another world that he must have realised was eminently marketable.

Accordingly it was under Pitt that Bowie took to studying mime under one of the UK's great stately homos – Lindsay Kemp.

'It was love at first sight for me, but I found out he was seeing a dear friend of mine, Natasha Korniloff, the show's costume designer, at the same time as having an affair with me,' Kemp told the *Guardian* years later. 'Of course I wasn't the only love in his life. There were scores, even then... I drank a bottle of whiskey and cut my wrist. They found me slumped on the floor... I'd been desperately in love.'

Nevertheless Ken Scott, who was the engineer and producer on several Bowie glam-era albums says, 'I don't remember him being camp at all at any time.'

Bowie, as was his wont, soaked up all he could from Kemp. He then toured last on the bill with Marc Bolan and T. Rex and at one point was booed off stage. Nothing seemed to be working for him.

Financially strapped, he got a job working a photocopier, while Decca and Apple rejected his songs. After failing the initial audition he also managed to land a part as an extra on the movie *The Virgin Soldiers* and appeared in a Lyons Maid ice cream ad directed by Rid-ley Scott.

Still unable to make ends meet, he moved in with divorcee Mary Finnigan and her two kids in 24 Foxgrove Road, Beckenham, stay-ing there rent free until she one day returned home to find she'd been replaced in her own house by the rampantly bisexual Mary Angela Barnett, or 'Angie' as she liked to be called.

And then, as if to erase the memory of his debut long player, he released another LP also called *David Bowie* – a negligible rock-folk mish-mash.

One track stands out, however – 'Space Oddity', an homage to Stanley Kubrick's 1968 epic picture *2001: A Space Odyssey* and the growing space programme. Initially, both George Martin and Tony Visconti (who had produced T. Rex and David Bowie's 1969 album) turned it down, so in stepped Gus Dudgeon. Featuring Rick Wakeman on keyboard and Herbie Flowers on bass, the song hit number five in the UK charts.

'I was always looking to see what I was supposed to do or be until the end of the Sixties, then it all came together in 1969 with "Space Oddity",' explained Bowie in a 1983 TV appearance. 'I'm quite a shy person and even more so on stage, so I created these characters and acted them out. A brilliant theatrical concept, I thought. But the character of Major Tom means a lot to me as he is the first credible character I created. For any writer that's a high point. But I had no ambition about going into space. I'm scared going down the end of the garden!'

Shortly after the record became a hit his dad, who had bought David the early rock 'n' roll records and supported his every move, died of lobar pneumonia on 5 August 1969. David was devastated.

Over the next year, however, in spite of his grief, David Bowie built up his team. On 20 March 1970, he married Angie, dropped Pitt as manager and moved to a production company, Gem, whose employee, the slightly suspect Tony Defries, took over the management reins.

David then formed the band Hype with Mick Ronson, Woody Woodmansey and Tony Visconti. 'This was my first costume band,' said Bowie. 'Where the trousers were as important as the music. We were one of the first glam rock acts for sure.'

By now he was well on the way down his own individual path. In April 1970 he recorded the mighty long player/concept album, *The Man Who Sold the World,* with Visconti producing, Ronson on guitar, Woodmansey on drums and Ralph Mace on Moog synthesiser.

More than a little camp and certainly androgynous, the cover photograph, taken by Keith MacMillan, hints at future controversy. It features Bowie with breast-length, flowing locks and wearing a long dress designed by Michael Fish. Resplendent on a chaise longue draped in an opulent turquoise fabric, he strikes a somewhat Pre-Raphaelite pose. It was an interesting concept in 1971, to say the least.

Hunky Dory, released just eight months later, features a cover designed by George Underwood that was influenced by a photo of

Marlene Dietrich. A quite brilliant album, it features some of Bowie's greatest songs such as 'Life on Mars', a parody of Sinatra's 'My Way', 'Kooks', a beautiful work written for his newborn son Duncan, and 'Oh! You Pretty Things', which alludes to Nietzsche, as does the dark and most metaphysical 'Quicksand'.

The album was also the first that Bowie co-produced in cahoots with the person he called his George Martin – Ken Stott – who produced all of his work up until *Diamond Dogs*, which Bowie produced himself. And even though future themes and infatuations were present in songs such as 'Changes' (a manifesto for his chameleonic personality), 'Andy Warhol' (high camp), and 'Queen Bitch' (about and dedicated to Lou Reed), the signature Ziggy look was yet to come.

'I was stage-managing Andy Warhol's play *Pork* starring the Warhol superstar drag queen Jayne County and Cherry Vanilla at the Roundhouse in August 1971,' said the late great New York photographer and band manager Leee Black Childers. 'Then we went to see David play at this little venue because on his record cover he had long hair like a girl and wore a dress.'

'David then was in his *Hunky Dory* phase,' explained Jayne County. 'It was really lame folk music and he sat down most of the time playing an acoustic guitar, had really long hair and was wearing a big hat and a kaftan.

'David was thrilled because he loved Warhol and the Velvet Underground. We met Angie and she came to the show every single night. We loved her as she was outrageous, trashy, used to grab our crotches, talked dirty and would dance with a fish. He just sat there. But they loved these crazy drag queens with the glitter on their faces and the platforms and sequinned hot pants 'cos they didn't look like women and didn't want to. Oh no! They were just these fabulous creatures of their own invention tottering around bitching at each other.

'Then the following year someone gave me the *Ziggy Stardust* album so I started looking at his press cuts and photos and saw that he had changed his look entirely and looked like one of us,' continues County. 'My hair was cut in this spiky almost Mohawk style and dyed this disgusting shade of purple red so I'm convinced he copied my hairstyle as it was so odd and accidental.

'He had hoisted his whole look from us individually. I remember watching his first American tour with Cyrinda Foxe (who is in the *Jean Genie* video and starred in Warhol's *Bad*) and she said, "Oh, David's wearing clothes just like… David's wearing my clothes!" And she was right. He was wearing the skin-tight black pants with the rhinestones, the woman's blouse tied in a little knot underneath his ribs and the large hooped earrings.

'If you ever wondered how David changed so abruptly from a hippie into this otherworldly camp androgynous entity called Ziggy Stardust,' adds County, 'well, darling, now you know.'

'I'm not an original thinker,' admitted Bowie. 'I'm a synthesiser of these things and ideas on society, refracting things that are in the air and producing some kind of glob of how we live at this particular time.'

But it wasn't just the clothes that Bowie absorbed from the excruciatingly hip Warhol cast.

'David and Angie had Tony Zanetta (who played Warhol) for dinner and a special dessert!' said Childers. 'He had sex with them both together. After that we thought we'd never see the Bowies again.'

'Sex wasn't any big deal for him and Angie,' said Tony Zanetta in the *Daily Mail*. 'It was like shaking hands at the end of the evening. David was a real seducer. He made you feel that you were the only person who exists. But after that, he would move on to the next.'

'I was hitting on everybody,' Bowie admitted in a 1997 BBC radio interview. 'I had a wonderfully irresponsible, promiscuous time.'

In September Bowie went to New York to sign to RCA USA and met Lou Reed, Warhol and Iggy Pop. Seen scribbling on Holiday Inn stationery, he explained to DJ Rodney Bingenheimer, 'I am writing about an imaginary character called Ziggy Stardust.' He'd simply bastardised Iggy's name and Childers's word for glitter.

Subsequently, when Bowie hit the big time he gave Tony Zanetta, Cyrinda Foxe, Cherry Vanilla and Childers rather wonderful well-paid jobs for which they were underqualified, and signed both Iggy and County to MainMan for hefty advances.

That November he started recording *The Rise and Fall of Ziggy Stardust and the Spiders from Mars*, and in the first month of 1972 had his hair styled in his famous Ziggy haircut by hairdresser Suzi Fussey. He dyed it red-hot red and kitted himself out in his soon-to-be trademark futuristic/glam kit. He also watched Kubrick's newly released *A Clockwork Orange*. Ziggy was born.

He then really set the tiger amongst the canaries by declaring in an interview with Michael Watts of the UK's bestselling music magazine *Melody Maker*, 'I'm gay and always have been, even when I was David Jones.'

Unsurprisingly this afforded him column inches galore, and while he vehemently denied it to his mum he camped it up all over the shop elsewhere.

'I think I was always a closet heterosexual,' clarified Bowie in 1993. 'I didn't ever feel that I was a real bisexual. I was making all the moves, actually trying it out with some guys. But for me, I was more magnetised by the whole gay scene, which was underground. I like this twilight world. I like the idea of these clubs and these people and everything about it being something that nobody knew anything about. So I made efforts to go and get into it.

'That phase only lasted up to about 1974. It more or less died with Ziggy. It was imperative that I find Ziggy and be him. The irony of it was that I was not gay. I was physical about it, but frankly it wasn't enjoyable. It was almost like I was testing myself. It wasn't something I was comfortable with at all. But it had to be done.'

In June 1972 David Bowie made the cover of the music papers with Mick Rock's shot of him picking the low-slung guitar of Mick Ronson à la faux fellatio in the Oxford Town Hall.

'I was all over poof rock,' recalled Mick Rock. 'That shot looking like David is blowing off Mick was the one, as there was all this talk of bisexuality and people were smashing their fucking closets down left and right. So this was the personal symbol of that moment.'

But none of the above was of any use to me back in 1972, as liking a singer who appeared on children's telly dressed in women's clothes, and who wore make-up and dyed his hair red, was positively incendiary. There was simply no way you could be seen buying a Bowie album, as that would incite bullying for the foreseeable future.

In 1972 I was what one might have called a junior suedehead. I had the cherry red Doctor Martens, the Levi's Sta-prest, the Brutus shirt and the centre-parted, collar-length hair, just like the kids on the cover of Richard Allen's novel *Suedehead*. In those days you either dressed like that and listened to reggae such as Dandy Livingstone and Johnny Nash, or you wore flares, leather biker jackets or army greatcoats with greasy long hair and had a penchant for substandard rock acts such as Status Quo. It was a time of gang warfare, and if you were caught in the wrong place at the wrong time in either kit your opposites would beat the shit out of you. Likewise, if you were partial to glam rock by the likes of the Sweet or T. Rex – who were mainly liked by girls – you were labelled a 'poofter' and given a dig. Therefore by liking Bowie you were skating on paper-thin ice in hobnail boots.

Accordingly, I kept my penchant a secret.

But then came summer and I, like most kids, hung out in the local park playing football with some boys three or four years my senior – Nigel Thomas, Raymond O'Neil, Roger Williams and Paul Sullivan – who'd dropped the suedehead look entirely and favoured long feather-cut hair, cheesecloth shirts, and baggy Brutus fader jeans. They always had a little gang of pretty girls wrapped around them who put the rather ugly skinhead gals I knew in the shade.

Soon I was dropping by Roger's house and listening to his new acquisition, *Ziggy Stardust* by David Bowie, savouring the funky 'Soul Love' and the rambunctious 'Suffragette City' while imbibing flagons of Brains Bitter.

Admittedly I was an impressionable young kid and I was in awe. I started growing my hair and saving up for a pair of bags, a Brutus spoon-collared shirt and a pair of wedges from Freeman, Hardy and Willis à la Bowie.

Then came 'John, I'm Only Dancing', released in September, which was a gentle but totally rocking R 'n' B groove. Its video, directed by photographer Mick Rock and featuring the outrageously camp Lindsay Kemp and a team of androgynous dancers, was banned by the BBC.

'In 1972 along came Doris, Mr Bowie,' remembers Mick Rock. 'I got wind of him as he was shouting, "Loook at me I'm a screaming poof!" and I thought, well that's interesting, that's a little strange, a little poncey. I think I'll have a little basin of that. But in those days that kind of thing wasn't everyone's cup of rosy.'

And I for one will second that. Round my way, liking Bowie meant that at some point you would almost certainly be physically attacked by thugs who took great delight in stamping all over their prey.

Regardless of this threat, there was no stopping me; my hair was growing, I'd bought the shirt and almost had enough savings for the trousers, too.

And then *The Man Who Sold the World* was re-released and more flagons appeared. Now we had mesmerising melodies and a faultless album from this bloke who could do no wrong. Next came 'Jean Genie', which reached number two in the charts and was all over the radio stations like a rash. Bowie was an overnight success after ten years of diligent effort with a song whose title was a word play on the gay icon Jean Genet, while for the lyrics he used the cut-up technique pioneered by another gay icon, the novelist William Burroughs. Needless to say, if you were a kid in my necks of the woods you needed cojones as big as footballs to admit a partiality for David Bowie.

By January I had my kit and the spiky-on-top-long-in-the-back, semi-mullet haircut, rendering me an alien in a sea of Doc Martens and Levi's. At school my clique of tearaways – siding with their older skinhead thug pals – ganged up on me, calling me 'Nancy boy' and 'poofter'. I took it on the chin, retreated, and no longer hit the town with the hard boys of a Saturday afternoon.

This lasted until the album *Aladdin Sane* was released in April and I loved it. Of course, my father was positively outraged when he saw the cover and even more enraged when he heard the song 'Time' and its legendary line '...falls wanking to the floor'! But still, I think it was this album that confirmed my need to be me and fuck the rest of them. So over the course of one sunny day, just before Easter, I physically attacked every last one of the so-called tough guys who had so enthusiastically berated me. They all bottled it and some even ran away. I was never the object of their ridicule again. In a way David Bowie and my penchant for his music gave me both the bottle and the single-mindedness to do this. Afterwards I was never quite the same.

As for *Aladdin Sane*, Mike Garson's incredible jazz-tinged piano, Linda Lewis's soul backing vocal and David Sanborn's sax hit my nail on its proverbial as I was just getting into soul music at that time, particularly anything on Philadelphia records, along with Al Green, Stevie Wonder, Marvin Gaye et al.

Bowie described *Aladdin Sane* as simply 'Ziggy goes to America'. Most of the tracks were observations he composed on the road during his 1972 US tour and the album undoubtedly established Bowie as a musical icon. It famously featured him with the now-trademark red and blue lightning bolt on his face that he said represented the duality of mind, while inside the gatefold he was naked and bereft of genitalia – although as photographer Brian Duffy told me, 'He was naked because the costumes didn't show up and the flash on the face was copied from the logo of a Panasonic kettle in the kitchen.'

'The make-up artist Pierre started to apply this tiny little flash on his face,' Duffy's studio manager Francis Newman recalled. 'And when Duffy saw it he said, "No, not fucking like that, like this." He literally drew it right across his face and said to Pierre, "Now fill that in." It was actually Duffy who did the initial shape – I'm not saying he did the actual make-up. It then took Pierre about an hour to apply properly. The red flash is so shiny because it was actually lipstick.'

One thing I realised early on was that almost all the people I knew who liked David Bowie were intelligent. They read books, studied his lyrics and were confident about being themselves, even if that meant taking the odd beating. On the other hand, those who didn't were so square they weren't worth acknowledging. Or they were morons. I realised that Bowie was a kind of litmus test. In short, if you liked him there was a good chance you were at least ever so slightly nonconformist and thus I could have a conversation with you.

Come that summer, June to be precise, a pretty girl in my class voiced her love for the Bowie single 'Life on Mars'. 'I have that on an LP called *Hunky Dory*,' I immediately piped up, only for the whole class to look at me as if I was the coolest cat on the block. Apparently disappointed that I had burst her bubble, the girl never spoke to me again. Whatever, the next day me and the few pals I had of my age were huddled around my Fidelity record player, taking in the man. They were digging the sounds but not knowing quite why, evidently still confused by this alien in make-up – a situation I certainly got some odd pleasure from.

While all this was happening, David Bowie decided to kill off Ziggy at his famous 'Last Stand' concert at the Hammersmith Odeon – which almost didn't happen after Steve Jones and Paul Cook of the Sex Pistols stole the band's back line for their own use (thus, in a way, Bowie helped create UK punk).

'David had to ditch Ziggy,' said Mick Rock. 'He was losing himself in the character and Ziggy was taking over. I saw it.'

Not that it mattered to me as by now it was summer 1973 and I'd added to my wardrobe the leather round-collared Budgie bomber jacket, another shirt and a pair of platforms and was jolly well up and running.

In November Bowie released *Pin Ups*, an album of covers that included the rather marvellous 'Sorrow'. Like his previous three singles it reached number three in the charts, while 'Jean Genie' had got to number two. He now had had three number one albums and another two in the top five. Bowie-mania had well and truly arrived.

His next album *Diamond Dogs* (featuring Leee Childers's artwork on the inside gatefold) is in many ways a swan song to Bowie's glam rock phase, while tunes such as the funky 'Big Brother' and the *Shaft*-like '1984' are a precursor to his 'plastic soul' era. Bowie was jumping the glam rock ship just before it became a joke and again hit number one in the UK charts.

By now it was 1974 and fifties-attired soul boys were walking the streets of London dressed in peg trousers and Hawaiian shirts, replete with wedge haircuts. They were frequenting clubs such as El Sombrero and Crackers, which pumped out soul and funk. Back in Wales we were following suit, but we weren't expecting the cover image or the music of David Bowie's magisterial *David Live* album. Gone was the spiky red hair and the outlandish costumes and in their place was a pure soul boy haircut and a bum freezer pegged trouser suit, while the album featured utterly brilliant renditions of all his greatest tunes, rendered by a first rate funk soul jazz band. Our gobs were well and truly smacked.

Bowie moved to New York in the spring of 1974, searching for anonymity in its avenues and streets. There he met virtuoso guitarist Carlos Alomar, a Puerto Rican New Yorker who'd toured with James Brown when he was just seventeen and later with Roy Ayers.

'He was the whitest guy I had ever seen, his skin was translucent and his hair was bright orange, but he was interested in everything to do with the New York experience,' Alomar told writer David Buckley. 'He came across as extremely humble, just a very nice person. I told him, "What you need is to come to my house and my wife can make you some nice chicken, rice and beans and put some meat on those bones." And surprisingly he said, "Sure." So he got a limousine parked right in front of my apartment house in Queens and we got together and hung out.'

Bowie swallowed up all New York had to offer, and vice versa. At the time the city was awash with cocaine and Bowie developed an insatiable appetite for the stuff, until his entire diet consisted of cocaine, peppers and milk, his weight eventually plummeting to a mere eighty pounds, which considering he claimed to be five feet, ten inches in height (I think he was probably a couple of inches shorter) is frightening.

Bowie, who claimed that apart from a bit of speed this was his first major drug affair, would often stay awake for seven or eight days on end at his lavish suite in Manhattan's Sherry-Netherland hotel. At one point he was 'taking so much it would have killed a horse', according to record producer Tony Visconti, who accompanied Bowie on the town alongside John Lennon. 'We did mountains of cocaine, it looked like the Matterhorn, obscenely big.'

Of course with excessive cocaine use comes excessive paranoia, which wasn't helped when Bowie discovered that manager Defries had contractually stitched him up. 'This is what ended their working relationship,' explained Visconti. 'Defries charged all of the company's wages and expenses solely to Bowie.' Defries later went on to lose $22 million in an offshore tax evasion scheme and then lost $9 million after he was sued by Capitol Records in 2011.

Bowie, destroyed by this revelation that his manager had been dishonest and had ruthlessly ripped him off, plunged deeper into the abyss. Aided by truckloads of Bolivian marching powder he sank into despair, isolation and a lack of confidence, believing that he could no longer make a record without imbibing huge amounts of chang. The BBC documentary *Cracked Actor* sees him freaked out in the back of a limo, while his appearance on *The Dick Cavett Show*, filmed at ABC Studios, New York, on 2 November 1974, saw the man coked off his perch, looking awkward and gurning. Still, no one batted an eyelid as at the time everyone in the music biz was at it. It was the Dom Perignon of drugs, expensive and glamorous, and Bowie was the King of Snort.

Incredibly, in spite of all this, he still managed to write and co-produce *Young Americans* (with Visconti), which does not sound anything like the work of a paranoid, agitated, delusional coked-out nutbag – quite the opposite. It is a relaxed, sophisticated and enormously assured funky affair that many regard as his finest work. Even more surprising is that according to Visconti *Young Americans* was 85 per cent live and most of the vocals were captured in one or two takes. 'Fame', featuring John Lennon and based on an Alomar riff, hit number one in the US billboard charts in July 1975, while the album achieved number two in the UK charts in March that year. 'There was no point in doing a straight take of black music so I put my own spin on it,' Bowie explained.

'I went to the local disco in Woking and would see all my mates from when we were skinheads or suedeheads in the early 1970s wearing the plastic sandals, the peg trousers and the Hawaiian and bowling shirts with the wedge haircuts,' said Paul Weller. 'They danced to Philly stuff but you'd also hear TVC 15 and *Young Americans* amongst it all. He nailed the link between British working-class youth who always follow Black American soul music and the style and fashions.

He always had his finger on the pulse and was a cut above everyone else.'

Indubitably, the release of *Young Americans* was spot-on for many a groovy Brit and coincided with what was the summer of soul in the UK; Hamilton Bohannon, Sister Sledge, Jackie Wilson and the Blackbyrds all hit the British top ten, while Van McCoy's 'The Hustle' reached number three. As for our gang, by September we'd started going to London's Kings Road in my pal Nigel Thomas's yellow Hillman Avenger to buy 1950s peg trousers before dancing to funk at Crackers in Wardour Street.

For me, Bowie hadn't taken a back seat; he just sat side by side with James Brown, the Fatback Band and the Ohio Players. Back home in Merthyr Tydfil the local thugs still felt the need to physically attack us, so I organised bus trips to Newport where I accidentally stumbled across a club called Scamps that played a lot of Bowie and Roxy. Pretty soon the club was *the* place to be in south Wales, attracting a fair-sized crew of Bowie freaks: Sean, Noddy, Mark Taylor, Mark Stephenson, Graham 'Spot' Williams, Colin Fisher, Steve Strange et al. In those days there were no style magazines so folk looked to the music press for inspiration, and most took Bowie or Bryan Ferry as their model, copying them down to the last detail. To dress exactly as our heroes was mustard.

In October 1975, as many were getting hip to Major Tom, Bowie achieved his first number one in the UK with a re-release of 'A Space Oddity'. His hair on the cover was decidedly punk rock.

Back in the real world, even though the *Young Americans* look was rather banal compared to previous Bowie attire, it still caused umbrage. At one point in early 1976 a gang of about twenty local thugs shouting 'Kill the Bowie freaks!' assaulted us as we exited Scamps and I ended up with a stitched upper lip, a night in the cells and a six-month suspended sentence for GBH when I was the one who was attacked. It seems that not even the judge liked Bowie fans.

Bowie himself was also subject to more attention than he was comfortable with. He now crossed all boards – he was adored by die-hard fans and the gay crowd, attracted black-music-loving soul boys of all colours, along with your more intelligent record-buying punter.

Bowie became the biggest star on the planet, albeit reluctantly, but the resultant attention was nigh on impossible for him to handle.

'To become famous was purely a means to acquire the resources to do what he wanted to do,' testifies Visconti. 'He wasn't at all interested in fame *per se*.' Or as the man himself said in 1974, 'I'm not content with being just a rock 'n' roll star. I need it at the moment so I can go off and do other things.'

But fame came to him, and by the plane-full. It got so bad that he couldn't leave his house, walk down the street or think without being accosted.

'Success was like going from zero to a hundred miles an hour in a few seconds for me,' explained Bowie. 'I was very frightened at first... it became like living in a very luxurious mental hospital where you are put in a padded room and meals are brought to you and every now and again you are let out to make money for everyone but yourself. It's good for getting concert tickets, backstage passes and tables at posh restaurants but apart from that it's a complete pain in the ass.'

Bowie's answer was to retreat further into himself and take more Charlie. Midway through 1975 he moved to LA and rented a small house on Doheny Drive with two huge sphinxes (Egyptian symbols of bisexuality and the occult) in the garden. He contented himself with drawing huge pentagrams on his wall and became interested in Aleister Crowley and the Hermetic Order of the Golden Dawn. He began storing his urine in the fridge so no other wizard could filch it and use it to enchant him. His long-time aide Coco Schwab would often find him slumped around the house and used to use the little mirror he chopped his coke out on to check he was still breathing.

Yet somehow he managed to prepare himself for his first starring role in a major motion picture as alien visitor Thomas Newton in Nicolas Roeg's *The Man Who Fell to Earth*. The director had spotted Bowie in the *Cracked Actor* BBC documentary. Bowie's huge cocaine problem had placed him way outside of society and its norms and into a detached twilight world that gave him a real-life weirdness that was perfect for the role.

On set, however, he was the consummate professional. Roeg allowed him to pick his own wardrobe and the singer was observant, punctual, knew his lines, and managed to maintain an entirely detached air that was perfect, while still doing mounds of coke. 'I actually was feeling as alienated as that character was,' he said in 1983. 'It was a pretty natural performance... A good *exhibition* of somebody literally falling apart in front of you. I was totally insecure with about ten grams [of cocaine] a day in me. I was stoned out of my mind from beginning to end. I'm so pleased I made that [film]. But I didn't really know what was being made at all.'

On its release *The Man Who Fell to Earth* fuelled a massive wave of Bowie lookalikes. I knew fans that watched the movie every night for two weeks, studiously memorising and noting down Bowie's every style nuance, then either getting his mufti copied or searching down similar kit. Some even copied his table tennis outfit, replete with visor.

After filming Bowie hung on to the character's uncommonly stylish look, along with his alien demeanour. As a result the Thin White Duke was born, a character who, according to Bowie, was a European ensconced in the USA and who, rather like Newton, was desperate to get home.

Once the shoot ended he wasted no time in escalating his drug habit. 'I'd stay up for seven or eight days on the trot,' he admitted in the 1990s. 'The impending tiredness and fatigue produces that hallucinogenic state quite naturally – well, half naturally. By the end of the week my whole life would be transformed into this bizarre, nihilistic fantasy world of oncoming doom, mythological characters and imminent totalitarianism.'

By now he was more or less anorexic and at one point phoned Angie claiming he'd been kidnapped by someone who wanted his semen so that they might impregnate themselves during a witches' sabbath. He also developed a worrying fascination with the Nazis and their alleged search for the Holy Grail. The plot was indeed lost, but it was only after he had his house exorcised that friends realised that he'd had a nervous breakdown.

Yet again he managed to pull himself together and in October 1975 started working on the *Station to Station* LP. 'We were in the studio and it was nuts,' testified guitarist Earl Slick. 'We often didn't start till 1 or 2am. I don't remember a lot about it.' Bowie said he couldn't remember recording it at all but, as the title track's lyrics suggest, seems cognisant of his addiction. 'It's not the side-effects of the cocaine, I'm thinking that it must be love, it's too late to be grateful, it's too late to be late again.'

Many consider *Station to Station* his finest thirty-eight minutes.

The album itself was released in January 1976 but the single 'Golden Years' appeared two months before and stands as an anthem of a generation. I cannot listen to the song without being whisked back to those halcyon days when we were all oh-so naïve and optimistic and no one could touch us. The album was experimental, fusing the two musical obsessions of the day – black music and electronica (Kraftwerk's *Autobahn* reached number four in the UK album charts in 1974, while George McCrae's electro-backed 'Rock Your Baby' topped the singles charts). Bowie was now king.

And then in May he played Wembley. Of course I couldn't afford the £2.75 ticket but at the last minute my great friend Roger Williams was struck down with pleurisy and gave the ticket to me, so around fifty of us Bowie fans, dressed to the nines, boarded our hired coach for the trip. A landmark concert, it wasn't only a shockingly brilliant performance (journalist Paul Gambaccini called it 'the finest performance by a white artist that I have ever seen') – it was where I saw the future.

The crowd was mainly soul boys and girls in pink peg trousers and wedge haircuts, but amongst them was a darker element – people in leather trousers with cropped hair and multiple earrings, Westwood cowboy T-shirts and bondage trousers, hacked hair with drainpipes and winkle-pickers. Amongst these were the Bromley Contingent (including Siouxsie Sioux), the Sex Pistols, and my future pal, Pistols co-manager Nils Stevenson.

Thoroughly intrigued, I knew where I was headed next style-wise. After the gig we went first to Louise's and then onto Chaguaramas in Neal Street, Covent Garden, which was then, unbeknownst to me, a trannie bar. All I recall was that the music was great, a girl with a deep voice chatted me up, and a glass of orange juice cost 60p (a fiver in today's money).

Unfortunately I missed the bus and had to hitchhike all the way back to Wales.

The punk ethic was already in the air, but it didn't have a name. My pals and I had already worshipped the Velvet Underground's 'banana' album, loved *Horses* by Patti Smith and *Here Come the Warm Jets* by Eno, and we played the Stooges to death (all of which we accessed after Bowie had referenced them). But the Bowie concert cemented our ardour. Consequently, my lovely mum knitted me a huge mohair jumper, made me a vinyl T-shirt with a zip across the front and pierced both my ears a few times. And so off I went into the fledgling punk scene while still attending funk clubs.

Many of the early soul boys, us included, wore early Westwood – the plastic-pocketed slacks, the ciré wet-look T-shirts – and had cropped bleached hair à la Lou Reed. I'd go as far as to say that punk was all about the DIY attitude and the trousers, while the music (apart from the political statements by the Sex Pistols and the Clash) was an entirely unnecessary interlude that got in the way of what was a rather exciting and interesting musical progression, namely black music fused with electro and Latin. Punk was the audio equivalent of genetically engineered foods – completely unnatural – and by the time the 'Anarchy' tour was underway in December 1976, the scene was getting silly. By February 1977 it was all over for me.

Bowie, of course, did not miss a trick. While punk reared its self-consciously recalcitrant head, he carried on regardless and moved from LA.

'I started getting really worried for my life,' stated Bowie in 1993. 'I came close to OD'ing several times. It was like being in a car and losing control of the steering. I resigned myself to going over the edge.'

He decamped to Europe – namely the Château d'Hérouville near Paris – and wrote and recorded not one but two works of genius, Iggy Pop's *The Idiot* and the mighty *Low*, for which he pulled in former Roxy synth maestro Brian Eno, brought Alomar and his guys over, and put Visconti in the co-production chair.

'I had to develop a new language so I discarded my characters and decided to work with Eno and found a soul mate,' said Bowie.

'I wanted to do something I *wanted* to do rather than what was expected of me.'

Later that year he moved to Berlin in search of anonymity.

'I went naked and stripped everything down to the barest essentials so I could build back up again,' he said. 'I gave away all my clothes, wore just jeans and check shirts and rode a bicycle. No one cared about a rock star in Berlin. It was my first taste of freedom from the trappings of fame in a good while.'

But Germany was a controversial choice of location. On his return to Britain from the US in May 1976 the *NME* had published a photo of him standing in a Mercedes convertible at Victoria station. It was accompanied by the headline 'Heil and Farewell', claiming he'd given a fascist salute. Given that Bowie had a mainly black rhythm section and had dated Ava Cherry, that was highly unlikely. Yet folk weren't happy, especially as he'd told a Stockholm journalist that he was the 'only alternative for the premier in England, Britain could benefit from a Fascist leader... Fascism really is Nationalism. I believe very strongly in fascism.'

A few weeks previously he had been detained at Russian customs when a cache of Nazi memorabilia was found in his suitcase. Oh dear! It was obvious that he had lost the plot, but detractors still claimed he'd long courted such absolutist philosophies. On *Hunky Dory* he referenced Friedrich Nietzsche's *Übermensch* – 'Gotta make way for the Homo Superior' – while some equated the *Aladdin Sane* logo with that of the SS.

Still, claiming an interest in German electronic music, he went to Berlin and lived in a flat above an auto parts shop in Schöneberg. Initially he planned to get healthy but was soon at it again, snorting, drinking and driving around the city with his new flatmate Iggy Pop. They hung out in gay and trannie bars and got mashed at clubs like the Dschungel and the Unlimited.

Both men had moved to escape Class A drugs, but unfortunately for Iggy Berlin was the heroin capital of Germany and coke was also ubiquitous. Whatever the case may be, Bowie certainly showed his resolve and delivered the goods with an album that was brave to say the least. *Low* was deeply uncommercial and mainly electronic, comprising 50 per cent instrumental tracks, yet it still reached number two and ten in the UK and US charts respectively, while the first single from the album, 'Sound and Vision', rose to number three in the UK charts.

'The most exciting thing about this was that I found I could still write without drugs,' proclaimed Bowie, who had cleaned his act up. 'It was an extremely rewarding time for me.'

As for yours truly, the album washed over punk rock like a huge tidal wave and reinforced my high opinion of the man. Meanwhile lacklustre music critics such as Charles Shaar Murray of the *NME* neither liked nor understood the release. But that was what we loved about Bowie – the idiots didn't get him.

Meanwhile Bowie toured with Iggy as a keyboard player. Between April and June 1977 he co-wrote and produced Iggy's *Lust for Life* album and straight afterwards wrote and co-produced his own monumental *Heroes* album.

For this he used the same line up as *Low* but added King Crimson guitarist Robert Fripp, whose virtuoso performance gave the album a fresh and decidedly uncommon edge. Released on 14 October 1977, it was devoid of all the peripheral style content and was again deftly unconventional, from the raucous opening track, 'Beauty and the Beast', through to its conclusion, 'The Secret Life of Arabia'. Between these tracks ambient, almost classical compositions such as the mighty 'Sense of Doubt' and the Japanese-tinged 'Moss Garden' amazed and astounded. And lest we forget, there is also the totally iconic title track 'Heroes', which has since become an anthem for all manner of causes. The German government, after Bowie's death, thanked him for helping to 'bring down the wall' with this song. Disgracefully, 'Heroes' only reached number twenty-four in the UK charts while ABBA was number one.

In the summer of 1978 Bowie played Earls Court and attracted the full retinue of Bowie freaks, many of whom had switched to full Westwood kit a few years before but now reverted back to Bowie circa 1975-77. After the show we went to Billy's, a seedy basement club run by a Jamaican pimp. It was underneath the Gargoyle Club in Meard Street, Soho, a hooker-infested back alley in this ganglion of nocturnal naughtiness. Billy's was where DJ Caroline from the club Louise's had moved her crowd and did a lesbian night every week.

Cut to the autumn, and I had just returned from a few months in California and was attending Camberwell School of Arts. One night I went back to Billy's on a Tuesday with my old pal Frank Kelly. The Welsh puppeteer and actor David Claridge (the man behind Roland Rat and the S&M organisation Skin Two) had started up a Bowie night on Tuesdays playing obscure Bowie bootlegs, Roxy Music and Kraftwerk.

Within weeks the club was so packed that Claridge got my other old friend from Wales, Steve Strange – who worked in his pal Helen's shop, PX – to do the door picking. Suddenly Claridge was replaced by Rusty Egan, who played more or less the same tunes, in addition to that year's biggest electro releases such as the Human League's 'Being Boiled' and Kraftwerk's 'The Model' and 'Neon Lights'. It was a rather obvious playlist but no one else was doing it then and it appealed to a crowd of die-hard Bowie fans for whom punk was entirely over and deemed naff.

After just a few months Billy's Bowie night closed. Vince, the six-foot, six-inch Jamaican gangster proprietor, wanted to put the door price up and as Strange and Egan were on a wage they wouldn't have benefited, so they decamped their Tuesday nights to the Blitz in Covent Garden – a trendy wine bar decorated in World War II fashion. And it was all pretty much the same apart from the press that the club attracted and the hordes of rubber-neckers who came to see the freaks but couldn't get past the stringent door policy of Strange and his security.

It was all very groovy. There was no house style or exact dress code, just a mad bunch of extroverts 'doing a Bowie' and dressing exactly as they pleased. It wasn't about conformity. It was about being *you*. 'The whole scenario was like a big, mad adventure with everyone just having a great time dressing up and going out,' recalls Princess Julia. 'I remember once making an outfit out of an old sheet and people loved it.' Contrary to the prevailing myth, it wasn't all frills and eyeliner.

The club for the most part catered to a motley crew of extroverts and resembled the canteen of MGM Studios circa 1953. 'There were a lot of male twentieth-century archetypes – cowboys, bikers, gauchos, screen idols, commandos, Italian futurists,' recalls Christos Tolera. 'It was very stylish and bizarre at the same time.'

Within the club you could be whoever you wanted to be. You could be a hero, as David Bowie put it, just for one day. And like him, none of us were content with what was mapped out for us. We all clubbed together and looked for something else.

'A lot of the Blitz regulars went on and did really well,' explained Steve Strange. 'Spandau Ballet, John Galliano, Stephen Jones, Kim Bowen, Sade, film director John Maybury, the artist Cerith Wyn Evans, broadcaster Robert Elms, artist Grayson Perry, GQ editor Dylan Jones, and me and you.'

Indeed, I started my own nights in December 1978, putting on parties in Toyah Willcox's run-down warehouse space called Mayhem Studios in Battersea, in partnership with Bob Elms, Graham Smith and Melissa Kaplan. They were a roaring success with our mob.

First called a Cult with No Name, then Blitz Kids, all we had in common was an adoration for Bowie, who continued to fuel our fires by releasing 'Beauty and the Beast', 'Breaking Glass', 'Boys Keep Swinging' and 'DJ' in the space of about eighteen months. In truth, so enamoured were my pals and I that we went and stayed in Berlin one summer in search of what had enthused the master.

But back in London things were changing. Our little gang had now been dubbed the New Romantics and, as with punk before it, the scene became utterly ridiculous, with gangs of sheep – mainly men – masquerading as individuals, copying last year's Strange look by dressing in frilly shirts, knee-length pants and ballet shoes, their hair big and vertical, their faces covered with white make-up and lipstick. It wasn't good. However we had already moved on and were now looking at silent movies for inspiration. I favoured either a gaucho look, influenced by Rudolph Valentino, or an Erich von Stroheim ensemble replete with jodhpurs, riding boots and monocle. Others chose to emulate Theda Bara, Douglas Fairbanks, Louise

Brooks or Harold Lloyd. For the inner core, futurism, electro and big hair were yesterday's news, while the Blitz's appeal was waning.

Our answer was to open a night at St Moritz and go back to playing Marlene Dietrich, tunes from the film *Cabaret*, Peggy Lee, Edith Piaf, Marilyn Monroe, Art Blakey and Tom Waits. It was without doubt a radical departure, but not for Bowie, who in March, three months after we opened, released 'The Alabama Song', written by Kurt Weill in 1929.

Yet we still went to the Blitz, as we weren't allowed in most venues. Then, just as it was truly on the way out and Hell was running two nights a week, Bowie turned up, and it was like the Pope dropping by to attend mass at a church in some remote village in the Philippines. Folk went nuts. Some were almost fainting and hyperventilating in the corner.

'I first clapped eyes on him in person at the Blitz when he came down in search of people for the video for "Ashes to Ashes",' recalls the artist Tracey Emin. 'Steve Strange ushered me upstairs where Bowie was sitting on the long table and people were fighting to get upstairs just to take a look at him.'

It really was hilarious. Naturally, I didn't make a twit of myself by trying to get upstairs. I just stood by the bar chuckling with Christos.

Bowie was not only there to check out what was happening but, as Emin said, to find a few characters for his forthcoming video shoot. Steve asked me to go along but as we were to meet at the Hilton at 4am a few days later and it wasn't paid, I wasn't at all keen. Eventually he settled on Darla Jane Gilroy, Judith Frankland and a girl I didn't know who looked entirely out of place.

'The four of us were told to meet outside the Hilton Hotel in London and we were all thinking, oh my god, we've got to be going somewhere fabulous like Barbados, somewhere hot and tropical,' recalled Strange. 'So we get to the hotel about 5am, then we get on this coach thinking, it's taking us to the airport. Then we're told we're going to Southend! The one glamorous thing about it was that David did close off the whole beach, but to be honest there weren't that many people around as it was absolutely freezing.'

I was hugely relieved when Steve told me this and even more so when I heard the song and saw the video as I thought both were utter shite and that Bowie dressing like a Pierrot was so New Romantic and old hat. Still, he clearly knew what he was doing, as the song reached number one. The track was from the album *Scary Monsters*, released in September 1980, which was by my estimation really outdated and for the most part instantly forgettable, while he looked like a bit of a chump on the cover image in his make-up and frills. At the time, after breaking it out in Hell, I was pioneering a return to the funk, while in the north of England and in New York groups like A Certain Ratio and James White and the Blacks were on the same wavelength.

Thus, finally, my love affair with Bowie had ended. I still played and adored all the old stuff, but the new recordings left me underwhelmed.

Later that year we opened another one-nighter at Le Kilt. By now the Blitz was over and New Romanticism was something that people from Birmingham loved. Down in the smoke our menu du jour was funk, funk and more funk, while the mufti I pioneered was decidedly manly and the polar opposite of the fey New Romantic look.

At the time, for my considerable sins, I was studying fashion at St Martins and started designing oversized zoot suits that I got made by a tailor. I grew a goatee beard, dragged out my 1940s hand-painted kipper ties, correspondent shoes and a beret, and listened to Miles Davis, Dizzy Gillespie, Tito Puente and James Brown. Previously I'd been influenced, but now it was my turn to be the influencer.

A few months after we opened, Bowie released 'Fashion' and while we agreed with the lyrics, we thought it stank – though I have since grown to like the song.

By 1981 I had signed my band Blue Rondo à la Turk to Virgin and our record 'Me and Mr Sanchez' – a storming Brazilian batucada – was racing up the charts, while the only other tune that was played on Radio One more than us was the absolutely dire 'Under Pressure' by Bowie and the loathsome Freddie Mercury. Bowie followed this up with the over-produced 'Cat People'.

Oddly, I became acquainted with Bowie himself around the same time that I found myself becoming less enamoured of his music. On

14 October 1982, I opened the Wag Club on Wardour Street, Soho, first as a one-nighter and then, in April, for seven nights a week. We played funk, jazz and Latin along with a smattering of hip-hop. In March Bowie had released 'Let's Dance', his most commercially successful tune to date which, albeit a pop song, certainly mirrored what we were doing (even though we'd never play it). He would pop into the Wag on a Saturday from time to time – mostly on his own – and we'd chat about art and music.

He never had a minder or entourage and I never called the paparazzi when he turned up. I was hardly going to shout it from the rooftops anyway as I knew that he'd leave and never return. No one ever bothered him, as he always seemed to blend in. I remember on one occasion a girl I knew said, 'That bloke you were talking to looked like David Bowie.' 'He was,' I replied. She never forgave me for not telling her. But then what was I supposed to do? Run around telling everyone? The only time he was noticed was when he turned up with Mick Jagger, but even then no one really bothered them. I took them in and offered them a drink. David asked for a pint of bitter, which we didn't sell behind the bar as in 1983 no one except your dad drank the stuff. So he asked for a bottle of Newcastle Brown Ale instead. I liked that.

Looking back, I should have been more fazed by his attentions. This was David freaking BOWIE for Christ's sake! But because I considered 'Let's Dance' too pop and 'China Girl' a complete waste of plastic I think it moderated any fanboy tendencies in me. Had it happened around the time of *Young Americans* it would have been a different story for sure. But this was the most commercial phase of Bowie's career and I confess that I was disappointed that the great man had succumbed to the lure of the filthy lucre and the desire for a 'pop' hit.

In 1983 I received an invite for his Serious Moonlight gig in Milton Keynes (the poster for which was remarkably like one of my illustrations on the Blue Rondo cover) and ended up watching it from the wings. Bowie was so friendly to me that I actually felt guilty about disliking his recent work.

He may have been approachable and affable but that still didn't make me feel any less embarrassed the next time I met him. I'd turned up at 5am in Maida Vale in the summer of 1984 thinking I was to be an extra on Julien Temple's elongated pop promo for the single 'Jazzin' for Blue Jean' (David loved the jazz night at the Wag), only to be introduced to a smart young actress named Louise. To my horror I promptly discovered that I was expected to not just walk with her down the street but to *speak lines of actual dialogue*.

What exacerbated my unease was that during the same scene Bowie was to be standing above us on a ladder pasting a poster of his alter ego in the film, Screaming Lord Byron, to a billboard. Worse still, it was drizzling – that horrible cold rain that's blighted many a UK holiday.

A dozen takes later, I whimpered to Julien, 'David Bowie's up a ladder waiting for me to get this right. I can't do this!' So David came down the ladder, wiped the rain off his face and assured me that all was well and that he understood my predicament as he'd had exactly the same problem on *The Man Who Fell to Earth*. Of course this was of absolutely no bleeding use to me whatsoever and it wasn't until take fifty-four that I sort of got it right.

Later in the day, maybe in an effort to help me salvage whatever self-respect I had left, David asked me to find him a backing band for the mimed performance of the song, soon to be filmed at the Rainbow Room above the old site of Biba on Kensington High Street. I was then asked to recruit an audience of London's finest for his performance and was backstage with him as he donned his extravagant, almost glam rock make-up and turban.

A few days later Julien Temple called me and asked if he could use the Wag to shoot a special version of the song for MTV because David liked the venue and its view over Chinatown. He then reiterated David's request that I find the audience and asked whether David could use my office as his dressing room, if it didn't put me out, of course. No prizes for guessing my answer, but on the day David's main concern was that he was an inconvenience and that I should carry on as if he wasn't there, which was of course impossible. But still he persisted, was constantly self-deprecating and insisted on making *me* a cup of tea!

The following year I worked with Julien again on the film *Absolute Beginners* and was fortunate to spend even more time with David. He'd turn up on set dressed in his windcheater and Converse and seemed totally unaware of the effect he had on the extras I'd gathered together, who were to the last huge Bowie fans. He also brought his fourteen-year-old son Duncan along and introduced him to the whole crew.

After that I didn't really listen to his music. I'd rather not think about 'Dancing in the Street', liked 'This Is Not America', but the *Tin Machine* era left me (and most others) thoroughly unimpressed. As a result I didn't even listen to *Black Tie, White Noise* at the time. Although listening to it now, it's safe to say it's a tad lacking, even if his voice is in fine fettle and the title track, along with 'Jump They Say' and 'Looking For Lester', stand up nicely (perhaps because of Lester Bowie's trumpet). His next effort, *Outside*, I liked as it's a barking mad mix of ambience, poetry and song and features Carlos Alomar and Mike Garson and personnel with Eno producing. *Earthling* was rather average, I thought, but it did see Bowie return to his old uncompromising self.

One night in April 1995 I bumped into him at the Atlantic Bar and we had a little chat, whereupon he invited me to the private view of his first solo art exhibition in Cork Street, Mayfair. I showed up and such was the scrum on the door that I turned away, ready to give up and go home, only for his PA, Coco Schwab, on David's instructions, to call after me and usher me past the hordes of fans and paparazzi. Inside we had a little chat, exchanged phone numbers and then he was whisked off to 'say hello to everyone', which he did with unparalleled diligence.

'In 1996 I was in a restaurant and someone came up to me and said, "I really like what you do." And I looked up and it was David Bowie,' recalls Tracey Emin. 'And we became friends. I went to Ireland then with him and Iman and then the last time I saw him he came round my house. He's a very funny person and extremely self-effacing. The type of man who has to be learning something all the time. He's a bit like his character in the film *The Man Who Fell to Earth* who constantly watches stacks of TVs on different channels all at the same time to absorb as much knowledge as possible. He was the first person I knew who was totally into the Internet and all it could give to you.'

In 1997, I began working at *GQ* as the style editor and recall how impressed my colleagues were when David, who was at the office for a photo shoot I believe, strolled up to my desk for a chat. Again, he was David Jones the bloke next door, seemingly impressed that I had reinvented myself as a journalist. He invited me to the Hanover Grand where he was performing the next night. Backstage, he got me a beer and treated me like an old friend. 'I'm knackered,' he confided. 'The problem is that I think I'm still twenty years of age.'

The last time we spoke was at some mad art happening in the meatpacking district in New York in the spring of 1999. He was his usual, self-deprecating funny self and seemed really happy to see me. I was enormously flattered. It still amazes me how much time he had for me. I was just this kid from Wales.

Unfortunately, I missed his legendary performance at Meltdown in 2002 and was really sad when his bass player Gail Ann Dorsey said that after his heart operation in 2004 he had decided not to play live again.

A couple of years ago I heard a whisper that David was ill and assumed it was his heart, but it was all very hush-hush and unspecific. It seems he didn't want anyone to know, didn't want sympathy, just wanted to get on with his life. All those around him respected his wishes and I inquired no further as such news was too much to take, but nevertheless the news of his death, when it came, unsettled me more than I thought it ever would. Accordingly, it has taken me a year to listen to his last two albums and while I find much of *The Next Day* not my cup of tea, 'Where Are We Now?' is a quiet, amazing song that haunts me constantly. As for *Black Star,* the fact that he used his own death as the premise for a work of art is a remarkable achievement, while the track 'Lazarus' brings a lump to my throat.

But as his last work underlines, David Bowie didn't just entertain, he intrigued and provoked, cross-pollinating his music with painting, literature, film, fashion and stage. From the outset he maintained that he was an artist who just happened to be working in pop.

If anyone was a maverick it was David Bowie. Throughout his entire career he did things his way, refusing to be anyone but himself, and he bestowed on millions of others, myself included, the unshakeable belief that they could do the same.

RIP David Bowie (8 January 1947 – 10 January 2016)

Jalal Nuriddin

Minutes after I meet Jalal Nuriddin, he raises his arms and kicks his foot in the air, touching his outstretched fingers. Pretty impressive for a seventy-year-old, I reckon. He is dressed head-to-foot in black leather, aviator shades, and a woollen hat over his steel-grey 'fro. This is the man Chuck D described as 'the undoubted godfather of rap', and he wasn't wrong.

As part of the Last Poets, Jalal, with his politically infused, socially aware poems dedicated to raising awareness of African-American history and culture – spoken over African percussion laced with an urban funk 'n' jazz sensibility – undoubtedly created the blueprint from which all rap is descended.

The band was led by Jalal, who had been jailed as a young man and offered an early release if he enlisted in the US army. Consequently he became a paratrooper, but was incarcerated again for refusing to salute the flag.

Given an honourable discharge, he had made the most of his time inside, learning the art of 'jail toast' (prison rap, most notably performed in *Dolemite*'s legendary 'Signifying Monkey'), embracing Islam and making the acquaintance of eventual fellow band members Umar Bin Hassan and Abiodun Oyewole.

Hanging out in Harlem, they joined the East Wind poetry workshop and started performing their raps, which Jalal then called 'spoa-graphics', on the streets. They officially formed the band on Malcolm X's birthday – 19 May 1969 – and attracted the attention of superlative jazz producer Alan Douglas, who signed them to his label and produced their bravura eponymous debut LP, *The Last Poets*.

The album soared into the US charts – number three in the US black singles and number twenty-nine in the pop chart – but before they could play live, Oyewole was sentenced to fourteen years for robbing a bank.

The band followed with the unimpeachable LP *This Is Madness* (1971), and the sublime *Chastisement*, an intoxicating mix of funk and cool jazz beneath a heady verbal concoction that Jalal called 'jaz-zoetry'. The following year Jalal, under the pseudonym Lightnin' Rod, released the seminal *Hustlers Convention*.

Sampled by the Wu-Tang Clan, Beastie Boys and Nas, and praised by Grandmaster Flash, Chuck D and Melle Mel, *Hustlers Convention* was all that hip-hop should ever be. 'I was snorting skag, while others played tag / and running through bitches like rags to riches,' goes the first title on the release, which precedes a gaudy representation of the ghetto, a prescient taste of things to come.

It was replete with the shoot-out finale that leaves the protagonists defeated by a system where 'the real hustlers were rippin' off billions / From the unsuspecting millions'. Similarly, Nuriddin never received the recognition or the financial reward he deserved for the work.

'It was probably the most influential record to set off all those early Bronx MCs,' says Chuck D. 'But very rarely does *Hustlers Convention* get mentioned in the annals. It's a missing piece of culture.'

'It's a cornerstone in the development of what is now a part of global culture. In the street somebody recited it and I thought it was amazing, the most epic jail toast of all time,' adds Fab Five Freddy. 'I memorised it and would recite it to friends on my block, then some-one told me it was based on a record. I stumbled upon that and passed it on. Hip street guys like Melle Mel knew about it. I could hear the influence in their raps.'

As the lyric goes: 'At the Hustlers Convention there's pick pockets and dope peddlers, murderers and thieves / card shark gamblers with aces up their sleeves / bank robbers, burglars, boozers and pimps / prostitutes, call girls and all kinds of nymphs / loan sharks, swindlers, counterfeiters and fences!'

Jalal Mansur Nuriddin released a further nine albums of the finest jazzoetry ever conceived. I considered it a privilege to be able to sit down with the great man over a plate or two of Chinese and chew some fat.

Chris Sullivan: Have you always been a man of music?

Jalal Nuriddin: Well, yeah. I grew up in music. I was born in bebop, raised on doo-wop, and I put the hip in hip-hop. Hip never plays out. Hop is an ingredient in beer, is what kangaroos and rabbits do, and is also a fifties dance, so I took a quantum leap and made it better.

CS: How did the Last Poets' sound evolve?

JN: It was the basic African rhythm combined with an African-American urban voice. I could rhyme before I could write, but my style was based on the blues. I started with jail toast, which was a combination of fable, fact, fiction, sex and violence and was designed to make you laugh.

Jail toast was various hustlers and players telling their life story. Some of it was fact, some of it was fancy. Most of it was exaggerated. It was like dissing rhymes, dirty jokes, and X-rated nursery rhymes. And there are only two masters of jail toasting: Redd Foxx and Dolemite. But nobody was saying anything that needed to be said or that was thought-provoking. I felt something new needed to be done that laid down the whys and wherefores of street life, its attractions and distractions. So when I was in the can I decided I was going to say what needed to be said, so wrote a few things down. Later, when I got out, we mixed it with an African drum sensibility, which was in our DNA. The Last Poets made that connection.

CS: How do you feel when people say you were the godfather of hip-hop?

JN: They commercialised the art form. It's just big business.

CS: What was the relationship with the Last Poets and other civil rights activists?

JN: We came out of human rights. If you have those, civil rights will follow. If you just have civil rights, that will depend on what people regard as civilisation, which differs from time to time and race to race.

CS: How do you feel about Obama?

JN: He found out that the office dictates his actions, not him. What Obama inherited was a *Titanic* in the North Sea, listing. And he managed to stabilise it. But he didn't get the credit, he got the blame.

CS: That's what people forget. He came into power in one of the worst economic and political depressions to hit America since the 1930s.

JN: Now we're in the year of the Horse, which is a good year for economics, so by summer we should start to see the world's economy improve. I do a lot of astrology, a lot of kung fu and a lot of acupuncture.

CS: What kung fu do you do?

JN: Bak Mei – white eyebrow.

CS: How long have you been doing that for?

JN: Since I was in my thirties. Now I just do it for self-defence, to keep the reflexes sharp and stay flexible. I live in an old folks' home 'cos it's cheap. I'm the healthiest guy in the building. Everybody else has a wheelchair.

CS: What about those doo-wop days? Where you one of these doo-wop street corner kind of guys?

JN: More like council estate hallway. The acoustics is better. I didn't aspire to be a doo-wop singer *per se* but I hung out with doo-wop singers because it kept me from gangbanging, and we could go to some other neighbourhoods without being killed.

CS: The 1950s were tough in New York?

JN: Sure, but the difference was that there was a code of honour that had to do with choice of weapons. No guns allowed. Either hand-to-hand or baseball bats or chains or car aerials were the weapons of choice at that time. If you were feeling vicious, you might use acid. But nobody had guns.

CS: And what were the prominent gangs in your neighbourhood?

JN: My gang, the Fort Green Chaplains, was the most prominent.

Including the brother clubs, we numbered around 1,500. We had it locked down.

CS: Who were the main rivals? Italian gangs, Puerto Ricans?

JN: The Bishops [another African-American gang] were the main rivals from Bedford-Stuyvesant. Other gangs were the Mau Maus and the Sand Street Angels.

CS: So how about your parents?

JN: Mom was a housewife who loved gospel. Pop was a World War II navy veteran. Shell-shocked, sick on a pension, but he was a poker player and did it like it was a job. He played three hands and he lost one. He only gambled to put food on the table. But he didn't talk.

CS: How did you gravitate from doo-wop to the Last Poets?

JN: At that time the Last Poets revolutionised *everything*. After us, all the R 'n' B singers were suddenly like, 'You know what? We got to start putting messages in our songs.'

Listen to Marvin Gaye's *What's Going On,* or 'The Ghetto' by Donny Hathaway, for example. The way I started was that I realised that doo-wop and soul was fine for the era that we were in, but it was no good for the Human Rights movement.

We needed a rally point, a battle cry. When I realised that, I said, 'We need to come up with a new art form that reflects where we're at now, otherwise we'll be stuck in this mode for the duration.'

So I took jail toasts, which as I explained was like the blues, and did my own version that told of the street.

CS: When did you start doing this?

JN: 1968. I started at a writer's workshop in Harlem where my aunt had a beauty parlour. A friend of mine told me to check it out, so I went and realised that nobody had what I had. There were no poets. I actually had to go search for somebody else on the same page as me. I found that poetry was in line with bebop. So later, I discovered that I could write lyrics to jazz because I applied myself. I'd done gigs with Eddie Jefferson at Smalls Paradise in Harlem. And Eddie said, 'Man, your stuff is good. You can write lyrics.'

CS: Did those guys influence you, the scat singers?

JN: Yeah, well, Eddie Jefferson and Babs Gonzales for sure.

CS: I love the way they wrote melodies and poetry to horn solos.

JN: Yes, exactly. That was going *on*. Then I met Herb Jeffries who was a singer in the Duke Ellington band. Herb told me, because he was Afro-Italian, those vowels could be elongated. Max Roach [Charlie Mingus's drummer] was another big influence. He was my mentor.

CS: So who, out of all those guys, do you think was your biggest influence?

JN: All of those jazz musicians. See, one third of my work contained jazz, and 'Bird's Word' [from the album *Chastisement*] was like a tribute. I played with him [Charlie 'Bird' Parker], Jimmy Smith, Nina Simone and Miles Davis. He was a Last Poets fan. So most of the company I was keeping was jazz musicians. Later on I would meet Stevie and Aretha. Paul Robeson was a huge influence. Then I met James Baldwin in Paris. He passed me the baton.

CS: Your first album was a huge seller. It was number twenty-nine in the pop charts, which in 1969 meant a lot of records.

JN: It was all done by word of mouth.

CS: Were you surprised when it sold so well?

JN: I was surprised that the record was even released.

CS: Where did the Last Poets' name come from?

JN: The name was taken from a South African poet named Little

Willie Kgositsile [aka Bra Willie], who wrote a poem containing the line in 1968 that says that this was the last age of poems and essays, that guns and rifles would take their place; therefore we must be the 'last poets' of this age. He'd fled apartheid in South Africa and came to Harlem.

CS: Is there anyone you would have liked to work with?

JN: Bird and Diz [laughs].

CS: When you were growing up, was that music around you a lot?

JN: I didn't have any brothers. But my cousins involved me with Bird and Diz from the age of about seven or eight. So they was up on bebop. I was up on doo-wop. And I said to myself, as a teenager, 'This music requires sitting down, listening and figuring out what they're doing. I'm not old enough to do that yet. I need to grow up to get this.' By the time I was twenty-one, I got out the army – I'm an ex-paratrooper – and then I looked at it again.

CS: Were you drafted for Vietnam?

JN: They were building up troops and preparing for the Vietnam War. I got into trouble with the law. I was gangbanging and was jailed for assault and battery. Next thing was, 'We won't let you out unless you register for the draft because your gang is notorious.'

But then my mother came and visited me, and she was all broke up about it. She don't deserve that. So I got out and got drafted. Then my homeboy was like, 'I'm going into the paratroopers.' I was like, 'More power to you.' He said, 'You're supposed to have courage. You from Fort Greene, too?' So I volunteered, went in and he didn't because he was too physically weak to pass the PT test.

CS: You must have just missed the Vietnam War, right?

JN: I missed it by three months. They went in August 1965. I got out April 1965.

CS: Would you have been a conscientious objector, do you think?

JN: I got out because I was a conscientious objector. I found out what they was getting ready to do! The platoon sergeant told me, because he liked me, 'Listen, we got two economies. We gotta have a war every ten years. This way, we put people to war and manufacture more money. We always win and there's prosperity for the next forty years. If we pick a fight, then we got to go back to war.' He'd done twenty years and had one more year to go, and he got killed.

CS: Do you think the powers allowed crack and heroin into the ghettos to destabilise the Black Panthers, the Crips (Community Revolution In Progress) and other black power groups?

JN: Hell, yeah! Damn right! It was genocide, the systematic destruction of a race of people by the djinns. The police turned their heads from the smugglers. As long as it was designated for the ghetto, then they was all right. That saved them the trouble of building prisons, but it destabilised the community and quashed any revolutionary thoughts, 'cos the people were too high to care. Prisons are big business now in the US. There's a whole poisonous industry revolving around prisons now, and whole communities that work there are reliant on them being full, so the judges and cops make sure that happens.

CS: Were you ever involved with the Black Panthers?

JN: No, they were trying to shake us down for our purse until we said, 'We ain't nobody you want to mess with. We want to give you something; we'll do it, but don't try to shake us down because we'll fight you. You ain't gonna tell us what to do!'

We were on the same page as them as far as our objective – the liberation of our people – but we weren't going to be told what to do. They were in California, we were New York.

CS: Tell me about *The Hustlers Convention*.

JN: I had to choose my subject matter carefully and articulate street life. I wrote it to direct kids who found hustlers glamorous away from the street. But they missed the point. It was a warning. I was telling young people to stay away from this.

The album was taken off the market two months after it was released (and sold on the periphery for the next forty years) because some thought it gave a bad example. They missed the point. It was written to glamourise and de-glamourise it. *Hustler's Convention* was hustled, the record itself was hustled, and I wrote it to prove a point. The point was, we're hustling and scuffling and scuttling, and we are the ones being hustled. You know, all that glitters is not gold. *The Hustler's Convention* is the legacy of slavery.

CS: Why did you choose the name Lightnin' Rod as a pseudonym for the album?

JN: A lightning rod is two things: it conducts energy when lightning strikes on the top of the building, and in the community a lightning rod is the one who blows the whistle when the community is being under-serviced, assaulted or being lied to.

CS: You pulled in some great musicians for the recording.

JN: Yeah, man – they was all the best, but some names your readers might recognise would be Bernard Purdie, Cándido, Johnny Pacheco, Eric Gale, Billy Preston, Cornell Dupree and of course Kool and the Gang, who are on three tracks.

CS: Wasn't Gil Scott-Heron a pupil of yours?

JN: I gave him one lesson as a student at Lincoln University. He took that and he ran with it, made a career out of it. It made him a commercial, mediocre poet. He didn't master his art, although he did he master the business of it. Master the art first, and then later you can master the business. Max Roach told me, 'Master your axe.' I spent twenty-five years mastering my axe – I learned the business of show business through trial and a lot of error.

CS: Tell me about Hendrix. You were in the army at the same time.

You did a great song with him – 'Doriella du Fontaine' – perhaps my favourite Hendrix track, with Buddy Miles no less.

JN: Jimi heard the preview of the Last Poets album. So he looked at the three poems and he said, 'You know what? I want to be the guy at the front with the Afro that win them riots. I wanna work for him. In fact he reminds me of me. He's saying what I'm playing.'

Jimi and me had quite a few things in common. We were young veterans and already in our twenties. We were revolutionaries. Jimi revolutionised the blues and I revolutionised the news.

So he wanted me to use his name to further my career. He didn't want no royalties. He wanted me to get all the money. He loved me. He was a fan of mine. I wasn't a fan of his. I respected him, but I wasn't a fan of his music *per se*. I was a fan of him being a rebel and being a master of his axe. I made that record – a jail toast – with him as Lightnin' Rod (which was my alter ego but is now a direct ego), and never got paid. I had to settle for the message and not the money.

CS: And how big a part did Malcolm X play in the formation in your music, your writing?

JN: Well, Malcolm was the man. He came up all the way from the bottom, 100 per cent, and his integrity was so intact that he beat the people that he was supposed to beat. He played all the right cards.

CS: Why did Islam take such a hold of Malcolm and a lot of black Americans in the 1950s and 1960s?

JN: Because it was not a philosophy of turning the other cheek. No cheek. Just heat and seek. Over the top is fanaticism. You know what I'm saying? But you know, there's a lot of history. They're really mad. It came as a result of the Crusades' horrible and violent excesses of Christianity. Opposition. Expansion. It held that kind of fascination and you didn't need to be intimidated. The Christianity that other slaves were taught made them docile. Islam is hostile, if it's attacked.

CS: What next?

JN: I'm doing a documentary about *The Hustlers Convention* itself with director Mike Todd. *The Hustlers Convention* is the grandfather of rap records… and I'm the grandfather of rap, courtesy of the *International Herald Tribune,* who gave me that title.

CS: And the book?

JN: I'm going to record my book. It's an autobiography in rhyme. So if I live long enough I will put it out because I need the money to take care of my old age.

CS: Are you looking for a publisher now?

JN: Yeah. I started it in Liverpool in 2000. I finished it in 2013. A fifty-page introduction, describing the chronology of the Last Poets, the Black Rights movement and the Human Rights movement and the Black Revolution in the 1960s. All that's in prose. I break down the civics and the government and congress and presidency and the constitution. I go into civics and how it all works. I want to restate how the US government works.

CS: I don't think anybody quite understands that.

JN: Aw, yeah. They know how it works, but they also need to know how it unworks.

Ed Bunker

Known in some Hollywood circles as 'the Man', Ed Bunker's prison novel *The Animal Factory* was made into an immensely well received movie of the same name, directed by Steve Buscemi and starring Willem Dafoe, in 2000. His three other novels have all been re-issued by No Exit Press, as has his memoir, *Mr Blue*.

Aged seventeen, Bunker was once the youngest-ever inmate of San Quentin State Prison, his parents' divorce having propelled him into a slowly descending spiral of boarding homes and military schools. The harsh discipline and his natural rebelliousness landed him in said penitentiary, even though his IQ had tested at 152.

His dire situation provoked the interest of the magnanimous Louise Wallis, wife of Hollywood producer Hal Wallis, who then introduced him to the likes of Jack Dempsey, Tennessee Williams, William Randolph Hearst and Aldous Huxley.

Encouraged by Wallis and spurred on by others such as Caryl Chessman, who he met in 'the pen', Bunker began to write.

On release from San Quentin, a parole violation put him on the FBI's most wanted list and after a protracted period as a fugitive, back to prison – this time Folsom. Impassioned by the injustice of his situation he wrote his first novel, *No Beast So Fierce*. Critically acclaimed, the book launched Bunker's career as a novelist and then screenwriter, after Dustin Hoffman made the book into the movie *Straight Time*.

Before his death in 2005 Bunker penned four novels and received an Oscar nomination for best screenplay for the film *Runaway Train*, starring Jon Voight. He also played Mr Blue in the movie *Reservoir Dogs*, and was the technical advisor on Michael Mann's movie *Heat*, teaching De Niro how to walk, dress and talk like a proper criminal – a subject that Bunker was eminently well versed in.

Having met Bunker on a number of occasions, one particular story springs to mind. One day he rang me up out of the blue, calling in my promise to take him out in London. We started off in a rather salubrious Japanese restaurant whereupon I found myself with two sets of chopsticks and Ed none. On offering the spare set to the man he answered, 'No, man. I'm into ecology.' And that, dear reader, is the curious dichotomy that was Edward Bunker.

Chris Sullivan: Have you ever killed anyone?

Edward Bunker: No, and I wouldn't like to do it, but I've been in situations where I would have as a criminal in prison and the under-world. I was never a dangerous person, but I was very psychopathic if someone was in my way and I wanted something. A couple of times I locked my mind to do it. I made the decision but they gave way, y' know? [In a] couple of desperate situations, I've stabbed a couple of people, shot someone – they didn't die – but it wasn't gratuitous. Today they kill for status. The most dangerous thing in the world is a fifteen-year-old black youth from the ghetto with a Magnum or a Glock.

Part of the problem is education. American youth score last in education tests. Young kids from the ghetto don't give a fuck; they deride and stigmatise education. In the ghetto you try and study and they say, 'Yo, you trying to be white, sucker?' The authorities say that education is good for you. It tastes like castor oil but you gotta get through it. The fact is, education is fucking wonderful, makes you fucking appreciate life, see more, experience more, makes every-thing better. You have frames of reference.

CS: Talking of which, I've read you've tested very high in IQ tests but seemed to have resisted formal education.

EB: Up until the age of ten I had what could be called a normal edu-cation, then I started to go to juvenile hall so I'd catch school one or two days at most. Luckily when I was ten I was a good two years or so ahead in school because, being [raised in] in homes, there was no education, but there'd be a teacher. It was intensive. I started read-ing when I was six and at seven really got going. I read everything I could get my fucking hands on from then on.

CS: And of course the odd book is handy in prison.

EB: Yeah, in most prisons there was always a big group of readers who passed on books. And there was a group of us who wanted to write – Jimmy Postman and Paul Allen to name two. Jimmy had the most talent – very facile, an excellent thief, richest guy in the pen. Y' know why he was the assistant dentist? He could get your teeth fixed.

CS: Do you think this inquisitiveness helped you succeed in crime in any way?

EB: Well it made me smarter, and I had been studying my craft since my youth. I was an insatiable learner... about just anything. I learned from the older guys in jail. One guy was an old-time card mechanic busted for dope. He hustled the cards, man, just to pay his way. He taught me how to make a slick sleeve, how to work, how to hand off, break off, deal from the bottom of the deck and shit. I had nothing better to do than to stay in my cell for days practising how to deal off the bottom. Another guy did the same with safe cracking. We all had a story to tell.

One of the reasons that I was successful, in that I had the nice car and the right clothes, was that unlike many other criminals I tended not to commit crimes on impulse. I would do all the preparatory work, go out looking, and sit on the location – really checking it out. I was meticulous in the scheduling, the planning. This *was* my hustle for a while. A guy would come out of the joint; he'd be a crazy man. I'd tell him to take it easy, put him in a room, tell him about my plan, tell him what to do, and then he'd take his time and go out and do it. Maybe he wasn't looking at a big strike, but maybe fifteen or twenty thousand dollars, and I would take 25 per cent of that.

CS: There are a lot of drug references in your books. Does the knowledge come from direct personal experience? It seems very accurate.

EB: There's not a lot I don't know about drugs.

CS: How easy is it to get quality drugs in American prisons?

EB: Pretty damn easy. My answer to people who say they're going to stop the smuggling of drugs is, 'Hell, fool, you can't even stop them getting into prisons!' If you've got the money you can get anything, same all over.

CS: In *Dog Eat Dog* one of the characters manages to run a whole cartel from behind the bars of a Mexican prison, replete with mistresses and all. How true to life is this?

EB: Shit, man! In Mexican prisons if you've got the cash you can live *exactly* as you want. There's all kinds of business, the drug barons are safe there from kidnapping to the US by the DEA. The drug dealers even shot the bishop down the airport and killed a presidential candidate in Tijuana. Twenty years ago some friends of mine went to Mexico and were caught trying to buy drugs. They were a thousand bucks short of the cash needed to get free, so one was handcuffed to a pipe in a room in a police station. The room was full of sacks of weed, tons of it. He spent his time there, two full days, rolling and smoking big fat joints out of brown paper.

CS: Can you explain the three-time loser ideology that in a way fuels your book, *Dog Eat Dog?*

EB: It's absurd. In California, for example, they've just made writing graffiti a felony, so if you've two violent crimes against you and you get caught in the act of committing graffiti, you are a three-time loser and go to prison for twenty-five years for writing your name on a toilet wall – it's insane. Let's say a guy steals a bicycle and gets caught by the owner. He might not shoot the owner if he's facing six months, but for twenty-five years as a three-time loser with no parole? Hell! He might as well shoot the guy. Not all would, but some would, most definitely.

CS: In *Dog Eat Dog* the protagonists are on a huge buzz after completing the job. Do you miss the adrenaline rush of crime?

EB: No, but I miss my friends. Some are dead and some are in prison. The thrill can be great, I suppose – that is, if the penalties weren't so bad. And I don't mean the violence. It has gotten so violent, which wasn't true when I was young. There was a great thrill being up on the roof, sawing a hole and hanging down like you were a leopard, free in the darkness and the shadows while everyone else is walking by with no idea that you are in there. That is the buzz. You're outside of society, a law unto yourself... until you get caught.

Richard Pryor

'Rumours of my death spread as far as New York newspapers,' remembered Richard Pryor. 'It's a bitch to be watching the nightly news and see the motherfuckers talking 'bout you in the past tense!'

News of the great comedian's demise had at this point spread throughout the civilised world, even pervading the sanctity of the man's own bedroom. He recalled his housekeeper walking in, making a lot of noise and squeezing his big toe when he failed to stir.

'"What you doing?" I'd scream. And she'd say, "Well, Mr Pryor, I thought you wasn't living anymore." And I'd say, "Why d'you think that?" And she'd say, "Cos you lying on the bed with you eyes closed an' all."'

You can see where his housekeeper was coming from. For decades Pryor had pushed the boat out so far out that it had begun to drift without direction or destination.

'It's amazing I didn't OD on heroin, get stuffed with coke, or die from AIDS,' said Pryor, the self-confessed Bard of Self-Destruction. 'Even I think it's remarkable that I'm still here.'

An undervalued master of understatement, Pryor failed to mention that he had also survived a humongous freebasing cocaine habit – once setting himself on fire after smoking the drug – seven marriages, and a quadruple heart bypass. At the time I spoke to him, he was living with multiple sclerosis.

'It was as if God had all this shit left over from the other afflictions he created and decided to throw it all into one disease called MS,' he said, before adding the punchline, 'Kinda like a Saturday night special. It's a motherfucker.'

Pryor was first diagnosed with MS in 1986 while shooting the movie *Critical Condition* in LA. Feeling unusually exhausted, he was resting on a chair between takes when Michael Apted, the director, called for him to take his place.

'I said, OK Michael,' recalled Pryor. 'But my brain told my legs to get up but the job order got lost around my waist. Nothing moved. My legs were on vacation.'

While the rest of the world thought Pryor a victim of a supersize cocaine habit, the proud comedian kept his ailment completely under wraps, and it wasn't until he teamed up with old colleague Gene

Wilder for *Another You* in 1991 that he realised it was time to tell the world.

'We were doing a scene in which I was supposed to have a run-in with a real live bear,' remembered Pryor. 'He was a trained bear but he was a big motherfucker with claws and teeth and shit. And he scared the shit out of me, but when the director shouted, "Run, Rich! Run!" I couldn't move. That was the beginning of me not being able to do the shit anymore.'

Part of the 'shit' he was not able to do was conduct an interview in person. So the fastest tongue in the west was reduced to responding to questions via email over several weeks. But Pryor had still not lost his edge or his considerable cojones.

'When I discovered I had MS I didn't think, "Why me?" Why bother? It's the hand that was dealt me... and I've had a great life – fuck yeah!'

The life of Richard Franklin Lennox Thomas Pryor III began on 1 December 1940, in Peoria, Illinois. He was born to Gertrude Thomas, a bookkeeper for the local brothel, and LeRoy Jr (aka Buck) Carter, an ex-Golden Gloves boxing champion turned pimp.

'Once I saw my mother in bed with a man. White dude. She didn't seem to mind. But it fucked me up,' stated Pryor. 'Tricks used to come through our neighbourhood. That's where I first met white people. They said, "Hello, little boy. Is your mother home? I'd like a blowjob."'

'She drank a lot. She'd be home for six months or so and then leave as if she was going shopping and not come back till six months later. I just thought it was nice to see her when she was home.'

Pryor's mother eventually abandoned him aged ten, leaving his moral, spiritual and physical wellbeing in the hands of his father's mother, Marie Carter, a barnstorming madam who ruled her brothel on 317 North Washington in Peoria with belt, buckle and brimstone.

'I lived in a neighbourhood with a lot of whorehouses,' wrote Pryor in his autobiography *Pryor Convictions*. 'Not many candy stores or banks. Just liquor stores and whorehouses.'

While sitting on his grandma's stoop shooting the breeze, he was exposed to all kinds of people – white, black, businessmen, politicians, junkies, winos and hookers.

'I remember a white dude used to come down and ask, "Do you have any girls who'll cover me with ice cream, and little boys that will lick it off?" And that was the mayor.'

He seems to have seen more as a child than most do in their lifetime.

'One night a man came in and cussed my grandmother,' he recalled. 'Buck heard it, grabbed a pistol and shot the man full of bullets. Blam! Blam! Blam! Scared the shit out of everyone in the place. But liquor makes you do strange things, like not die when you're supposed to. The man was pissed and managed to crawl across the floor and cut Buck on his leg. My father was crippled the rest of his life.'

After being raped by a teenage neighbour, sexually abused by a priest and losing his cherry to a hooker called Penny, Pryor found he had a flair for comedy.

'I first noticed I could make people laugh when I slipped in dog shit and made my grandmother laugh!' he says. 'Then I spent all day making up shit. Some kids sang on the street corner, I talked. But I was in every gang in Peoria, which had about five. I was only tough for about half a minute, no more.'

Pryor now had the bug – the entertaining bug. Consequently, the classroom became his stage.

'I sat in the back row and entertained my neighbours as if I was at the Comedy Store working out a new routine. One day he [his teacher Mr Fink] got real fed up. He grabbed me by the scruff of the neck and took me downstairs. Just to show I had a sense of humour I took a swing at him. He opened the front door and literally threw my ass on the ground. Threw me out of school for good.'

After his expulsion, the fourteen-year-old would-be comedian drifted. At first he took a job as cleaner in a strip club. 'The problem was I liked the show more than the work,' he wrote. Then he tried his arm as a shoeshine boy, a meat packer and, finally, purely to get out of Peoria, joined the army.

'I thought the army was like hunting, camping, a little fishing. But

I learned to kill from a guy who killed in World War II, and they couldn't stop him. So they gave him a job. "Can't let him on the streets, so we'll let him train these guys for World War Three."'

Pryor was stationed in Germany. One day his closest friend ended up in a fight with a white guy who promptly gave him a proper pasting.

'The white boy seriously hurt my guy's ass,' wrote Pryor. 'A crowd gathered. I knew my guy was going down if something didn't happen. From within a crowd of soldiers I reached into my pocket and drew out my switchblade. Pushed the button. Flifft! I waited for the right moment. Then I stabbed the motherfucker in the back six or seven times... I was lucky. Lucky I didn't kill that white guy and luckier still they didn't kill me.'

Consequently he was dishonourably discharged. 'I was disappointed that I hadn't connected with the service,' said Pryor. 'I'd hoped to start a new career. Something with more security than working at the packing plant... Instead I settled into the most popular career among young uneducated black men – unemployment.'

Soon he blagged his way into entertaining at Harold's Club (a 'black and tan' club, meaning both blacks and whites went there) in Peoria, where he claimed to be both a singer and a pianist, neither of which he was or ever had been.

Using the only four chords he knew, augmented by whatever lyrics came into his head, he impressed the club's owner, who was more appreciative of his sheer nerve than his ability. Grateful to find himself casually employed, he soon realised that the audience responded better to his jokes than his singing.

'Talking was much easier than making up songs. I told jokes, did impressions of Dean Martin, Jerry Lewis and Sammy Davis Jr, and sometimes I simply picked up a book or the newspaper and read the shit out in a strange voice while adding my asides.'

In 1962 he started at Collins Corner – a predominantly black club – as emcee. Shortly afterwards he cut his teeth touring 'the black belt', the unofficial coloured club circuit, in Pittsburgh. After an altercation with a female singer he spent thirty-five days in prison. Once back on the streets he moved to New York in 1963 with just $10 in his pocket.

'Before long I became a regular act at the Bitter End, Papa Hud's, and the Living Room, and introduced myself to Woody Allen at the Café Au Go Go,' he recalls. 'Woody said, "Stick around, watch me and you'll learn something." But oddly I learned more from a hooker in Baltimore.'

That particular lady took Pryor to her house and played him an album by Lenny Bruce. 'That destroyed me,' admitted Pryor. 'I went fucking crazy.'

Crazy or not, that didn't stop Pryor emulating Bill Cosby – then the biggest black stand-up in the country – until he became known as just another pale imitation of the straight-playing comic.

'I went for the money,' he confessed. 'Even though there was a world of junkies and winos, pool hustlers and prostitutes, women and family screaming in my brain to get out.'

Even though a copycat act, he appealed to the rather staid TV executives who'd rather go for formulaic than new. You can imagine their conversation: 'We can't get Cosby so let's get Pryor. He's black isn't he? They're all the same anyway.'

TV offers flew in and, as he readily admits, he 'entered the mainstream'. On the other hand, his personal life remained less conventional.

He became involved with Tia Maria, a prostitute who introduced him to his true love – cocaine – and soon after he was imbibing *ad nauseam*.

'Somebody told me that if you put coke on your dick you could fuck all night,' he wrote. 'Shouldn't have told me. My dick had a Jones. Six hundred dollars a day just to get my dick hard.'

The coke had an altogether different effect on Tia Maria.

'She liked to take all her clothes off, climb out the apartment window and walk on the ledge of her building,' recounts Prior. 'With her titties blowing in the wind, she yelled at people in the street.'

Still, it was she who kicked him out after he confessed to having had sex with her lesbian lover.

His next paramour, Maxine Silverman, stabbed him through his upper arm. When she was nine months pregnant with his child, he saw the writing on the wall, panicked and ran to Mexico to block out his misgivings. On his way back he was arrested for possession of marijuana and thrown in jail.

'I was in jail in California,' he wrote in his memoir. 'When they'd arrest you they'd be serious. They'd look in your asshole… What you be looking for in my ass? There ain't nothing in my ass! If I had a pussy, I might dig it. You can hide something in your pussy. But in my ass? What am I gonna hide in my asshole? A pistol?'

After posting his own bail (he'd forgotten that he had $7,500 in his pocket) he arrived back to find his daughter Elizabeth had been born. Not surprisingly the couple split up shortly afterwards.

By now Pryor was moving in circles he'd never dreamed of. Singer Bobby Darin threw a party for him welcoming him to LA. He guested on *The Merv Griffin Show* with Jerry Lewis and had a spitting competition while Groucho Marx gave him advice. 'Do you want a career to be proud of?' asked Marx. 'Or do you want to end up like a spitting wad like Jerry Lewis?'

Even though the money was rolling in faster than he could count, Pryor was suffering a major identity crisis. Things came to a head in Las Vegas in 1967 when, now snorting mountains of cocaine, he suffered a nervous breakdown on stage at the Aladdin while performing in front of Dean Martin.

'The fog rolled in,' said Pryor. 'Then I finally asked the sold-out crowd, "What the fuck am I doing here?" Then I walked off stage.

'The breakdown was the only way I could shed the phoney image and start building my self respect,' said Pryor. 'I read a copy of Malcolm X's collected speeches and I really searched for the truth.'

On 13 January 1968, Pryor married a rich hippie chick called Shelley Bonis. Meanwhile his stage act became increasingly radical.

'Each outing was like jazz,' he stated impenitently. 'I was searching for the perfect note. Then one day I repeated the most offensive, humiliating, disgraceful, distasteful, ugly and nasty word ever used in the context of black people: nigger. I decided to take the sting out of it. "Hello, I'm Richard Pryor. I'm a nigger. Nigger, nigger, nigger, nigger." It was the truth and it made me feel *free* to say it.'

323

Of course many clubs weren't hip to this new, irreverent and controversial version of himself, so back he went to New York and found work at the Village Gate – NYC's most progressive club – where he opened for and befriended Miles Davis. The jazz supremo subsequently introduced him to his coke dealer, who Pryor claimed sold 'the purest shit I'd ever had!'

Now he had the proper 'taste', so back in LA he snorted up a snowstorm, staying out for weeks on end and getting up to 'some real sordid shit'.

This was 1968, a tumultuous time in the US. Martin Luther King was assassinated on 4 April, followed by Robert Kennedy on 6 June, while the Tet Offensive had turned the tide of popular opinion against the war in Vietnam.

It was also a traumatic period for Pryor. His wife Shelley tried to kill him and there was a warrant out for his arrest for failure to pay child maintenance to Maxine.

'I got in my car and aimed the motherfucker north. I wanted to go to Berkeley. I didn't know why there, except I had it in my head.'

Back then Berkeley – just over the bridge from San Francisco, where free love, LSD, and the hippie movement were in full unrestrained bloom – was the undoubted hub of intellectual black radicalism. It also neighboured Oakland, where the Black Panthers were based.

Pryor was soon hanging out with Angela Davis (the black communist freedom fighter), snorting Bolivia's finest with Huey Newton, the Panthers' 'Minister of Defence', and hanging out with African-American wordsmith Ishmael Reed.

'By the end of 1970 I just felt full. I knew it was time to go back and resume my career as Richard Pryor, comedian. For the first time in my life I had a sense of Richard Pryor the comedian. I knew what I stood for. I knew what I had to do. I had to go back and tell the truth.'

As a stand-up he was groundbreaking. Few had reeled out monologues on the subject of 'getting high, fucking my wife's girlfriend, and rednecks looking for pussy'. And, even though he upset a few apple carts, he soon became comedy's hottest yet eminently provocative ticket.

In 1971 Pryor recorded his first concert film, the seminal *Live and Smokin'*, and explored areas hitherto unadventured. With routines entitled 'Black Cat with Neat Hair' and 'Coloured Guys Have Big Ones', Pryor singlehandedly set the tone for much black comedy to come, inspiring a vast slew of copycats.

'I got more free drugs and a lot more pussy after *Live and Smokin'*', acknowledged Pryor. 'But that piece scared a lot of people.'

After *Live and Smokin'*, offers for film work poured in. First came a big role in the Billie Holiday biopic *Lady Sings the Blues*. He then wrote *Blazing Saddles* with Mel Brooks (he came up with the fart scene and the idea for a black cowboy), but was turned down for its lead role. ('They saw me as a volatile, vulgar, profane black man who wisecracked about getting high and screwing white women.')

He also had a short-lived relationship with a transvestite, but 'after two weeks of being gay, enough was enough and I went back to being a horny heterosexual.'

In 1974 he was imprisoned, first for a bunch of traffic warrants, then for tax evasion, while his third album, *That Nigger's Crazy*, sold over 1 million copies.

By now he was rolling. He did a five-week stint at the Comedy Store in LA and a legendary performance on *Saturday Night Live* with John Belushi and Chevy Chase. Now a household name, by the time he co-starred in Paul Schrader's monumental heist flick *Blue Collar* in 1978, he had notched up some eighteen appearances in films as diverse as *Car Wash*, *Silver Streak* and *Greased Lightning*.

'As befitted my stature, I spent $500,000 on a Spanish-style hacienda in Northridge with an electronic gate, a pool, tennis court, guest house and a miniature horse,' he said. 'But you know what? One of the scariest things in life is to get what you wish for. I don't give a fuck about nothing. I don't know nothing. I don't know shit. The IRS have busted me. I been in prison nine times, man. I don't give a fuck. Richard Pryor is a criminal. I've sucked white pussy. Man, I've done it all. People say I'm as good as Charlie Chaplin but he don't say shit. Motherfucker don't even talk.'

After being invited by Lily Tomlin to appear at a star-studded gay rights benefit at the Hollywood Bowl, Pryor, incensed by the way he'd seen a black act on the bill treated compared to their white counterparts, took the mike and said, 'You Hollywood faggots can kiss my rich, happy black ass.'

Incredibly he then got his own TV show, remarried and was again divorced within a year.

Over the next few years Pryor's cocaine abuse reached new heights – or rather lows – thanks to his new-found friend freebase, a pure form of cocaine smoked in a pipe.

'I can't remember how much I did,' admitted Pryor. 'But shee-it, motherfucker! It was a lot!' Conservative estimates put Pryor's Charlie bill well past the $1,000 a day – $350,000 a year – mark. But it wasn't his wallet that suffered, it was the man.

'It started out innocently enough. Every now and then,' bemoaned Pryor casually. 'Then I fell in love with the pipe. It controlled everything I did. The motherfucker would say, "Don't answer the phone, Rich – we got smokin' to do."'

In 1978 Pryor was once again arrested after he had shot his wife's car in an attempt to arrest her understandable departure.

'I thought it was fair myself,' chuckled Pryor. 'She was going to leave me so I shot the car. I shot the tyre – BOOM! Another tyre said, "Ahhh!" I shot another [and] it went, "Ohhh!" I shot the motor. But the motor fell out. It said, "Fuck it!"

'If you want to get a cop to respond quickly, all you have to say is, "Hello, Officer. I want to report a black man with a gun." It's like announcing the start of hunting season at an NRA convention. The cops arrived so fast I barely had time to smoke my stash.'

Whatever Richard Pryor was shooting, smoking or sniffing, nothing could impede his rise to the top. In 1979 he recorded and released *Richard Pryor: Live in Concert,* which confirmed his place as the world's greatest-ever stand up, launched a sea of imitators and became the most essential videotape of the 1980s. It was passed around college dorms faster than a case of the clap, sold millions and was *the* must-have item for the common-or-garden hep cat. If you didn't know Pryor you just weren't happening.

But by 1980 his freebasing addiction had snowballed while his paranoia – a direct result of the drug – knew no bounds. 'I left all my guns right out in the open so when the bogey man bust in my house... he could see 'em,' he said. 'I thought everyone was stealing from me. I continued to smoke until I ran out of coke. I was suffering serious dementia. Miserably alone. Frightened. Then I thought, "OK, I'll set myself on fire."'

Dousing himself in cognac, Pryor set himself alight, dived through the bedroom window and ran down the street like a Mexican jumping bean.

'You know what I noticed?' he said. 'When you run down the street on fire, people get out of your way.'

With third-degree burns covering 50 per cent of his body, Pryor suffered a long and painful rehabilitation, but exited hospital feeling on top of the world having ditched his old friend and nemesis – cocaine.

The movie *Stir Crazy* with Gene Wilder topped $100 million at the box office and he presented an Oscar at the 1981 awards, while *Bustin' Loose* became the most watched film in the States. All was looking good. Too good for our Richard.

'Then one day I returned from Hawaii,' sighed Pryor. 'And even though the house had been cleaned of all the drugs and paraphernalia eight months earlier, I could sniff it like a bloodhound. I looked in my super, super secret stash and there it was. One perfect little rock. I found my glass pipe and climbed on board the old self-destructive roller coaster without anybody knowing it.'

In 1982 Richard flew to London to play the villain in *Superman III*.

'The movie was a piece of shit,' he admits, 'but before I'd even read the script I was offered $4 million – more than any black actor had ever been paid. I told my agent, "For a piece of shit, it smells great."'

Armed with such a fee, Pryor flew back to the US and was soon up to his old tricks. Then, out of the blue, he had his Damascene moment.

'I took my kids to Hawaii,' he reminisced. 'And Rain – my daughter – was standing in the doorway. "Daddy," she said. "Come with us." I really wanted the kids to go so I could smoke my shit. Then the strangest thing happened. Left alone, I had a moment of clarity. I asked myself what was I doing. I saw the pitifulness of my situation. So I tossed all the shit into the garbage for real. No hiding the pipe in one drawer, a rock in another. I chucked it.

'Grabbing my cigarettes, I shuffled to the sand – my kids looking at me as if I was an alien. But then it was great. Rain taught me how to float. The water slapped the shore and I was in the middle of it. And do you know what? I was grateful to be there.'

Back in LA, having kicked the coke, he saw all the previously strewn pieces of his life slowly come back together and admitted in rehab that he was indeed an addict. In 1986 *Jo Jo Dancer, Your Life Is Calling*, a semi-autobiographical movie of his life that he wrote, directed and starred in, hit the screen. Tragically, a few months later he was diagnosed with MS, which he said stood for 'More Shit'.

'I found that my life, instead of ending because of MS, has only changed,' said the now-retired comedian. 'Perhaps it was God's way of telling me to chill, look at the trees, sniff the flowers rather than the coke, and see what it's like to be a human being. Or perhaps God was thinking, "Shit, why did I have to go give this Pryor more funny muscles than me? I'll drag the motherfucker back down to earth!"'

Pryor died of a heart attack on 10 December 2005, eight months after I conducted this interview for the Independent. *I think it was the last interview he did.*

To the very end of his life he was as sharp as a razor, an extraordinary and wonderfully maverick human being who had even suggested a rather innovative way of distributing his ashes.

'Sprinkle my ashes in about two pounds of cocaine,' he once remarked. 'Then snort me up!'

Iggy Pop

Prior to this interview (conducted in October 2003), the last time I saw Iggy Pop was in October 1981 when he stayed at my flat in Kentish Town. The reason he was visiting my place was because he was seeing a friend of my American wife Holli, a New Yorker who was staying with us at the time. Iggy didn't want to go to a hotel because he'd played a gig in Marseilles a few nights before and, after declaring on stage that all French men were faggots, was given a good hiding. Consequently, he simply wanted a place to stay that was away from all the limelight and hullabaloo.

He arrived at mine in the early hours of the morning having just played London's Rainbow Theatre, and waltzed in on his own carrying a small leather holdall that contained very little for someone who was on a European tour. A soon as he got in he took his shirt off, showed off his bruises, had a drink with us and then retired to bed with his paramour, only to keep us awake most of the night with the rhythmic and unabated sound of fornication.

I must have dropped off to sleep at around 5am, only for the man himself to knock on my bedroom door a couple of hours later. 'Hey, man,' he growled, his incredibly deep tones hitting rock bottom. 'Sorry to bother you but I need to get some curve-wazz-eee-aye.'

Still half-asleep, I couldn't work out who he was at first, let alone what he was saying. But eventually I sussed that he was in need of some strong drink – Napoleonic brandy to be precise – and needed it fast.

Now, getting hold of such a thing on a Sunday in 1981 in North London wasn't easy – indeed it was virtually impossible – as back then it was illegal to sell booze before midday. But I got dressed and asked him how much he wanted.

'Get me one of those small bottles, man,' he said. 'The ones you can stick in your pocket.'

So off I went to break a really stupid law.

Luckily for him, the Greek corner shop down the road was open early for once and I was quite friendly with Kostas, the old proprietor. After much cajoling, coaxing and explaining that it was for an American pop star, he sold me the bottle but told me to hide it under my coat – 'In case those bloody cops peeps see you, innit.'

I gave Iggy his brandy and went back to bed.

Half an hour later he was knocking my door again, and I was soon back at Kostas's shop. 'Why you not buy a big bottle?' he asked, to which I had no answer.

In hindsight it was classic alcoholic-in-denial behaviour, as ordering a big one would have voiced both an admission and acceptance of his addiction. Lest we forget, one rarely sees street drinkers with a big bottle.

Anyway, that afternoon, by which time Jim (as he is known to his friends) was well and truly sozzled, he sat at my kitchen table in a maudlin mood.

'I'm too old for this shit, man,' he said. 'I'm thirty-fucking-four and shouldn't be getting the shit kicked outta me!'

Evidently he'd had his fill of getting battered and living the rock 'n' roll lifestyle, something that he seemed perfectly created for. I suggested that a rather more sombre approach to life, coupled with an album of Sinatra covers, might be more appropriate for a man of his advancing years (I was twenty-one at the time) and that he should slow down.

'But how can I, man?' he answered incredulously. 'I *am* rock 'n' roll!' A salient point that few would contest (although a few years later he did record a duet with Debbie Harry – *Well, Did You Evah*, the great Sinatra-Crosby number from the 1956 film *High Society*).

That same night, a good friend of mine from the Blitz Club, Francesca von Thyssen, was throwing a party in her palatial Seymour Road home (coincidentally just a few doors up from where the Stooges recorded *Raw Power* with Bowie in 1971). And so off we went.

Iggy, as was his wont, left the party with only a shirt on, despite it being December and thus very cold. Soon after, he'd lost the shirt too and having been introduced to Anita Pallenberg and Marianne Faithfull disappeared with them into the night, leaving his battered black leather holdall – containing his passport and a spare change of clothes – in my flat.

The next day I received a call from David Bowie, who came to my flat with his PA Coco Schwab to get the bag. And that was the last time I saw Iggy Pop in the flesh until this interview. Of course he has no recollection of me or his stay in North London when we meet.

'Yeah, man... weeeeell,' he explains rather sheepishly when reminded of the episode, elongating the last word like a spoon out of syrup. 'I've left bags all over the world. I didn't start hanging on to anything until I became an old git. And I should remember that, man, but I can't. Nothing.

'But there's a lot I can't remember from that period. As for the beating – that's what happens when you're an intemperate person with a big mouth. Recently it's been a bit smoother. It's been some time since I've been jumped.'

This chat with one of rock 'n' roll's greatest living legends is part of the promotional trail for director Jim Jarmusch's *Coffee and Cigarettes*, a series of short films disguised as a feature (or vice versa).

In this remarkable series of vignettes scripted by Jarmusch, Iggy plays a version of himself as he chats with Tom Waits. They are one of many duos who gather around a table to drink coffee, smoke or discuss cigarettes, and chew the fat over subjects that include, in characteristic Jarmusch fashion, Elvis, conspiracy theories, Paris in the twenties, the inventions of Nikola Tesla, and the use of nicotine as an insecticide.

Other members of the cast include Bill Murray, Cate Blanchett, Steve Buscemi and Alfred Molina, to name just a few.

'We did the piece about ten years ago and it was one of the first of the series Jim did and it was hard,' says Pop. 'Jim is no pushover. He takes a pretty hard look at you when he lays out the script direction and it was a challenge. He didn't show Tom or I the script until just before midnight on the eve of the morning shoot, and so we really didn't have time to examine what we were doing, which was wise, especially in my case as I would have probably ruined it. There were some difficulties, but at the end of the day it makes for a more interesting piece.'

Many might be shocked to see the godfather of punk eating humble pie, as served up by the abrasive Waits, but the thoroughly likeable and charming Pop is even more amazed that his rep as a rabble rouser lives on.

'It was hard playing myself but not myself, and everything was scripted, but it's still interesting that people *still* do get the wrong idea of me,' he says. 'And because I've been living in my butt for my whole life I tend to forget how I'm perceived.

'I just worked with an older, more distinguished gentleman and he was really very non-committal and I was told it was because he expected me to chew his head off. Then I realised there's still all that hanging around. I've never associated anyone's on-stage persona with how they are in person, but some people are exactly fucking it – the same on and off stage. [And you think], oh no! It's the same fucking shit. But then again some aren't. Some are completely different. It's almost like method acting.'

Pop has been at the coalface of rock 'n' roll for some forty years. 'Music came naturally,' he declares. 'My dad loaned me the money to buy a drum kit as they were the least sedentary thing I was offered. I couldn't see myself with a clarinet or a violin. If they'd have offered me a piano I might have gone for that; and I would have gone crazy if somebody had offered me a guitar when I was twelve.

'But the drums were the best thing they had, so I went for that and I had a friend who had a guitar and an amplifier so we played as a two-piece, learned some Ray Charles songs and entered the school talent show. And right away my life transformed: people suddenly liked me! For the first time in my life something that I loved emotionally and physically started to look a little more plausible.'

They started a high school band called the Iguanas, at which point Iggy began to suspect that he might have some creative ability lurking in his subconscious. He enjoyed what he was doing and was 'seduced' by the idea of making music that was fuelled by all the great bands around at the time.

'We were hearing the Stones, the Beatles and Bob Dylan at the peak of their creativity and we also had the last wave of the very finely crafted American black music such as the Ronettes, Dionne Warwick, all the stuff on Stax. And later I got into jazz and Bo Diddley and Chuck Berry and I was charmed and seduced.

'Then there's also all the benefits, such as girls will talk to you,' he adds after a moment's thought. 'And you don't have to be at the office at 9am. So I kinda dropped out of everything but music when I was in high school. Once you got out of high school it looked to me as if there was gonna be more high school until you die, and I wasn't going for that.'

Encouraged by Jim Morrison's example, Iggy (who started life as James Osterberg Jr) ditched the drums in favour of vocals and formed the Stooges in 1967 with Scott and Ron Asheton and bass player Dave Alexander.

'Ron was someone who was a year ahead of me in juvenile delinquency and a year behind me in age,' reflects Pop with a chuckle. 'His brother and Dave the bass player and their friend Roy used to hang out in front of the drug store on the main drag right across the street from where I worked in a record store. I described all this in the song 'Dum Dum Boys'. They smoked and always wore these very tight, too-short pants that showed off their ankles.

'But Ron was in this cover band,' he continues. 'And he was the only guy in this band that looked kind of ill, kind of off-colour, unkempt and dirty. He looked like a lot of the good musicians I was seeing on the covers of albums I liked that were coming out of Memphis, Tennessee, or London, England, like the Rolling Stones.

'In fact I've never met a convincing musician that didn't look ill and dirty, and Ron had those two things very well covered! That's just the way he was. He could come out of the bath and look dirty and always looked a little unwell. So I said to myself, "Wow, this guy could go all the way!" And you had his brother

[Scott], who looked like a teen idol – athletic – and I knew that one day he'd be one of hell of a drummer. So he kept bugging me to give him lessons and I'd say, "Well, some day, kid. One day!"'

That day eventually arrived and the band evolved into the Stooges, a name that came about after an LSD session. 'We'd been up all night taking psychedelics together, mainly because that is what we did, man – only because we didn't know how to hang out any other way,' explains Pop. 'I, believe it or not, was the ambitious one who didn't want to waste a trip without getting something out of it. So I said, "Well, what are we gonna call our band?", because we didn't have a name then.

'After a lot of chat and a lot of throwing names around, Ron said, "We'll be like the Stooges except we'll be the Psychedelic Stooges." Ron had already spent about a thousand million man hours watching the Three Stooges' films since he was twelve so it was inescapable that anything creative he did in his life was going to hark back to the Three Goddamn fucking Stooges!'

At first they tried to emulate the rhythm and blues and Delta blues acts Pop had seen in Chicago, but soon moved on. 'We were really influenced by a little vanguard of avant-garde musicians: John Cage and particularly Harry Partch [an experimental Californian musician and microtonal pioneer] who was very key. We wanted to create mayhem – an assault of sound concept that would confuse and question what music was. I really could put my thumb on a vacuum cleaner and pull music out of it. Other than that we were into the simpler British groups: the Animals, the Stones, the Kinks, the Who – those groups were very important for us, as well as American garage music like Count Five, the Strangeloves and the Sonics and Bob Dylan for the lyrics and the way he used his voice.'

Still, it took a while for Pop to get to grips with vocalising. 'I don't think I gave it real thought until we got a record deal, and then everything changed and I considered what I was doing a great deal.

'Still, it was some time before I opened my mouth and made noises that were something that was really exciting, and that I was ready to share with the world. When we started, I could never really hear myself sing, either at our rehearsals or gigs, so I just pulled together all the elements that I thought I wanted to sound like and practised in my room when I thought nobody was listening.'

One outfit Pop is sorely indebted to is MC5. 'Without them there would be no Stooges,' he admits. 'And of course there's their manager John Sinclair, an artistic ex-con – a sort of proto Suge Knight figure. He took a lot of not-so-imaginative lower middle-class Detroit people and a lot of drifting, ignorant semi-suburban people like ourselves and turned us on to a lot of shit. Through him I first heard Coltrane, Archie Shepp and first rubbed shoulders with the [likes of] Warhol and Ken Kesey.'

Sinclair, using MC5 as his spearhead, went on to create his very own political party.

'My favourite thing,' remembers Iggy, 'was that they published a purple postcard with a white panther leaping on the front, and on the back it said, "White Panthers People's Party – Our Platform: 'Rock 'n' Roll, Dope and Fucking in the Streets."'

'And they distributed these on the streets of Ann Arbor, this little bucolic college town. But you've got to hand it to them for sheer balls. Did he think everybody was going to drop what he or she was doing and go fuck in the streets? When they got to be the White Panther Party it became a bit silly. When I look back, it was something I was willing to support, but the rock band and John were not ready for political responsibility in such a puritan country. That landed John in jail with a ten-year sentence, man. It certainly was not the two joints he had in his pocket.'

For a while the Stooges played second fiddle to the rampaging MC5, supporting them in concert all over Michigan. One such appearance in 1969 attracted the attentions of the Velvet Underground's Welshman, John Cale, who, completely enamoured of their enigmatic frontman, went on to produce the Stooges' self-titled debut album.

Yet even though the album contained *the* seminal proto-punk song, 'I Wanna Be Your Dog', it failed to sell due to an almost blanket ban by radio stations, who considered the band to be evil incarnate.

'I always thought, when we put out our first thing, there must be about fifty thousand people in America who would be interested in this,' explains Pop. 'And we sold thirty-five thousand. I thought that was pretty good. That's what I was told we sold anyway. Of course, that could have been a lie too – the whole industry's corrupt, man.'

Consequently, the band were dropped by their record label Elektra and in 1971, burdened by, as Pop admits, expansive Class A drug habits, they split.

Two years later Danny Fields – who had worked for Elektra and later managed the Ramones and MC5 – told Iggy that they had been mentioned in *Melody Maker*, where David Bowie cited the band as one of his favourite acts. Subsequently, Bowie tracked the band down, dragged them back to the UK and produced the massively influential but commercially unsuccessful Iggy and the Stooges album, *Raw Power*.

'Everybody wanted me to get rid of the Stooges and do something with sensible people,' he chuckles. 'So out of everyone who approached me, the most convincing and colourful and smartest people were David Bowie and his manager, Tony Defries, who I met. They wanted me to work with some English musicians but eventually they gave up and let me bring the Stooges over.

'Then Tony pointed out that the album we were going to do wasn't up to scratch, so as everything from Marc Bolan to *Exile on Main Street* to Led Zeppelin, Mott the Hoople and David Bowie was all recycled Chuck Berry, we took Chuck Berry and Little Richard and filtered it through to who we were, and that's kinda what *Raw Power* is.'

It was around this time that the band played their now legendary performance at the Kings Cross Theatre. 'The audience were not wildly enthusiastic but were really stunned by this animal force on stage,' recalls photographer Mick Rock, who photographed the concert. 'They were like, "What the fuck is going on here then?" No one in the UK had ever seen Iggy before and I was the only photographer there.

'I met him through Bowie, which was amazing because this was the summer that Bowie really took off, but he still found the time to help push Iggy and Lou – who were the godfathers of punk. In person Iggy is kind of shy, modest and rather contemplative. He has all this art in his house and books, but boy, when he hit that fucking stage it was like, fuck everybody and everything!'

In certain circles the Stooges were the cat's pyjamas, a vivid portent of the future. But yet again the combination of drug abuse, poor sales and financial pressure caused the band to break up – this time for good.

'The first album sold enough as far as I was concerned and by the second I was so into it I didn't really care or pay any attention to all that sales crap!' he snarls.

'It never bothered me. My dream was just to do something really cool and really good. There wasn't much million-selling music that I liked, and what I did like was by people who were much more accomplished than us, so I knew that wasn't going to happen and that wasn't our intention anyway.

'And as far as all the trash that sold millions, we didn't really pay any attention because we knew we were better and I always thought I'd rather just sell a few than create a pile of shit. But I knew we weren't the Ronettes. They could sing better than I could, but I thought we sounded pretty cool. I listen back to it after all these years and think it's better than I realised at the time. And that took a long while to sink in.

'Since [then] I've seen that the whole music business is so corrupt. The record company owns the master and owns the right to massage the accounts in order to pay the artist as little as they can, so the artist gets zilch while having to fend off a whole panoply of crooks – lawyers, agents, girlfriends, drug dealers, managers. It's fucking criminal, man.'

With his band in tatters Iggy lost himself in drink and drugs. Homeless on the streets of LA, he finally checked himself into the Neuropsychiatric Hospital in Los Angeles until his guardian angel, David Bowie, appeared again to help him kick heroin, drag him out of the shit and take him to Munich where together they produced two legendary Iggy albums, *The Idiot* (started in Paris) and *Lust for Life*.

'It's very simple,' clarifies Pop. 'David saved me from professional and maybe personal extermination as he really liked what I did, was keen to get on board and was full of the best intentions. To be fair, he resurrected me. Back then he was more like a benefactor than a friend. Sorta like Professor Higgins in *Pygmalion* saying to you, "Young man, please, you are from the Detroit area of the USA. Now I think you should write a song about automobile manufacturing."'

Undoubtedly one of the tracks that they produced together is one of the all-time great rock songs. 'We heard this beep from the Armed Forces Network telecast as this was before you had all these channels in Europe. This beep that came on before their shows. So we took that as our rhythm and added a bit of Motown. David wrote the chord progression on a ukulele and said, "Let's call it 'Lust for Life'. You can write some lyrics for that."'

Both albums are seminal. 'Nightclubbing', a song on *The Idiot*, was recorded with a cheap synthesiser and an early drum machine as that was the only equipment available in the studio after all else had been packed up. 'David told me that he couldn't put a record out with just that, but I told him I could and that was that.'

Since then Pop has been cited as the godfather, perhaps even the creator, of that whole milieu known collectively as punk. Certainly he influenced everyone who can claim any punk credentials.

'Well, I thought it was good because it's kept the Stooges alive,' smiles Pop. 'People say we influenced them and people are still listening to our stuff perhaps because of that. I thought the Sex Pistols and the Ramones were very, very good indeed. The Clash bettered us musically but their vibe didn't get me quite as much. But they're the three that I liked. Then there's the

Damned, the Adverts, the Minutemen. And the Buzzcocks were also an excellent band.'

The Stooges reformed in 2003, finally making a good chunk of change. 'Well, we finally did it and did the shows for a lot of money at last,' he smiles. 'So we all were able to buy houses and cars, get girlfriends and live well off of it. And it was all very emotional for me because it's been a long journey for us and we were sounding really bloody good and got to the point where we could headline small festivals, support on big ones and do our own shows anywhere in the world.'

Lest we forget, Pop also has an acting career to fall back on. 'David Bowie is to blame for getting me into acting,' he bemoans. 'He urged me to give it a shot. "You can be in the movies, blah, blah, blah." When I lived in New York City, around 1984, I assiduously began to apply and promote myself, which is what people really do there, and actually did some acting classes for a year, which was not an altogether pleasant experience.'

After taking said classes, Iggy doggedly attended auditions and put the word out that he was available for work, until finally Martin Scorsese tested him.

That initial test failed to impress the Oscar-winning director, but he did get another chance. 'I got a part in *The Colour of Money* because Scorsese said he liked the way I stuck out my tongue,' says Pop. 'For a while I took almost anything, including American TV shows. The only thing I wouldn't play is musicians or junkie dads. That's where I drew the line. I usually get roles from someone who is a fan of the music or my book and wants to get a "character" in the film.'

Such was the case with Jarmusch.

'I kind of fitted into that role because I am sort of the last of the coffee and cigarettes generation,' he says. 'When I started the Stooges there was a hippie coffee house called Mark's Café that was very much a gathering place, and coffee and cigarettes were very important to us. And now we have Starbucks!

'Originally Jim filmed these pieces for MTV, but soon MTV

banned [on-screen] smoking and that was the end of that. Before that, cigarettes were all over MTV. This cigarette hysteria, this banning wouldn't have happened if the Soviet Union hadn't disintegrated, but once that was broken up this country needed a new devil and it was cigarettes. And now we have another new one, with a beard and a sheet over his head. It's ridiculous.'

Since Pop filmed the Jarmusch vignette over a decade ago he has appeared in Johnny Depp's *The Brave*, Tim Pope's *The Crow* and was even the voice of a newborn baby in *The Rugrats Movie*. But it seems that acting is definitely not his bag.

'Compared to music it's hell work,' states the renegade rocker. 'You are not the boss. You literally have to speak when spoken to. You have to wait loads and loads. It helped me keep my music going and I learned a lot – such as good old-fashioned discipline and as much humility as I could stand. But there's no immediate payback, no thrill of the sweat and the noise of a gig. It's just the pits, dude.'

The pits or not, it seems that Mr Pop, as his performance in *Coffee and Cigarettes* illustrates, has just the knack for the job, but I can't see him taking up acting instead of music.

Maybe the last word should go to Iggy, or Jim, as he prefers to be called.

'Hey, man, I was made for playing live, man. It's what I live for, dude. There's no buzz like it.'

Fela Kuti

For many years Fela Kuti's name slipped off the musical radar, but after the release in 2014 of *Finding Fela*, a documentary on the great man by Oscar-winning director Alex Gibney, the full extent of the Nigerian's genius was realised and a surge of interest quite rightly followed.

Capitalising on the film, Knitting Factory Records re-released Kuti's complete catalogue of almost fifty albums online and on CD, followed by a brace of vinyl. Furthermore, radio jocks such as Lauren Laverne, Cerys Matthews and DJ Edu dug deep into the incendiary African's archive and played his music on their shows, while producer and musician Brian Eno released a classic Kuti seven-vinyl LP box-set that he himself compiled.

'I remember the first time I listened [to Fela's album *Afrodisiac*] and how dazzled I was by the groove and the rhythmic complexity, and by the raw, harsh sounds of the brass, like Mack trucks hurtling across highways with their horns blaring,' recalls Eno in an interview for the film's release. 'Everything I thought I knew about music at that point was up in the air again. When I met Talking Heads I told them that this was the music of the future, and it still is. Robert Wyatt [Soft Machine] sent me a cassette of Fela, which he entitled *Jazz from Another Planet,* and it was. This is what I'd have liked jazz to have become.'

As with most quality music, Kuti's work still sounds contemporary and enormously pertinent.

'You can listen to Fela today and still be stunned by the power of his music,' explains director Gibney. 'And even though his lyrics in the likes of "Beasts of No Nation" are very angry, emotive and anti-corruption, the music is hypnotic, beautiful and peaceful. There is something spiritual about it. He used music as a weapon and instinctively knew that when you reach people on a musical level you connect in a deeper way.

'And what makes Fela so special and relevant is that he understood that to get his hugely political message across, it wasn't enough to say, "This is what I stand for," so he invented his own art form, his own musical genre that transcends his time.'

Indeed, Fela Kuti's life now seems more myth than reality, almost a work of fiction that most writers would never dare make up. The ultimate rebel and diehard malcontent, he was the greatest, most influential African musical artist of the twentieth century, sold millions of records worldwide and pioneered his own musical form, Afrobeat – a bracing, mesmerising hybrid of sullied funk, powerful jazz and traditional African rhythms realised by a band comprising drummers, percussionists, bass guitar players, a mighty horn section and a bevy of beautiful gyrating backing singers.

A dancer, saxophonist and composer, he was also an angry and intense militant who lambasted and embarrassed the right-wing Nigerian junta from the 1970s to the 1990s. Billing himself as 'the Black President, the Chief of the Shrine', he was hailed a hero throughout the African continent. Kuti was imprisoned, beaten and tortured for his troubles, but still helped move Nigeria towards democracy and advanced a fresh pan-African political ideology. He also advocated traditional Yoruba culture, married twenty-seven women in one day (employing a sex rota to keep them all happy), ran for president and smoked more spliff *per diem* than a room full of Rastafarians.

If Afrobeat, the form Kuti created, sounds fresher than ever, then his contentious lyrics seem entirely alien in an era where, for many, the pinnacle of musical achievement is winning *The X Factor* or *The Voice*.

Kuti put his life on the line to address moral discrepancies, much the same as Bob Marley used his music to stir his maligned countrymen, or The Clash stood up to Thatcher's maltreatment of the working classes.

'Fela Kuti's music is more relevant than ever,' informs Fela's former manager Rikki Stein, sitting in his London home. 'The messages contained in his songs, that deal with mismanagement, corruption and social injustice, still apply, and not only in his homeland, Nigeria, but also in many, many other parts of the world.

'There is definitely a paucity of artists who use music as a means of addressing social issues. These days most singers seem content writing lyrics about being happy or saying "I wanna party all night long," etc., but very few deal with issues that should be addressed or find it appropriate to use their skills as musicians to address social issues.'

Today Fela would have a lot to complain about. Nigerians now have the worst reputation for drug trafficking of any nationality in the world. Cocaine from the Andes and heroin from Afghanistan arrives by the ton at West Africa's ports, airports and border crossings, and is promptly smuggled into the UK – where Nigerians are rapidly taking control of drug distribution – and the US, where officials estimate that 40 per cent of the heroin is smuggled in by Nigerian drug rings.

And even though there is little evidence of recent collusion, cooperation in hugely corrupt Nigeria between political figures and drug barons cannot be ruled out. In fact, in 2007 the heads of the country's drug enforcement agency (NDLEA) were themselves found to be involved in trafficking. As a result, officials also estimate that 37 per cent of the population in Kano, Nigeria's second city, are drug abusers.

According to a March 2013 editorial in *Punch* – Nigeria's most widely read newspaper – money from the Nigerian drug trade also funds the radical Islamic group Boko Haram. Almost a year later the newspaper led with the headline, 'No Boko Haram links with drug barons – NDLEA.' Ho hum.

Needless to say, corruption still reigns in Fela's birthplace. Thus, his music is even more appropriate than ever.

'Fela spoke up then and would today, no matter the risks,' asserts Stein. 'He was the bravest of men who devoted his life and put his balls on the line on a daily basis to challenge and question the Nigerian military juntas during the seventies, eighties and nineties. And they beat him. They beat him badly. He was covered in scars from these beatings but he was fearless. He used to say, "Well they didn't kill me did they?"'

Undoubtedly they would have killed him if they could. Instead, he was arrested some 200 times and beaten senseless on numerous occasions. They even murdered his seventy-eight-year-old mother by throwing her out of a third-storey window. And yet he still carried on lambasting the Nigerian junta.

'The difference with Fela was that he was just *one* man, a musician, against the massive, mighty and vindictive Nigerian military junta who would kill you without a blink of an eye,' adds Stein.

Could you ever imagine Kanye West, Pharrell or Alex Turner behaving in such a manner? It's utterly unthinkable.

'Really I can't imagine a rock star today who would challenge everything and risk imprisonment, even death, to get a moral point across and then get his house burned down and still carry on,' reflects Gibney. 'And to Fela's credit, as an internationally successful artist, he could have kicked back in London or Paris, but stayed in Lagos and put himself right in the cross-hairs of his enemies in ways that were ultimately very damaging.'

He was born Olufela Olusegun Oludotun Ransome-Kuti in Abeokuta, Nigeria, on 15 October 1938, to Reverend Israel Oludotun 'Daudu' Ransome – an Anglican pastor and respected member of the Nigerian elite – and Funmilayo 'Bere' Ransome, a fiery feminist politician who won the Lenin Peace Prize in 1970.

In 1958 Fela, aged twenty, was parcelled off to London to follow in the footsteps of his elder doctor brothers. Instead he enrolled in the Trinity College of Music and became a regular at the city's fledgling jazz clubs, such as Ronnie Scott's and the Flamingo. He took up the saxophone, married Remilekun Taylor, had three children – Femi, Yeni and Sola – and stayed for five years. In 1963 – three years after Nigeria gained its independence from the UK – he returned to Lagos full of optimism, swiftly started his own band, Koola Lobitos, and settled in.

But the tranquillity was not to last as the onerous shit-storm created by British colonisation soon hit the fan. As well as ignoring the 300 or so autonomous tribes that existed before they arrived, the Brits had fuelled the fire by dividing Nigeria into three regions: north, west and east, inhabited by the Islamic authoritarian Hausa-Fulani, the Yoruba, who although monarchist were less autocratic, and the democratic Christian Igbo respectively.

Thus, when the Brits left it all went off. A series of coups d'état, beginning in January 1966, ensued and consequently tens of thousands of civilian Igbo Christians in the north were killed by the

Islamic Hausa, allowing Murtala Mohammed and the Sandhurst-trained General Yakubu 'Jack' Dan-Yumma Gowon to step in and create their own twisted, corrupt military dictatorship.

Not surprisingly, in May 1967 the remaining Igbo Christians proclaimed the secession of the eastern region from Nigeria and its dictatorship as the Republic of Biafra. Coupled with the discovery of oil in the region, this prompted a horribly excessive low-tech war. Two million civilians, including many women and children, died mainly from the famine deliberately caused by Nigeria (heavily armed by Britain and Russia), which stated that food blockades and starvation were legitimate weapons of war. They shot down planes bringing in grain to the beleaguered starving and withheld all food supplies, even though the Biafran famine was front-page news all over the globe.

'There are forces let loose in Biafra,' wrote the *Sunday Times Magazine*, the UK's most sympathetic publication to the Biafran cause, 'that white men cannot understand.' In 1970, after two and a half years of heinous conflict, the severely under-armed Biafran forces (who at times went into battle with just ten bullets per man) capitulated, agreed to a ceasefire and were dragged kicking and screaming into the corrupt Nigerian state.

Disillusioned, Kuti took his band to the US for a ten-month tour where he met Sandra Izsadore, a Black Panther associate. Izsadore introduced him to the Black Power literature of Malcolm X and Eldridge Cleaver and the funk of James Brown. He then changed the name of his band to Africa '70 and returned to Lagos, coining the term 'Afrobeat' and churning out hit records.

One such record was *Why Black Man Dey Suffer,* which features former Cream drummer Ginger Baker, who had been a friend of Kuti in London in the early 1960s, hanging out at the jazz clubs when he was studying at Trinity College of Music.

With money now pouring in, Fela set up the African equivalent of a hippie commune – comprising some one hundred people – and launched his own nightclub in Lagos, the Shrine, where his band played almost nightly. Paul McCartney attended the club in 1973 and described the combo as 'the best band I've ever seen live. I just couldn't stop weeping with joy. It was a very moving experience.'

Fela then discovered that the former Beatle wanted to employ his musicians so jumped on stage and accused him of 'stealing black man's music'. 'So I had to say, "Do us a favour, Fela, we do OK,"' said McCartney later. 'We're all right as it is. We sell a couple of records here and there.'

Now Fela was firing. He adopted the middle name Anikulapo ('one who carries death in the pouch') and morphed into a freedom-fighting militant who used his music to speak out against the insidious corruption of the Nigerian stratocracy. He sang in pidgin English so that the whole of Africa might understand him. Ipso facto, the authorities sent in the troops, who arrested him, gave him a good pasting and then burned his house to the ground.

'I was just scared and couldn't understand why he was beaten and why they attacked him so often,' explains Femi Kuti, watching from the sidelines, who was barely in his teens at the time. 'I couldn't understand role of the government who seemed like this invisible wicked force.'

The one recording that really shook things up was his inimitable 1976 hit *Zombie*, which employed a mesmerising Afro-funk groove and compared the Nigerian soldier to a moronic zombie: '...Zombie no go turn, unless you tell am to turn (Zombie) Zombie no go think, unless you tell am to think (Zombie)... no break, no job, no sense, A joro, jara, joro Tell am to go kill.'

'The record was a massive hit all over Africa and caused riots,' recalls Stein. 'And every time someone saw a soldier they'd shout "Zombie, Zombie!" and do Fela's robot dance in mockery.'

The dictatorship reacted on 18 February 1977 by sending 1,000 troops into Fela's commune. Now the biggest recording artist in Africa, he had named the compound the Kalakuta ('Rascal') Republic, and declared it an independent state divorced from Nigeria and its junta. The soldiers set fire to the compound, destroyed all of his recordings, bludgeoned the men and raped the women. They then killed his mother, Funmilayo, while Fela was dragged by his genitals into the courtyard and battered to a pulp by the soldiers. It was only the intervention of an officer that saved him from death. The common soldier despised Fela.

'The only thing that keep him alive was the unconditional love that the African general public had for him,' clarifies Stein. 'There would have been riots had they killed him.'

After Kalakuta, Kuti simply upped the polemic. He wrote a song, 'Coffin for Head of State', dispatched his mother's coffin to the house of then-president General Olusegun Obasanjo, and left it on his doorstep. His next step was to pen a successful tune entitled 'Unknown Soldier', whose lyrics berated the official inquiry which found that Kalakuta was razed to the ground by 'an exasperated and unknown soldier'.

'Soldiers now rule Africa,' proclaimed Fela in an interview on national German TV. 'And they are not legal because they are not elected. They follow the white man and want to make us slaves and put us in bondage. They do not care about Africa. They are only concerned with their own wealth and making it bigger. They are totally corrupt.'

Fela and co then moved into the Crossroads Hotel in 1978 where, in protest against the westernisation of African culture, he married twenty-seven women in one ceremony (he later restricted himself to just twelve). He also formed his very own political party, Movement of the People, and put himself up for president in Nigeria's first elections, held on 11 August 1979. While touring Europe his band, which he hadn't paid, deserted him, claiming he was using his live shows to fund his political campaign.

'Fela was not good at paying,' attests Stein. 'He wasn't mean as when we travelled he'd give me a brown paper bag filled with money and he'd tip that person and this person until all was gone. He used his money for what he thought was appropriate at that moment.'

The following year, Fela formed a new band, Egypt '80, and toured the world with an entourage of seventy men and women.

'They were wild people,' laughs Stein. 'We [Fela and the band] were banned from most five-star hotels in the world, not because they were wicked, but would forget to turn the bath tap off and flood the hotel, or burn a bed by dropping a hot iron on the sheets. They also smoked weed *all* the time, while there'd be the girls running through the corridors naked. But we never missed a plane.'

One time that Fela did the miss the plane, however, was when he was detained at Lagos airport in November 1984 for currency smuggling.

'One of his gang carried £3,000 on him as Fela didn't carry money and if he did it was down his balls as he never carried a wallet or had pockets in his pants,' remembers Stein. 'So Fela filled in the necessary forms but had no money on him to give to the customs guy who asked for "something", so the form was "lost" and Fela was arrested and detained while his band was on the plane that soon took off.'

The judge sentenced Fela to five years in prison. He served twenty months. The judge later admitted that the military had forced his hand and was sacked.

'In prison I played no games, I didn't talk much,' remembered Fela. 'I just meditated and kept to myself.'

'Even after his release they continued to arrest him and tried to charge him with murder, armed robbery all kinds of shit,' says Stein, who now looks after Kuti's estate. 'They couldn't nail him because he was innocent.'

Even though Fela continued to release albums and tour relentlessly (with his own personal witch doctor), preaching the merits of polygamy, sex and marijuana, while attacking the Nigerian establishment, the sentence took its toll along with the regular thrashings he endured.

'He was in real pain,' reflects Stein. 'By the late 1980s, all the beatings started to take their toll so he could hardly pick his saxophone up.'

Unsurprisingly, Kuti slowed down.

Rumours spread that Kuti was suffering from an unknown illness, but he refused tests to determine what caused his skin lesions, weight loss and extreme fatigue. On 2 August 1997, Kuti died at the age of fifty-eight. His brother Dr Beko Ransome-Kuti then publicly announced that the cause of death was AIDS. Fela had always claimed that AIDS was a 'white man's disease'.

'It seemed like Fela was immortal, but AIDS killed him,' reflects Gibney. 'It was like his lesson to the whole of Africa that said, "If AIDS can kill me it can kill you."'

His death prompted the World Health Organisation to investigate Nigeria's AIDS problem. It was later discovered that the Nigerian government had concealed the country's AIDS crisis by hiding the results of blood tests and lying to worldwide health officials about the number of cases reported. As a result, the Nigerian government admitted that at least 2.25 million people carried the human immunodeficiency virus in Nigeria.

Fela's funeral was attended by an estimated one million people, causing utter chaos and bringing the whole of Lagos to a halt for two days.

'Everywhere was full of people,' remembers Stein. 'In trees, in windows, on top of cars. Our journey that normally would have taken twenty minutes took eight hours. It was incredible.'

No one can doubt the potency of Kuti's legacy.

'He registered in people's consciousness the importance of resistance and made them aware,' says Gibney. 'His legacy in Nigeria is still very apparent even years after his death, even though he did not solve Nigeria's problems – just look at the government today and the corruption and how Boko Haram is running roughshod.'

'Someone once asked [Fela's son] Femi Kuti what he felt about his father's contribution,' says Stein. 'And he said that he "took a lot of licks, was arrested 200 times and they beat the shit out of him, but now I can raise the same issues and not get any licks at all." In other words he opened the door for people to be able to talk. Whether that talk has any consequence is another matter.

'Today too many artists consider music purely as a means to make money and achieve fame, rather than a means to affect thought or social change,' continues Stein. 'Fela said, "music is the weapon of the future".'

So how would Stein sum up Fela, his close friend and client?

'He was a *big* someone. And he was the bravest, most amazing man you could ever meet, but also the funniest; he had this incredibly ironic wit. We'd spend most of our time rolling about on the floor laughing.

'But even more simply,' continues Stein after a melancholic pause, 'he was a man who loved to make music, laugh, fuck and eat.'

Siouxsie Sioux

'I am already sick to the back teeth of this anniversary,' says legendary diva Siouxsie Sioux. 'And that's putting it mildly. There's one almost every year for this or for that and often they are just an excuse for them to sell more stuff. It's like, enough already.'

As one of the original 'Class of '76', Siouxsie has been bombarded with requests [in 2006] for interviews and photo calls in this, the universally acknowledged thirtieth anniversary of punk. And even though her record company has seen fit to re-release her first four albums with the Banshees – *The Scream, Join Hands, Kaleidoscope* and *Juju*, plus a DVD of *Nocturne*, their live concert at the Royal Albert Hall in 1983 – the enigmatic singer has resisted almost every adjuration.

'I've always hated the term punk, and have never wanted to be lumped in with it,' she explains, effortlessly stylish in trademark bible-black hair and Gaultier dress, sitting in the bar of a London hotel. 'But it was the perfect name for those who wanted to be called a punk band [she pronounces the word "band" to mimic a bleating sheep].

'It was for followers and those who needed to belong to something. I have always disliked any kind of label because it short-changes anything with quality because it makes it appear to conform to a uniform and an idea, when ironically what we did was about not conforming and defying categorisation. It wasn't even a movement; it was just the right time, right place, and right chemistry. And it was like an explosion, like a big bang, where all these different systems had their different effects.

'The term punk was so lazy and so inaccurate,' she continues. 'But looking back nothing can really describe quite how single minded, out there and isolated the entire key people were. Thirty years ago, walking down the street as we did was like walking the gauntlet as you risked getting the shit beaten out of you, and often you did. But punk was the perfect name for those who needed something to belong to.

'We were the only people into what we were into, but now it is all so homogenised and there is very little rebellion as everything now has too much help and comes too easy and before you know it, it is deemed fashionable.'

Siouxsie and the Banshees first appeared on stage on 20 September 1976, at the Anarchy in the UK Punk Special at London's 100 Club supporting the Clash and the Sex Pistols and were, even according to punk standards, nothing if not unconventional.

'I was just starting with the bass and Siouxsie wanted to sing together with Billy Idol; we had an idea for a band but hadn't done much about it,' says founder and long-term Banshee Steve Severin. 'Then Malcolm [McLaren] said he was putting on this punk festival at the 100 Club and he needed to fill a slot. So Billy said, "We'll do it!"'

But with days to go before their debut, Idol dropped out and in stepped Marco Pirroni (later of the Ants) on guitar and the ill-fated Sid Vicious on drums.

'The Clash let us rehearse in their space in Camden,' remembers Severin. 'But after ten minutes Sid, who couldn't play drums *at all*, got bored and said, "OK, let's just make a racket – who cares?" So we thought we'd make all this noise while Siouxsie recited the Lord's Prayer and lyrics from all these other horrible songs and then Marco would break into "Smoke on the Water" which was the only song he knew. It was a big piss-take. It was horrible. A twenty-minute barrage of awful, dreadful noise.'

'One thing that people forget is that a lot of the places we went to were predominantly gay,' recalls Sioux. 'And they played this new kind of dance music by the likes of Brass Construction and John Handy and Disco-Tex and the Sex-O-Lettes, and we used to dance together doing the hustle or a sort of jive thing, but to soul music.'

In the summer of '76 Siouxsie could do no wrong. Along with Severin, Soo Catwoman, Idol and the rest of what would become known as the 'Bromley Contingent', she had turned heads since the scene's inception and had famously stolen the limelight from the Sex Pistols by turning up at their Screen on the Green appearance clad only in full-on fetish underwear, fishnets and a cupless bra exposing her bare breasts. She had 'star' written all over her.

Born Susan Janet Ballion, Siouxsie Sioux was raised along with her older brother and sister in seriously suburban Chislehurst in Kent. Her parents had met in the Belgian Congo. Her mother was a bilingual secretary, while her father, a laboratory technician who milked serum from poisonous snakes, died when Siouxsie was just fourteen.

'I was always quite aware of us being different from the rest of our street,' she recalls. 'So I started coming up to the West End with my sister who was a go-go dancer, and she introduced me to a lot of people in clubs like the Sombrero in Kensington, who were a lot more interesting than those in Chislehurst. And so I started travelling up on my own, walking down the Kings Road and hanging out at Let It Rock, Malcolm and Vivienne's shop before they opened Sex. I must have been about seventeen at the time.'

It was during one of her London excursions that Siouxsie sealed her fate.

'It was at a Roxy Music concert at Wembley Empire Pool in October 1975 that I met Siouxsie,' remembers Severin. 'She had some mad outfit she'd hired for the night and I had this dyed white hair and a 1950s Lurex jacket. It was a match made in heaven as we both saw ourselves as carrying on the tradition of glamorous art rock – the Velvets, David Bowie and Roxy, with a bit of Kraftwerk and Can thrown in for good measure. We never fitted in anywhere and never wanted to.'

Maybe it was this refusal to kowtow to what was fast becoming a commoditised punk caricature that kept Siouxsie and the Banshees (now with Kenny Morris on drums and John McKay on guitar) unsigned for almost two years after the 100 Club engagement, even though they were one of the country's biggest live draws. 'By the time we were signed,' she says, 'I wanted nothing to do with punk. Zips, mohicans and safety pins were yet another uniform sold in the back pages of music papers – punk was a joke.

'All these punk acts are, in my opinion, pathetic,' she chides after a sip of her coffee. 'It's got that nice harmlessness about it. They are just like a pastiche of the past. For many, punk was the last time there was something that happened that wasn't encouraged by the music industry, it was the loose cannon, the runaway train, and it certainly cannot happen again and it's ludicrous to even consider that it could. People like Iggy, and us to some extent, we all deliberately threw a big spanner into the works and it was all about just getting off on that.'

Siouxsie and the Banshees' first single, 'Hong Kong Garden' – a perverse love song to a Chinese takeaway in Chislehurst – hit number seven in the charts on 13 September 1978, almost two years to the day after the 100 Club date. They followed its success with their first album, *The Scream*. Both critically and commercially massive, it provoked fanatical approbation the world over.

'We lived pretty much on our own island and were as influenced by film as we were by music and that has always been true,' she explains. 'Our aim has always been to create drama and tension within our music. I've never liked pure entertainment, films that are just an easy ride. I have always liked opinionated films or ones with a twist or something that one can think about afterwards. I still love a Disney cartoon though, *Snow White* being my all-time favourite. But it wouldn't have been so great if it didn't have the wicked stepmother, from whom I've borrowed a few style pointers.

'Then we released our second album, *Join Hands*, in September 1979,' she says, her voice belying the many problems the band encountered during the making of this uncompromising and at times sombre work.

'People said it was a difficult album, but is it fuck? It's bloody great! It doesn't matter what was going on behind the scenes because it was a really consolidated album that still sounds modern today. We were lonely and isolated and that comes across in the music. It's an extreme record but a very brave one and that's why I've still got a soft spot for it and I am grateful that I have been able to ignore the bad press.'

The 'bad' press to which she refers focused on the very public break-up of the band that occurred just after the record's release. Drummer Morris and guitarist McKay left just hours before a concert in Aberdeen after a scuffle had broken out between the band in one of the city's record shops. 'If you ever see them,' Siouxsie told the bewildered crowd that evening, 'you have my permission to beat the shit out of them.'

But rising out of the rubble, Siouxsie and Severin, joined by new drummer Budgie and the late lamented guitarist John McGeoch, went from strength to strength with their next album, *Kaleidoscope*, which followed in the wake of two staggeringly successful singles – 'Happy House' and 'Christine', the latter having entered the charts at number five in August 1980.

'It really felt like a solid, unified group at the time,' recalls the singer. 'A lot could be said without anybody saying it, while *Juju,* our next album, had a really strong identity, which the bands that came in our wake tried to mimic, but they simply ended up diluting it.'

Throughout the 1980s Siouxsie's influence as a style icon knew no bounds. She became the face that launched a million goths, spawned a nation of lookalikes and attracted a massive international following with the Banshees while exploring an altogether more indulgent path with her new husband, Banshee drummer Budgie, and their band the Creatures.

'At one point I was scheduled to be the black Madonna – the Queen of Goth,' she chuckles. 'Once people start asking me to conform in any way it is like a red rag to a bull and I rebel in the exact opposite direction. But I refused to be categorised. I like my freedom too much. I will not be held back by others' expectations and that is that.'

After two decades together, in 1996 Severin and Siouxsie ended their musical collaboration shortly after completing *The Rapture*, an album partly produced by one of the most influential people in her career: John Cale of the Velvet Underground. It was a fitting finale to a legendary association.

'A lot of people were really upset when we split up,' remembers Siouxsie. 'But being in a band you live in each other's pockets and for stupid reasons it becomes joyless, and petty grudges are held onto and there came a point when there was too much bad water under the bridge.

'The Seven Year Itch tour with Steve [Severin] in 2003 was an attempt at reconciliation, to mend the bridges and purify the water, and we gave it a go, but some things cannot be mended. But looking back on the Seven Year Itch tour we had this Japanese band and stayed in Japan at the end, and via our support band met Leonard Eto, this famous Kodo drummer.

'We said goodbye to the band and met Leonard, booked a studio and went in, and in an afternoon I knew we had an album. It was amazing to see and get these new ideas. Back home it sounded amazing and we went with it, and the resulting tour was a realisation of this and all of our influences. Some of it sounded like Cab Calloway, some fifties tracks like 'Godzilla' really come into their own with this band.'

In October 2004 Siouxsie saw the summation of all her previous work in one single evening when she performed some twenty-seven classic Banshees and Creatures songs live at the Royal Festival Hall, backed by a classical orchestra. The DVD of the concert, entitled *Dreamshow*, topped the music DVD charts for the better part of a year.

'It was the perfect realisation of all of our past work and I was in heaven,' she beams. 'It really was my wish list, my letter to Santa. We had Leonard Eto, a percussion section, a brass section, a ten-piece orchestra, backing singers and our band. I was like, OK, there's not much time to rehearse, it could be really crap and it would be like "Help, is there anyone out there?" But it kicked ass as we had this attitude that we were playing this fucking dump.

'Everyone was panicking. I was obsessive because of the violent air conditioning. I get hot and sweaty and the costume I use is composed of layers that expose the chest and neck and I'm like, do not blow cold air on me!

'I walked off halfway through because I was bloody freezing my tits off, but they plugged up the holes and I came back on. At the time I was so ill as well. I had given up smoking and it was if my body went on strike and I was incredibly ill with asthma, bronchitis and sinusitis. I had an operation to clear my nose. I was on steroids and was taking heavy-duty Clarityn tablets. I felt like shit. My tongue was coated and I was puffing out because of the drugs. The Clarityn was making me really cranky.'

Eventually she went back to smoking and the symptoms cleared.

'One doctor, a chest specialist, said that there is a minuscule amount of people for who, when they give up smoking, everything goes wrong, and I was one of them,' she says. 'So I've started again and I am a lot better thank you very much.'

Understandably, Siouxsie was delighted with the way the concert panned out.

'It was truly magnificent as it was a dream come true,' she enthuses. 'I made it clear to the orchestra that they should listen and play it not like a classical concert and stick rigidly to the sheet music. And it looked as if we'd had some cohesive game plan all along – as if we had written stuff down and planned something, God forbid! I was like, "This is very, very adult." I was *more* than pleasantly surprised.'

Indeed, Siouxsie and her band were taken aback by how their music was translated.

'With all of us [in the band] self-taught, we were amazed by how these real musicians understood us and how they translated our ideas. Often I've been guilty of reacting against styles just because they've become popular, but listening to this as a whole sounds as if I meant to do it.'

Siouxsie was so enamoured of the experience that, spurred on by the Dream Show, she is spending much of her time in London away from her home near Toulouse, preparing for her next project.

'I enjoyed working with an orchestra and the drummers on the Dream Show so much that I wanted to work with lots of different people on what is ostensibly a solo album,' she says. 'I am here in London meeting with loads of different collaborators but I don't really want to talk about it because I don't want to jinx it.

'The only thing I would say is that it is the best thing since sliced bread and it is scheduled for mid-2007 but will take as long as it takes. But we need to be funded. I'd love to take it to Moscow, New York, Tokyo. But at the moment it's impossible as we funded the whole thing ourselves. Fucking hell! It cost us an arm and a leg and we are still out of pocket. It is a legacy we've left behind, though, so I mustn't grumble.'

She admits to missing her house and four cats in France.

'I moved to France because of the space, the final frontier where no one can hear you scream. Touring continually and coming back to a small flat, albeit in nice Notting Hill, was very dispiriting. In France I open my window every morning and see butterflies, blue tits, black-birds and kingfishers. And I have my garden.

'We had water and a little nut feeder over the well so the cats can't get at them. I just saw a hoopoe, an African bird, and my first king-fisher last week. Maybe that is how I can still be myself and not get sucked into what everyone else is doing, because I am away from it all and get left alone.

'I don't want houses everywhere and all the cars and all the accoutrements. I keep it simple. I'm away from the constant bombardment of rubbish.

'I feel that things have regressed, as everything is all so cynical. Everyone wants to be the next big thing. There is this self-promotion and self-glorification; I find it all a bit tawdry. Very few of the original mobs have survived to continue being interested in what they are doing. I first of all please myself and that keeps me interested in what I am doing. That is paramount. I need to enjoy what I do and would like it to be extremely successful, but I know that you have to lose certain things to become so. A part of me hopes I can do what I do and get lucky, while another says that it's great for me just to survive doing what I love and live the lifestyle I like.'

But Siouxsie, although seeking a simple possession-free existence, still sees the music business for what it is.

'Why should musicians get a raw deal?' she asks. 'In what other business do you have to fund everything? Dance, film and theatre are all funded, but with music you have to pay for everything yourself. And when you get a record deal, you pay for the record to be made out of an advance loaned to you in lieu from your royalties, then you get fourteen per cent at most and the record company gets the rest.

'And what about photo rights?' she continues. 'Someone can come and take your photo without your permission and then own that image and the copyright of that picture of me forever. But it does not go the other way. I have to get permission from the photographer to use photos of me, but they can just do whatever they want with my face. It doesn't happen with the moving image.'

I ask her what advice she would you give to someone who looks up to her.

'My advice to any young girl like me would be: "Don't listen to what they say!" No, but seriously, it would be to dress and do whatever makes you happy and do not let convention hold you back. But that entire search for something else, for conformity, has gone too far. Botox – we need expression, so use your eyebrows! Everything is about sex! It's overkill – it's obsessed. And I don't understand this label thing – when I see one I cut it out. And as for wearing them on the outside, I do not get that at all.'

We idly shoot the breeze, talking about the passage of time.

'It seems like a long time since 1976 doesn't it?' she chuckles. 'I saw my brother recently and we went to our old house and there was a woman on the street who I recognised and she said, "Suzy? Is it you?" And then she went on to say that there used to be these teenagers that camped outside my house for days on end, and there was this young boy who looked like I did and she told him, "She doesn't live there anymore, you know," and he answered, "I know, I'm just taking in the vibes." How funny is that?

'A lot of people ask me now,' she concludes, 'if recalcitrance was the only reason we did what we did initially, and I answer, "Yes, absolutely!" It warmed the cockles of my heart and to some extent it still does.'

Siouxsie Sioux is an example to us all.

Jacques Mesrine

As for a life of crime, I made a choice, and from the moment I am dead I will no longer be guilty of anything because I will have paid for my actions. And in the end I want to remain an example, perhaps a bad example. What's terrible is that some will make of me a hero, even though there are no heroes in the criminal way of life. There are only men who live on the margins, who do not accept the laws because the laws are made for those who are rich and powerful. Me, I chose to have the good life through crime, by attacking in almost every case only the very wealthy and the well off. I have been richer than any of them because I've had... the courage of my convictions and to be what I chose to be, all the way to the end.

– Jacques Mesrine in a recorded message to his girlfriend Sylvia Jeanjacquot, to be listened to after his death

Jacques Mesrine did indeed pay for his actions. He met his demise in a scene that might have been the climax of a preposterous 1970s gangster flick. It was around midday on 2 November 1979, that a gold BMW driven by a well-dressed man in a fake beard and wig pulled up behind a covered lorry at a set of traffic lights in Porte de Clignancourt, a grim Parisian quarter familiar to generations of tourists due to its tacky flea market.

Within seconds the lorry's tarpaulin was pulled up and four men opened fire on the car, discharging fifty-two shots, fourteen of which struck the chest and head of the bewigged man, while his passenger, girlfriend Sylvia Jeanjacquot, was severely injured.

This was no gangland assassination. The gunmen were French policemen and the driver of the car was none other than Jacques Mesrine – the career criminal who could boast the ignominious honour of being Public Enemy Number One in both France and Canada.

Certainly Mesrine was no friend of the police. He had taunted them for twenty years, fleeced more French banks than any man before or since, escaped from almost every prison the authorities dared put him in, robbed only the wealthy, kidnapped hifalutin billionaires, posed for pictures in *Paris Match* and bragged about his exploits in print.

'With a boy like Mesrine you don't get him with a bunch of violets,' said Robert Broussard, the police commissioner who pursued the scoundrel for a decade, and was said to have part-orchestrated the execution. 'You don't mess around. You just get him.'

Known as 'the Robin Hood of the Paris Streets' and 'the Man with a Thousand Faces', Mesrine gave some of his ill-gotten gains to the homeless. He was good-looking, often courteous and kind – even to those he robbed – but could also be vicious and unrepentant. He had a string of gorgeous girlfriends, penned two books and a collection of poems, loved fine wine and good food and often robbed banks dressed in the most fashionable clothes. A master of disguise, he would shave his head, grow a beard, wear glasses and don multiple wigs for rapid changes of appearance, and planned his robberies with military precision.

'Undeniably Mesrine committed some unpardonable acts at times and he also pulled off some exceptionally daring deeds,' attests Vincent Cassel, who played him in the 2008 movie *Mesrine*. 'Some will think he's despicable and reactionary, some will like the fact that he followed his own path right to the end, shouldered the responsibility, and will identify with him. Even after nine months of shooting the film, I found it hard to judge him.'

Yet Mesrine's beginnings were relatively ordinary. He was not the product of a tough ghetto, nor did he emanate from a family steeped in crime. He was born on 28 December 1936, in the middle-class Parisian suburb of Clichy-la-Garenne, where his father worked in the lace industry. Apart from suffering the cruelties of German occupation until he was nine years of age, he seems to have had a happy childhood. But something was certainly stirring within him, something different, something disruptive. The first rumbling of discontent manifested when he was expelled from his respectable Catholic school for 'aggressive' behaviour aged fourteen and moved to a local high school.

He later claimed that his 'whole youth had been conditioned by the gangster films that I'd watched as a kid.'

Aged sixteen he was drawn like a moth to the debauched flame that was Pigalle – the capital's red light district and centre of criminal activity – where he lost his virginity to a prostitute named Sarah and got his first potent whiff of the Mephistophelean criminal life.

He soon formed his own little gang of delinquents and, after beating up his headmaster, was expelled from high school and ran away from home. He arrived back in Paris with his tail between his legs.

'My parents were waiting for me on the railway station platform,' wrote Mesrine in his memoirs, *The Killing Instinct,* in which he positioned himself as 'a kamikaze of crime'.

'As soon as I saw them I threw myself in their arms. My father whirled me round and gave me a gentle kick. "That's all you deserve," he said. "Come on, big adventurer. Let's go home."'

Lest we forget, even public enemies were children once.

Enrolled in a different school, he did well for a while but was soon truanting, forging sick notes and school reports, and stealing cars for fun. Consequently, he was expelled again. He started work, quit and then, aged eighteen – displaying an impetuosity and a twisted sense of honour that would mark his future – married his girlfriend of one month, Lydia De Souza, who he knew was pregnant by another boy. Unsurprisingly, they divorced a year later.

Ultimately he appears to have been an honourable youth who loved his parents and who might possibly have straightened himself out eventually. All changed in 1956, however, when, aged twenty, he was conscripted and chose to fight in the Algerian War.

'It was Algeria that changed him,' stressed his tearful mother in an interview with French TV after his death. 'He came back a different boy.'

While in Algeria, the French, renowned for their inexcusable torture and execution of anyone even suspected of insurrection, nurtured Mesrine's less palatable side and made him a commando. He witnessed atrocities unimaginable to most, saw his comrades die, and was ordered to execute Algerian prisoners by putting a bullet in their head after they had been mercilessly tortured, committing acts he was unquestionably not proud of.

One thing he discovered while in Algeria was that he liked to fight in battle, loved the adrenaline rush of raw combat and was thus decorated with the Cross for Military Valour by de Gaulle. But as he wrote, 'I saw too many men die to believe they died for a just cause. What concerned me was that other people's lives, as well as my own, don't matter.

'At the age of twenty I'd been sent to war in the name of freedom. Society had used me like a pawn; it had taken advantage of my youth. It had drawn out my inner violence and exploited it to turn me into a good soldier and a good killer. I could accept that a man would die to defend his country against an invader, but that a government let its youth croak for a colonial war, knowing how useless that sacrifice was, I couldn't accept it. The very idea was unbearable.'

On returning to Paris in 1956, the disenfranchised former soldier was soon able to weigh up the pros and cons of Gallic morality. He had taken part in the criminal slaughter of a population all in the name of imperial zeal. He had seen his superiors order teenage soldiers to execute men, women and children at point-blank range. He was not a happy bunny.

'He made a decision,' explained Broussard in an interview for the French TV show *Daily Motion* in 2001. 'After leaving the army aged twenty-three he decided to become a criminal. He wanted, even then, to be king, to be number one, to have international standing.'

But for Mesrine it was a lot more than that. His decision to become a career criminal enabled him to play havoc with the society that had abused the naïvety of his comrades.

'The tipping point was definitely the war,' attests Martine Malinbaum, Mesrine's lawyer between 1976 and 1978. 'It gave him a taste for action and showed him that he wasn't like everyone else.'

By 1959 he was engaged in another war of his own creation: Jacques Mesrine versus the French establishment.

'Society had sent me back to civilian life without worrying about the impact of the war on my mental state,' he said. 'So I was going to attack it and make it pay the price for what it had destroyed in me.'

He began by burgling 'a place at random in a fancy Paris neighbourhood'. He then murdered a pimp named Ahmed who had badly beaten Sarah – the prostitute who had taken his cherry. Meanwhile he existed as a minor criminal on the periphery of the far-right-wing terrorist group, the OAS (Organisation de l'Armée Secrète) and was robbing the rich with zeal.

But as fast as the money came in, it went out. 'The gambling vice turned into a drug,' he admitted. 'The green velvet, the "bancos", the tense atmosphere of the gamblers waiting for the right card… All of that anchored in me like a destructive tumour. I had lost all notion of the value of money.'

On the morning of 7 June 1961, his girlfriend Maria de la Soledad, a simple Spanish lass with no links to the criminal life whatsoever, gave birth to a girl named Sabrina. Yet despite his wife's protests this new arrival didn't stop Mesrine committing robberies or behaving like a chump. Marital fights ensued. Soledad attempted suicide. So in 1962 Mesrine married her, shortly after robbing his first bank. Despite his meticulous planning for the robbery he was caught and imprisoned for eighteen months.

On his release Mesrine went straight. He worked at an architectural design company constructing models (where he learned a very valuable lesson in how to read and interpret blueprints), but was fired in 1964 due to cuts. Of course, this did not go down at all well with Mesrine.

'Since society refused me the right to earn a living,' he waxed. 'I was going to attack it again.'

At first he worked a fake currency scheme in Switzerland, and then planned a big robbery of the house of the military governor in Palma, Majorca. Caught red-handed in the man's house, he was arrested and sentenced to only six months because, as he later claimed, he persuaded the Spanish he was working with French Intelligence.

'I could not believe my bluff worked,' he later chuckled. 'I played it down and even told them I was a plain thief but they looked at my military record, thought it was a double bluff and made their own conclusion that I was a covert agent for the French.'

In April 1966, Maria – or Sole, as he called her – gave birth to his son, Boris Mesrine.

'In spite of that birth I doubled my criminal activity,' he wrote. 'I was in love with action. Confronted with that mistress Sole had no power.'

Subsequently, he rose to the top of his game, displaying an amazing propensity to dispense his peculiar brand of justice and attendant violence that amazed his contemporaries and was matched only by his facility to rob banks. Without doubt, Mesrine was now a major player in the Paris underworld, admired and feared. But such notoriety comes at a price. He became embroiled in gang warfare. His confederates were murdered and disposed of, while Mesrine himself narrowly escaped death in a classic gangland hit.

Mesrine had just got into his car, only for a gunman to appear and walk towards him, firing his revolver. Mesrine ducked as a shot shattered his windscreen. Another four bullets pierced his car door while another ripped through his thigh.

'Other men died or disappeared,' he said. 'Blood washes away blood. Sometimes you kill a man who could have been your friend had he not been on the other side.'

For their own safety Mesrine stopped taking his children out and wisely moved out of the line of fire to Tenerife to manage a friend's restaurant. Life was idyllic; he had more than enough money to survive and few anxieties. But he still hungered after 'the life'.

'I was involved in a few trafficking deals,' he said. 'But I missed the action.'

And there's the rub. Mesrine was addicted not only to crime but to risky, life-threatening, high-octane blags. Accordingly, he and Sole argued relentlessly until she threatened suicide again. It was the final straw for their increasingly tumultuous relationship.

'I realised that if I stayed I'd end up killing her,' he admitted. 'I flew to Rome. I never saw her again.'

Meanwhile his wife, mentally damaged by Mesrine, gave up their kids to Mesrine's parents to raise.

'Free from Sole I dove into my world head first,' he explained in his memoir. 'I knew that I was responsible for the collapse of my marriage, but remorse wasn't one of my states of mind. Over the years I had become tough and dangerous. I was feared and I got a certain satisfaction from that. I could be gentle in front of kids and old people but my world was a jungle where the strong man is respected.'

Women were a huge part of Mesrine's life. They loved him and he them; the charismatic robber was seldom without a paramour for long.

In 1966 he met Jeanne Schneider, aka Janou. It was love at first sight, his first words to her being, 'Me Tarzan, you Jane.' Actually, 'Me Clyde, you Bonnie' would have been more apt as Janou, a bit of a naughty girl, had spent a year in jail for theft and, once released, turned to prostitution.

Nevertheless they tried to go straight and together they ran an inn for a while – until two pimps turned up claiming ownership of her. Mesrine captured them, tied them up and executed them both. She then took to carrying a gun and together they robbed all sorts, including a gambling den owned by exactly the kind of people you don't mess with.

As a result, they left France to go on a tour of Spain, Italy and Portugal. While in the latter Mesrine discovered that back in France he was wanted for armed robbery and a murder (which he described as 'a settling of scores'), so in February 1968 they fled to Quebec and planned to abide by the law.

Despite hoping for a fresh start, Mesrine was refused a visa because of his extensive criminal record and given ten days to leave the country. He wrote in his book, 'You can't start a new life, it just goes on, with a past that is denied any future.'

Somehow he managed to overcome such trivialities and, a few weeks after arriving, responded to an ad from multi-millionaire textile and grocery magnate Georges Deslauriers, who was looking for a cook and a woman to organise events at his estate. Since Janou was pretty and Mesrine knew his way around a kitchen, they got the job and went on the straight and narrow, but they were soon sacked after a disagreement with the man's aged gardener.

Mesrine responded by kidnapping Deslauriers and demanding a £200,000 ransom, but he botched it by using knockout drops that were inert, enabling the man to escape. With seemingly the entire Canadian police force on their tail they bolted to Texas and were eventually arrested in Arkansas, where they were detained for ten days in the squalid city jail.

When two Canadian coppers eventually appeared, Mesrine gave

himself up for extradition, along with Janou. On his return, pressured by a Canadian television crew to comment, he recalled General de Gaulle's famously undiplomatic remark of 1967, sneering, '*Vive le Québec libre*.'

For the botched kidnapping Mesrine and Janou were sentenced to ten and five years respectively, to be served in the Percé prison in Quebec.

But on 17 August 1969, after just two weeks, they escaped. They were caught twenty-four hours later. Mesrine was then transferred to the maximum-security wing of the Saint-Vincent-de-Paul prison, whose architects had striven to create a lock-up that no one could escape from.

Three years later, in 1972, Mesrine absconded again with dazzling aplomb, having teamed up with Québécois terrorist Jean-Paul Mercier. After four days on the lam they robbed two banks in one day, another twice in three days, and fifteen days later attacked the maximum-security wing.

'We made our decision,' wrote Mesrine. 'We would take over the maximum-security wing and free all the prisoners. I made a list of the weapons we needed: ten M1 rifles with thirty bullet clips, five sub-machine guns, a shotgun, a sniper rifle, and two pump-action seven-shot .12 calibres. I let our friends know that we would attack the prison at 2pm on September 3... We passed and I saw our friends walking across the courtyard and the beefed-up surveillance.'

But as they drove past the enclosure they were spotted. Armed guards and police pursued them from all sides, machine guns blazing. Madcap Mesrine decided to attack anyway and opened fire on his pursuers, while guards in the watchtower opened fire on him, riddling the car with bullets and wounding Mercier in the process.

'We left in a rain of bullets,' said Mesrine. 'We had failed. All our friends had helplessly witnessed one of the worst shootouts Quebec had ever seen.'

A few days later, whilst out in the woods doing a bit of shooting practice, Mercier and Mesrine were apprehended by two forest rangers – Médéric Côté, sixty-two, and Ernest Saint-Pierre, fifty. The former, having more bravery than sense, went for his gun after he discovered a veritable arsenal in Mesrine's car, so the criminals shot and killed them, Mesrine finishing them off with shots to the head.

Every police officer available was charged to find him and his accomplice, yet just a few days later the daring duo still managed to squeeze in a few spirited bank heists. (For the record, they had robbed nine since they escaped.)

It seemed that the writing was very much on the wall, so they crossed the border to the US and made their way first to New York and then down to Venezuela. Meanwhile Janou, despite Mesrine promising to get her out legally, languished in a women's prison facility in Canada.

Returning to France in 1972, the inveterate felon wasted no time in returning to his old ways. 'He developed his own style then,' explained Jean-François Richet. 'He would rob several banks in a row – waiting for the police sirens and then getting into the car to take down a bank on the next street over.'

'Since my return we held up about twenty banks,' wrote Mesrine. 'I'd even done one hold-up on my own, just for the hell of it.'

On one occasion he cased a bank next to a barber's shop then told the police of his plans to break into it. Having carried out this task, he managed to sneak into the barber's, disguised himself in fake wig, glasses and a tunic covered in hair clippings, and patiently waited for the police to arrive at the scene.

He then approached a policeman in the street and asked him what was going on.

'It's Mesrine,' the clueless copper replied.

'When are you going to catch this menace?' said Mesrine, tutting at their ineptitude.

Revelling in his ability to wind up the police, he bragged relentlessly about this particular escapade. To be sure, such flagrant disrespect did not go down too well with *les flics,* and by 8 March 1973, he was caught again. But knowing he would soon be apprehended, Mesrine had already planned a daring escape. 'What do you bet me,' he taunted his police escort, 'that I'll be out in three months?'

On 6 June he was taken to the Palais de Justice in Compiègne. Feigning an attack of diarrhoea he was allowed to use the toilet, found the gun behind the cistern that his accomplice had hidden weeks before and hid it in his belt. Marched back into the court, when asked to answer the charges he jumped over the dock, grabbed the judge and, using him as a human shield, made his getaway in a hail of gunfire.

'I knew I'd be arrested and I knew that they would try me for an old charge first in Compiègne so I decided to organise my escape before my arrest,' he laughed.

Having enjoyed just a few months on the lam, a former partner in crime revealed his whereabouts to the police and, on 28 September 1973, hordes of armed coppers surrounded his apartment.

'He knew he was under siege,' said arresting officer Broussard. 'So I gave him the choice: "Come out unarmed or die." To which he asked if I was Commissaire Broussard with the beard and would I approach unarmed – which I did. He then opened the door with the biggest cigar I'd ever seen in his mouth, invited me in and offered me a glass of champagne.'

No one could now deny that Mesrine had every right to the title of Public Enemy Number One.

It was then, while awaiting trial, that Mesrine found his appetite for media assiduity. After reading an article in *L'Express* that was not to his fancy, he sent a threatening letter to the writer responsible, which prompted his appearance on the front page of the publication. Seeing a chance to vent his considerable angst, he began writing long letters to the press about prison conditions.

On a roll, he then authored his memoir, entitled *L'Instinct De Mort* (*The Killing Instinct*) in which he admitted to thirty-nine killings (mainly other villains and the odd cop who got in the way), described his every blag in detail, and clarified his life's philosophy. Mesrine spent a lot of time in solitary.

At his trial he played to the balcony and put up a bravura performance that fuelled the press's fascination even further. 'And what did you do with the money you took in the hold-up?' asked the judge. 'I put it in the bank, your honour,' quipped Mesrine. 'That's still the safest place to keep it.'

No matter how funny he found himself, Mesrine was still sentenced to some twenty years behind bars in a high-security prison. Whilst incarcerated he wrote letters to friends and talked openly of escape, prompting La Santé, already the most secure prison in France, to build a new wing to hold him.

On 3 May 1978, the prison governor was tipped off that Mesrine was going to attempt escape two days later. He laughed it off as a practical joke.

Indeed, Mesrine did not break out on the fifth, because it was raining. Instead, he postponed his escape until the eighth, when he produced a gun, stole keys and, along with notorious escapee François Besse and another man, got out of a cellblock and onto a fenced-off footpath. They forced workmen to give them a ladder, took an armed guard by surprise, scaled the thirty-foot exterior wall, hooked a grappling iron onto the top of the ladder and slid down the rope.

The third man over the wall was shot dead by police while Mesrine and Besse stole a horse and dodged the police barricade.

They were the first two men ever to escape from La Santé.

Eight days later the pair held up a gun shop in Paris. Ten days after that, on 26 May, they robbed a casino in Deauville.

Still incensed by the indignity of incarceration, Mesrine went on a publicity drive. He granted interviews with publications such as the hugely popular *Paris Match* and *Libération*, emphasising that he was rebelling against injustice and battling to abolish maximum security and solitary confinement. He then went a step further and in 1978 was on the cover of an August issue of *Paris Match*. In the article he brazenly elaborated on his exploits and the insufficiency of the police and the powers that be.

'For four years, I repeated to everyone that I was going to "break" [out of prison] with guns in my hand,' Mesrine told *Paris Match* reporter Isabelle de Wangen. 'It was more than a trap; it was a method of working – intoxication. Of course they believed me, but if you trigger a warning signal a hundred times, when it really sounds like the right day, nobody believes in it anymore. I am a specialist in escape.'

He also spoke of the Deauville robbery.

'In Deauville, it did not happen the way we wanted. We thought we would take 100 million. Attacking a casino means attacking the empire of vice. The only way to rob a casino is to go in with a gun. We stole 13 million and not seven-and-a-half as was said. It's not much, but it's better than working for Renault.'

He added, 'Some people like golf or skiing. My relaxation is armed robbery.'

An incorrigible publicity hound, he never missed an opportunity to bolster these articles with photographs of himself brandishing a gun, face uncovered. One paragraph in *Paris Match* particularly incensed the constabulary.

'Now it's war,' he was quoted as saying. 'The police must know that I will not surrender. I do not want to go back to prison. I will shoot, and too bad if unfortunately there are innocent [people] behind my bullets. I will not fire the first shot. But I will leave some bodies on the pavement. If I'm locked up in a place with people, I'll get them out. I do not want hostages. But do not miss me.

'I say this without hatred. There is no hatred; it's a question of survival. They want my life and I defend it. I do not defy the police but I want my freedom. The cops do their job and in the end there is a certain mutual respect. A guy like Broussard, I do not like him, but I respect him. He's a worthy opponent.'

And so he infuriated not only the police but also the whole of his country's establishment, who demanded his arrest. His answer, in November 1978, was to attempt to kidnap the judge who had sentenced him, demanding that if all top security prisons in France were not closed he would begin assassinating magistrates.

But the kidnapping of the judge backfired, with Mesrine only just evading capture by running down the stairs and shouting, 'Quick! Mesrine's up there!' to the oncoming police as he sped past them. A young policeman was later found handcuffed to a drainpipe weeping with embarrassment.

Still, not even these near escapes from capture or narrowly missed assignations with the Grim Reaper deterred the renegade former paratrooper. It seems that imprisonment had incensed him beyond belief. Once mad, bad and dangerous to know he was now wild, wilful and on a death wish. As such, François Besse dissociated himself from Mesrine and disappeared. Mesrine, meanwhile, laid low for a while, living the high life, before re-emerging on 21 June 1979 to kidnap the millionaire property tycoon Henri Lelièvre. For this he managed to extract a ransom of six million francs.

But the tide was turning for Mesrine. Infuriated by a piece written by right-wing journalist and former policeman Jacques Tillier, he lured the scribe to a cave, undressed him, beat him senseless, shot him three times and left him for dead. In a misguided attempt to justify his actions, Mesrine then sent a wordy letter to *Le Monde*, accompanied by Polaroids of the naked bloodied writer with his hands tied behind his back. This time the country was overcome with loathing. In one fell swoop Mesrine had lost public support.

Indeed this and the kidnapping of Lelièvre not only attracted the attention of the press but of French President Giscard d'Estaing, who told his minister of the interior: 'We really have to finish this Mesrine off.'

Just a few days later Mesrine was controversially shot dead. He was just one month shy of his forty-third birthday.

The operation that ended Mesrine's life caused an outcry, even though the police, who were praised by d'Estaing, pronounced it a success. The question is: was he given the chance to capitulate or was he was gunned down in cold blood?

'The police gave him the chance to surrender,' testified Broussard, for once seeming less than honest in his TV interview. 'But instead of keeping still he got down out of the way of the machine guns and reached for a little bag where he had two hand grenades.'

'I will swear blind that the police told him to get out of the car after he was already dead,' maintained eyewitness Guy Penet in an interview for the same programme. 'I heard "Don't move, you've had it" after the gunfire. I have maintained that for twenty-two years and that is what I saw.'

After Mesrine died the authorities found a cassette tape in a drawer in his apartment addressed to his last love, Sylvia Jeanjacquot.

'Hello darling,' he said. 'If you [hear] this I'll have been killed by the police, which is nothing we didn't expect. I died with a gun in my hand, and even though I might not have had the time to use it, if I had I would have.'

Jeanjacquot was also shot. Her arm was damaged for life and she lost an eye. Sadly, her pet poodle was less fortunate, dying heroically in a hail of bullets.

Martin Scorsese

I will never forget the first time I saw a Martin Scorsese picture. It was in 1976, during the hottest summer on record. Every Monday my pals would bowl up to our local flea pit, the Scala cinema in Merthyr Tydfil, where the air conditioning was an open back door and half the audience were there to sleep off a whole day's boozing.

We usually turned up without knowing what was playing beforehand. Some weeks we'd see something great, such as *Thunderbolt and Lightfoot*; other weeks something not so great, like *Sleeper*. On this occasion we moseyed on up in the pouring rain to find that *Taxi Driver* was showing and so, thinking it another *Death Wish,* paid our twenty-five pence, sat down and had our gobs smacked senseless.

Here was this mad-arsed picture inhabited by lowlifes, hookers, pimps and druggies that told of a febrile Travis Bickle, a troubled Vietnam vet suffering from insomnia, who is obsessed by the city's squalor and the indefinite need to either purify or destroy. It was unlike anything I had ever seen before.

'I remember when *Taxi Driver* was first released, some reviews said it was an exploitation film because there's a lot of violence in it,' chuckled Scorsese, sitting comfortably in a very big chair in the Directors Guild of America in New York's Upper West Side in 2004. 'But for me the whole film is very much based on the impressions I had as a result of growing up in New York and living in this city which was bankrupt morally and otherwise and was simmering with tension. But *Taxi Driver* was exactly what we wanted – the three of us. I was the director, Robert De Niro was the actor and Paul Schrader wrote the script.'

The story behind the script is worthy of an article itself. The writer had split with his wife, his union and his job, and lost his apartment. Homeless, he drove around the streets alone for days on end. 'Then I realised I hadn't actually spoken to anybody in weeks,' informed Schrader, interviewed at London's Dorchester hotel seven years later, in 2011. 'And then this metaphor came into my head of the taxi car and the seclusion and the paranoia. Then I wrote it very, very quickly, but as self-therapy, and not to be made. I just wanted to get this ugly thing out of me. Then the script was sold and it became this film that is now regarded as a classic.'

A few months after I'd seen *Taxi Driver*, my friends and I, while on one of our many excursions to London in search of ladies who liked narrow trousers, found ourselves with a few hours to kill before we hit the nightspots. So we ducked into the Academy Arts cinema on Oxford Street and, to my unbridled delight, caught Scorsese's *Mean Streets* just as the opening credits rolled.

I loved *Taxi Driver,* but *Mean Streets* was pretty near perfect. Here was a filmmaker who was talking to me and every other young ne'er-do-well in the world who ducked and dived and had pals who were dangerous to hang out with. Scorsese knew his subjects and so did we.

'The film was written for Harvey Keitel, whose character Charlie, I've since realised, is based on my father, who was also named Charlie,' said the director, who wrote the script with Mardik Martin.

'Johnny Boy is based on [my dad's] brother Joe, who lived underneath us on the second floor. My father came from a family of eight or nine and Uncle Joe was the youngest and was constantly getting in trouble. And my father was the one who, out of respect for the family name, had to go and have what we call a "sit down" to make peace with the people Joe had upset.'

A galvanising piece of personal filmmaking, *Mean Streets'* strength lies in its depiction of a gang of guys from a working-class neighbourhood (Little Italy in lower Manhattan) that could just as well have been in Merthyr or Moscow.

Certainly, Scorsese knew exactly what he was talking about. Both his parents hailed from Palermo and the family lived on Little Italy's Elizabeth Street – a locale controlled by the omnipresent 'made men' who held court in the area's little restaurants and cafés.

'The other interesting figure in *Mean Streets* is the heavily mobbed-up Giovanni, who runs the restaurant,' said the director. 'I saw my first displays of his kind of power when I was about nine years old, in this little restaurant. There was one particular guy (who I believe was killed in 1968) who was a very powerful mafia figure. He didn't have to say anything. He didn't have to do anything. He'd just walk in a room and everything would stop. I've never forgotten that.'

Scorsese has often been criticised for presenting Italian Americans as hoods and gangsters.

'A lot of friends, when they saw the movie, would say, "Oh, it's about wise guys, but not everybody's like that,"' he recalled. 'And yes, that's true, but I'm telling the story from my point of view, from what my perception was.'

Essentially, *Mean Streets* is about responsibility. 'It's about being your brother's keeper,' said Scorsese. 'It's about what's right and what's wrong morally. And it has to do with borrowing money, and disrespect. And that is that. I made the film about a period of my life when I was going to Washington Square College at the same time as hanging out with the same kind of guys you see in the picture, who were my friends I grew up with.'

De Niro's incredible rendering of Johnny Boy, the screw-up hoodlum, makes the film. This was De Niro at his best – wiry, mercurial and dangerously charismatic – before the method swallowed him.

'It was Bobby who came up with that improvisation with Keitel in the back room of the bar which really pulls the film together,' said Scorsese of the famous 'Joey Clams' scene. 'It's one of the longest in the film and is pivotal. Bobby is something else there. He really impressed me.'

Of course, Scorsese is himself a fan – a fan of great film. 'For me film was all about European cinema, Italian mainly,' he enthused. 'Every Friday night when I was four or five years old, my parents, grandparents and *all* my uncles would come over to our tenement (we had a sixteen-inch black-and-white TV), and watch Vittorio De Sica's *The Bicycle Thief*, Roberto Rossellini's *Paisà* and *Open City* — all these great subtitled pictures. I understood the language. I understood what they were doing. I was captivated.'

It was on TV that he first watched some of the movies that left their mark on him. There was *The Third Man* by Carol Reed, *Letter from an Unknown Woman* by Max Ophüls and *The Southerner* by Jean

Renoir. But it wasn't until he was taken to the cinema that a whole new world opened up for him.

'I suffered from asthma so was taken away from sports, and the only thing they could do was take me to a movie theatre,' he recalled with a smile. 'And when I was in that theatre, boy that was peace. That was heaven. The next thing that had a similar effect to that was the church, particularly Saint Patrick's Old Cathedral on Mott Street. For me, it's the cinema and the church.'

The former infatuation led him to Washington Square College where he started making his first short films in 1963 and 1964, inspired by the great John Cassavetes. 'He made us feel that you could pick up a camera, go in the street and shoot and make a movie.'

He made his first feature, *Who's That Knocking at My Door*, starring Harvey Keitel, in 1967, and in 1972 was hired by Roger Corman to direct the lacklustre *Boxcar Bertha*. A year later he'd shot *Mean Streets*.

After *Mean Streets*, I was like a teenage girl waiting for her Beiberesque pop idol to release his next album and I regularly scoured the Sundays for news of Scorsese's next picture. At last, in 1977, I queued in the rain to watch *New York, New York* on its opening night. My expectations perhaps too high, I was hugely disenchanted. Apart from De Niro's Hawaiian shirts, peg trousers and correspondents, I felt it missed the mark by a city block.

However crestfallen I might have been, I still lived in hope and was richly rewarded three years later, in April 1980, when I saw *Raging Bull* at the Odeon in Leicester Square on its opening night. I was so blown away I watched it again a few days later. Quintessential Scorsese, *Raging Bull* is believed by many to be the director's greatest work but, curiously, he almost turned the job down.

In truth, the film was De Niro's obsession and in his eyes the only man fit to sit in the director's chair was Scorsese, who in 1978 was 'like a brother'. Still, Scorsese couldn't see why the actor was so intent on making a picture based on Jake LaMotta's ghosted autobiography, *Raging Bull: My Story*.

Furthermore, Scorsese was in a bad way. He'd just finished making *The Last Waltz*, a film about legendary drug fiends the Band, and collapsed bleeding from his mouth, nose and rectum. The combustible mix of prescription drugs, asthma medicines and the mounds of cocaine he was doing had destroyed the thrombocytes (which are crucial for normal blood clotting) in his blood, leaving an impending threat of brain haemorrhage. His girlfriend at the time, Isabella Rossellini, didn't think he'd survive.

'I went through that rough period of my own,' Scorsese told *Vanity Fair*. 'But came out the other side alive and finally understood Bob's obsession.'

Now that it suddenly made sense, it appealed to him on every level. Scorsese riffed on the almost Old Testament subplot regarding LaMotta's incomprehensible jealousy over his wife, Vikki, who he imagined was having an affair with his brother, Joey, who he consequently beat to a bloody pulp. He was drawn to Jake's Catholic masochism and his facility to take vicious thrashings but remain standing before, out of nowhere, knocking his exhausted opponent flat on his ass.

As Scorsese often said, 'Jake LaMotta fought as if he didn't deserve to live.' And he was attracted to the overriding fact that Jake was a victim of his father – who pushed him into unlicensed bouts as a kid to earn a crust – and the mafia hoods (Clay/Liston fight fixers Frankie Carbo and Blinky Palermo) who forced him to throw his 1947 fight with Billy Fox.

But above all he was drawn because, as he said, *Mean Streets* and *Raging Bull* are 'really the same movie'.

After Paul Schrader took Mardik Martin's original script and made it sing, he, De Niro and Scorsese finished it on the Caribbean island of Saint Martin, by which time the director had recuperated and fully embraced the project.

The film opened in 1980 to exalted reviews, but due to the lack of a proper advertising campaign the box office was lukewarm. Ten days after *Raging Bull* opened, *Heaven's Gate*, the prototypical megaflop, was released by the same studio, United Artists. 'The era of big-budget personal filmmaking was over,' Scorsese told the *Guardian* remorsefully. 'I was going to move on to other things – go to Italy and make documentaries. I didn't think there was any place for me in Hollywood anymore.'

Nevertheless, the picture was nominated for eight Academy Awards and has since been voted the best film of the 1980s in numerous critics' polls. It's also regarded by many critics as one of the finest American films ever made and was ranked number one in the greatest movies ever made in reader polls conducted by both *Empire* magazine and the *New York Times*.

Criminally, Scorsese did not get the 1980 Academy Award for best director, although De Niro received the best actor gong for his portrait of LaMotta, who critic Pauline Kael described as 'a swollen puppet with only bits and pieces of a character inside'.

We all wondered how Marty could follow up this monumental work. But follow it he did, with *The King of Comedy*, an amazingly prophetic study of fame in which wannabe stand-up star Rupert Pupkin, who lives in a world of make-believe, kidnaps his idol, the pompous talk show host Jerry Langford (Jerry Lewis simply playing himself). The ransom is an appearance on Jerry's show, which will guarantee Pupkin fame. Angry, lonely, satirical, *The King of Comedy* is a stunning tour de force that sees Scorsese and De Niro at the very top of their game.

As was his wont, De Niro reportedly polished his stand-up skills in open-mike sessions in small comedy clubs, while Scorsese watched endless talk show reruns. But it wasn't until the two men visited Blue Mountain – a Broadway clothing store with a sign above the door that said 'Shirt Maker to the Stars' and a mannequin in the window – that they nailed Pupkin's oddball appearance.

'It had everything,' Scorsese confirmed. 'The face, moustache and the red shirt, red tie and everything. We said, that's him. Let's do it.'

Again I'd queued to see the movie on its first night. This time it was in New York on a freezing evening in February 1983. It was so bitterly cold – minus twenty degrees as I recall – that my brilliantine froze to my head, while my feet felt like somebody else's. But it was worth it.

At the time I was married to a New Yorker named Holli, a big face on the downtown club scene who had lived in the East Village for years, so we were entirely conversant with the city's arty underbelly. Accordingly, news of Scorsese's next project, *After Hours*, set amongst the bars and lofts South of Houston Street, intrigued us no end, especially as our friends were in it.

After Hours tells the story of a paranoid, nerdish data processor, Paul Hackett (Griffin Dunne), who arranges a date with a waitress (Rosanna Arquette) he has just met in a café. Unable to pay his cab fare on the way to her apartment (which she shares with a couple of S&M freaks) he ends up getting stranded in SoHo amongst the barking mad, drug-crazed locals, eventually falling foul to a vigilante mob led by a Mister Softee ice cream truck. A nocturnal oddity with a superb soundtrack that includes everything from Bad Brains to Peggy Lee, it is an extraordinary piece of filmmaking.

Scorsese (who we'd see in the clubs all the time) recreated this world of ours with unerring accuracy. Watching it now is like travelling back in time to the utter nuttiness that was lower Manhattan circa 1985.

By now a new Scorsese movie was not just a film release, it was an event looked forward to by every hep cat on the block. Hardly surprising since he had made seven features in thirteen years, of which only one failed to find the target.

Still, my feelings of dismay were to return, as no matter how much I loved *The Hustler,* I could not see why anyone would want to make its sequel, *The Color of Money*, especially one starring that thoroughly talentless wardrobe, Tom Cruise.

Apparently it was the director's attempt to move into commercial filmmaking. I found it facile and annoying. Next up was *The Last Temptation of Christ*, adapted from Nikos Kazantzakis's controversial 1951 novel by Paul Schrader, which quite admirably upset millions of half-wit Christians, looks incredible and is a brave piece of filmmaking – albeit one that somehow doesn't engage with its audience.

At this point I thought Scorsese – a filmmaker synonymous with the more colourful, seamier side of big city life: boxing rings, bars, nightclubs, pool halls, taxi cabs – had lost the plot and was wandering the desert with a bunch of method actors in sandals and long robes. It was like losing an old friend.

I needn't have worried, though. He then came up trumps with *Goodfellas,* a veritable masterpiece based on the memoir of Henry

Hill, a mafia thug turned informer. Seduced and forsaken by 'the life', Hill worked his way up through the mob hierarchy and connived with vicious fellow lowlifes (such as Jimmy 'the Gent' Conway, played by De Niro, and Tommy DeVito, incredibly rendered by the superlative Joe Pesci), only to fall from grace with a bang.

'I saw this review [of *Wiseguy*] which talked about Henry Hill being a guy on different levels of the underworld,' reflected the director. 'And that's what made it valuable. I like diaries. I'm fond of James Boswell's London diaries. It tells you a lot about a place and time. *Mean Streets* is a street corner, stealing a quarter or stealing twenty-five cents to get a pack of cigarettes. *Goodfellas* started on that level but then went a lot further.

'But the very powerful point in *Goodfellas* is that these guys are trapped in that system. [The] only way he [Hill] would get out is he's gonna be killed. And then he realised [he'd] better talk. And because *Goodfellas* touches on something very dangerous that younger people might admire or emulate, we showed, in the last hour of the film, that the life is anything but a good life.'

Like all of Scorsese's best movies there is always the standout scene that we all remember and quote years afterwards. On this occasion it's Joe Pesci's 'You think I'm a funny guy?' scene.

'Joe Pesci improvised that,' reflected the director, still impressed. 'He told me this story that happened to him. With a friend, a guy he knew. A made man. Joe was laughing and the guy says, "Yeah, yeah, real funny. Funny guy. So you think I'm a funny guy?" And then Joe had to use his wits to get out of the situation, take a chance and say you're putting me on. You know, I'd almost had you.

'So Joe said, "I'm dead either way. I can't leave the room. The whole room is stopped. Everybody's looking at me. I better call him on it." That's a true story. A guy who knows all about "the life", when asked what film summed it up, he said *Goodfellas* because of that scene. He said that's the lifestyle. It could turn like that on a dime and you're dead. And that's what you have to know. I'm interested in that kind of historical detail – it's like anthropology.'

Admittedly I was apprehensive about his next film, a remake of the 1962 classic *Cape Fear,* directed by J. Lee Thompson. Thankfully

De Niro pulled off his reprisal of Bob Mitchum's ex-con, Max Cady, with aplomb, turning him into a tightly coiled, predatory Nietzschean superman. A work of overwhelming cinematic brutality, it grabs you by the throat from the getgo, its grip tightening until the astonishing climax, after which you can, at last, breathe again.

After that came 1993's *The Age of Innocence*, which left me cold and bombed. But he bounced back yet again in 1995 with *Casino,* written by *Goodfellas* writer Nick Pileggi, which was a platform for another bravura De Niro performance as casino boss Sam 'Ace' Rothstein, and follows the same path as *Goodfellas* with its 'live by the sword die by the sword' *leitmotif.*

'Take *Casino*, there's the scene where Joe Pesci's character and his younger brother are killed by their closest friends with baseball bats in a cornfield,' Scorsese informed the *Guardian* in 2003. 'That way of life that we depicted, that's where it really ends – your closest friend smashing you in the head with a baseball bat. Not even a gun. Not cutting your throat. If you want to live in that lifestyle, that's where you're going to go.'

Notably, *Casino* was the last film De Niro did with Scorsese. Neither has been quite so efficacious since.

In 2002 Scorsese released *Gangs of New York* and found a new leading man in Leonardo DiCaprio. But casting the baby-faced youngster as a nineteenth-century New York gang member was never a good idea. In truth the whole film, however ambitious, was never going to work. Scorsese attempted to squeeze almost every detail from Herbert Asbury's seminal 350-page book of the same name into his 167 minutes (and spent his entire 100-million-bucks budget), when a re-enactment of just one chapter of the book would have sufficed. I was particularly disappointed.

Since then, I've felt let down by *The Aviator*, thought *The Departed* OK (not a patch on the Hong Kong original, *Infernal Affairs),* while *Hugo* didn't float my boat. As for his music documentaries, I never found them that interesting. I was again on the verge of losing faith.

Yet, as he's proved time and again, you can't keep this diminutive New Yorker down. In 2013 he surprised us all with the deliciously politically incorrect *Wolf of Wall Street*, in which DiCaprio shone, thanks in part to the faultless script of *Sopranos* and *Boardwalk Empire* writer Terence Winter. Basically *Goodfellas* on Wall Street, it swapped Italian mobsters with a bunch of dubious stockbrokers, guys who make $12 million in three minutes at a company where hired dwarves are tossed around to lift employee morale and snorting anthills of Bolivian marching powder is encouraged. It was a return to that familiar ground that Scorsese does better than anyone else.

Amazingly, out of the twenty-two feature length dramas Scorsese has directed, there are nine that are seminal films – five of which are downright classics. He has in fact created his very own milieu, a genre known as 'Scorsesesque', which the *New York Times* defines as films that feature 'Fluid camera work cut to an eclectic soundtrack with themes of Catholic guilt, the Italian American identity and pervasive violence and are usually set in the American Northeast.'

'It is as simple as saying Raoul Walsh only did films about men and professions,' admitted Scorsese. 'There's the famous line about a love story that Jack Warner said about Raoul Walsh. "A love story? A love story for Raoul Walsh is a whorehouse burning down."'

For the coming year [2015], Martin Charles Scorsese has a busy slate. He has just shot an untitled rock 'n' roll TV project in New York for HBO starring Juno Temple (the ill-fated *Vinyl*), is preparing to shoot *Silence*, an adaptation of Shūsaku Endō's novel about two seventeenth-century Jesuit missionaries in Japan starring Liam Neeson, and is reported to be prepping a biopic of Frank Sinatra.

Looks like I've got a bit more queuing up to do.

Richard Kuklinski ('The Iceman')

About ten years ago I was trawling through the TV channels late one Friday evening and came across an HBO documentary based on interviews with a six-foot, five-inch, three-hundred-pound bear of a man.

Bearded and bald, he sat there in the maximum security Trenton State Prison, New Jersey, and told tales of murder committed with all manner of instruments. Although he had been convicted of killing five men, he claimed he had carried out at least a hundred mob hits, for which he was handsomely remunerated.

A riveting and haunting documentary that has stuck with me ever since, it was called *The Iceman Confesses: Secrets of a Mafia Hitman*, and the man's name was Richard Kuklinski – New York's most prolific freelance assassin, who worked on and off for the city's Five Families, as well as Newark's DeCavalcante family (the inspiration for the Sopranos), for some thirty years.

More reminiscent of a soldier explaining military tactics that kill thousands than a common-or-garden assassin, he was cool, calm, collected, and extremely rational. As New Jersey Assistant Attorney General Robert J. Carroll attests in the documentary, 'Richard Kuklinski is not a serial killer. He is not driven by perverse sexual desires. He does not drink or smoke. He is a predator who kills for greed.'

Accordingly, Kuklinski claimed that he would never kill a child and 'most likely wouldn't kill a woman', unless she was a professional hitwoman or gangster. After the documentary, I sat and thought about Kuklinski and concluded that the man was purely an assassin working in a war between crime families. The only difference between him and a Navy Seal assassin (like those who killed Osama bin Laden, for example) was that the people he worked for had not been voted into power.

Like many heads of state and royal families, crime families and syndicates had initially come to power via extreme acts of violence and the ability to pay mercenaries such as Kuklinski to kill their rivals. And oddly, even though we're not supposed to *like* such cold-blooded murderers, this man was certainly not unlikeable. There was something puzzlingly endearing about his sincerity, candour and lack of remorse or need for forgiveness, not to mention a total lack of braggadocio.

Many others have agreed, including Israeli film director Ariel Vromen. 'I was amazed by the story,' he recalls. 'The weirdest feeling that I had was that I liked the guy.' Subsequently, Vromen penned a screenplay based on the prison interviews, which has now been made into a quite excellent film entitled *The Iceman*.

'Richard Kuklinski was not part of The [mafia] Family; he was an outside contractor,' explains producer Ehud Bleiberg. 'He was contradictory. He was a family man with his family, but on the other side he was different. He killed people so that no one knew they had been killed. He operated for two decades without anyone knowing who he was.'

In the film, Kuklinski is played by Michael Shannon, who first came to my attention as Larry Oster-Berg in director David Caffrey's oddball comedy *Grand Theft Parsons* (which tells of two men who steal Gram Parsons's corpse). He was also convincing as the creepily obsessive Agent Nelson Van Alden in *Boardwalk Empire*. The six-foot, four-inch Shannon delivers a quite remarkable performance. 'I guess any time I take a job, I'm not afraid to dig into something, no matter how ugly it may be,' said Shannon. 'To me, that's where the stories are – that ugly, dark, confused place. Those, unfortunately, for better or for worse, tend to be the most interesting stories. People are fascinated by them... The value of making this movie is to give you some idea of what Richard Kuklinski's life might have been like. Here's a fellow that people are intrigued by and want to know more about. Hopefully, we're giving them that insight.'

Kuklinski was born on 11 April 1935, in an apartment on 3rd Street, Jersey City, New Jersey. His parents' neglectfulness and cruelty virtually guaranteed a bleak future for their children. When Kuklinski was just five years old, his father Stanley, a drunken tyrannical Polish-born railway worker, beat Richard's eleven-year-old sibling Florian to death. His parents told him and the police that the boy had fallen down the stairs. Later in life his younger brother Joseph was convicted of raping and murdering a twelve-year-old girl. When asked about Joseph's crimes, Richard replied: 'We come from the same father.'

His mother was apparently cut from the same cloth. 'My mother was cancer,' he explains in the documentary. 'She destroyed everything. She'd hit me with a broomstick so hard that one day the stick broke on my back.' Born Anna McNally, Kuklinski's mother had a turbulent childhood herself, seeing her Irish father die of pneumonia and her mother killed by a truck on 10th Street. Raised in the Sacred Heart Orphanage, Jersey City, on a diet of fire, brimstone and damnation, she was regularly beaten by the sadistic nuns and lost her virginity to a priest who raped her when she was ten. Most would conclude that she never had a chance either. Still pathologically religious, however, she beat the ethic into Richard who, now that his elder brother was dead, was regularly battered within an inch of his life by his father, causing welts and bruises so severe that often the young boy had to miss school for weeks.

Unsurprisingly, Richard grew into a painfully shy child lacking in both self-confidence and self-worth – the world to him an ugly dark place filled to the brim with pain, suffering and religious hypocrisy. Thus, other boys on the block singled him out. On one occasion his father saw him being bullied so hit him across the face with his belt and sent him out again to fight the two Irish brothers who had picked on him.

'No kid a mine's gonna be a chicken shit,' he roared. Catching the siblings off guard, Richard gave them a ferocious beating. That afternoon the young adolescent realised that force came first and that the meek definitely did not inherit the earth.

But the bullying did not end there. With Stanley spending all the family's money on alcohol and hookers, his sons' clothing left a lot to be desired. Ragged and dirty, with holes in their shoes, they became the butt of the tough immigrant kids' jokes. As for their religious zealot mother, Anna, she was only interested in lighting holy candles in church, her children's appearance or wellbeing of no concern to her.

At St Mary's School, the severely dyslexic Richard was beaten by the nuns. Finally his father left the family home for good while his mother retreated further and further into the bowels of absurdity, embracing religion more than ever. She pushed Kuklinski into becoming an altar boy and a priest made sexual overtures to him. Fired with religious mania, she rarely fed her offspring and consequently the lanky young boy took to stealing food for his younger brother and sister, who looked on him as the sole provider.

Given all of the above, it's hardly surprising that Richard Kuklinski turned his burning anger to stray local animals. He would tie two cats together by their tails, hang them over a clothesline and watch them tear each other apart. He would set dogs on fire with petrol or bludgeon them to death with lead pipes. The killer who would become known as the Iceman had been created. All he had to do now was actually kill a human being.

When he was twelve years old a gang from the projects picked a fight with him. They beat him so badly on one occasion that he couldn't leave his home for a week. The gang's leader, Charley Lane, had been the most vicious when beating the boy. Richard's answer was to take a two-foot long wooden pole and lie in wait for the older bully, confront him, and then beat him to death.

An avid reader of true crime magazines, Kuklinski knew that the authorities could identify Lane by either his teeth or fingerprints, so he drove the corpse out to a remote South Jersey marshland called the Pine Barrens, cut off the dead teenager's fingers, knocked his teeth out, and dropped the body into a pond. He was thirteen.

'As a young guy I realised that if you hurt someone they will leave you alone,' he explained to Dr Park Dietz, who interviewed him for the documentary. 'Good guys finish last. I'd taken enough as a kid so I attacked, and to everyone's surprise I was no longer taking but giving it. I learned it was better to give than receive. I didn't mean to kill Charley and I felt bad. I was upset. I was sad at first but then I felt this rush because for once I had control. It was like, "If you mess with me I will hurt you!"'

One such aggressor was a Jersey City copper named Doyle, who berated Kuklinski after he had beaten him repeatedly at pool. Outside the pool hall Doyle fell asleep in his car, so Richard torched the car with him in it.

'I could smell his burning flesh and hear his screams as I walked around the corner,' he says. 'It didn't bother me. I liked it. He made me mad.'

He later said that the bullying Doyle reminded him of his father. 'Stanley was a first-grade sadistic prick,' he said. 'He should never have been allowed to have children. I've wondered thousands a times why I didn't kill him.'

Soon Kuklinski had his own gang comprising three Poles, an Italian and an Irish kid. They called themselves the Coming Up Roses, and each had a tattoo of a tiny roll of parchment with said name written on their left hand between thumb and forefinger. They each swore an oath of loyalty and set about holding up liquor stores, hijacking lorries and burgling the homes of the wealthy.

The money piled in and Richard, describing himself as 'nigger rich', always had a roll of notes, gambled incessantly and dressed in garish bespoke yellow or pink suits. If anyone was foolish enough to criticise his attire he would pull out his knife and stab them. Word soon spread that if you fucked with the Polack (as he became known) chances are you'd end up on a slab. Inevitably, it wasn't long before the local mob got wind of him.

Carmine 'Meatball' Genovese summoned the gang for a meet at his house, handed them a black-and-white photograph, an address and a contract to kill. Richard carried out the assignment with ease. Soon he and his gang were doing 'jobs' all over, until two of his gang stupidly robbed a card game sponsored by a made man in the DeCavalcante family, Albert Perenti, who then ordered Kuklinski to kill the pair of them – the two people who he was closest to in the world. It was him or them, so he shot them both. 'They didn't suffer,' he later said. 'They were dead before they knew what hit them.'

Word reached the DeCavalcantes that Kuklinski was a reliable killer. Now there was no going back. A new career as a mafia hitman beckoned. He was nineteen years of age.

Genovese had asked Kuklinski to kill a man, make him suffer (which he did by slowly smashing his ankles and knees with a hatchet) and bring back a piece of the victim. Kuklinski duly returned with his victim's head in a bag and left with his reputation as a highly efficient contract killer cemented, plus $10,000 in cash in his pocket.

As the contracts rolled in, Kuklinski warmed to the role.

'Richard became addicted to killing people,' writes author Philip Carlo in his biography of Kuklinski, *The Ice Man: Confessions of a Mafia Contract Killer*. 'After he committed a murder he felt relaxed, whole and good, at peace with himself and the world. Murder became like a fix of pure heroin for him.'

Nevertheless, in 1962 Kuklinski married Barbara Pedrici (played by Winona Ryder in the 2012 movie), gave up drinking and gambling and became, as he says, 'A working stiff, a civilian.' He found a job in a film lab in Manhattan, got the bus into work every day and printed off Disney cartoons, making ninety dollars a week. It wasn't long however before he sprang an angle and began pirating the films and making a bit on the side, but after Barbara gave birth to a girl, Kuklinski was in financial trouble.

'The harder I worked, it seemed the less we had,' he told Philip Carlo. 'I felt like I was drowning and no matter how hard I tried I couldn't stay afloat. This straight life wasn't for me.'

It wasn't long before Kuklinski was hijacking lorries and using his printing expertise to pirate and trade in porno films. The latter activity brought him to the attention of Gambino associate and head of a gang of contract killers Roy DeMeo (amazingly well rendered by Ray Liotta in the movie), who in August 1973, under the watchful eyes of his large muscular goons, pistol-whipped Kuklinski over a debt, giving him thirty-eight stitches in head wounds.

A few days later, the money paid in full, the Polack made the journey to Brooklyn to see DeMeo face to face at his headquarters, the Gemini Lounge, which served not only as a bar but also the venue where DeMeo, a former apprentice butcher, and his crew dismembered the many men they had killed, sometimes at the rate of two a day.

By now both DeMeo and the Polack had made enquiries about each other and both were aware of the other's capabilities. Before they parted company they shook hands and agreed that they would make money together.

According to Kuklinski, DeMeo subsequently took him out for a drive. They parked on a city street whereupon DeMeo pointed to a man walking his dog and told Kuklinski to kill him. He didn't know the man. He was a stranger and this was a test. So Kuklinski got out and shot the pedestrian in the back of the head. From that moment on, Kuklinski was DeMeo's secret weapon – a lethal freelance six-foot, five-inch murderer with a knack of not getting caught who could get to anyone anywhere.

A few weeks later, at the behest of DeMeo and Gambino *capo* Anthony 'Nino' Frank Gaggi, Kuklinski killed associate Paul Rothenberg, followed by a slew of others, sometimes travelling first class to destinations both domestic and abroad.

By 1975 Kuklinski was fulfilling four to six contracts a month for the family at approximately $20,000 a pop – he claimed to have killed Teamsters leader Jimmy Hoffa – while also working as debt collector-cum-enforcer, but because he had taken to gambling again he was still forever chasing the buck.

'It went out faster than it came in,' he said. He spent hundreds of thousands of dollars going to Vegas to see Liberace – his favourite entertainer – and bought cars and lavish gifts for his family. For Kuklinski, money was there to be spent.

In spring 1977 in a converted basement of a Gambino lieutenant on Bay 17th Street, Bensonhurst, a few drops of blood were taken from DeMeo's finger, an oath was made and he became a *sgarrista* – soldier – of said family. The honour was bestowed by boss Paul Castellano to thank DeMeo for forging an alliance with a gang of cutthroat Irish-American criminals known as the Westies, led by Jimmy Coonan and second-in-command Mickey Featherstone.

Now a made man, DeMeo became the Gambinos' undisputed assassin *par excellence*, and when a special job came in he contacted the Polack, or 'the Big Guy', as he liked to call him. Thus, via association, Kuklinski became the *de facto* East Coast wise guy's contract killer of choice.

'Richard Kuklinski went undetected for decades because he killed with guns, poison, knives, bats, explosives, garrottes, fists, crossbows, chainsaws and even a bomb attached to a remote-control toy car, disposing of the bodies far from where the murders took place,' attests New Jersey state trooper Pat Kane in the documentary. 'He was one of the most dangerous criminals in the history of New Jersey and New York.'

Kuklinski's favourite method of disposing dead bodies was to drop the corpse in a fifty-five-gallon oil drum, although he often dismembered them and sometimes placed the bodies in the trunks of cars, which were then crushed in a junkyard. He sometimes left bodies sitting on park benches, and even fed victims whilst still alive to giant rats living in a Pennsylvania cave.

Often Kuklinski wondered why he was capable of such atrocities.

'I've always felt like an outsider,' he told Carlo. 'Like I don't belong, and now, because of these things I did, I was feeling that way again… For the most part it didn't bother me, but why, I wondered, am I like this? I mean so cold, so indifferent to people's feeling… I thought about going to a psychiatrist to see if I could get some help or medication but I couldn't do that. I mean, what would I say to a shrink? "I torture and kill people for money and I like my work?" I don't think so.'

According to Carlo, 'Richard was bipolar and should have been taking medication to stabilise his behaviour, his sudden highs and lows. But going to see a psychiatrist was out of the question. He'd be admitting something was wrong with him, and he'd never do that.'

In 1980 Kuklinski met fellow hitman, the certifiable Robert Pronge (a fantastic turn by Chris Evans in the movie), nicknamed 'Mister Softee' who, to appear inconspicuous, sold ice cream from his Mister Softee ice cream truck and stored corpses in its deep freeze. Pronge (who Kuklinski later shot dead) was a morbid dyed-in-the-wool homicidal freak who sold Kuklinski remote-controlled hand grenades and taught him the intricacies of cyanide as a murder weapon.

'Unless you're looking for cyanide as a cause of death it's really almost impossible to detect,' states Michael Baden, a New York medical examiner. 'And it is also lethal. You can kill someone just by tipping it on their clothes.'

On one occasion in 1981, Kuklinski followed his mark, Bonanno family lieutenant Tony Scavelli, to the upmarket nightclub Xenon (Studio 54's main rival, where Madonna's then boyfriend Jellybean Benitez was DJ) on West 45th Street, and as he passed the man dancing on the side of the packed dance floor, stuck him with a syringe full of cyanide. He died within seconds and poison was not suspected.

And all the while everyone – his family and neighbours included – thought he was a businessman. No one suspected he was the Iceman – so called because of his penchant for freezing bodies to mask the time of death. He did not hang out with wise guys – Roy DeMeo only had his pager – and he was not on the police or FBI radar. To all intents and purposes he was an average family man, albeit a very large one.

'My family made me feel as if I had achieved something,' he elucidates in the documentary. 'I was proud that I could provide for them. It maybe wasn't the best way to do that, but it was the only way I knew and I never allowed any threat to them in any way.'

'We were the perfect all-American family,' explained his wife Barbara in an interview. 'We had wonderful times. He just wanted to be home all the time and hated going away, rarely went out with friends.'

Indeed Kuklinski admitted that he had few friends and, apart from his family, the only person he thought wasn't out to murder him was his buddy Phil Solimene. Kuklinski also regretfully claims in the HBO interview that Solimene was the only friend he didn't kill.

Unfortunately for Kuklinski, Solimene also became a police informant and ratted on him. New Jersey state policeman Pat Kane, who had worked for six years trying to nail Kuklinski, had turned Solimene, who introduced the Iceman to Special Agent Dominick Polifrone. The latter, posing as a mobster out to hire the contract killer, met and taped him talking about his grizzly modus operandi.

Kuklinski later explained that he spoke openly only because he intended to kill Polifrone the first chance he had so that his words would have been of no consequence. On 17 December 1986, Kuklinski met again with the agent in an effort to obtain cyanide for the planned hit. Two hours later, as Kuklinski was leaving his home, all hell broke loose as some fifty armed police swooped on his car. It took five officers to subdue him.

Two years later, a New Jersey court convicted Kuklinski of five murders and sentenced him to consecutive life sentences. He would have been ineligible for parole until he was aged 110. In 2003, his guilty plea for the 1980 slaying of Peter Calabro, a New York City police detective – a crime for which Sammy 'the Bull' Gravano was also charged – added a futile thirty years to his sentence.

It was only while he was in prison that Kuklinski's complexity and contradictions came to light. At one point he claims to have no regrets. 'I would have liked to have been someone different and had a better outlook on life but can't change yesterday.'

Kuklinski died aged seventy at 120am on 5 March 2006, the timing of his death considered suspicious. He was due to testify that Gambino underboss Gravano (whose testimony had brought down John Gotti) had contracted him to kill New York Police Department Detective Peter Calabro. A few days after the hit man's death, prosecutors were forced to drop all charges against Gravano as without Kuklinski's testimony there was insufficient evidence.

Kuklinski had told family members that he thought 'they' were poisoning him, but after an examination of his autopsy by forensic pathologist Michael Baden it was concluded he died of natural causes.

Both the documentary and the movie end in the same way, with Kuklinski near tears.

'I've never felt sorry for anything I've done other than hurting my family,' he concludes. 'I am not looking for forgiveness and am not repenting. No, I'm wrong. I do want my family to forgive me. Oh boy [his voice falters], oh shit... this would never be me. I feel for my family. Phew! Do you see the Iceman crying – not very macho... But I have hurt the only people that matter to me.'

In a 1992 column in the *Washington Post*, Tom Shales called Kuklinski 'the ultimate misanthrope, unapologetic and irredeemable... after watching, you may feel some minds are better left impenetrable.'

Lemmy

Lemmy of Motörhead was one of the great rock 'n' roll characters of all time – a man who stuck to his guns and lived his life in a way that is a credit to us all.

I first met him during the post-punk era at the infamous Speakeasy Club on Margaret Street, W1 and then regularly drank with him at the Portobello Gold of a weekday afternoon throughout the eighties. After he moved to LA in the late eighties he often popped in to the nightclub I ran – the Wag – for a few drinks and whatever else we could muster when he was in London.

Consequently, when I was offered the chance to interview him a few years back, I jumped at it. Initially, I sold the piece as 'Lemmy: The Style Icon' – hence the style questions, which he duly answered with a wry smile – but we covered a lot more than that.

He was staying at the Royal Garden Hotel in Kensington but, obviously, just wheeled himself out for the interviews without knowing who was to interview him. As I walked into the suite Lemmy was in the bathroom so I waited with the PR lady. As he came out I was relieved to see that he had not changed one iota – his black cowboy shirt open, his long hair dyed jet black, a ciggie dangling from his mouth. He was looking down and said, 'Hang on a minute I've lost me fucking…' bent down, picked something up, and looked at us. And as the PR lady politely said, 'Lemmy this is…' he looked up…

Lemmy: FUCK me!! It's you, you old Welsh cunt! If I'd have known it was fuckin' you I'd have got more booze and gear in… fucking hell. Sit down, you Welsh bastard.

Lemmy pours two large Jack Daniel's, waves the PR lady away, shuts the door behind her, chops out two railway lines of white powder and gives me a rolled up $2 bill.

Lemmy: You can keep that. I don't want you catching my fucking cold. They say a $2 bill is lucky in the US.

Not wanting to be rude, I partake of what appears to be rather strong speed, gulp down the JD and look up. Lemmy is beaming.

Lemmy: Right, get the fucking tape on and get this interview done; then we can crack on.

Looking at the miracle of nature that is Lemmy, one question springs to mind.

Chris Sullivan: Did you think you'd be still at it with Motörhead all these years on?

Lemmy: I never thought I'd be doing this for this long. I've never even considered time. I just do what I do. No one ever thinks that – you just look at the next few years and see how it goes.

CS: How do you feel about being described as a legendary rock animal?

Lemmy: Oh all that shit. Well I just do what I do. The secrets of success are find out what you do best and do it. And what I do best is Motörhead. Oh! Do you want another drink? [He pours] Do want some ice? [He picks up the ice] Oh sorry, mind the fingers.

CS: It is quite amazing that you've kept it up for so long.

Lemmy: Well… we do it very well. I am very happy with where we are at the moment. We are at the top of the second echelon. You don't want to be top of the first echelon, as people will never leave you alone.

CS: You could keep going forever?

Lemmy: Yes. Well, as long as my forever is.

CS: What caused you to start a band?

Lemmy: I saw that the bands got all the girls. That's fair enough an ambition. Drink yourself into a stupor, travel the world and get all the chicks – nothing wrong with that. Getting away from Colwyn Bay was another good incentive.

CS: But everybody likes Motörhead – right across the board.

Lemmy: Yes, well this year certainly. You wait, next we'll be out of fashion again.

CS: Why do you think everyone likes you?

Lemmy: Because I don't give them any bullshit. I always figured that if you treat people decently they would treat you decent back. You get the occasional obstruction but that's how life is. There is no better saying than, 'Do unto others as you'd like to be treated yourself', and that's how I live my life anyway. Well most of the time... there are some times you can't resist being a twat to twats.

CS: Do you write the songs? I love the lyrics to 'Eat the Rich'.

Lemmy: Yeah man, 'I eat you baby. Eat two and get one free. Shetland pony, extra pepperoni. I'll eat you baby and you eat me. Eat you baby, get one free. Shetland pony extra pepperoni just pick up the phone...' I write all the lyrics and I especially like that one.

CS: What is your favourite item of clothing?

Lemmy: A bow and arrow because it is so clean and so lean.

CS: You've always had a very definite style; how would you describe it?

Lemmy: I suppose I'd describe my style as mid-sixties cowboy, basically. Kirk Douglas chic. I haven't changed in years because, in my opinion, if you find something you like, you should stick with it. A lot of people just go for the latest fashion and look really stupid because it doesn't suit them, because they haven't got the body or the taste for it, and they look like twats. It's as if they have had a head transplant. I think everyone should find out what suits him or her, and what he or she feel comfortable with, and stick with it.

CS: Have you ever been considered fashionable?

Lemmy: I'm not fashionable in the slightest. Oh no. No, no, no. I have never even tried. I might be fashionable in a room full of Motör-head fans, but that is it. All these new groovy types wear our T-shirts, but that is because it's a great logo. I always say if we could have sold as many albums as T-shirts we'd have been OK. We get a lump sum for the shirts.

He chops out another line and pours me another drink. We demolish both.

CS: Where do you shop?

Lemmy: I don't shop. I get everything made because I know exactly what I want and I can't be bothered trudging around shops looking for stuff.

CS: What's your favourite item?

Lemmy: Shoes by Pascal Cooper – he's a famous shoemaker in LA – makes my boots. They are fucking magic. I have quite a few pairs.

CS: Do you buy vintage stuff?

Lemmy: I like new clothes. The only vintage clothes I have are mine. I have stuff going back years. I have a great collection of left boots as I always wear the right out first but never throw them away. I've got white ones, black ones – all left foot. Maybe one day when I lose a leg they'll come in handy. Well, that's what I'm thinking any-way. I have a flat full of shit and most is hopeless to me.

CS: Is there anybody who you've always looked up to style-wise?

Lemmy: Kirk Douglas always looked great. I am not sure what well dressed is. Is it that you are a slave to the fashion? Or is it that you look good in what you wear? I think the latter. But I don't know who I think dresses well. Some people dress well for them and that's all you can say. Some people are like mutton dressed as lamb and, to be honest, you might say that about me sometimes.

CS: What's the most dosh you've spent on an item of clothing?

Lemmy: The most money I've ever spent on clothes is my boots that cost me $600, which is great considering you can have any pattern on them you want. I go in and draw what I want and he makes them.

CS: Is there anything you own that wouldn't wear out of the house?

Lemmy: The only thing I'd like to wear but can't is my SS uniform. I collect that stuff and have a really good one, but it doesn't go down so well in mixed company. Unfortunately, the bad guys had the best uniforms – the Confederates the same – sharp grey and yellow. Napoleon – the same. It's always true; the bad guys have the best uniforms. I collect them for artistic reasons, purely because of the way they look. I don't agree with what Hitler said – it was fucking rubbish. These guys in the US started calling me a Nazi and then I said I have three girlfriends in LA and they are all black. You can't get less Nazi than that. Imagine if I was at the Nuremberg rally: 'And here's my girlfriend, Mein Führer…'

CS: Anything you'd like to get made?

Lemmy: The only thing I'm considering having made is a pair of false tits. I have always wondered about them. I'd have them on my back so the missus will have something to play with.

CS: What do the women in your life like you to wear?

Lemmy: Well, if they're good women, nothing – naked is always fun. A light dusting with face powder, maybe.

He chops out another few lines and pours me another drink. We destroy both.

CS: You started in the punk period and have always been loved by punks – why is that?

Lemmy: We started at the same time as punk and a lot of punks love us, but I always thought we sounded more like a rock 'n' roll band. Maybe our attitude is a bit more punk.

CS: What have you bought most over the years?

Lemmy: I wear black, mostly. I wear a lot of cowboy shirts that I pick up from all over the states. I have plain ones, embroidered ones.

CS: What about male jewellery?

Lemmy: I used to wear a lot of rings. I used to wear them on every finger and on one thumb, but not so much anymore. I have this pendant that Slim Jim of the Stray Cats saw in a stall in Nepal and so he got it for me. It's carved out of some sort of bone.

CS: How do you feel about tattoos?

Lemmy: I've got three tattoos and have been planning to get another for about ten years but I can't think of anything I really want. It's a big decision, as you can't change it like your shirt. People tend to make bad decisions with things like that so not having one avoids all that.

CS: What do you think of male grooming?

Lemmy: I use aftershave. But you don't need it. I like good quality soap. I try and stay away from moisturiser. I think it makes you look old.

CS: Do you wax?

Lemmy: I have never found the need to wax. I occasionally shave my bollocks and that's about it.

CS: Do you wear cologne?

Lemmy: I wear Allure aftershave cologne by Coco Chanel. Funnily enough, the initials and logo of Coco Chanel is the same as King

Carol the First of Romania. Exactly the same. Perhaps she was Romanian.

CS: How do you keep fit?

Lemmy: Being on stage with Motörhead is a pretty good workout. Two hours of exercising the diaphragm and the legs is ample. I have two more tours coming up. One in America with Judas Priest and Heaven and Hell, followed by another American one on our own, and then another here and Germany. I haven't got a clue how many dates that is but it's enough to keep me as fit as I need to be. Playing live is what I do. Travelling all over the world playing music to people and leaving them with a smile.

CS: Do you like watches?

Lemmy: I don't really like wearing watches, I have this Rolex that was given to me by my agent but if you take it off, it stops. What's the use of that? It's fucking useless.

CS: How about an iPod?

Lemmy: I have an iPod but I don't really use it as my roadie put all this music on it that I can't bear. He put Dr Dre on it so that's not much use for me.

CS: What car do you drive?

Lemmy: Even though I live in LA, I don't drive a car because I kept crashing them. It was too expensive. I gave up in 1966. That was the last time I drove on the road. I had a 1952 Chevy Coupe in 1966 – a monster it was – it cost me £36. Valve radio, power steering, and power brakes. And that was in 1952, when we were making Ford Poplars. Even though the car was American I still couldn't drive it as I was used to gear and it was automatic, and I changed down into reverse and crashed it. 'Kachunga, kachunga,' it went. Not a pretty sight. I just gave the car and the keys to a bloke at a petrol station and walked off.

CS: Is there one item you wear all the time?

Lemmy: The only thing I wear all the time is trousers because otherwise people tend to point at you if you don't. I have been on stage in my Y-fronts and it went down OK…

CS: Any fashion tips for the youth of today?

Lemmy: My fashion tip to anyone is don't wear anything you could really be embarrassed about later. Think really hard about it because someone will always remember.

He chops out another few lines and pours me another drink. We demolish both.

CS: You were a roadie for Hendrix I believe. What was that like?

Lemmy: I roadied for Hendrix and the Nice but I couldn't tell you what it was like, man. I was on acid all the time. Everybody was on it. I didn't know anyone who wasn't on it. It was a very different time then. The acid was fucking strong then as well. When the acid came out in the acid house in the late eighties, it wasn't the same. We used to go to Richmond Park and we used to talk to the trees and the deer. You knew it was time to stop when the tree wins the argument.

CS: And Hawkwind?

Lemmy: Jesus H. Christ! We used to do a lot of acid in Hawkwind. We used to go on stage tripping. I gave it up in 1975 because of their runs – it was repeating itself – like most drugs when you do them too often. But I only had one bad trip though from '67 till '75. I was out of it all the time so that's not too bad.

CS: Did it teach you anything?

Lemmy: The one useful thing about that was that it taught me to function, no matter what condition I was fucking in. I could always deliver the gig. I got fired from Hawkwind for getting busted. So

I started Motörhead. But when we get a new guy in Motörhead I always tell them, 'I don't care what you do after the show, it's your time, but when the show is on you must deliver the show. I don't care if you're tripping or speeding, whatever, but you have to deliver the fucking show!' And that is why we are different from everybody else these days.

CS: What about all these teetotal bands you get these days?

Lemmy: Fucking shite. They go, 'I'm not drinking so neither can you!' But what the fuck is that? 'What if you want to stop. Don't tell me to fucking stop 'cos I am not you.' You go backstage at these gigs and there are twelve bottles of mineral water and some wholemeal fucking bread. That's not rock 'n' roll – fuck off! Rock 'n' roll is not being able to stand up but still being able to play your music.

CS: You've been known to like a bit of speed.

Lemmy: Oh yeah. I was taking speed before acid. We used to take these liquid meth ampoules thirty years ago. Speed is just a functional drug that will get you up on stage when you are really knackered. You're like, 'I can't go on.' So it's like, 'Well have some of this.' Next thing you're on stage and you're off. You cannot do that on cocaine. Coke will make you stand up and look at the wall. I've tried all the drugs I could get my hands on – except smack and morphine – and I've never injected… that's the beginning of the fucking end. Speed made sense. Doing gig after gig back when we started was how it started. We did fifty-three gigs in fifty-six days with Saxon in 1969 – that is ridiculous – nobody does that being high on life. I don't care how many fucking vegetables you eat – you need a bit of help to do that.

CS: How was Yugoslavia in 1965?

Lemmy: We had dinner with Tito – he was at the far end of the table. It was a cultural exchange; England got the Red Army Orchestra but I think the Yugoslavians got the better deal. They went mad. Kids were setting their shirts alight. They had never seen an electric guitar before. They just wanted to touch it. But they had bad luck with that war. They always hated each other. We'd be in Slovakia and they'd say, like, 'these fucking Croats, they're all assassins', and we'd say 'it's the same country' and they'd answer, 'no it's not – we fucking hate them!' Fact is, the Brits made a country after World War I and stuck 'em all together and they hated it. Look at them now – they're all split up and they're happy. How could we have thought that it would work? But that's how fucking arrogant we were. Don't get me started on the British Empire.

CS: I heard you spoke to the Welsh Assembly.

Lemmy: Yes, and for the Conservatives as well. They'd seen some Channel 4 documentary where I said I hated heroin and they thought, well let's get him in and make him the voice of our party to attract the young vote, but I didn't play by the rules I'm afraid.

CS: What did you say?

Lemmy: I told him that it should be legalised because they have thrown the police at it for thirty years and now there's more smack on the streets than ever. And I fucking hate the shit and I've seen it up close with friends of mine. Evil shit. But at least if it was legal you could keep track of it. Because it would be the same powder, no one would be getting hotshots. It seems reasonable to me. I absolutely hate it but I cannot see a better way. About three weeks after I said this a load of college professors wrote in and said they agree. You cut out the dealers and all the shooting will stop.

CS: Yes, I agree – you don't have turf wars with pharmacists. Boots versus Vantage Pharmacy over drugs.

Lemmy: [Laughs uproariously] You can imagine them hiring hit men. I want you to go round to Superdrug and shoot 'em up. A league of eight pharmacists gets together.

He chops out another four lines and pours me another drink. We demolish all with aplomb.

Lemmy: You've done that before I see?

CS: Once or twice. How would you describe your politics?

Lemmy: I hate them all, man. They are all lying, thieving bastards. As soon as they become the government they can't resist; they take all these free flights and big houses and big cars. Course they are going to take them. But they are all bastards because they are not sharing it with ME! There is only one politician who always told the truth and that was fucking Hitler. He kept all his promises. He said he was going to kill all the Jews ten years before in a book that was available to everybody and, when he did, they all said, 'What a surprise.' He said he was going to make Germany big again and he did. He said he was going to solve unemployment and he did that. Even Kennedy didn't keep all his promises. He was the only one. Kind of unfortunate isn't it really? The only example of an honest politician is Adolf fucking Hitler. Every one of them is a thieving fucking prince. Gordon fucking Brown, that bastard – a fucking rat – and Tony Blair, he's the same. Glad they're gone but now Cameron and fucking Clegg! Thatcher is starting to look pretty good here. When she went down I told people, 'you're gonna miss that woman', and they laughed at me. Tony Blair put the Poll Tax through as the Community Charge and no one noticed. Fucking arsehole. Nobody brought him down. Why do they always have to shoot the good guys? Why can't they shoot the arseholes? It's a disgrace. Fucking Blair sold the country into slavery. Bastard should be imprisoned for life. Evil cunt!

CS: How do you get the Motörhead sound?

Lemmy: Well they are making my amp now, which is great. It's fucking loud. They're also making a Lemmy bass, which is hand carved on the front. Originally, I had a Rickenbacker and the pickups weren't so good so I got a Gibson Thunderbird pickup, which was a monster. Then it wore out. I have always had different pickups. Basically turn it all the way up and hit it really hard. I had these controls on me bass that went up to thirteen – that was good.

CS: But you ended up singing as well?

Lemmy: I never wanted to be a singer. The singer left and the rest said go on you do it. I like singing now though. I've got a lot better at it.

CS: Why is your mike so high?

Lemmy: It's more comfortable, man. I don't know how anybody sings with their head down. It's really hard.

He chops out another few lines, but a lot bigger than the rest, and pours me another drink, much larger than the others. We demolish all.

CS: I first met you at the Speakeasy.

Lemmy: Yeah, I fucking remember. You were a fucking kid then. How old? Seventeen?

CS: Spot on.

Lemmy: Lot of water under the bridge since then hey? I used to go to the Speakeasy all the time. I also used to go to the Embassy with Phil Lynott, which was funny because it was a gay club; and then all these punks started coming while all the other guys had these fucking tutus on. It was great fun because gay people have the best sense of humour. Murderous sense of humour. Really fucking funny. 'Ooh I can't wait for you dear.' They are really fucking funny. I used to live above a team of gay guys. There was Johnny who was like this leather-jacketed tough guy and then there was Mickey his lover, who was this little fella with a bald head and stubble, and Johnny used to beat him up so he used to come to my door and say 'Johnny's beat me up again' and I'd invite him in for a cup of tea. Then one night there was this drag queens' ball at the Lyceum and Mickey always went as Liz Taylor and I was sitting there on the windowsill of my flat tripping and Liz Taylor walks in through my door and she hikes up her skirt, dives on me bed and asks, 'Do you think I look all right dear?' Fucking great. That night Johnny couldn't do enough for him.

I got no problem with gay people. I don't understand why people do. They're not up your leg are they? If they're into my thing I'll tell them to stop but apart from that, fair enough.

CS: But your audiences were always mixed. I've seen punks, goths, and all sorts.

Lemmy: Yeah. In Toronto we had this kid with this hair that stood out for about a foot with spikes and everyone was standing about ten feet away from him and I told the audience, 'you should be shaking his hand'. He stands up for self-expression. He's got the nerve to come here with all you cunts and he knew how you would treat him and then they were like, 'Oh all right then.' I'm like, you have to tell them.

CS: But, as I said, punks love you.

Lemmy: We always sounded a bit like a punk band and a bit like a rock 'n' roll band. But now we sound like Motörhead. As we fucking well should after almost forty years. Christ was younger than us when he fucking died.

CS: And had the same haircut as you.

Lemmy: If you believe the fucking hype. Contemporary observers have said he was short, hunched over, and had a bald head. People weren't that good looking back then. I don't really go for all that walking over water stuff, looking like a film star. Not if he was Israeli. If he was Egyptian he might have looked cute, as they know about make-up.

CS: Did you know that Jesus and the apostles anointed themselves with liquid hashish mixed with olive oil? No wonder they thought he was walking on water.

Lemmy: Bloody fortunate that, hey! It was really shallow like the Serpentine. You fall out of the boat and it's only up to your fucking knees.

He chops out another line and pours me another drink. We demolish both.

CS: You live in LA now.

Lemmy: I have been there eighteen years. It's fucking miserable in London now. It's like Hull. Raining all the fucking time. Whatever weathers you fucking got, it's always raining. People ask me, 'Why did you move to LA?' And I say, 'Well the sun shines all the time so the chicks wear less clothing because of this and everything is half price – any questions?' And they go, 'No.' I should have gone twenty years before. The gas has gone up to four dollars and they're screaming. Here it's twelve fucking dollars. They knew it was going wrong when they changed it to litres. A fucking con like when the country went decimal. A shilling was suddenly five pence and it was twelve pence before. Those bastards.

CS: How did you get your name?

Lemmy: I think my name is a Welsh insult. I got it when I was in primary school in Wales. All these years later and I still really don't know what the fuck it means. People say it's 'cos I used to say, 'lemmy have a couple o' bob for the fruit machine', but I don't remember that.

CS: That'll do.

Lemmy: Thank fuck for that. Now we can talk some real shit [he laughs uproariously again].

Subsequently, he showed me his collection of hand-made cowboy boots and we continued to indulge until very, very late and parted with a big hug. As I reached the door I turned to wave goodbye. Lemmy gave me the thumbs up, swigged on his bottle of JD and shouted:

'Look after yourself, you old Welsh bastard…'

And those were the last words he said to me.

RIP Lemmy… one top bloke.

Mickey Rourke

My second interview with Mickey Rourke took place around the time of the release of *The Wrestler*, in which he delivers an astonishing turn as Randy 'the Ram' Robinson, a grappler on the verge of physical and cerebral collapse.

At the time most film journalists, including yours truly, would have wagered that the Best Actor Academy Award was his; not that you would have been given favourable odds as almost every bookie in the world concurred. Rourke, after all, had already bagged a BAFTA and a Golden Globe for the role, as well as fifteen other best actor awards from various critics' circles across the USA.

He thoroughly deserved each and every accolade. Rourke's rendering of the fifty-something has-been wrestler is ranked as one of the greatest screen performances of all time. Yet it is a small and remarkably exact portrait whose beauty lies in the tiniest details. In short, this thoroughly disenfranchised grappler, once the number one wrestling star on primetime TV and now working behind a supermarket deli counter, reflects Rourke himself.

It was a frosty January morning in 2009 at Blakes Hotel in South Kensington when we met, and even though the comparisons between the actor and Randy were legion, he could not have looked more different. Gone was the dyed, long blond hair. Absent were the huge pumped biceps, while a sharp pinstripe suit had thankfully replaced the Spandex leotard. In addition he sported a pair of plastic-framed spectacles more suited to a 1950s BBC newsreader than a Hollywood movie star. If it wasn't for his low, slow, deliberate East Coast growl I might have thought he was a different chap entirely.

Not wanting to waste time I got right down to it and asked him if he thought he would win the Oscar he had been nominated for.

'Well, I don't know,' he replied, shaking his head and rubbing his goatee. 'It's voted for by the Academy, people from the movie business, and I pissed them all off. I was good at that. It came easy to me. I stupidly said that acting wasn't a job for a real man. I threatened producers, raged at directors, forgot my agent's name. Man, I really burned my bridges. And a lot of people have long memories, so...'

Indeed, during my previous interview with him, back in 2002, he had pissed *me* off, too. Mickey Rourke has a reputation for being a rather difficult interviewee, but I'd always thought him a fine chap and a huge talent. I had actually hung out with him on a few nights in the 1980s in Paris and London when I ran a nightclub.

So when I saw him on the up again I pitched an interview with him to coincide with Jonas Åkerlund's directorial debut, *Spun*. In this hard core re-enactment of the revolting world of crystal meth, Rourke steals the show as 'the Cook', with a performance that illustrates the 'powder power' that only the man with the gear can have.

After three postponements I turned up at his hotel and waited for an hour, only for him not to show. The interview was then re-scheduled. Again I arrived bang on time and, after half an hour of energetic thumb-twiddling (the deadline for the article was two days later), in he finally walked.

Dressed that day in an old-school sweat suit, he looked a lot smaller than he did on screen and had obviously been up most of the night. But he still didn't look quite as bad as I'd expected. His face still had the look of a hastily arranged plate of cold meats – the type your granny put together when the priest popped round – but certainly not deserving of the description by now-defunct website awfulplasticsurgery.com, who called him 'one of the scariest plastic surgery victims of all time.'

What was more apparent back then was that Rourke was achingly reminiscent of a man who had lost his dog and found a mouse. He spoke in a low, expressionless monotone, like a supplicant sinner in a confessional box, his enthusiasm rising only when the Marlboro Reds arrived. He instantly lit one up, sucking on it as if his life depended on it, and then asked me who the interview was for. When I answered *Jack* (an erstwhile men's lifestyle magazine) he asked, 'Is that a gay magazine?'

I needn't have answered, but did so in a deadpan, half-joking and half-entirely bloody serious manner.

'I don't think they'd let me write for a gay mag,' I said, and without pausing went on to ask him about his great line in *Spun,* where he recalled his mother who says, after drowning a litter of puppies, 'I kill what I can't take care of.'

'Is that what you did with your life?' I enquired.

After taking another expressive drag on his fag he looked up. 'Yeah,' he groaned. 'That's right, that's a great analogy. I've never heard such a parallel. I guess I did. I just sort of had it with the bullshit. Most of the bullshit was me though. I made up a lot of excuses, blamed it on a lot of other things other than me, you know.

'I just needed some time to grow up and be responsible. But I wasn't equipped for fame so the party kept going, the motorcycles got louder, and work became less and less important. I didn't really have a childhood – because I worked my whole life – so when I had a little bit of success, I went ballistic and had the childhood I never had. And it kept going on.'

He was born Philip Andre Rourke Jr on 16 September 1952, in Schenectady, New York, the son of Annette (née Cameron), a lady of French-Canadian, English and German ancestry, and Phillip Andre Rourke, of Irish and German descent.

When he was six years old, his parents divorced. A year later his mother married Eugene Addis, a Miami Beach police officer, and moved to Miami Shores, Florida. Rourke has said on numerous occasions that he had a real rough time as a kid and that his stepdad was physically abusive to both him and his brother.

When I asked if his upbringing was tough, he looked up and gazed at the annoying parrot in a cage across the room. 'No, it was pretty normal.'

Mmm, yes, OK then. Back to the notes.

'Do you think fame is overrated?' I asked.

'It depends on who's doing the overrating,' he said. And then repeated himself: 'I guess it depends on who's doing the overrating.'

I sat back and thought to myself, 'He's said this twice, so is it a trick answer?'

Confused, I offered the suggestion that it must be better than working on an assembly line.

'But some guys like working on an assembly line... for thirty years,' he replied.

To which I responded, 'Personally I have never met anyone who liked working on an assembly line for even a week. And according to my dad, who for the record really did work on an assembly line for forty years, it is one job that is massively overrated.'

Apart from a surge of semi-enthusiasm when we talked about his boxing it was all rather humdrum – as though he was going through the motions. And then, without a by your leave, he asked me the time. Perturbed, anxious, worried and sweating, I reluctantly informed him that it was 10:25 a.m.

'I have to go in four minutes,' he declared.

Quick as a flash, hoping for a nice philosophical quote to end the piece, I replied, 'Do you think your experiences have made you a stronger person?'

After a pause that seemed like hours he replied, 'I'd have to think about that. I don't have any answers for the big questions – just the small ones.'

I regrouped my anxious brain and asked him the admittedly age-old question, 'What advice would you give a young actor or young person?'

'Well, I don't think I'm the man to give advice,' he answered. And before I could state the obvious – that after all he's been through, he was exactly the man to give that advice – he was up on his feet.

'Well, I've got to go,' he said. 'It was a pleasure to meet you, my friend.'

And then he left.

And that was jolly well that, all seventeen glorious minutes of it. At first I was rather peeved, but then I realised that he's not a bad man. Just a down-to-earth-guy who was given too much too soon and screwed up – something we all do occasionally.

I considered what it's like to have to meet total strangers and talk about yourself all bloody day. Then I pondered the fact that he has made some great movies that I have really enjoyed and he must have had cojones the size of cannon balls to go back into the ring aged forty after being a Hollywood pin-up. And who cares if he opted to have cosmetic surgery performed by someone known as 'the Butcher?'

More importantly, he is still a great actor with a formidable canon of work. Rourke, just like the rest of us, is simply a human being, albeit a complex one.

And as I sat there in Blakes Hotel six years later for our second interview, all of the above was spinning around in my head. Will he show, or won't he? Will he be taciturn, noncommittal and reserved?

I needn't have worried. Rourke, on this occasion, was a different man, even though I will admit that this time the interview didn't get off to the best start.

As I went to sit down on what I thought was a cushion on the couch, the actor dived across the room and grabbed me. It wasn't, in fact, a cushion; it was his beloved chihuahua Loki wearing a Burberry dog-coat, who I'd have almost certainly killed had I sat on her.

Realising how close a miss it was I apologised profusely, but Rourke was as nonchalant as I was distraught. 'No problem, man,' he said quietly. 'Have a cup of tea and relax.'

And so he poured me a cup of tea, his rather large hands dwarfing the tiny porcelain teacup.

Minutes later he was pouring his heart out to me, describing how close his life had been to Randy in *The Wrestler*.

'I lost everything: my house, my career, my wife,' he explained, visibly wincing. 'My life was a disaster zone. In fact nobody really knew just how broke I was. I was paying $500 a month for a one-room apartment with a yard for my dogs. A friend used to give me a couple of hundred dollars a month just to buy something to eat. I'd be calling up my ex-wife and crying like a fucking baby.'

There is one particularly poignant scene in the film in which a tearful Randy tells his daughter Stephanie (Evan Rachel Wood) that it was he who was supposed to look after everybody, to sort everything out, but, as always, he screwed up – a reflection of Rourke's own life. There was a time when he was incapable of looking after anything, be it himself, his life, or his career.

And lest we forget, Rourke had a lot more going for him than a TV wrestler. After studying in the famed Actors Studio in New York he moved to Hollywood and became, during the 1980s, one of the biggest stars in the world, commanding millions of bucks for a movie.

But it wasn't just the pay cheque. Following superb turns in such films as *Diner*, Francis Ford Coppola's *Rumble Fish*, *9½ Weeks* and *Angel Heart*, he was the coolest cat on the block. Frequently seen swanning around swish Parisian nightclubs with a *Vogue* model on each arm, he could do no wrong. That is, until he did. And did repeatedly.

'I started screwing up around [the time of] *Angel Heart*,' admitted the now remarkably humble actor. 'I was out of control and didn't think the party was going to end. I could stay in any hotel I wanted, buy anything [he once bought six Cadillacs for cash and gave them all away], and take my entourage out to dinner. My big mansion in Beverly Hills was like *Halloween III*. Elvis on acid. The motorcycles, the nightlife, the pussy… you know, it was all blinding.

'My brother and me had six motorcycles each. We had a confederate flag and a Jolly Roger over the garage. Neighbours were moving out on each side almost monthly. I surrounded myself with a bunch of retards and idiots, guys from the street, and it brought me down, because they were goofballs, and villains and stuff. But I had a great time nevertheless, and when you're having fun you don't think it's going to end, and when it does, it's real scary.'

When his career hit the skids, the minions, sycophants and hangers-on soon disappeared. 'I didn't have any more entourage, no assistants,' he said. 'I lost my big fucking house and I had to go to the supermarket. So I'm in there for the first time, pushing a cart, getting my fucking supper.

'I remember going, "This sucks!" I used to have people to do that. I'm sort of OK going to the supermarket now, but you always get recognised in the fucking supermarket, even though I'd always go to the twenty-four-hour Ralphs in gay town that's open all night long. But you get all kinds of people shopping at 3am there.'

Rourke could not have engineered a better demise if he tried. He famously allowed some of the era's greatest film roles to pass him by, turning down Kevin Costner's role as Eliot Ness in *The Untouchables*, Tom Cruise's part in *Rain Man* and a turn in *The Silence of the Lambs*.

'I remember Dustin Hoffman calling me up and telling me he wanted me to do this movie, *Rain Man*, and I didn't even return his call,' he said. 'Tarantino – he called once. I think it was the script for *Pulp Fiction*, the part Bruce Willis played. I didn't even read the script.'

Added to this rather negligent approach to reading scripts was a puzzling arrogance, heavily seasoned with belligerence.

'I allowed myself to get very proud and angry because I could do the acting,' he explained. 'I thought I'd have to be dead not to fucking work here. And that's wrong. It was poor judgement on my part, very arrogant, because it's a business. And I refused to see it that way. I wasn't equipped or educated enough to see it as a business, that I had to take care of the shop. I didn't see that I should have taken this commercial movie because it would have made $200 million, but I should have. That would have given me the juice to do the other stuff that I wanted to do.'

As *Angel Heart* director Alan Parker said at the time, 'Working with Mickey is a nightmare. He is very dangerous on set because you never know what he is going to do.'

Pouring oil on the fire, Rourke then embarked on an explosive six-year relationship with future wife Carré Otis, his co-star in *Wild Orchid*. It ended with Rourke being charged with spousal abuse while she sunk into chronic heroin addiction. 'I really loved her,' he declared, touching her name tattooed on his arm. 'But we were like fire and fucking fire. And then she left. I waited for her to come back, and then when Joey [Rourke's brother] died, I gave up.

'But I've never had a drinking or drug problem,' explained Rourke, 'My thing was always being a hard guy, which seems to scare them more than the drugs. But hey, I don't want to be a hard man anymore. It's killed me. When my ex-wife had a heroin problem, I went and dealt with her dealers and put people in hospitals. I took the law into my own hands. That got into the papers and stuff. I got nailed for fucking someone up in a public place. I got fired from a movie once for putting a heroin dealer in hospital.'

So hopelessly unravelled had his life become that his friends eventually urged him to seek psychiatric help. The subsequent treatment opened up a veritable can of vipers that, once understood, put his whole life into some kind of tolerable perspective.

'I came from a very violent background,' he explained. 'So I became very hard. I realised that I had made myself that way to deal with a feeling of abandonment and shame. I didn't know why my father abandoned me when I was a little kid and never came to see us. I didn't know why my mother married a physically and mentally abusive cop, let things happen to me and my little brother Joe and never did anything about it.

'I tried to protect Joe when I got older,' he said, the emotion showing. 'Even though I was just a year older, I really felt like his dad because we were extremely close and I looked out for him.' Rourke stopped, sobbed and wiped a tear from his eye. 'All of this I kept inside.'

After five years of therapy three days a week, Rourke realised that this silence was a part of his problem.

'The anxiety will come out eventually,' he said, composing himself. 'For me it was not vocally but by being belligerent. I blamed everyone in Hollywood and identified him or her with this authority figure that had beaten me with a stick. I spent so long studying really hard to become a fine actor and threw it all away because I think I got the adulation and the fame so easily that it was like, "Where were you when I needed you? I'm a man now. I don't need you. I needed someone to go fishing with."'

'So what about your mother?' I asked.

'She got diagnosed with Alzheimer's three months ago and she doesn't remember what happened, so now I'm OK with her,' he replied. 'But I was angry with her for my whole life. I am not angry with anybody now. I'm just so grateful for this second chance.

'You have to remember that everything was gone and I was left in a room on my own. I walked past a mirror one day and saw myself and I was like, "Holy shit!" Because I didn't realise how I looked. I looked like a mad man and I didn't want that anymore because I had nothing. But I didn't want to change because it was like, "Change into what?" I was glad of who I was, in a way. I just took it too far. But I'm a proud man. I'm a man's man. I'm an old-fashioned man and that's the way it is.'

Despite being handed a second chance, it hasn't been a walk in the park for Rourke, although he is grateful. 'This part was a gift from God,' he said. 'I had heard good things about [Darren] Aronofsky. Hollywood wants him to do the big budget stuff but he does his own thing, beats his own drum and hangs his balls over the fence.

'Then when I met him he held his finger up and said, "Nobody wants me to do this movie with you as you're not a star anymore and you fucked up your career for twenty years." I said, "Ok, I heard that one." Then he said, "Listen, if I get the money to do this you're gonna listen to everything I say and you are not going to disrespect me. Also, I can't pay you." And I thought, well, you got balls to say that – this is my kind of man.'

For the role, Rourke, then fifty-six, trained for three months as a professional wrestler and put on thirty-six pounds of muscle, yet it was not the physical rigours that gave him cause for concern.

'Reading the script was like, "I hate this. I hate the man – what a piece of shit." It was painful, but I stepped away from the character for a while and thought about it. Aronofsky wanted me to do the movie initially but the money guys didn't want me, so they replaced me with a movie star. Then something happened between Darren and him and next thing we were talking again and I was back in.

'Then I met Darren and I knew he was going to make me work and make me go to some very dark places and it would be very painful, both emotionally and physically. So at first I really didn't know if I wanted to work that hard, for that long, for free. But the bright Mickey, not the stupid Mickey, said to me, "With this kid you'd better go to work." So when the part came around again I was like, "Oh fuck, yeah, let's go!"

'Darren gave me the courtesy of allowing me to rewrite my role myself, which was very gratifying – like the stuff with Evan and all the personal stuff at the end. But it wasn't that difficult for me to write for Randy, as I'd been there myself. There was a lot to add. But I'm so glad I did it because it is the best work I have ever done in the best film of my career.'

Rourke did all his own stunts in the picture, even to the point of cutting himself across the forehead with a concealed razor blade, a trick commonly referred to by wrestlers as 'gigging'.

'I can only hurt myself when my woman leaves me, but the day that we had to do it I wasn't upset about anything. Then Darren said, "Listen, you don't have to do that if you don't want to. We'll get around it." So I was like, "Fuck that, let's do it."'

'We shot a lot of the wrestling scenes in real gyms and at real wrestling events, and after three months of training as a wrestler some of the moves that we incorporated were added which were very difficult. Thank God I was able to nail them because at times there were 3,000 people watching.'

Evidently no stranger to either pain or appearing live, the errant actor, after falling foul of Hollywood, controversially re-entered the ring as a professional boxer at the age of thirty-nine. Not the most obvious career move, I suggested.

'I went back because of shame,' he said. 'I was a really good amateur and took a year off due to early concussion – really bad concussion. I grew up in a gym in Miami, same gym as Ali. Angelo Dundee's gym. I was an amateur for seven years, and then I stopped. I had 142 amateur fights and lost three. I was very lucky because I had power in both hands. I was very strong and that's always been a big asset of mine. I was good at it.'

Rourke's intention was to have just one fight, but that spiralled into eight until he was advised to stop because of neurological problems.

'I was three fights away from a title fight and I will never know what would have happened,' he explained. 'I had already turned forty and was fighting guys twenty years younger. I didn't lose any pro fights but I got my arse properly kicked every day in the gym. I sparred with Roberto Durán and James [Toney], who kicked my ass for eighteen months, but now I look at [Toney] as the guy who beat [Evander] Holyfield and think, "Hey, I'm not so bad."'

'He broke my cheekbone, with headgear on. I had my nose broken twice. I had five operations on my nose and one operation on a smashed cheekbone. I had to have cartilage taken from my ear to rebuild my nose. Today I still cannot feel the tip of my nose. The worst thing is that my hands shake because I broke the fourth or fifth metacarpal.

'The short-term memory stuff only affects me when I drink and

I have no problem going up stairs, only when going down. I also had to have a couple of operations to scrape the cartilage out because the scar tissue was healing wrong. That was one of the most painful operations I ever had. The worst was hemorrhoids.'

At one point there was much speculation regarding the state of Rourke's face. Was it a result of the boxing or bad cosmetic surgery?

'Well, most of it was to mend the mess of my face because of the boxing, but I made a few mistakes here and there and went to the wrong guy to put my face back together.'

But sometimes it takes more time to mend a broken career than a broken face – a fact that Rourke readily admits.

'I said a lot of things I shouldn't have said that people won't let me forget,' he sighed. 'I shouldn't have said that acting is not a man's job. I remember Mel Gibson had something to say about that, but he should have said it to my face. It's not man's work compared to the work I did all my life: construction, lifting, where you got to sweat your ass off for $100 a day.

'For the money you get paid, [acting] is relatively easy. I didn't mean it was for faggots; I got a lot of respect for a certain kind of acting. Monty Clift, look what he went through [he pauses for a moment]. And I know that's my therapist talking, but it just shows it's working, right? Oh yeah, quite often I hear my therapist coming out of my mouth. My therapist's leaving town for a week! What am I going to do?'

At this point his publicist came in to remind Rourke that he was due in David Bailey's studio for a cover shoot and called an end to the interview. But Mickey was having none of it. 'I ain't finished talking to my friend here,' he barked.

'But all I've done, the ups and the fucking downs, has prepared me for this role,' he continued. 'God works in mysterious ways. I had to learn my lessons the hard way for a higher reason and I feel very, very thankful and blessed that I have been given a second chance. And it was very tough the second time around, very hard work.

'One thing I do know is that I will never return to my old ways as that is a very dark place to be and I never want to go back there again. If I can keep myself healthy and mentally disciplined, get rid of the anger, I think I can do some of my best work. People ask, "What's your favourite movie?" And I say, "I haven't made it yet."'

We shot the breeze for a few minutes until the publicist re-entered. Rourke groaned and stood up. I congratulated him again on his performance in *The Wrestler*.

'Thank you,' he replied, gripping my hand tightly and looking me straight in the eye with due sincerity. 'It was a real pleasure to meet you again, my friend. Make sure you come to the premiere. I'll get them to send you a couple of tickets.'

I wished him luck, assured him that the Oscar would be on his mantlepiece in six months, and asked him for a final comment.

'Oh yeah,' he said, putting his coat on. 'As Bette Davis once said, "Getting old ain't for sissies."'

Of course, Rourke did not win the Oscar. It went to Sean Penn as Harvey Milk, which was a fine performance but not a patch on Rourke's. And so he was right. Hollywood *does* appear to have a long memory.

Since *The Wrestler* he hasn't done anything to match that performance or any of his other memorable roles. He starred in *Sin City*, got fourth billing on *War Pigs* behind Luke Goss and Dolph Lundgren, starred in the lacklustre *Blunt Force Trauma*, appeared in *Weaponized* alongside that other car crash, Tom Sizemore, and at the time of writing has finished a boxing movie, *Tiger*, alongside a relatively unknown cast.

Most of the press he gets nowadays seems focused on how unrecognisable he is from his days as a heartthrob. But at least he is not living in one room. At least he can afford to pay his therapist, and at least he is working.

On a final note, a few days before the premiere I received a phone call telling me that the film company was biking two tickets over to me. So I went along and was delighted to see Mickey receive a standing ovation. He deserved that.

Despite his failings, his fallibilities, his peccadilloes and his myriad imperfections, I really like Mickey Rourke.

Liam Gallagher

You never know what to expect from Liam Gallagher. We've all heard about his swaggering braggadocio, his ban from Qantas airlines after an argument over a scone, his penchant for attacking irritating cyclists, or the time he headbutted an Aussie fan who bugged him.

And who can possibly forget his appearance at the 2010 Brit Awards? Receiving the 'Best Album of 30 Years' award from Noddy Holder for *(What's the Story) Morning Glory?*, he omitted to mention his brother Noel when thanking the other band members of Oasis, then threw the trophy into the audience.

Presenter Peter Kay was seen to mutter, 'What a knob head!', prompting Gallagher to post a characteristically scathing reply on Twitter.

'Listen up fat f**k,' he wrote. 'As a real northerner I was brought up 2 say shit 2 people's faces not behind their back. Live forever LG.'

Yet there are countless examples to be found online of the man's sharp intelligence and wit – quotes that, though punctuated with expletives, are the stuff of legend. And anyone who has ever watched Oasis perform live will testify that the band's success was not only due to Noel's songwriting prowess but Liam's massive stage presence. You'll never meet anyone like Liam Gallagher. He is a bona fide star and a total one-off. Ergo, I was most happy to interview him.

Of course, our first assignation fell foul. I turned up to meet him at 9.45am at the location of a magazine shoot in West London, only to discover that he had turned up early to get the shots out of the way before our chat.

Looking on, I saw a man comfortable with himself, who didn't ask to see any of the photographs and just got on with it. Indeed, while most shoots take at least an hour, Gallagher was done in half that time.

At one point I nodded to him as he went to change his outfit. He gulped and looked at me as if he was going to throw up, which apparently he did a couple of minutes later on the pavement outside the studio, just as soon as the shoot ended. As I would later discover, the cause of this was not a heavy session the night before. It was a stomach bug.

Rebel Rebel

A week later I'm sitting outside a pub on the edge of Hampstead Heath waiting for the man again. Bang on time – at 12 noon – he bowls up dressed in jeans and a parka from his rather exceptional clothes line Pretty Green. Taken from the title of a Paul Weller song, it not only describes his coat but also his pallor as he exited last week's photo shoot.

Strolling into the pub now he shakes my hand, smiles, acknowledges the waitress – 'All right luv, 'ow you doing?' – then takes me into the back room.

'Sorry about last week, man,' he says, his broad Manc accent undiminished after years down south. 'I was feeling really ill and it was so hot. I didn't want to do this and not give it me best, you know what I mean, I want to do it right.'

So adamant is he in his endeavours that while I order a pint of bitter, he orders a bottle of water. Turning up on time, apologising, drinking water – whatever next? This is certainly not what I'd expected from the legendary Liam 'excess in all areas' Gallagher, the man the tabloids love to hate and the nearest thing Britain has to a proper old-school rock star.

'I've knocked all that [makes a scooping sign indicating cocaine use] on the head since last November,' he says, unprompted. 'I'll have a little drink now and again but all these people say, "I will never do it again." But I say I'm not doing it for the time being, I'm having a rest. The minute you say you are going to try and stop doing anything, you've had it.

'You must remember that I've caned it for twenty years and not just on the sauce,' he continues, swaying back and forth in his seat, looking around restlessly. 'Caning it not just with drink but with all sorts, and this is a nice change. I've had a great time and now I'm having a break. All that doesn't work [when you have] kids, man. You wake up the next day after a session and it's tits, you're looking for bits of your kids' homework and football boots, you know what I mean, you're all over the place – it's fucking rubbish.'

Rumour has it that Mr Gallagher, now thirty-six, has even taken up running, knocking out a good ten miles a day. 'Yeah, mate,' he

430

says. 'Every day I'm up at six for a run over the Heath – it's fucking beautiful. I love it.'

Along with Gallagher's new fitness regime comes an unexpected interest in gardening. 'I've got a shed but there's nothing much in it,' he says. 'Just a Flymo, which I am seriously going to get into soon. Get back to me in a year when I've got a bit of time off and you might see some mad gardening shit going on.'

Now living on the edge of Hampstead Heath in a house painted in the blue and white colours of his beloved Manchester City, he has two sons. Gene, aged eight, lives with him and his second wife Nicole Appleton, formerly of the girl band All Saints, while Lennon, ten, who attends the same school as his brother, vacillates between Liam's house and his mum's, Gallagher's ex, Patsy Kensit. He also has an eleven-year-old daughter, Molly, by singer Lisa Moorish.

'I love being a dad,' he says in earnest. 'Family is the most important thing in the world and the kids are nuts. I did all the nappy changing, all that. I am hopeless at putting up light fittings and stuff but I do my bit elsewhere. I'm up at six every morning with my kids. I do the school run. It sorts my head out in the week. I fucking love it.

'What I do know is that there are a lot of parents out there who shouldn't be allowed to have kids,' he adds. 'But that's life. What the fuck can you do? You got these kids torturing and killing other kids – it's gotta be something [to do] with the parents.'

As a father of two boys living in the big city, Gallagher understandably has something to say on the subject of teenage knife crime. 'Knives are too much,' he says, looking genuinely concerned. 'But they've always been around. When I was in school I got in a scrap and got hit over the head with a hammer and it didn't do me much harm. But it's hard to make sense of the equation, and all you can do is hope for the best and hope your kids don't get involved.'

'All these hoodies look like shit anyway,' he adds after a swig on his water. 'They're walking around like some mad fucking monk. I suppose that was me once, only I was dressed better. They should get some Pretty Green gear on them.'

Pretty Green is a project that Gallagher has really thrown his weight behind. More so, some have suggested, than his band. Featuring beautifully constructed peacoats, button-down shirts in the softest Egyptian cotton, corduroy suits, and zip-up collarless bomber jackets constructed from Kobe leather – the softest in the world – it is Mod-influenced semi-casual wear made to luxurious Jermyn Street specifications.

'We just went for it, man,' explains Gallagher, who conceived the line with tailor Nick Holland. 'I wanted it to be the best 'cos there's no point in fucking about is there? And if it doesn't look good on me then I'm not having it. I'm not a fashion man. I've never done fashion before, but I know what looks good and what I like and that is as far as it goes.

'It's more about style really than fashion. Because it's me I won't take any notice of trends. It's what I like. And if people like it, they do, and if they don't, at least I've got a nice wardrobe out of it. It's not about making money. I just wanted to make things that I couldn't find.

'I love clothes and the music, but I won't force people to buy it,' he continues. 'If you can't afford it, fucking save up like I did. There were days when you wanted something and you didn't have the money, so you'd have to wait to get it, and then you appreciate stuff. It makes you a better man.'

The look of a band, he is at pains to point out, is just as important as the tunes.

'You can write a decent tune but if you look like a dick, that doesn't cut it with me. There's plenty of bands I've heard and thought, "Fucking hell, if they look good, man, if they look cool, then we're over." Then you see them on TV and go, "Thank fuck, they look shit." If you look good *and* you've got the tunes then you're away man.'

Suddenly he sticks his foot on the table to reveal his faux (I hope) leopard-skin Yves Saint Laurent Tod's-style loafers. 'People are having a pop at these!' he says, incredulously. 'I think they are the nuts, man. These are my pride and joy. I fucking love 'em.'

Indeed, no one can doubt that Gallagher has his own unique look, one which evolved when he was a teenager in a working-class Manchester suburb. 'It's what you do when you've got fuck all,' he says. 'When we saved up a bit of money we bought clobber: Dunlop Green Flash, Lacoste, Levi's. You work all week and then on the weekends you can have a bit of style, be the rock star, look the bollocks, know what I mean?'

Born William John Paul Gallagher on 21 September 1972, in Burnage, Manchester, he was the third and final child to Irish parents Thomas and Peggy. 'I'd go to church with me mum and then go home and see her get proper battered by my dad. She left him when I was ten,' he says.

At fifteen he was expelled from school for fighting, then found a job creosoting fences. He was known to sell knock-off Stone Island and Calvin Klein gear from a huge holdall to folks down on New Mount Street. After a spell establishing himself as a top Manc stylemonger, he found himself, aged nineteen, singing in the band Rain alongside school pal Paul 'Guigsy' McGuigan and Paul 'Bonehead' Arthurs.

Older brother Noel soon joined the group and started writing the songs. Renamed Oasis under his guidance, they released their first album *Definitely Maybe* in 1994, which became the fastest selling debut LP to date. To their credit, they have enjoyed an unprecedented twenty-two successive top ten hit singles, while it was once estimated that the two brothers were together worth a staggering £77 million.

Such a meteoric rise – from living in a house with 'no carpets' to filthy-rich rock royalty – might have fazed many an eighteen-year-old, but not Liam Gallagher.

'It was fucking great,' he recalls with a grin. 'It didn't freak me out at all. I'd been digging holes in Manchester for the last four years so I was ready for it. I was like [he gets up and mimes throwing a spade into the corner], "Here's that fucking spade, you can have it!" Felt good to me, man.

'But I think we succeeded because we were real,' he says. 'Not taking yourself too seriously but taking the music very seriously. But for the rest of it we were having a laugh. Getting everyone at it. At least that's what I thought it was anyway. You tell it how it is, how you think it is. There's no point in doing it any other way. We just did what we liked and dressed as we liked and made the music we liked. We weren't built on a career plan – we just did it and it happened. And if it didn't fucking happen, it didn't.'

Gallagher's attitude to style, dress and music is best illustrated by his favourite film *Quadrophenia*. 'It still stands up,' he enthuses. 'It's the bollocks! The music, the clothes, the people, what they were into. It's fucking tops. It's the height of British style. Better than the Madchester scene or the Britpop shit or anything else.

'The clothes were cool, and all they had was a scooter and a house party to go to in Brighton. There's too much going on these days. There's too much choice and not enough quality, you know what I mean? It's fucking shite.'

As he will readily admit, he has little time for contemporary bands, style or culture.

'I listen to the Beatles, Stones, Kinks, Neil Young, a bit of Stone Roses and the Pistols, definitely. But what I really, really despise is this new disease of Indie shit. Fucking student music – the likes of Bloc Party. It's nonsense. They don't keep me awake at night but it's just shite and they can fucking have it, mate.'

'What about grunge?' I enquire, almost knowing the answer.

'Fucking gypos!' he barks disdainfully, looking like he's eaten a bad prawn. 'The thing is, man, you can make your clothes look like they've been worn in and as if they had a bit of character, but underneath you've got to have a fucking wash, you know what I mean? I can wear the same jeans for a week, but you have to have a wash. Those fuckers wear those same clothes all the time and they don't wash so it's like, "Where's the park bench and the Special Brew?"'

He's on a roll now and his vituperation turns, naturally, to footwear.

'Another thing I hate is fucking pointed shoes,' he says. 'Not for me, man. They're for girls. I don't like these skin-tight jeans either. I don't mind a bit of slim, but I can't tell whether they are a boy or a girl. Are you a fucking chick or a bloke? In my opinion a girl has to look like a girl and a lad look like a lad.'

While he's on the subject of androgyny – or, rather, his aversion to it – I decide to mention Michael Jackson.

'He was a genius without a doubt,' he says. 'Not my kind of music. I preferred him when he was in the Jackson Five, but then he turned into a bit of a nutjob. But it was always on the cards wasn't it? He loved being in America for a start and anyone who has their own fairground in their back garden has to go fucking nuts. I have a couple of trees and a garden shed so it keeps me well on the ground. At least I ain't got a fucking Ferris wheel. Bound to drive you mad!'

At the mention of almost any band, Gallagher is off and running.

'I met Bono and [the] Edge and they're all alright, apart from being on CNN all the frigging time,' he says of the U2 frontmen. 'I'm sure they're not bad people but musically I'm not having them. People say we haven't done much in our eighteen years musically, but we've done a lot more than them. They are just fucking dreadful. The production is terrible, the songs are shite and I just don't get it.

'Also I have never seen a U2 fan, not ever. I have never seen anyone with a U2 shirt or been around someone's house that has a U2 record. I mean where do these "fans" come from? Where are they? I reckon they buy them. With all the money they've made they just buy a load of people and every time they do a gig they get a big old shovel [he gets up and mimes some more shovel action] and pile them in to their gigs to make them look good.'

He takes another swig on his water and looks around. Then he's off again…

'I never got the Clash, either. *Never Mind the Bollocks* is the ultimate punk record, but the Clash [being] into all that reggae, man! I never got it. I know that a lot of punks were into all that and I don't mind a bit of reggae, but not done by punks!'

In jest I ask him if there is anything that *really* gets on his wick?

'Fuck yeah, man, loads!' he grins. 'I could go on all day.'

He cites George Harrison, John Lennon ('the coolest nerd in the world'), Brian Jones of the Rolling Stones and Paul Weller as being the most stylish chaps in history.

Who, I enquire, is the most overrated?

'That has to be Noel Gallagher,' he answers with a smile. 'He dresses like Liz Hurley's son. On the posh vibe. Loves a cardigan and all that. He's had some of the Pretty Green gear when we were almost on speaking terms. But I don't think he is happy about this Pretty Green stuff 'cos a few of my mates were backstage wearing it and he was like, "What the fuck are you wearing that for?" And my mates were like, "'Cos you fucking can't." There's not much to dislike, it's not in your face. But fuck him anyway. His fashion sense is massively overrated.'

At this point, despite being warned not to ask him about the Oasis split, I carry on regardless and pop the question.

Sitting back in his chair, he looks over my shoulder to his companion, manager/bodyguard Steve Allen, who emits a big sigh.

'I'd love to talk to you about it but I can't because I haven't had the time yet, after eighteen years in Oasis, to think about the situation,' says Gallagher. 'It's just been a month and I have to sit down and work it out because as far as I'm concerned my comments would be on my musical headstone. I'm as gutted as anyone else, but when I'm ready you will hear my side of the story. It wasn't a shock to me that we split. But there's been enough shit said about us so I am going to wait before I say anything.'

Perhaps his recently acquired reticence is because of the repercussions whenever he and his brother air their dirty laundry in public. In an interview he did with the *NME* he talked about them not speaking all year, of them travelling separately, of Noel's jealousy regarding his clothes line. He also claimed, 'He doesn't like me and I don't like him,' adding, 'It takes a lot more than blood to be my brother.'

Just four days after the article was published, Noel Gallagher walked.

Yet even though he is not up for discussing the minutiae of the band's split, his activity on Twitter certainly tells much of the tale. During the Oasis world tour his posts (followed by some 75,000 people at the time of writing) start off rather innocuously, mentioning Pretty Green and thanking fans who came to the concerts. But as the gruelling ten-month tour rolled on, signs of strain started to show.

Firstly Noel, in an interview with Q magazine published at the end of April, laid his cards on the table, saying, 'I don't like him and he doesn't like me, that much is evident.'

A subsequent tweet by Liam stated, 'I can't wait to fly to Miami with a big mouth who calls himself a rock star. I've had more fun with a tin of sardines.'

He followed this with, 'Just heard through the grapevine that Noel G is playing guitar on The Nolan sisters comeback tour… B Jesus.'

Things got even worse after Liam threw a wobbler during a gig at the Roundhouse on 21 July in London and had a pop at a 'soft lad in the pointy shoes' in the audience for throwing beer in his general direction. He followed it up by walking off stage then coming back, causing Noel to snipe into his microphone, 'Well, well, well. I think someone is in a bad mood!'

'Whatshisname [Liam] exploded with pretend rage the minute he walked on,' blogged Noel on the band's website the next day. 'Strange cat. Probably on his man period.'

'Regarding shortarse's comments on my behaviour at the round-house,' responded Liam on Twitter, 'Pretend rage? It's called rock and roll darling, you wanna try it sometime!'

In August a thoroughly enraged Liam posted a succession of crip-pling broadsides in the space of a couple of hours, including this one: 'Just seen photos of the fool on the bill, outside some kebab house, acting like a right cock. Grow up lad.'

Such jibes would be bad enough if said on the phone without being posted on a website for all to see. Noel's response was to openly state that the forthcoming concert at the V festival would be the band's last.

'Finally reports in smartarses column about Oasis last British gig ever,' responded Liam. 'The kid's talking out his arse.'

On the day of the festival, Liam allegedly came down with viral laryngitis and was advised by doctors not to take to the stage. One can only imagine the older brother's irritation as he had for years berated his sibling for smoking too much, not looking after his voice, and generally caning it.

'I can only apologise – although I don't know why, it was nothing to do with me,' Noel said in a letter posted on the official Oasis website. 'I was match fit and ready to be brilliant. Alas, other people in the group weren't up to it.'

Just a few days later the shit hit the fan in Paris where the band were due to play the Rock en Seine festival. Liam travelled in on the Eurostar, accompanied only by Steve Allen, his personal minder and business partner in Pretty Green. As soon as he reached the venue the arguments began.

Scottish singer songwriter Amy Macdonald, who was performing at the same gig, wrote on Twitter, 'Oasis cancelled with just one minute to stage this time. Liam smashed Noel's guitar, huuuge fight!'

Other sources maintain, however, that before he left the scene, Noel smashed Liam's prized acoustic guitar – a present from his wife Nicole. Just two hours later Noel wrote again on the band's site, 'It's with some sadness and great relief to tell you that I quit Oasis tonight. People will write and say what they like, but I simply could not go on working with Liam a day longer.'

His final entry a day later was even more pointed. 'I feel you have the right to know that the level of verbal and violent intimidation towards me, my family, friends and comrades has become intolerable. And the lack of support and understanding from my management and band mates has left me with no other option than to get me cape and seek pastures new.'

'You see, that's the beauty of Oasis,' he tells me. 'It took the members of Oasis to knock it on the head and not the fucking people who were knocking us down, saying we wouldn't last. But we did, and for eighteen years.

'But no one got to us except for us – we got to ourselves. And eighteen years is a long time, man, especially when a lot of people are on your case saying you're shit and all that. We were the only ones that brought Oasis down and not all those cunts. I am very proud of that.'

Maybe the last comment on the matter should come from the brothers' mum Peggy, who, when asked recently about the split, answered, 'They love each other. They've had fights before and got over it.'

Whether the squabbling siblings eventually make their peace or not, Liam Gallagher remains one of the all-time truly great characters of British pop music – a man who stands head and shoulders above his contemporaries and is, at the very least, on equal standing with his heroes.

Although he's a darn sight funnier than any of them.

Nong Toom

Imagine climbing into a Thai boxing ring to fight in front of a crowd of loud, macho, mad-bag, gambling Siamese geezers, only for your opponent to step out in full girlie make-up, batter you to a pulp, knock you to the floor and whoop your ass. Not ideal for your macho boxer. Almost unbelievable, in fact. But it happened and it happened to countless boxers who fought the infamous Nong Toom, the transgender boxer who fought her way to the top of her profession and into the body of a woman, having used her purse to pay for her sex change.

'I first of all started boxing to help my family and pay for my own education,' remembers Nong Toom – the subject of the new Thai film *Beautiful Boxer*. 'But after a while I saw that I could earn a lot of money fighting and thought I would also save to get a sex change because as long as I can remember that is all I have ever wanted. I always felt like a woman trapped inside this man's body, and so I fought in the ring to get out.'

The film follows Toom – whose real name is Parinya Charoenphol – from boyhood to Buddhist monk to pugilistic fame and then the inevitable sex change.

'My first fight was very difficult because I was so scared and worried about getting hurt,' recalls Toom, now an actress and a model. 'But I just kept punching and the other guy eventually fell down and I won. I realised then that I could do something. That I had a gift. For many of us Thai people, especially in the rural areas, there are very few career choices for those without an education.'

But the transition from choosing boxing as a career to actually stepping into the professional ring is sheer unadulterated hell, involving a dedication to the form that most mere mortals are unable to follow. 'In the beginning the training was so very hard I felt sick,' recalls Toom. 'I really wanted to give up, leave the training camp and go home, but after a while the training became a part of me – almost like a ritual – and I got used to it by pushing myself out of my body until it was like meditation.'

And what of the other boxers in the training camp? How did they react to her obviously feminine countenance?

'I just felt very shy so avoided all eye contact or any communication with them at all. But it was hard keeping my secret. It was very frustrating as I could not behave like a woman and be myself with all the boxers around, so I became very subdued and quiet.

'But after a while I could not hold it in anymore, my femininity escaped and I was unable to hide so I started to wear make-up. I felt a lot happier and more beautiful but the other boxers were very confused and some were not very happy, but what could they do?'

As Toom moved up through the ranks her fame spread, attracting the attentions of boxers from all over Thailand. 'Some just laughed at me while others would say, "Don't worry, I won't punch you too hard," and blow me kisses, but I knew that I would soon show them what I had been trained to do. Then after I knocked them down I would try to make friends with them or sometimes kiss them gently on the forehead when they were knocked out, just to show I meant no harm – but this didn't always go down so well.'

But it wasn't only her fellow combatants that caused Toom anguish.

'The audiences found it really weird and laughed at me from the very beginning,' she bemoans. 'As I was so naïve I thought the audience thought me cute and I was happy to make them laugh, but after while I was hurt by the negative reactions, especially from the press. But when you're in the ring, who cares? Other people's reactions do not count. It's just you and your opponent and nothing else. I had this dream to make myself a woman and that pushed me forward and kept me winning.'

Such was her incredible drive that Toom soon found herself boxing at Lumpinee stadium – the Mecca of Thai boxing – becoming one of the country's top fighters. 'It is very difficult to get there as there are so many great kick boxers from so many different provinces,' states Toom. 'But I got there.'

As Toom's fame increased so did her desire for womanhood, so she started taking hormones. 'I knew that they would soften my muscles and make me weaker but I had to take them,' she explains. 'It was one of the most conflicting moments of my life and soon I wasn't doing so well, but I had made enough by then to pay for my operation.'

Stepping into a ring is one thing but undergoing a sex change is another matter. 'The hardest part is the decision,' states Toom, speaking at her home in Bangkok.

'When you decide you have to be sure as the change is totally irreversible. The operation is easy as you have the anaesthetic and you wake up feeling a bit sore, but it is not as hard as finding the courage and making the decision.

'It is a real emotional nightmare. But for me I have no regrets. I never felt whole. It was as if I was a man who had lost his manhood. I felt as if there was always something missing and now I feel whole and happy.'

Now that Nong Toom is legally a woman, the young of Thailand – who mob her in search of photos and autographs – afford her much admiration. 'I think they like me not just because I am now a woman,' says Toom. 'It is because I have done what I wanted to do, even though I am from a very poor background. My life shows that if you have the will and the courage you can get what you want, and for many Thai people this is important and it gives them hope. And that makes me feel that everything I have done has been worthwhile.'

Daniel Day-Lewis

On meeting actor Daniel Day-Lewis, one gets the distinct impression that, whether successful or not, he has no other option than to do things his way. A man who subconsciously defies convention at every turn, he is rarely seen at Hollywood shindigs, only acts in films he really believes in, and doesn't give two hoots about money or fame.

Furthermore, since 1997 he has lived as far from the madding crowd as possible, basing himself in Ireland's wild and wet, though awe-inspiring Wicklow Mountains with his writer-director wife Rebecca Miller – daughter of US playwright Arthur Miller – and his two teenage boys Ronan and Cashel. A several-year hiatus between movies is par for the course for the London-born actor, who is known to choose his projects carefully and sparingly.

'Others might use that frenzy to find who they are,' said the affable and entirely down-to-earth actor as he sat in the Soho Hotel dressed in black jeans, a T-shirt and scuffed steel-toe-cap work boots, his long curly hair barely concealing the large gold hoop earrings he sports in each ear. 'But I need tranquillity and absolute quiet after a film and that is that.'

His modus operandi is certainly effective. He is the only man ever to win three Best Actor Academy Awards – an achievement all the more remarkable as he's made just seventeen films in thirty-four years (compare this with, say, Christopher Lee, who starred in 135 films in as many years and never won an Oscar). He made his last film, *Lincoln*, over four years ago [at the time of writing in 2015], presumably because he is waiting for the right part to come along.

'When I look back and try to work out why I did each role, I reinvent the answer each time because I never really thought about why I should do them.' He smiled. 'They just seemed right. [In] each case it is just that sense of something, it's a sense of inevitability. And I have always had that very strong feeling towards what I do.'

Indeed Day-Lewis has throughout his career picked roles that were not only extremely challenging but also completely disparate. Who could forget his rendering of Hawkeye (a white man raised by Mohican Indians) in *The Last of the Mohicans*, Michael Mann's brilliant

adaptation of James Fenimore Cooper's classic novel set in eigh-
teenth-century America?

'It took me about six months to get myself in shape then it all fell
off during the last few weeks of the production,' he explained. 'I did
a hell of a lot of running around for that. If you notice, I get progres-
sively thinner throughout the film because all I did was run.'

And then there is his performance as Gerry Conlon, a Belfast
Catholic wrongly convicted of a terrorist bombing in *In the Name of
the Father*.

'It was a thoroughly exhausting shoot, mentally draining,' he said.
'But I felt so strongly towards the case that I felt duty bound to give
it my all.'

Other roles, such as that of the psychopathic gang leader Bill the
Butcher in Martin Scorsese's *Gangs of New York* (2002), drove him to
distraction.

'At first I was reluctant [to do the film] because I had been out of
the game for five years,' he admitted. 'I'd got married and had children and wasn't sure that I was ready to get back into it, because
when you go into that tunnel with someone you have to be sure
you're not looking for the escape hatch half way through.

'I knew what doing the part would entail as I knew what I am like
and Martin didn't need to convince me. He told me the story on the
phone and I thought, here we go, not again. But I had to need to
know I was up for it because I don't want to let anyone down, especially not him as when you work with him it's hard work and you
have to be an ally, to be someone you can count on and who has the
strength of purpose to sustain you through eight months of mayhem.

'And of course I had to prepare, so I just went mad and remembered the halcyon days of fighting on the terraces at the Den, memories that stood me in good stead as Bill the Butcher. He was a bit of
a punk and a marvellous character and a joy to be – although not so
good for my physical or mental health.'

Perhaps one of the reasons he is able to play everything from gangsters to boxers to presidents and deliver such unimpeachable performances each time is because of this upbringing, which is as unusual
as the man himself.

'My parents, give them their due, even though their experiences were very far removed from what I was experiencing, in that neither of them would ever have considered setting foot on the terraces of the Den, neither were snobs and were completely open and believed that there was work that had to be done to break down these rigid demarcations of society.'

He grew up in Greenwich, south-east London, and despite being the son of the Poet Laureate Cecil Day-Lewis (whose ancestors hailed from Ireland and England) and actress Jill Balcon, the daughter of Michael Balcon (who founded Ealing Studios and was of eastern European Jewish descent), he was hardly sheltered.

Anyone familiar with the geography of south-east London will readily inform you that, however fine and dandy Greenwich might be, it's an area surrounded by infinitely less salubrious boroughs, which were once home to many of London's dockworkers. Bombed severely during World War II, their streets were replaced by sprawling council estates.

As a young teenager, Day-Lewis soon found himself strolling these places and, being both posh and Jewish, had to defend himself physically. He has admitted to having been a somewhat disorderly youth, prone to shoplifting, petty crime and other such antics.

'I was fascinated by the streets that were close by – Lewisham, New Cross, Deptford – and I roamed the streets of South London and supported Millwall with great gusto and was on the terraces every Saturday with the rest of the lads,' he recalled. 'That part of my life means a lot to me – that time before I went to boarding school, when I was roaming the streets of Deptford. It was heaven, just discovering that world.'

Nevertheless his parents, seeing their wayward son advancing rapidly towards a life less ordinary, and certainly more hazardous, sent him to the Sevenoaks boarding school in Kent where he lasted just two years.

Transferred at the age of fourteen to Bedales, a famously liberal private school in Hampshire, he dabbled in drama and soon acquired his first role as a vandal in John Schlesinger's watershed kitchen-sink drama *Sunday Bloody Sunday*. He was overjoyed. 'They paid me a

couple of quid a day to smash up a few cars,' he chuckled. 'I was fourteen and in heaven.'

During his school breaks, however, he was back on the streets,
extracting more out of his experiences than your average Joe.

'It was such an important part of my life and it was the first time
that I understood anything about this society we live in,' he smiled
fondly, looking out the window, as if recalling a particular mischievous incident. 'Luckily my youth coincided with a wave of dramatist
social commentators: Barrie Keeffe, Nigel Williams, Lindsay Anderson and, of course, Ken Loach. I was hugely influenced by these
guys.

'And once I discovered great film I was voracious. I just devoured
all I could get my hands on. I looked up in awe at Michel Simon in
L'Atalante; Jean-Louis Barrault in *Les Enfants du Paradis*; Jean Gabin
is marvellous in *Le Quai des Brumes*. But there were the British actors
who influenced me as well: Richard Harris in *This Sporting Life*;
Albert Finney in *Saturday Night and Sunday Morning*; Tom Courte-
nay in *The Loneliness of the Long Distance Runner*, David Bradley in
Kes, everyone in Ken Loach's films. And lest we forget there were
the Americans: Brando, Montgomery Clift – so many great actors to
aspire to.'

In 1973, at the age of sixteen, Day-Lewis walked into a cinema
and saw Martin Scorsese's seminal *Mean Streets,* the story of a gang of
young New York Italian tough guys.

'You could *not* imagine the effect that had on me,' he recalled, sip-
ping his black coffee. 'I was this young and slightly wayward guy
from South London who just didn't know what to do with his life. It
was like a light going on in my head. It was so influential for me as
a young person, never mind as a young actor. Then I saw that there
could be a purpose for this work, this acting, and that it wasn't all
about prancing around on stage in tights.'

Consequently the young man put his foot down and after leaving
school joined the Bristol Old Vic Theatre School. He performed with
them before going on to cut his teeth in film and TV.

It was director Stephen Frears who first saw the young thespian's
true potential and cast him as Johnny, a tough London right-wing

extremist street kid who embarks on a romantic relationship with the son of a left-wing Pakistani journalist in Thatcher's Britain.

'You could see the producer's bewilderment,' he chuckled. '*My Beautiful Launderette* felt to me as if we were like a continuation of this tradition of looking at this ludicrous divided society we inhabit. I loved the sense of mischief and it's a very sustaining feeling to feel you are all partaking of this mischievous enterprise – it really felt like that on *Launderette*.'

I mentioned the famed snogging scene and how an actor friend of mine (who will remain nameless) was thoroughly fazed when he was suddenly called upon to passionately kiss a male actor in front of the camera.

'Well what a sheltered life he must have had,' chuckled Day-Lewis. 'He obviously doesn't get out enough!'

Day-Lewis loves to dwell in dichotomy. 'I did the Merchant Ivory adaptation of E. M. Forster's *A Room with a View* the same time as *Launderette,* and I believe they premiered in New York on the same day. I relished the opportunity to do both. In *Launderette* I was this working-class outcast and in *Room* I was this upper-class twit. It was great, great fun.'

But there are roles that he doesn't look back upon with such fondness, such as the adaptation of Milan Kundera's overrated, confusing novel *The Unbearable Lightness of Being* (or as I rechristened it *The Unbearable Heaviness of Reading*). I confessed to disliking the book, which deterred me from watching the film.

'I made it against my better judgement,' he admitted with a groan. 'People ask me about those sex scenes and I say I shouldn't have done them and I shouldn't have done the film – there is a sense of despair in those scenes and it left me feeling a little bit down in the mouth.

'I don't think I was ready for such a powerful and complex role. Part of my job was to be preoccupied and overwhelmed by Kundera's world and be immersed in it, and the film took six months to make, which is a long time to live with those complex themes and for me it was very hard going.'

Enjoying himself both creatively and otherwise on set is of paramount importance, and that entails not only empathising with the characters themselves, but also suffering the same hardships and enjoying the same pleasures.

'I love the pure pleasure of doing the work no matter if that work involves some kind of discomfort, even though I don't see it as discomfort,' he clarified. 'And it's not that one deals with the problems so much as one deals with the day-to-day challenges of the character. It's a big game. It's not life and death. Acting and theatre and film are just one big game and some people forget that. I understand that some might not understand the lengths that I go to, but does it really *fucking* matter?'

For those unacquainted with those lengths, Day-Lewis's preparation has been the cause of much hyperbole and, occasionally, scorn. He crudely tattooed his own hands and trained for three years as a professional pugilist in preparation for *The Boxer* (1997), built his character's dwelling out of seventeenth-century implements for *The Crucible* (1996) then lived in it for three months without electricity or running water, and remained in a wheelchair and in character for the duration of the shoot as the cerebral palsied Irish writer Christy Brown in 1989's *My Left Foot,* for which he received his first Oscar.

'A very dear friend of mine, my agent Julian who is sadly no longer with us, was quite unsettled when he came to visit me on the set of *My Left Foot,*' grinned the actor. 'This was because I was "in character" all the time and, apart from anything else, he couldn't understand a word I was saying.

'So after our one-sided conversation he walked off and had a very quiet aperitif in a local hostelry. It was at that moment that he opened his eyes and knew what he was dealing with and never asked any questions from then on and just let me get on with it. He thought, "OK, he is a little odd but I'll leave him be," and we had a great relationship.'

Unsurprisingly he is sick to death of the likes of me asking about his method.

'Nothing I say in answer to these questions will make the work better or worse, but I understand the impulse that causes people to even consider why I do what I do. But that thirst for information as to what I do and how I do it has been developed and encouraged by I don't know what.

'I was on Parkinson and I knew he would ask me about all this and I thought I was ready for it and I wasn't at all and so made a right knob of myself.'

But I, for one, get his drift. It has to be easier rendering a character if one walks a few miles in their shoes, albeit with pebbles in them.

'I love it when people like you say that my approach is not unusual.' He smiled. 'But you'd be surprised how few do. For me, it seems obvious as that is what I do, and I think, well, if people think it's odd then what can I do? But a part of me thinks what difference does it make?

'I've *always* been intrigued by the life I have never experienced,' he said. 'I go with that feeling but more than anything else I enjoy it. It is a game. But the way people would have it, it is like a game of self-chastisement and it has never been that way for me as it is a plea-surable and intriguing game.'

It seems like common sense to me, although describing it as enjoy-able might be stretching it a tad.

'What I tended to do in the past was keep my mouth shut,' he con-fided. 'But then people speak on your behalf, which creates a whole absurdity around it. So then you try to talk a bit to address the bal-ance and then you make an even bigger dick of yourself. So essen-tially there's nothing to say.'

In 2007 he received his second Oscar for his bravura rendering of renegade oil man Daniel Plainview in Paul Thomas Anderson's *There Will Be Blood*. Again he remained in character day and night throughout filming, having worked on becoming the man for three whole years.

How long he was in full-blown character?

'I really don't know – maybe twelve to fourteen weeks. I don't know, ask someone else,' he answered, looking truly bemused. 'Luckily I had my family with me and to be honest the joy about great work is that you are not looking for the finishing line – quite the opposite – and one of the great things about such work is that you lose yourself as [with] all artistic endeavour. My wife and kids went a bit crazy as I was there all the time. All creative work involves the loss of the self, and it's like time out of time – a period when I lose myself and the clocks stop and this is the joy.

'You go to these great lengths to imagine another world and another time; and you go to those lengths to imagine a man living in those times and having spent your imagination on that it seems more fun to live there than jumping in and out. That is the playground that you've created so why not stay there and play?

'It gets rid of that specious notion of playing between times, which often people talk about – waiting for the next shot – I don't buy that. Whatever you can do to give yourself a sense of continuity, right from the work before you start – and there is no limit to the amount of time that you take to discover a whole life – I'm happy doing it and could do it forever. It's quite alarming when someone then says you have to go to work.'

Day-Lewis oozed Plainview's seething malevolence, so considering the actor is such an affable chap, where did it come from?

'We all have murderous thoughts throughout the day if not the week, do we not?' he mused. 'Any form of coexistence we live under involves some repression. We have to do that – it's part of the deal – and we all have some of that in us. And what's more invigorating than to unleash it? But I cannot account for where any of this comes from me – it comes from the unconscious and I cannot account for what ferments in my unconscious. That part of the work doesn't take part in the conscious. One just hopes there is a cave somewhere that you can ransack.'

After talking to him for a while it all starts to make total sense. He is a visceral actor who pulls performances partly from research but mostly from within.

'My preference is that, that day when someone sticks a tripod in front of you with a camera on the top, it is not day one,' he clarified. 'It begins way before, with the work prior to filming.

'I wasn't working in isolation as Paul [Anderson] and I were in very close touch, but still it's like a little secret that you have to share with yourself and then 200 people. It's quite an alarming moment and they're like, "Who the fuck is that and what is he doing – well he seems to know what he's doing so let him get on with it." And of course, they're all there with all the kit on, the anoraks and hiking boots and lots of pens in all these pockets – it's terrifying.'

Considering that his wife and children accompany him on set wherever he goes, I would have thought that they'd be far more terrified seeing their beloved husband and father morph into a misanthropic, mercurial monster for months on end.

'They think it's a right laugh and both boys did a pretty decent impersonation of me,' he grinned, still obviously amused. 'And my wife is amazingly tolerant. I knew that from the word go. She just believes, like I do, that if you are attempting anything of a creative nature, no rules apply. I don't ask her how she comes up with her stories. I just read them and love them. And that is all I need to know. And I really would rather not know.'

He admits however that sometimes stepping out of character can be problematic.

'Absurd as it might seem,' he laughed, tilting back for a moment and then leaning forward, as if sharing a secret, 'when you've been someone else for that amount of time, conceiving such an enterprise, it's even more absurd when it's all over. Then the joke is on all of us because once a curiosity is unleashed you can't just tie it up again. There is a period of leakage.

'Plainview probably had a lot of leakage, or rather seepage. And that is why there was no Mrs Plainview in sight. But it does take time to leave your man as there is no great part of you that wants to stop doing that work and no matter how much you're begging for it to stop you need someone to put a restraining order on it and yourself.'

Since Plainview, Day-Lewis has taken on just two roles, one as Italian film director Guido Contini in *Nine* (2009), the other as the title role in Steven Spielberg's 2012 epic *Lincoln*, which gave him his third Best Actor Academy Award.

But never mind the countless accolades. When I first interviewed Daniel Day-Lewis he had just delivered a cracking turn as an overprotective father in *The Ballad of Jack and Rose* (written and directed by his wife). Naturally the conversation swung round to parenthood, his boys and my recently born son Finbar.

Interviewing him a few years later for *There Will Be Blood*, he bounced into the room, full of more beans than a Mexican dinner, and straight away asked, 'How's Finbar?'

Now how many Oscar-winning actors would do that?

A mutual friend told me just the other day that Day-Lewis now has a building firm that indulges his need to work with his hands. And he has recently announced that his last movie will be Paul Thomas Anderson's *Phantom Thread*, set in the London fashion scene of the 1950s and due for release in Autumn 2017.

Needless to say, Day-Lewis is unlike any other actor. He's not even like any other person. No, siree. Daniel Day-Lewis is a total one-off.

Thanks

Both Chris Sullivan and Unbound would like to thank the numerous magazines that commissioned the author to write many of these pieces. Particular thanks go to The Independent, Big Issue, Jocks and Nerds, GQ, The Times and Sunday Times, Dazed and Confused, Esquire, Italian Vogue and The Guardian.

Unbound
Liberating ideas

Unbound is the world's first crowdfunding publisher, established in 2011.

We believe that wonderful things can happen when you clear a path for people who share a passion. That's why we've built a platform that brings together readers and authors to crowdfund books they believe in – and give fresh ideas that don't fit the traditional mould the chance they deserve.

This book is in your hands because readers made it possible. Everyone who pledged their support is listed below. Join them by visiting unbound.com and supporting a book today.

Archer Adams
Jonathan Akeroyd
Victoria Al-Din
Alan Alderson
David Alexander
Hargreaves Alison
Chris Altree

Patrons

Christopher Campbell
Stewart Campbell-Clark
Felicity Cannell
Melissa Caplan
Paul Caren
Chris Carlson
Steven Cassidy
Gregory Cathcart
Terry Challingsworth
Pietro Cheli
Mick Clark
Sophie Clinch
Dave Coghill
Nick Coleman
Madeleine Collins
Sean Collins
Chris Collins
Rachel Condry
Philip Connor
Ray Conroy
Fraser Cooke
Suzie Cooke
Keith Cooper
Daniel Cooper-Kamodsky
Meredith Coral
Joseph Corre
Andrew Cotterill
Bryan Cowie
Ken Cox
Matt Cox
John Crawford
Nicole Croft
Michelle Daley
Smiler Darren Castle
Carol Dartnell
Cocks David

Patrons

Julian Greaves
Chris Greenwood
Clive Hadley
Steven Hall
Jacqueline Hancher
Jezz Harkin
Pete Harris
Mary Hart
Dave Harvey
Craig Hawes
David Hawkes
Lesley Hayter
Zane Hayward
David Hebblethwaite
Laurence Hegarty
John Hibberd
Carol Higgins
David Hitchcock
Steve Hogg
Tim Holmes
Paul Howden
Charles Howgego
Simon Hui Kin Onn
Mike Hunkin
Kim Hunt
Jemima Hunt
Andrew Ingram
Tobin Ireland
Patricia Irvine
Hagar Itzikson
Andrew James
Dean James
clive jennings
David Jimenez
Paul Jobson
Finn Johannsen

Patrons

Philip John
David (shapersofthe80s) Johnson
Jacque Johnson
Allison Jones
Nik Kealy
Peter Kelly
Marie Kelly Jones
Christina Kennedy
Peter Kent
Joanne Kilgour
Michael Kinder
Monika Klama
Ben Knight
Juha Kolari
James Lambert
Trevor Lang
Clive Langer
Per Larsson
Julie Law
Daisy Lawrence
Jimmy Leach
Dawn Ledwidge
Mike Leigh
Steve Lewis
Paul Linney
Helen Lisle-Taylor
Elizabeth Little
Kristin Lockhart
Steve Loft
Frederick Londonderry
Paul Lonergan
Terry Loring
Alisdair Lynch
Sophy Lynn
Claire Lyons
Tommy Mack

Patrons

Catherine Makin
Warren Marsh
Chris Martin
Columba Martin
Les Masco
Sarah Matheson
Bert McCloud
Paul McGoldrick
Aidan McManus
Andrew Mcneill
Alessandro Meteori
Simon Milne
Robert Milton
Monsoonphoto
Jim Mooney
Kris Moore
Mark Morfett
Vincent Moses
Shirley Moth
Peter Nash
Peter Nash
Rex Nayman
Cory Neal
Alison Newman
Steve Norman
Suzanna Nuthall
Brendan O'Sullivan
Eddie OCallaghan
Georgia Odd
Anna-Maja Oléhn
Gregory Olver
John Oswin
Michael Paley
Cindy Palmano
Laarni Grace Paras
Kevin Parker

Patrons

Emily Parsons
Trafford Parsons
Samuel Pattinson
Peppermint Patty
Nancy Pearce
John Pearson
Penny Pepper
Nigel Peters
Gary Phillips
Paul Philpott
Donna Pinel
Jack Pinter
Marco Pirroni
Justin Pollard
Harriet Posner
Roland Power
Janet Pretty
Neil Pretty
Laura Pritchard
Anita Prosser
Lesley Purcell
Heather Quin
John Quinn
Frank Radcliffe
Sean Regan
Mark Reilly
Samantha Reynolds
Jill Richards
Thomas Richardson
Lloyd Ridgeway
Richard Rodriguez
Kevin Rogers
Mark Rudd
Alistair Rush
Roy Russell
Philip Sands

Pub Crawlers

Marc Albert
David Allder
Ed Allen
Simon Andrews
Janet Awe
Jason Bacon
Jason Ballinger
Matt Barker
Steve Beech
Peter Benton
Owen Blackhurst
Dean Bradley
Richard W H Bray
Ben Buchanan
Alex Bucke
Michael Bush
Zoe Butt
Georgina Calder
Andy Carroll
Fiona Cartledge
Andy Checker
Belinda Chorley
Russell Clarke, the Rock'n'Roll Routemaster
Stuart Coalwood
Stevyn Colgan

Pub Crawlers

Mhari Colvin
J.J. Connolly
Tom Conran
Nicci Cuff
Mark Daniels
Neil Davies
Camilla Deakin
Simon Dimmock
Sofia Donoghue
Ricky Dowles
Lesley Edgar
Sebastiaan Eldritch-Böersen
Leo Elstob
Nick Embiricos
Miles English
Graham Evans
Jeremy Evans
Alan Every
Bridge Fazio
Lois Feltell
Keith Ford
Aldo Framingo
Timothy Frost
Jane Garry
Richard Garry
Iestyn George
Peter Golding
Perry Haines
Louise Haisman
Andrew Hale
Jonathan Hill
Iain Hill
Jon Hobbs
Michael Holden
Ann Holmes
Will Holt

Pub Crawlers

Karen Howarth
Ivor Howells
David Hughes
Mark Huxley
Rhiannon Ifans
Jess Jethwa
Veronica John
Chris Jordan
Pauli Karkkainen
Dan Kieran
Andy King
Antony Knight
Barbara Knox
Graham Lentz
C Lewis
Dave Little
Franceska Luther King
Gautam Malkani
Sandra Mattocks
Jill McComish
John McGuire
Katherine McIntosh
Andrew Mills
John Mitchinson
Valentine Morby
Sarah morris
Steve Murray
Joe Nahmad
Susie Newman
Lyn Pagano
Gabriella Palmano
Yianni Papas
Jamie Petrie
Alexander Keith Potter
Gareth Potter
Keith Power

Pub Crawlers

Harry Pye / John Harlow
Jeanette Ramsden
Gladys Rashbrook
Allan P Russell
Kevin Saunders
Gabrielle Seymour
Bobbie Smith
Derek Moulder & Jacqueline Soltau
Adam Stone
Amanda Sullivan
Marcus Sweeney-Bird
Alan Teixeira
Steve Thorogood
Ian Townsend
Amelia Troubridge
Nick True
Michelle Tuft-Smith
Liam Tuke
Shaun Usher
Samantha Vavrik
Neil Warner
Geoff Waugh
Rob West
Paul Whelan
Simon White
Mitchell Wilson